Economic Development and Islamic Finance

DIRECTIONS IN DEVELOPMENT
Finance

Economic Development and Islamic Finance

Zamir Iqbal and Abbas Mirakhor, Editors

THE WORLD BANK
Washington, D.C.

© 2013 International Bank for Reconstruction and Development / The World Bank
1818 H Street NW, Washington DC 20433
Telephone: 202-473-1000; Internet: www.worldbank.org

Some rights reserved

1 2 3 4 16 15 14 13

This work is a product of the staff of The World Bank with external contributions. Note that The World Bank does not necessarily own each component of the content included in the work. The World Bank therefore does not warrant that the use of the content contained in the work will not infringe on the rights of third parties. The risk of claims resulting from such infringement rests solely with you.

The findings, interpretations, and conclusions expressed in this work do not necessarily reflect the views of The World Bank, its Board of Executive Directors, or the governments they represent. The World Bank does not guarantee the accuracy of the data included in this work. The boundaries, colors, denominations, and other information shown on any map in this work do not imply any judgment on the part of The World Bank concerning the legal status of any territory or the endorsement or acceptance of such boundaries.

Nothing herein shall constitute or be considered to be a limitation upon or waiver of the privileges and immunities of The World Bank, all of which are specifically reserved.

Rights and Permissions

This work is available under the Creative Commons Attribution 3.0 Unported license (CC BY 3.0) **http://creativecommons.org/licenses/by/3.0.** Under the Creative Commons Attribution license, you are free to copy, distribute, transmit, and adapt this work, including for commercial purposes, under the following conditions:

Attribution—Please cite the work as follows: Iqbal, Zamir, and Abbas Mirakhor, eds. 2013. *Economic Development and Islamic Finance.* Directions in Development. Washington, DC: World Bank. doi:10.1596/978-0-8213-9953-8. License: Creative Commons Attribution CC BY 3.0

Translations—If you create a translation of this work, please add the following disclaimer along with the attribution: *This translation was not created by The World Bank and should not be considered an official World Bank translation. The World Bank shall not be liable for any content or error in this translation.*

All queries on rights and licenses should be addressed to the Office of the Publisher, The World Bank, 1818 H Street NW, Washington, DC 20433, USA; fax: 202-522-2625; e-mail: pubrights@worldbank.org.

ISBN (paper): 978-0-8213-9953-8
ISBN (electronic): 978-0-8213-9954-5
DOI: 10.1596/978-0-8213-9953-8

Cover photos: © Giorgio Fochesato / iStockphoto.com. Used with permission; further permission required for reuse.
Cover design: Naylor Design.

Library of Congress Cataloging-in-Publication Data

Economic development and Islamic finance / [edited by] Zamir Iqbal and Abbas Mirakhor.
    pages cm
ISBN 978-0-8213-9953-8 — ISBN 978-0-8213-9954-5 (ebook)
  1. Finance—Islamic countries. 2. Finance—Religious aspects—Islam. 3. Economic development—Islamic countries. I. Iqbal, Zamir. II. Mirakhor, Abbas.
  HG187.4.E26 2013
  332.0917'67—dc23
                                                                                                        2013013763

Contents

Foreword		*xi*
Acknowledgments		*xiii*
Contributors		*xv*
Abbreviations		*xix*
Overview		1
	Views on Economic Development	3
	The Islamic Concept of Economic Development	5
	Summary of Chapters	10
	References	22
PART 1	**Theoretical Foundation**	**23**
Chapter 1	Epistemological Foundation of Finance: Islamic and Conventional	25
	Abbas Mirakhor and Wang Yong Bao	
	An Ideal Conventional Financial System	26
	An Ideal Islamic Finance System	31
	Achieving the Ideal: Uncertainty, Risk, and Equity Markets	41
	Summary and Conclusion	53
	References	57
	Background Reading	60
Chapter 2	Islamic Finance Revisited: Conceptual and Analytical Issues from the Perspective of Conventional Economics	67
	Andrew Sheng and Ajit Singh	
	Introduction	67
	The Central Tenet of Islamic Finance: Absolute Prohibition against Interest Rates	69
	Ethical Foundations of Islamic Finance	76
	Modigliani and Miller Theorems	78
	Risk Sharing, Risk Shifting, and the Risks of Bankruptcy	81
	The Stock Market and Islamic Finance	82

	Interim Summary of the Main Findings and Two Further Questions	83
	Islamic Finance and Economic Development	85
	The Real Challenge of Islamic Finance	86
	Conclusion	87
	Notes	88
	References	88
Chapter 3	**The Foundational Market Principles of Islam, Knightian Uncertainty, and Economic Justice**	**93**
	S. Nuri Erbaş and Abbas Mirakhor	
	Introduction	93
	The Foundational Islamic Market Principles	97
	Knightian Uncertainty and the Islamic View of Uncertainty	99
	Institutional Development, Trust, and Uncertainty	101
	Islamic Contracts and Risk Sharing	106
	Research Agenda for Islamic Economics: A Proposal	118
	Concluding Remarks	119
	Notes	120
	References	125
PART 2	**Developmental Aspects**	**131**
Chapter 4	**Finance and Development in Islam: A Historical Perspective and a Brief Look Forward**	**133**
	Murat Çizakça	
	Introduction	133
	Basic Characteristics of an Islamic Economy and Finance	134
	Implementation	135
	Historical Evidence	136
	Stagnation and Decline	141
	Relevance for Today: What Needs to Be Done?	143
	Conclusion	145
	Notes	146
	References	147
Chapter 5	**Economic Development in Islam**	**151**
	Hossein Askari	
	The Evolution of Western Thinking on Development	152
	Economic Development in Islam	158
	Concluding Comments	175
	Notes	175
	References	176

Chapter 6	Islam's Perspective on Financial Inclusion	179
	Zamir Iqbal and Abbas Mirakhor	
	What Is Financial Inclusion and Why Is It Important?	181
	Issues with the Conventional Approach to Financial Inclusion	183
	The Concept of Financial Inclusion in Islam	185
	Redistributive Instruments of Islam	188
	Public Policy Implications	191
	Government as the Risk Manager Promoting Risk Sharing	192
	Need for Developing a Supportive Institutional Framework	193
	Institutionalization of Islamic Redistributive Instruments	195
	Conclusion	198
	Notes	199
	References	200
Chapter 7	Financial Inclusion and Islamic Finance: Organizational Formats, Products, Outreach, and Sustainability	203
	Habib Ahmed	
	Introduction	203
	Inclusive Finance: Scope and Constraints	205
	Islamic Finance and Inclusive Finance	209
	Islamic Inclusive Finance: An Overview and Comparison	213
	Organizational Formats, Services, Outreach, and Sustainability	220
	Conclusion	224
	Notes	225
	References	226
Chapter 8	Theory and Instruments of Social Safety Nets and Social Insurance in Islamic Finance: *Takaful* and *Ta'min*	231
	Kamaruddin Sharif and Wang Yong Bao	
	Islamic Social Safety Nets	232
	The Institutional Framework of Social Safety Nets in Islam	234
	The Concept of Social Security in Islam	239
	Social Insurance: *Takaful* and *Ta'min*	241
	Takaful in Practice	245
	Conclusion	248
	Notes	248
	References	249
Chapter 9	Islamic Capital Markets and Development	253
	Obiyathulla Ismath Bacha and Abbas Mirakhor	
	Introduction	253

	Are Capital Markets Necessary?	253
	Issues Concerning Capital Markets	255
	Concept of Islamic Capital Markets	257
	Equity and *Sukuk* Markets in an Islamic Capital Market	260
	The Reality of Capital Markets in the Muslim World	268
	Concluding Remarks: Implementing the Risk-Sharing Framework	270
	Notes	272
	References	272
Chapter 10	**Islamic Stock Markets in a Global Context**	**275**
	Andrew Sheng and Ajit Singh	
	Introduction	275
	Do Stock Markets Help Economic Development?	278
	Lessons for Islamic Stock Markets	280
	Stock Markets and Economic Efficiency: Further Lessons for Islamic Stock Markets	284
	Issues of Globalization and of Long-Term Growth for Islamic Stock Markets	289
	Conclusion	291
	Notes	292
	References	293
PART 3	**Policy Formulation**	**297**
Chapter 11	**A Survey of the Economic Development of OIC Countries**	**299**
	Hossein Askari and Scheherazade Rehman	
	Introduction	299
	Fundamental Islamic Economic Doctrines	300
	The Performance of OIC Countries	306
	Concluding Remarks on Islam and Economic Performance and Prosperity	317
	Notes	322
	References	323
Chapter 12	**Islam and Development: Policy Challenges**	**325**
	Azura Othman and Abbas Mirakhor	
	Introduction	325
	The Islamic Economy and the Role of the State	326
	Policy Tools in Macroeconomic Management	328
	Policy Instruments in an Islamic Economy	332
	Challenges in Policy Implementation	338
	Summary	342
	Notes	343
	References	344

Glossary of Arabic Terms 345

Boxes
O.1 Basic Principles of an Islamic Economic and Financial System 4
12.1 The Malaysian Financial Services Master Plan (2001–10) and the Malaysian Financial Sector Blueprint (2011–20) 341

Figures
O.1 Growth of Islamic Banking and Conventional Banking Assets in Selected Countries, 2006–10 2
O.2 Total *Sukuk* Issuance, 2002–12 3
7.1 The Basic Structure of *Takaful* Models 212
8.1 Dynamics of Poverty Reduction 247
11.1 U.N. Human Development Index (HDI) Trends 307
11.2 U.N. Education Index 308
11.3 Gender Inequality 309
11.4 U.N. Health Index 310
11.5 U.N. Income (Wealth) Index 311
11.6 Gini Coefficient 312
11.7 Poverty 313
11.8 Environment Index, 2010 314
12.1 A Transmission Mechanism in a Conventional Economy 330
12.2 A Transmission Mechanism in an Islamic Economy 338

Tables
O.1 Total Islamic Banking Assets 2
3.1 Banking Crises in Predominantly Muslim and Non-Muslim Countries, 1800–2008 110
7.1 Organizational Types and Services Provided 222
7.2 Criteria Used to Rank Outreach and Sustainability 223
7.3 Outreach of Different Organizations 223
7.4 Sustainability of Different Organizations 223
7.5 Inclusive Finance, Outreach, and Sustainability 223
8.1 Increase in Regional Growth Rates in *Takaful*, 2010–11 245
10.1 Financing of Corporate Growth in 19 Developing Economies and 22 Advanced Economies, 1995–2000 282
11.1 Overall Islamicity Index Rank by Economy 315
11.2 Summary Results of the Islamicity Index (I^2) by Country Subgroup 318
11.3 Economic Islamicity Index (EI^2) Rankings by Economy 318
11.4 Economic Islamicity (EI^2) Index Ranking Averages of All Countries and Various Subgroups 321

Foreword

This book highlights the strong synergies between the current thinking in development economics and an Islamic economic and finance approach to development based on the inherent inclusivity of Islamic financial instruments; the two share a common goal of balanced and equitable growth.

Following a description of the conceptual similarities in principles and approach, including income distribution and redistribution, financial inclusion, and growth, the book suggests possible lessons from Islamic economics and finance for policy makers and development economics researchers.

It challenges readers to learn from Islamic capital market instruments in a global context, arguing that the risk-sharing approach of Islamic finance is more stable than conventional capital markets' practices, which are inherently unstable because of their bias toward leverage-creating debt-based instruments.

Questions of distribution of wealth are very much at the forefront of today's social and economic debates. The authors of this book point to ways in which the Islamic economic system approaches these issues. The book introduces new theoretical ground based on the analysis of John Maynard Keynes on employment, interest, and money, which inadvertently provides the best rationale for some of the basic precepts of Islamic economics. The book also explains how the emphasis of Keynesian analysis on profit and loss sharing encourages investment, which contributes to growth and full employment, as does its emphasis on redistribution of wealth.

This book establishes an excellent link between finance and economic development. It highlights poverty eradication as the principal objective of an Islamic economic system; thus, institutions providing financial services can play an important role in achieving this goal. It also shows how redistribution elements in the Islamic financial system, such as *Zakat* (alms giving), *Qard al-hassan* (benevolent loans), and *Waqf* (charitable endowment), can be integrated into Islamic inclusive finance to resolve problems of outreach and sustainability. This is in addition to serving as complementary vehicles to poverty alleviation efforts.

I would like to commend the work of Professor Abbas Mirakhor and Dr. Zamir Iqbal, as well as the contributions of the distinguished team of authors, for this addition to the literature on the application and use of Islamic finance and economic theory in development economics. They have made a timely contribution to current debates on financial regulation, inclusion, and development.

Dr. Mahmoud Mohieldin
President's Special Envoy
The World Bank

Acknowledgments

The World Bank would like to thank the International Centre for Education in Islamic Finance (INCEIF) for its significant support and co-funding of the publication.

The authors are grateful to Dr. Tunc Uyanik, Director of Financial Systems Global Practice, Financial and Private Sector Development Vice Presidency, World Bank, for conceiving and sponsoring this project. His guidance and generous support was a major source of encouragement for us.

We are indebted to Liudmila Uvarova, Knowledge Management Officer, Financial Systems Global Practice, World Bank, whose diligence and hard work made the completion of this project possible. Special thanks to Mee Jung Kim, Junior Professional Associate, East Asia Financial and Private Sector Development Department, World Bank, for her assistance.

We are also thankful to the manuscript editor, Nancy Morrison, whose drive to perfection and attention to detail significantly improved the manuscript.

Contributors

Habib Ahmed is the Sharjah Chair in Islamic Law and Finance at Durham University, the United Kingdom. Before joining Durham University in August 2008, he worked at the National Commercial Bank and Islamic Development Bank Group (IRTI) in Saudi Arabia and taught at the University of Connecticut, National University of Singapore, and University of Bahrain. Professor Ahmed has authored/edited more than 65 publications, including articles in international refereed journals, books, and other academic papers/monographs. His current research interests include contemporary applications of Islamic commercial law, product development in Islamic finance, inclusive finance, and the integration of *waqf* and the financial sector.

Hossein Askari is Iran Professor of International Business and International Affairs at the George Washington University. He served for nearly three years on the Executive Board of the International Monetary Fund (IMF) and was Special Advisor to the Minister of Finance of Saudi Arabia. During the mid-1980s, he was director of the team that developed the first comprehensive energy plan for Saudi Arabia. He has written extensively on economic development in the Middle East, Islamic economics and finance, international trade and finance, agricultural economics, oil economics, and economic sanctions. He holds a PhD in economics from the Massachusetts Institute of Technology.

Obiyathulla Ismath Bacha is professor of finance and the head of the Graduate Studies Department at the International Centre for Education in Islamic Finance (INCEIF), Malaysia, and President of the Malaysian Finance Association. He received his doctor of business administration (finance), MBA, and MA in economics from Boston University, and his undergraduate degree from the Science University of Malaysia. Professor Obiyathulla has published extensively in academic journals and has authored a textbook on financial derivatives. His most recent work is a co-authored textbook on Islamic capital markets.

Wang Yong Bao received his first PhD in Islamic jurisprudence and its principles from International Islamic University Malaysia (IIUM) in 2005 and received his second PhD in Islamic civilization (IIUM) in 2006. He joined Xi'an International Studies University China in 2008 and INCEIF in 2011, where he has taught graduate level courses on Shari'ah aspects of business and finance, Shari'ah rules in financial transactions, and Shari'ah issues in finance. He is the author of a number of articles and books on Shari'ah and Islamic civilization.

Murat Çizakça is professor of Islamic finance and comparative economic history at INCEIF, Malaysia. He is also a member of the Executive Board (Giunta), Istituto Storia Economica (F. Datini), Prato, Italy. He served as the Third Allianz Visiting Professor for Islamic Studies at the Institut für Geschichte und Kultur des Nahen Orients, L.M.U. Munich University (2006), and is a former fellow of the Institute of Advanced Studies (Wissenschaftskolleg), Berlin (1997–98). Dr. Çizakça received his PhD (economics) from the University of Pennsylvania. He is the author of several books on Islamic finance.

S. Nuri Erbaş, a native of Turkey, holds BA (1975) and MA (1976) degrees in economics from Bogazici University in Istanbul and a PhD in economics (1982) from Columbia University in New York. He taught at the University of Hawaii at Manoa and the University of Houston (1982–89). He was an economist at IMF and also served on IMF's Board as advisor (1989–2009). He taught at INCEIF and the University of Maryland as visiting professor and lecturer (2010–11). He has published in the areas of macroeconomics, monetary theory, public finance, international trade and finance, labor markets, and decision-making in uncertainty and ambiguity.

Zamir Iqbal works as lead investment officer with the Quantitative Strategies, Risk, and Analytics department in the Treasury of the World Bank in Washington, D.C. He holds a PhD in international finance from the George Washington University. His research interests include Islamic finance, financial engineering, and risk management. He has written extensively on Islamic finance and has co-authored several books on Islamic finance. He is chairholder of the YTI Chair of Islamic Finance and Banking at Universiti Sans Islam Malaysia (USIM). He is currently also serving as professional faculty at the Carey Business School of The Johns Hopkins University.

Abbas Mirakhor has been the First Holder of the INCEIF Chair of Islamic Finance since January 2012. A former Executive Director of IMF and acknowledged worldwide as a specialist in Islamic finance, Dr. Mirakhor was appointed to the Order of Companion of Volta for service to Ghana by the President of Ghana in 2005. In 2003, he received the Islamic Development Bank Annual Prize for Research in Islamic Economics, which he shared with Dr. Mohsin Khan, another well-known economist at the IMF. The President of Pakistan conferred on him the Quaid-e Azam star for service to Pakistan in 1997.

Azura Othman is a PhD candidate in Islamic finance at INCEIF, Malaysia. Before that, she was an executive director with PricewaterhouseCoopers Taxation Services, Malaysia. She has over 18 years of experience as a tax consultant, with extensive assignments relating to Islamic finance engaging with the Malaysian Ministry of Finance, the Inland Revenue, and the Central Bank of

Malaysia. She holds a degree in accounting and finance from the London School of Economics and Political Science, is a Fellow of the Association of Chartered Certified Accountants (U.K.), member of the Malaysian Institute of Accountants, and council member of the Association of Chartered Islamic Finance Professionals.

Scheherazade Rehman is the Steve Ross Professorial Fellow of International Finance and Director of the European Union Research Center at the George Washington University. She is a Senior Research Fulbright Scholar and an expert on global financial markets, financial crises, and the Eurozone. Previously she served as a foreign exchange trader in the Middle East. Dr. Rehman regularly guests on national and international televised programs (PBS-Newshour, BBC WorldNews, CNBC, Al-Jazeera, Reuters, C-Span, Colbert Report, VOA). Her latest book (co-authored) is titled *Corruption and Its Manifestation in the Persian Gulf* (2010). She regularly blogs for *U.S. News & World Report*.

Kamaruddin Sharif is a professor of *Takaful* and wealth planning at INCEIF, Malaysia. He holds a doctorate degree in insurance and risk management from Ohio State University, Columbus, Ohio (1985). Dr. Kamaruddin spent about 28 years as an academician, mainly at Universiti Kebangsaan Malaysia. In September 1993, he was appointed as the first principal officer (CEO) of MNI Takaful Sdn. Bhd., the second Islamic insurance company in Malaysia. Over the years, Dr. Kamaruddin had been involved in research and consulting projects, mostly in the area of insurance, *Takaful*, and risk management. He is the author of numerous papers and several journal articles and books.

Andrew Sheng is the President of the Fung Global Institute and the Chief Adviser to the China Banking Regulatory Commission. He served as Chairman of the Securities and Futures Commission of Hong Kong (1998–2005), and as a central banker with the Hong Kong Monetary Authority and Bank Negara, Malaysia. He also worked with the World Bank (1989–93) and chaired the Technical Committee of the International Organization of Securities Commissions (2003–05). He has published widely on monetary, economic, and financial issues, and is a regular contributor to leading economic magazines and newspapers in China and the Asian region. He has an honorary doctorate in economics from the University of Bristol.

Ajit Singh is Emeritus Professor of Economics at Cambridge University and a Life Fellow of Queens' College. He was the fifth holder of the Tun Ismail Ali Chair at the University of Malaya and is the first holder of the Manmohan Singh Chair at Punjab University. He was a senior economic adviser to the governments of Mexico and Tanzania and has advised almost all the UN developmental agencies. Professor Singh has more than 200 research publications. His research falls into three areas: (1) modern business enterprise, corporate finance, and the market for corporate control; (2) de-industrialisation, structural changes, and employment; and (3) liberalization and globalization of financial and product markets and emerging countries.

Abbreviations

AAOIFI	Accounting and Auditing Organisation for Islamic Financial Institutions
ARM	adjustable rate mortgage
ATM	automatic teller machine
BAIK	Koperasi Baytul Ikhtiar
BMT	Baitul Maal Tamwil
BNM	Bank Negara Malaysia
BOT	Build-Operate-Transfer
BPR	Badan Perkreditan Rakyat
BPRS	Bank Perkreditan Rakyat Syari'ah
BR	Bank Rakyat
CAPM	capital asset pricing model
CBO	community-based organization
CIESIN	Center for International Earth Science Information Network
EI	Education Index
EI^2	Economic Islamicity Index
EMH	efficient market hypothesis
EPI	Environmental Performance Index
ETFs	exchange-traded funds
FAO	Food and Agriculture Organization
FBS	Funeral Benefit Scheme
FI	financial institution
FSB	Financial Sector Blueprint
FSMP	Financial Sector Master Plan
GCC	Gulf Cooperation Council
GDP	gross domestic product
GE	general equilibrium
GNI	gross national income
GNP	gross national product

HDI	Human Development Index
HPI²	Human and Political Rights Islamicity Index
I²	Islamicity Index
IBBL	Islamic Bank Bangladesh Limited
IBF	Islamic Bank Foundation
ICC	International Chamber of Commerce
ICM	Islamic capital market
IFC	International Finance Corporation
IFIS	Islamic Finance Information Services
IFSB	Islamic Financial Services Board
II	Income (Wealth) Index
IILM	International Islamic Liquidity Management
IMF	International Monetary Fund
INCEIF	International Centre for Education in Islamic Finance
IPO	initial public offering
IRI²	International Relations Islamicity Index
ISRA	Institute for Education in Islamic Finance
LBO	leveraged buyout
LEI	Life Expectancy Index
LGI²	Legal and Governance Islamicity Index
MENA	Middle East and North Africa
MFI	microfinance institution
MIAN	Microinsurance Association of Netherlands
MIFC	Malaysia International Islamic Financial Centre
MM	Modigliani and Miller
MPT	modern portfolio theory
MSMEs	micro, small, and medium enterprises
NGO	nongovernmental organization
NIE	new institutional economics
OECD	Organisation for Economic Co-operation and Development
OIC	Organization of Islamic Cooperation
PLS	profit-loss sharing
PPP	purchasing power parity
R&D	research and development
RB	regional briefing note
RDS	Rural Development Scheme
REIT	real estate investment trust
ROA	return on assets
ROE	return on equity

SAR	special administrative region
SDI	Subsidy Dependence Index
SIBL	Social Investment Bank Limited
SMEs	small and medium enterprises
SOE	state-owned enterprise
TFP	total factor productivity
TO	*Takaful* operator
TTTFS	Takaful T&T Friendly Society
UN	United Nations
UNICEF	United Nations Children's Fund
WACC	weighted average cost of capital
WDI	World Development Indicators

Overview

Over the last three decades, the concepts of Islamic finance and Islamic economics have captured the attention of researchers. The growing market for transactions compatible with Islamic law (*Shari'ah*) is further evidence of growing interest in this mode of finance. Although Islamic finance is one of the fastest growing segments of emerging global financial markets, it is often stated that the market is far below its true potential. At the same time, the concepts of Islamic finance are not fully explained and exploited—especially in the areas of economic development, inclusion, access to finance, and public policy. Against this background, this volume is a humble attempt to highlight some of the key features of Islamic finance relevant to economic development. The objective of the volume is to improve understanding of the perspective of Islamic finance on economic development, social and economic justice, human welfare, and economic growth.

We are grateful to all the contributors of the volume, who worked with great dedication and commitment on their assigned topics. We hope that readers will benefit from the experience and knowledge of the contributing authors in deepening their appreciation and understanding of core principles of Islamic teaching concerning economics and finance. We also hope that the ideas presented in the volume are equally beneficial to researchers and the policy makers interested in both Islamic and conventional literature.

Although the principles of Islamic finance go back several centuries, and Islamic finance has been practiced in some form since the inception of Islam, its practice in modern financial markets became recognized only in the 1980s, and began to represent a meaningful share of global financial activity only around the beginning of this century. Over the last two decades, by some estimates, the total volume of Islamic financial assets has grown by 15–20 percent a year and now exceeds $1.3 trillion (Ernst & Young 2012). Following on from the significant developments that have occurred in what we view as the core area for this market—the predominantly Muslim countries—we are now witnessing the globalization of Islamic finance. In recent years, significant interest in Islamic finance has emerged in the world's leading conventional financial centers, including London, New York, and Hong Kong, and Western investors are increasingly considering investment in Islamic financial products.

The growth of this market has been driven by the high demand for Shari'ah-compliant products, as well as the increasing liquidity in the Gulf region due to high oil revenues. Table O.1 shows the growth trend in Islamic finance for the banking sectors by different regions, with estimates of total Islamic banking assets reaching $1.8 trillion by the end of 2013 (Ernst & Young 2012). Figure O.1 shows how the growth of the Islamic financial sector in the 2006–10 period surpassed the growth of the conventional financial sector in all segments of the market, ranging from commercial banking, investment banking, and fund management to insurance in several Muslim-majority countries (Deutsche Bank 2011).

One of the recent developments in Islamic finance is the introduction of Islamic bonds, or *sukuk*, which are structured as a securitized product. The key feature of *sukuk* is that they are structured following the principle of linking the financial return to a real sector activity. As a result, the bonds are backed by real assets or projects, and the investors' return is based on the performance of underlying assets. Figure O.2 shows the total number of *sukuk* and their volume over the last ten years, which is testimony to the rapid growth of this market, and its quick recovery during the global downturn. The *sukuk* market has been used by both the public (sovereign and quasi-sovereign) sector and corporate sector to

Table O.1 Total Islamic Banking Assets
$ billion

Global Islamic banking assets, 2011	1,334
Growth estimates by region through 2013	
Southeast Asia	89
Gulf Cooperation Council (GCC) countries	131
Rest of the world	257
Global Islamic banking assets (2013, est.)	1,811

Source: Ernst & Young 2012.

Figure O.1 Growth of Islamic Banking and Conventional Banking Assets in Selected Countries, 2006–10
Percent

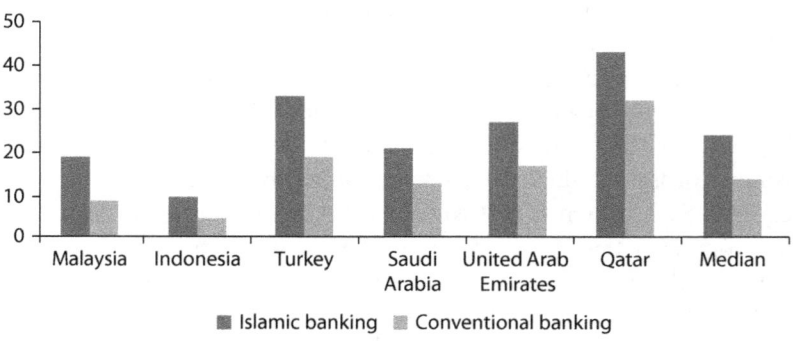

Source: Deutsche Bank 2011.

Figure O.2 Total *Sukuk* Issuance, 2002–12

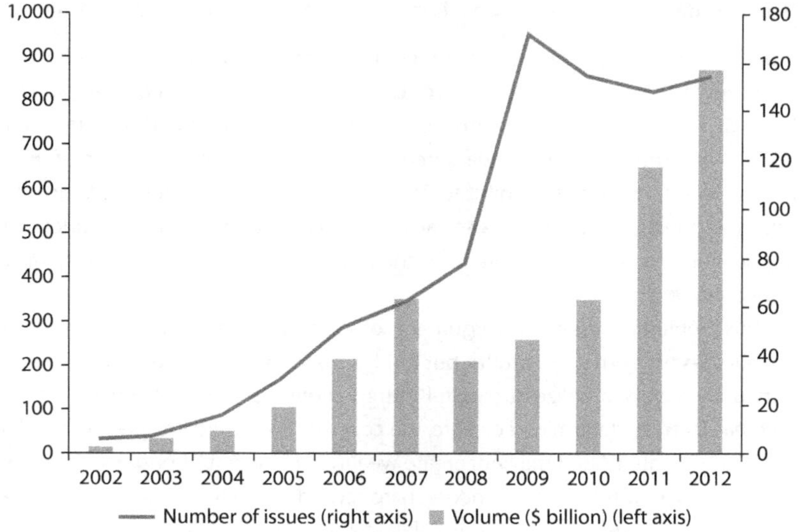

Source: Islamic Finance Information Services (IFIS).

mobilize finance. Although the size of the *sukuk* market relative to conventional bonds market is very small, there is great potential for further expansion, development, and innovation of this market, which could unleash the true potential of Islamic finance.

Views on Economic Development

A world view—a conception of how the world works—will determine the values and preferences that determine actions and decisions. In the realm of economics, finance, and development, the underlying world will also stimulate the actual behavior of economic agents. There is an important difference in the world view and nature of the norms assumed by modern conventional economics and those in Islamic economics.

Modern economic theory describes the ideal pattern of behavior of people in commercial endeavors, to which they should strive to conform in order to achieve economic growth and development. The ideals follow certain norms and are shaped by a world view that is motivated by rationality and act in conformity with the maximization principle.

The Islamic view of economics, finance, and development has an added dimension in the form of moral and spiritual values (see box O.1). In order to appreciate the concept of the Islamic economic theory of development, it is useful to examine the Western or conventional concept of economic development to provide the context and benchmark for this discussion.

In a conventional system, the concept of economic development is centered mainly on the pursuit of personal gain, in the form of satisfaction, utility, or profit. The motivation that conditions the economic conduct of the people

Box O.1 Basic Principles of an Islamic Economic and Financial System

Prohibition of interest. The central tenet of the system is a prohibition of *riba*, a term literally meaning "an excess" and interpreted as "any unjustifiable increase of capital whether in loans or sales." More precisely, any positive, fixed, predetermined rate tied to the maturity and the amount of principal (guaranteed regardless of the performance of the investment) is considered *riba* and is prohibited. The general consensus among Islamic scholars is that *riba* covers not only usury but also the charging of "interest" as widely practiced. The direct implication of prohibition of interest is the prohibition of pure debt security with a predetermined interest rate.

This prohibition is based on arguments of social justice, equality, and property rights. Islam encourages the earning of profits, but forbids the charging of interest because profits, determined ex post, symbolize successful entrepreneurship and creation of additional wealth, whereas interest, determined ex ante, is a cost that is accrued irrespective of the outcome of business operations and may not create wealth in the event of business losses. Social justice demands that borrowers and lenders share rewards as well as losses in an equitable fashion and that the process of wealth accumulation and distribution in the economy be fair and representative of true productivity.

Risk sharing. Because interest is prohibited, pure debt security is eliminated from the system. Therefore, suppliers of funds become investors instead of creditors. The provider of financial capital and the entrepreneur share business risks in return for shares of the profits and losses.

Asset-based transactions. The prohibition of debt and encouragement of risk sharing suggests a financial system where there is a direct link between the real and the financial sector. As a result, the system promotes the "materiality" aspect, which requires linking financing directly with the underlying asset so that the financing activity is clearly and closely identified with the real sector activity. There are strong linkages between the performance of the asset and the return on capital used to finance it.

Money as "potential" capital. Money is treated as "potential" capital: that is, it becomes actual capital only when it joins with other resources to undertake a productive activity. Islam recognizes the time value of money, but only when it acts actively as capital, not when it is "potential" capital.

Prohibition of speculative behavior. An Islamic financial system discourages hoarding and prohibits transactions featuring extreme uncertainties, gambling, and risks.

Sanctity of contracts and preservation of property rights. Islam upholds contractual obligations and the disclosure of information as a sacred duty. This feature is intended to reduce the risk of asymmetric information and moral hazard. Islam places great importance on preservation of property rights; defines a balance between rights of individuals, society, and the state; and strongly prohibits encroachment of anyone's property rights.

Source: Iqbal and Mirakhor 2011.

within this system is the promotion of self-interest, which is seen as eminently rational. This motivation relies solely on logical and scientific reasons and the concept of natural order. Profit maximization is one of the focal points of this motivation. The pursuit of self-interest in a conventional economy may not necessarily lead to improvements in the general well-being of society. Monopolistic situations may develop; price distortions, speculation, and hoarding of goods may ensue, and can result in certain segments of the society being deprived in favor of others with more influence in the market. It follows that in a conventional economy, the well-being of the society as a whole is not central in the pursuit of economic development.

The conventional world view separates the worldly and spiritual affairs of life. Thus, the concept of economic development is devoid of any spiritual values. Absolute freedom is granted to individuals in their economic pursuits, which in most circumstances focus on the material interest alone. Any incentive structures or sanctions put in place to guide human behavior in the economy are based on man-made rules and are subject to discretionary changes and influence.

Traditionally, in a conventional system, the process of economic development is centered on the quest for increasing economic prosperity, as evidenced by early discussions on economic development following World War II, which focused mainly on the structural transformation of economies toward increasing the level of productivity and per capita income. Over time, the Western approach to economic development has started to recognize the wider dimension of human development. Human solidarity, belonging, well-being, sharing, concern for others, basic human entitlements, and modest living are some of the dimensions increasingly being emphasized (Mirakhor and Askari 2010).

Adam Smith, a leading explicator of the self-interest motive, has often been quoted in terms of his views on rules of market behavior. What have not been widely quoted are his views contained in the *Theory of Moral Sentiments* (1759), in which Smith emphasizes the moral foundations of economic relations, such as belief in the One Creator, accountability and compliance to the rules prescribed by the Creator, and internalization of the rules by being consciously aware of the ever-presence of the Creator—moral foundations that share much with Islam (Mirakhor and Askari 2010). Smith believed that justice and fairness are embedded in the rules of the Creator and are achieved by fully complying with these rules. Crucially, the moral values emphasized in an Islamic economic system are not alien to conventional economics, but are a neglected feature that is gaining renewed interest among conventional economists.

The Islamic Concept of Economic Development

The concepts of economic and human development in Islam are not time-dependent, as Islam is an immutable rules-based system. The rules of behavior for humans and society to achieve material and nonmaterial progress are grounded by the rules prescribed in the Qur'an. The Islamic concept of development covers three interrelated dimensions: individual human development, physical-material development, and development of the human collectivity (Mirakhor and Askari 2010). The first dimension is the most important, and specifies a dynamic process of the growth of individuals toward realizing their full potential given by the Creator. The second dimension refers to the utilization of natural resources provided by the Creator to meet the material needs of individuals and society. The third dimension refers to the progress of the human collectivity toward full integration and unity. The first dimension—which starts from an intense awareness of oneself and the Creator, such that every action is taken in compliance with the rules prescribed by the Creator—will lead to harmony and unity with the rest of humanity and creation. Failure for the three dimensions to proceed in tandem leads to harmful distortions.

The achievement of the three dimensions is reflected in the principal teaching of Islam, which is justice and equity. Every rule in Islam enjoins activities that serve to remove obstacles from the path of humans toward individual and collective well-being and spiritual fulfillment, in line with the Creator. Consequently, the development in the human collectivity and the physical-material realm will be achieved as the actions and decisions of humans are taken in consonance with the well-being of the society and the environment, as well.

Islam has given humans a unique position among all creation as Allah (swt's) vicegerent on earth, which confers on them responsibilities toward their own individual well-being and development, as well as that of the rest of creation. Concurrently, humans are to create a just and moral social order on earth. Similar to the conventional economic system, there will be reward and retribution for rule-compliance and rule violation: however, the rules are divine and absolute. Rules in the Islamic economic system lead to actions that embed the interest of society and the rest of Creation, as well as humanity's own self-interest, in conformance with the will of the Creator.

The Qur'an is the fountainhead of all Islamic thinking, including thoughts that relate to the structure and operations of an ideal Islamic economy and its financial system. Scholars provide further elaboration of the rules in Islamic jurisprudence within the framework of the Qur'an and *Sunnah* (the sayings and the practices of the Beloved Messenger). From these sources, the rules relating to the conduct of participants in an economy are derived, including the rules relating to contracts, property rights, trusts, cooperation, consultation, justice, distribution, and redistribution.

Contracts and Trust
Islam forcefully anchors all socioeconomic relations in contracts. Constant awareness of the ever-presence of the Creator will encourage faithfulness to the contract with the Creator, as the rules of the Creator become internalized in the individual's every action and decision. The Qur'an encourages individuals to fulfill their contracts and render the trusts given to them. Faithfulness to contracts and fulfillment of their terms is essential to ensure transparency and unhindered flow of information. Compliance to contractual obligations provides certainty in the formation of expectations, prevents conflicts, coordinates actions,

promotes social cohesion, and strengthens social order. It is through the condition of trust that contracts can be fulfilled. Without trust, contracts become difficult to negotiate and conclude, and hence costly to monitor and enforce. When trust is weak, administrative mechanisms are needed to enforce contracts, and these mechanisms can be complex and expensive. In such cases, transaction costs become high; as a result, there is less trade and fewer market participants. Faithfulness to contracts requires commitment, which in turn requires a high sense of diligence toward complying with the rules of the Creator. When all humans act in accordance with the prescribed rules, then all transactions will be completed according to contractual expectations. Under such a system, regulations will be kept to a minimum.

Cooperation and Consultation

Achievement of trust among participants facilitates cooperation and smooth running of the economy. Through cooperation, there will be mutual consultations in matters pertaining to human relations. In a series of verses in the Qur'an, Islam urges humans to establish a collective, unified, and successful social life, undertake cooperative social action, and maintain social solidarity within society. Islam discourages working in isolation, which can lead to social disunity. Instead, humans are encouraged to make decisions through a *shura* (collective consultation). Through consultations, impulsive behavior and reactions can be kept in check.

Property Rights

The rules relating to property rights hinge on the principle that the ultimate property rights to everything in this world belong to Allah. These rights include all the value added to the store of wealth, as the human's capabilities that made these additions possible also belong to Allah. As the vicegerents of Allah, humans are acting only as the trustees to natural and created wealth. Humans are able to gain legitimate property rights only through their own creative labor or through transfer (such as exchange, trade, gifts, or inheritance). Therefore, gaining instantaneous claim to property rights without commensurate effort is prohibited unless the property is acquired through gifts and/or inheritance. Once the wealth is acquired, there are obligations for it to be used for lawful purposes and not to be wasted, squandered, or used opulently or ostentatiously.

Additionally, the Creator provides sustenance to all Creation without discrimination, implying that all humans have equal opportunity and rights to the resources created. It is only the differences in individual human abilities and capabilities that lead to differentiated results. Therefore, income inequality is bound to exist. However, the rights of the less able to the wealth of the more able remain intact. By recognizing the fact that created resources are available equally to all and the rights to these are immutable, any amount of wealth that is amassed that exceeds an individual's moderate needs is the right due to other individuals who are less able. These rights to the less able must be redeemed through redistributive transfers, such as *zakat*, *infaq fi sabil Allah*, and *sadaqah*.

Those who are unable to work should be given adequate income to cover their basic needs, irrespective of the level of their productive effort, as explicitly stated in the Qur'an. In Islam, collective humanity has priority rights over the created resources. Therefore, while individual possession of wealth is allowed, protected, and preserved, it should not come into conflict with humanity's collective interests and well-being. The rules of property rights as a distinct feature of the Islamic economic system lead to the rules of distribution and redistribution.

Distribution and Redistribution

The issues of poverty and distributive justice are directly related to economic growth and human development (Naqvi 2003). Therefore, one of the central concerns of Islamic economics is to bring about distributive justice and maximize social welfare. Inequality, brought about by the different capabilities of humans to access and work with the created resources, if not corrected, will pass from one generation to the next and lead to wealth accumulation by a few at the expense of poverty and misery for a large part of the society. In a truly Islamic economy, such a situation will not be allowed, as Islam places great importance on the preservation of human dignity. Every human has the right to live a decent life in order to carry on his or her work and responsibilities toward his or her family, society, and the Creator. Accordingly, there must be a mechanism to ensure that the dignity of the less able is preserved. The Qur'an has made provisions for income and wealth to be shared among the members of the society through the rules of distribution and redistribution.

The rules of distribution and redistribution are the most important economic institutions in Islam for achieving social justice. These rules seek to achieve development in the human collectivity and create a balanced society that avoids excessive wealth and extreme poverty. The governing rule of distribution requires that each is paid according to the contribution to what the society is able to produce. The rule governing distribution and redistribution ordains that the more economically able redeem the rights of the less able in the form of *sadaqah*. To motivate this transfer, incentives structures are put in place in the form of multiple returns, implying that the income and wealth of the giver will not diminish but increase as a result of this giving. To ensure the distribution of wealth to the next generation, Islam prescribes the rules of inheritance, which distribute the wealth of a person to his/her heirs on his/her passing, thus ensuring that the wealth is shared among the progeny. The objective of the rules of distribution and redistribution is to ensure that the wealth is circulated within the society. The flow of wealth and resources is needed for the growth of the economy.

These features of an Islamic economy frame Islam's position on economic progress, which places great emphasis on societal implications—and starts from faithfulness and active awareness of the Supremacy of the Creator and internalizing the rules aimed at achieving social solidarity and unity.

Characteristics of an Islamic Economic System

After examining the conventional and Islamic concepts of economic development, the characteristics, structure, and logic of an Islamic economic system can be understood. While much of the next section focuses on the ideal system, such an ideal does not exist today. Instead, different countries have adopted various features of the ideal system. These can be referred to as "hybrid" systems. Such a system has characteristics of the Islamic and capitalistic market systems. Thus, the hybrid system recognizes the interdependencies between the individual's self-interest and that the interests of society. It utilizes the institution of the state to regulate the economy so as to align the interests of the individual and society. It is a market-based economy similar to a capitalist economy, but with an emphasis on social welfare measures adopted by the state. It modifies the capitalist system by moving from a system that is usurious to a system that shares risks among the participants in the economy. At the same time, it recognizes the individual's right to own property. In this economy, features of an Islamic system coexist with policy and institutional frameworks that are features of market capitalism. The aspiration to move toward full compliance to the rules as prescribed by the Qur'an also is present. This is a system in transition from a capitalistic economy toward becoming an ideal Islamic economic system.

An Islamic economic system is a rule-based system. It does not treat economic activity independent of values prescribed by the Qur'an and *Sunnah*. The central aim of Islam is to establish a just, moral, and viable social order through the agency of man (Al Hasani and Mirakhor 2003). Under such a system, economic activities are built on foundations of justice, where everyone is given what is rightly due to them and everything is put in its rightful place. The rights on wealth bestowed on individuals are given with the condition that the use is conducted in accordance with the rules of Allah (swt). Honoring contracts and agreements is obligatory in all circumstances. As a result, there is great transparency in the market, where participants must disclose full information to avoid harm, disputes, or damage arising from any trade or market activities. Reduced uncertainty makes it easier to make informed market decisions. Transparency increases coordination and makes behavior predictable. Coordination also arises from reciprocity and the high level of trust among participants, which will also promote cooperation. Cooperation is the basis for the concept of sharing, which reduces the risk for individuals and spreads it among participants.

The organizing principle of Islamic finance in an Islamic economy is transaction based on exchange, where real asset is exchanged for real asset. Hence transactions are based on the real economy. When it comes to finance, no dealings with *riba* (interest) are allowed. The epistemological roots of risk sharing as an organizing principle of the Islamic financial system are discernible from verse 275 of chapter 2 of the Qur'an, which decrees that all economic and financial transactions are conducted via contracts of exchange (*al-Bay'*) and not through interest-based debt contracts (*riba*). According to this verse, requiring contracts to be based on exchange constitutes a necessary condition, and "no-*riba*" as the sufficient condition in an Islamic financial system. By focusing on trade and exchange in commodities and assets, Islam encourages risk sharing, which promotes social solidarity. The prohibition of interest-based transactions stems from the fact that interest-based debt contracts are instruments of risk shifting. In such a contract, the creditor acquires a claim on the property rights of the debtor without losing the claim on the property rights to the money lent, regardless of the outcome of the contract. Another important implication of risk sharing is the rate of return to financing is determined ex post (after the investment has been made) by the rate of return on real activity.

The features of an Islamic economy will also change the behavior of society. There will be greater consultation; hence there will be no impulsive-compulsive reaction in financial dealings. At the same time, the labor force in an Islamic economy will work under a rule of trust and full understanding of contracts and obligations. Workers also share in the gains achieved through the risk, based on their own productive efforts, which is a better incentive system than a fixed wage. Workers will be treated with respect, which reflects the importance of human dignity in Islam.

Summary of Chapters

In *chapter 1*, Abbas Mirakhor and Wang Yong Bao discuss the epistemological roots of conventional and Islamic finance. (Epistemology deals with the question of what we know about a phenomenon and how we know it.) Given that an economic system determines the features of a financial system, the origin of a financial system is better understood by knowing the epistemology of its economic system. The epistemology of the contemporary conventional economic system is usually traced to Adam Smith's conception of an economy, which is embedded in his view of a moral-ethical system that gives rise to the competitive market economy envisioned in the *Wealth of Nations* (1776). Kenneth Arrow and his principle co-authors, Gerard Debreu and Frank Hahn, attempted to provide an analytically rigorous proof of what they saw as the vision of Smith for an economy.

The authors argue that the work of Arrow-Debreu-Hahn is fundamentally about optimal risk sharing in a decentralized market economy. It addresses the question of how best to allocate risk in an economy; the answer is that risk should be allocated to those who can best bear it. The economy-finance nexus defined by the Arrow-Debreu-Hahn general equilibrium models were risk-sharing conceptualizations in which securities represented contingent financial claims on the real sector. Comparing the origin of the conventional financial system, the authors make the case that risk sharing is the objective of Islamic finance. The essential function of Islamic financial instruments is spreading and allocating risk among market participants, rather than allowing it to concentrate among the borrowing class. The authors discuss the roots of risk sharing in the tenets of Islam and how compliance with and commitment to a set of rules—among them, property rights, contracts, trust, virtues of prudence, concern for other people, justice, and benevolence—can insure social order and cohesion. Islamic finance provides the risk-sharing mechanism across the financial system in three main ways: through risk-sharing instruments in the financial sector; redistributive risk-sharing instruments that the economically more able segment of the society utilize to share the risks faced by the less able segment of the population; and the inheritance rules, by which the wealth of a person at the time of death is distributed among current and future generations of inheritors.

The authors conclude that stock markets are an effective instrument of international risk sharing, as well as a tool of individual and firm risk management. Therefore, active involvement of governments in creating a vibrant and efficient stock market, and their participation in that market by financing a portion of their budget with equity, can create the incentives and motivation for further development of more effective risk-sharing instruments of Islamic finance. The chapter suggests that government can enhance the credibility and appeal of the stock market by financing part of its budget by issuing equity shares that would be traded in the market. Government can also mount a public information campaign to educate the population regarding the risk-sharing characteristics of the stock market. This strategy was adopted in the United Kingdom, with considerable success. Such an enhanced stock market could serve the high end of the time-risk-return profile of the transactions menu.

In *chapter 2*, Andrew Sheng and Ajit Singh provide a perspective of conventional modern economists who seek to relate the concepts of Islamic and conventional finance, and to examine certain important questions that arise from the interaction between these systems. The chapter discusses the main tenets of Islamic finance, as well as those of modern economics, including the implications of interest rates and those of Modigliani and Miller theorems. One of the notable observations of the chapter is that John Maynard Keynes' analysis of employment, interest, and money provides, inadvertently, the best rationale for some of the basic precepts of Islamic finance.

An economic system where capital is rewarded according to its earning capacity could be entirely adequate for achieving sufficient savings and investments for economic growth, and for allocating them efficiently. The main proposition of Islamic finance is that the return to capital is determined after the investment period is concluded (ex post) and should be based on the return to economic activity in which the capital was employed. Savings and investment should be determined by this ex post rate of return on capital. Indeed, research has shown that the Islamic system can be based entirely on equity capital, without debt, and is therefore often more stable than the conventional system based on debt. This discussion raises an important question for conventional economists: whether an economic system requires an ex ante interest rate to function efficiently. Sheng and Singh endorse the argument by Mirakhor (2011) that the Arrow-Debreu-Hahn system of general equilibrium, together with its welfare properties, does not have a predetermined (ex ante) interest rate in the analysis. This system is totally viable, and is indeed the crowning glory of modern economics.

With respect to economic development, the authors challenge any unsubstantiated claims that Islamic principles are counter-growth. They argue that the traditional Islamic emphasis on profitability encourages investment, which contributes to growth and full employment, as does its emphasis on redistribution of wealth. Interpersonal redistribution, rather than being a negative force for accumulation and economic development, becomes, in the current era, a positive force for maintaining aggregate demand for achieving full employment. It is therefore arguable that Islamic finance in general does not necessarily have negative consequences for economic growth, but rather quite the opposite.

Finally, Sheng and Singh conclude that there is no inevitable conflict between the two systems, and cooperation between them is eminently desirable and feasible. Islamic finance has long represented a distinct approach to economic thinking and financial practice and provides a potentially complete system. One can envisage a future in which the two systems—the Western and the Islamic—each with its distinct characteristics, run in parallel, offering individuals and businesses open choices between the two. The conventional and Islamic finance could cooperate and even compete to produce the best outcome for common projects, such as the provision of cheap banking for the world's poor or for investment in environmental undertakings. There is wide consensus that the world's poor should have wider access to finance, and this may be more appropriate under the Islamic finance system because of its more ethical basis.

In *chapter 3*, S. Nuri Erbaş and Abbas Mirakhor provide a brief taxonomy of the foundational Islamic market principles and evaluate them in the context of institutional and behavioral economics in the context of Knightian uncertainty. In the normative sense, the chapter interprets *preferred* economic behavior as moral behavior, while in the objective sense, the authors interpret preferred economic behavior as such behavior that reduces uncertainty and increases individual and social welfare, in the same way the concept is understood in welfare economics. The authors skillfully develop a robust analytical context to analyze the economic impact of religion on the basis of three fundamental factors that play a role in economic development: incentives, uncertainty, and justice. It appears this is the missing context underlying the search for a testable causality going from religion to economic development.

There is a need to examine the market principles embedded in a specific religion and their particular influence on *preferred* economic behavior. Among the Abrahamic traditions, an example *par excellence* is Islam, because the Qur'an and the Traditions of the Messenger specify a comprehensive set of rules relating to economic incentives, uncertainty, and justice. Those rules cover contracts, property rights, market organization, moral behavior in the face of uncertainty, and redistribution of wealth. Islamic principles protect property rights, ordain adherence to contracts, and provide incentives for investment and growth. The chapter argues that Islamic rules for moral market behavior are economically substantiated in the context of uncertainty; moreover, observance by procedurally rational decision makers can reduce uncertainty and aversion to ambiguity.

In addressing uncertainty or Knightian uncertainty, Erbaş and Mirakhor argue that human economic behavior, whether based on rationality or morality, cannot be reduced to prespecified probability distributions that trivialize uncertainty as a random walk. With perfect information and foresight, errant or immoral intent can be terminated and sanctioned before it becomes behavior. But humans must submit that capacity to the highest authority. The economic function of moral behavior and the social trust it generates is analytically meaningful in the context of substantive uncertainty emanating from unknown and unknowable contingencies and human responses to them over space and time.

The chapter argues that it is in the context of Knightian uncertainty that the economic function of beliefs, norms, rules, institutions, and their transmittal from generation to generation becomes substantiated. Faith-based rules may also reduce economic uncertainty by establishing behavioral reference points and by promoting social trust, cooperation, and solidarity—and thus generating positive externalities. The chapter proposes that a fundamental analytical context in which to explore the correlation between religion and economic progress is human decision behavior in the context of substantive uncertainty, and the scriptural guidance that religion provides to reduce it.

The authors conclude that the foundational Islamic moral principles and institutional structures are market-oriented. They incentivize economic progress and reduce uncertainty by providing guidance for preferred market behavior. They can also achieve a significant measure of economic justice without undermining incentives and property rights. For much of their economic history, Muslims structured their markets in accordance with the rich legacy of the market institutions in the traditions of the Qur'an and the Messenger. Those institutions were rule-based, market-oriented, and innovative. History gives proof that Islamic societies thrived, and some grew into global economic powers. That rich legacy was not sustained, resulting in a state of underdevelopment relative to the West in the last two centuries and relative to other countries that have made great strides in economic development more recently. The historical reasons for the decline are complex, including warfare, devastating invasions, geography, decline of scientific thought, moral and institutional decay resulting in erosion of social trust, internecine power struggles and despotic rule, and predatory taxation to finance wars and indulgence.

Finally, the authors observe that social trust is built on society's belief in justice in general and economic justice in particular. Lack of economic justice undermines trust and incentives to invest in human and physical capital and takes the form of predatory competition; corruption; risk of expropriation; upward mobility based on arbitrary social position (ascription) rather than achievement; restricted access to markets, financing and education; and widespread poverty. Economic justice is a fundamental moral issue that emanates from uneven accumulation of wealth through market-based economic progress, even though progress may improve the welfare of nearly all income classes.

In *chapter 4*, Murat Çizakça accounts for finance and development in Islam from a historical perspective and examines how the classical principles of Islamic finance and economy, together with the institutions that applied these principles, have led to economic development. He poses the key question: Is there any historical evidence of sustained and significant economic development in the Islamic world?

The author postulates that the economic and financial principles enshrined in the classical Islamic sources undoubtedly point to a vibrant capitalist system, but with a blend of Islamic moral and ethical principles. All the legal and institutional prerequisites for financing and administering production and exchange in a capitalist framework were in place in the Islamic world long before the Europeans started utilizing them in full. Such institutions were highly efficient because of lower transaction costs.

First and the foremost, the author addresses the question of how the prohibition of interest was observed and, by implication, how the different factors of production were combined. The simple answer is the classical principles of an Islamic economy were applied in real life through various economic, financial, and social institutions. For example, sharing profits, risks, and losses between the capitalist and the entrepreneur was made possible by the institution of business partnerships; through these partnerships the capital owned by the capitalist could be deployed to the entrepreneurs. Thus sharing risks, profits, and losses replaced the notion of lending capital at a predetermined rate of interest. Innovative application of partnership-based instruments, particularly *mudarabah* (agent-principal partnership), became essential for financing an entrepreneur. This concept was incorporated into the various instruments in Europe, where it came to be known as *commenda*. It is generally agreed that *commenda* was the most important business partnership of medieval Europe and that it played a crucial role in triggering the "commercial revolution."

Another historical development in the Muslim world was expansion of international trade, which could not have been possible without a sophisticated maritime law. Çizakça notes that the institution of maritime law was originally provided by Muslims, and this Islamic law of maritime trade was transferred to Europe through various compilations. It was expansion of international trade that necessitated a whole spectrum of new financial instruments, such as bills of exchange, letters of credit (*suftaja*), promissory notes, ordinary checks, and double-entry book keeping—all known to the Muslims. Historians are in general agreement that medieval Europe simply borrowed these instruments from the Muslims. Without these financial instruments, long-distance trade would simply have been impossible.

Despite modest government revenues, important social services to the society were made possible by *waqf* (endowments). *Waqf* establishes, finances, and maintains the most essential services any civilized society needs—often for centuries. Foremost among them are the institutions of learning and health: in short, institutions that enhance human capital.

In *chapter 5*, Hossein Askari discusses the evolution of the concept of economic development—from a concern for social order, to the role of civil society, culture, and state, to development as material well-being, with ethics, freedom, development of the self, income equality, environmental preservation, and sustainability factored in. The three rules that new institutional economics considers crucial to economic growth—protection of property rights, the enforcement of contracts, and good governance—are emphasized in Islam. However, the network of rules in Islam that guarantees development goes further.

While Western economic thinking on development has changed over the last 60 or so years, basically rediscovering Adam Smith and recognizing the central importance of human well-being to the development process, Islamic thinking on development finds strong roots in rules prescribed by the Qur'an. Islam is a rules-based system with a prescribed method for humans and society to achieve material and nonmaterial progress and development grounded in compliance with rules and effective institutions. The Islamic concept of development has three dimensions: individual self-development; the physical development of the earth; and the development of the human collectivity, which includes both. The first specifies a dynamic process of the growth of the human toward perfection. The second specifies the utilization of natural resources to develop the earth to provide for the material needs of the individual and all of humanity. The third concept encompasses the progress of the human collectivity toward full integration and unity. Together they constitute the rules-based compliance system, which is intended to assure progress on the three interrelated dimensions of development.

The three dimensions of development are closely interrelated, to the point where balanced progress in all three dimensions is needed to achieve development. The four basic elements of the Western concept of development—scarcity, rationality, and the roles of the state and of the market—are perceived somewhat differently in Islam. All three dimensions of Islamic development assign heavy responsibility to individuals and society—with both held responsible for any lack of development. Balanced development is defined as balanced progress in all three dimensions. Progress is balanced if it is accompanied by justice, both in its general (*ádl*) and in its interpersonal (*qist*) dimension. The objective of such balanced development is to achieve progress on the path to perfection by humans, through compliance with rules. Enforcement of the prescribed rules is accomplished by an internal and an external mechanism. The love of humans for one another is a part of their adoration of the Creator, and each human is responsible for ensuring that others are rule-compliant. It is also the duty of the state and its apparatus to enforce rule-compliance. The governance structure envisaged in Islam requires full transparency and accountability by the state and the full participation of all members.

In *chapter 6*, Zamir Iqbal and Abbas Mirakhor provide an Islamic perspective on financial inclusion and argue that the core principles of Islam place great emphasis on social justice, inclusion, and sharing of resources between the haves and the have-nots. Islamic finance addresses the issue of financial inclusion from two directions: one by promoting risk-sharing contracts that provide a viable alternative to conventional debt-based financing, and the other through specific instruments of redistribution of the wealth among the society. Risk-sharing financing instruments and redistributive instruments complement each other to offer a comprehensive approach to enhancing financial inclusion, eradicating poverty, and building a healthy and vibrant economy. They help reduce the poor's income-consumption correlation. In other words, the poor are not forced to rely on their low-level income (or even absence of income) to maintain a decent level of subsistence living for themselves and their families.

Conventional finance has developed mechanisms such as microfinance, small and medium enterprise (SME) financing, and microinsurance to enhance financial inclusion. Conventional techniques have been only partially successful in enhancing the access and are not without challenges. Islamic finance, based on the concept of risk sharing, offers a set of financial instruments promoting risk sharing rather than risk shifting in the financial system. In addition, Islam advocates redistributive instruments such as *zakat* (obligatory tax for social welfare), *sadaqah* (voluntary charity), and *Qard-al-hassan* (benevolent loans), through which the economically more able segment of the society shares the risks facing the less able segment of the population. Such instruments of wealth redistribution are used to redeem the rights of the less able by means of the income and wealth of the more able. These are not instruments of charity, altruism, or beneficence, but are instruments of redemption of rights and repayment of obligations. In addition, the inheritance rules specify how the wealth of a person is distributed among current and future generations of inheritors.

Iqbal and Mirakhor remind us that access to finance is hampered by informational asymmetries and market imperfections that need to be removed before financing may be enhanced. When it comes to Muslim developing countries where the financial sector is not very developed and the formal financial sector is underdeveloped, it is important to pay attention to improving institutions critical for financial sector development. Improved access to finance in many developing countries is constrained by underdeveloped institutional framework, inadequate regulations, and lack of specialist supervisory capacity. Policy makers need to take steps to enhance key institutions, such as the legal, informational, and regulatory bodies in the country.

The authors conclude that Islamic finance provides a comprehensive framework to enhance financial inclusion by promoting microfinance, SME financing, and microinsurance structured on the principles of risk sharing, and through Islam's redistributive channels, which are grossly underutilized in Muslim countries. Redistributive instruments need to be developed as proper institutions to optimize the function of such instruments. Institutionalizing of these instruments would require improving the enabling environment, strengthening the legal framework, and making collection and distribution of Islamic redistributive instruments more transparent. Applications of financial engineering can devise innovative ways to develop hybrids of risk-sharing and redistributive instruments to enhance access to finance to promote economic development.

In *chapter 7*, Habib Ahmed addresses financial inclusion, but from a different angle. His focus is on organizational formats, products, outreach, and sustainability of Shari'ah-compliant solutions. Ahmed focuses mainly at the micro-level organizational features and identifies some regulatory issues affecting their operations. He looks at the issues from six dimensions: (1) organizational formats, by examining the legal status of the organization; (2) the regulatory regime, which defines the scope of Islamic financial products that different organizations can offer and also determines the conditions under which certain financial products are permitted; (3) the sources of funds, which will vary depending on the organizational format and type of business; (4) products and services offered for financial inclusion through savings opportunities, financing, and insurance for the poor; (5) outreach, in terms of both width (the number of clients served) and depth (the proportion of poor served); and finally, (6) sustainability, indicating the ability of the financial institution to sustain its activities without subsidies.

Ahmed highlights the trade-off between outreach and sustainability, since both are closely related to the organizational features used to deliver the financial services to the poor. Typical organizational structures include commercial firms, nongovernmental organizations (NGOs), mutuals or cooperatives, and the community-based organizations (CBOs). The chapter provides a very useful survey of Shari'ah-compliant microfinance and microinsurance organizations with varying structures, to indicate the factors contributing to their success. These include an NGO, Rescue, based in Bangladesh; a cooperative in Trinidad and Tobago, Takaful T&T Friendly Society (TTTFS); a nonprofit organization, Peramu Foundation, based in Indonesia; a commercial bank (Islamic Bank Bangladesh Limited, IBBL) with a Rural Development Scheme (RDS), based in Bangladesh; a rural bank, Bank Perkerditan Rakyat Syari'ah (BPRS), in Indonesia; and a cooperative bank, Bank Rakyat's ArRahnu Programme, in Malaysia.

Provision of different Islamic financial services by various organizations presents interesting perspectives on the various issues. The chapter finds that organizations that have a poverty alleviation approach are able to fulfill outreach much better than the organizations with commercial approaches. Specifically, in terms of depth of outreach, all three nonprofit organizations in the sample (Rescue, TTTFS, and Peramu) have a ranking of good, while the commercial organizations (BPRS and Bank Rakyat [BR]) have a ranking of poor. In terms of the ranking of sustainability, the commercial organizations perform better than organizations with a poverty alleviation approach. One key feature related to access to funds is that the commercial organizations depend on their own funds (particularly deposits), while the poverty-focused organizations depend on donations or subsidized funds. Thus, lack of availability of funds can be a constraint to expanding the scale of operations in poverty-focused organizations. In terms of provision of services, outreach and sustainability, and use of *zakah* (plural of *zakat*)/*awqaf* (endowments), the results indicate that nonprofit organizations appear to serve the poor better than for-profit organizations. However, nonprofits face problems of sustainability partly because they serve the poor and partly because they do not have access to funds.

The chapter concludes that eradication of poverty is considered an important objective of an Islamic economic system; thus, institutions providing financial services can play an important role in achieving this goal. Examination of six organizations providing inclusive Islamic financial services documents the trade-off between the outreach and sustainability. The results show that nonprofit organizations adopt the poverty approach and rank well on outreach, but have problems with sustainability. For-profit organizations are sustainable but rank low in terms of outreach. *Zakah* and *awqaf* can be integrated in Islamic inclusive finance to resolve the outreach and sustainability problems. While the nonprofit organizational models appear to serve the poor better than the for-profit organizations, the weakness of the former is sustainability. This can partly be resolved by using *zakat* and *waqf* as additional complementary funds to support their activities. For-profit organizations can expand outreach by using funds from these sources to cover provision of financial services to the poor.

In *chapter 8*, Kamaruddin Sharif and Wang Yong Bao provide insight into Islam's perspective on social safety sets and social insurance. The chapter notes that Islam views poverty not only as a social disgrace but also an avenue to apostasy, against which the poor need protection. Despite the fact that all Muslims are to believe in *Qadha-o-Qadr* (the Divine Decree and the Will of God), they must look for ways and means to mitigate risk and to avoid misfortunes and sufferings wherever possible and to minimize their financial losses should such disasters occur.

Islam always links social safety and security with two subsystems. The first is the distribution system based on the individual's capacity; hence Islam urges or obliges the members of society to struggle to ensure their own adequacy independently. By doing so, the members will simultaneously enjoy their rights as well as fulfill their duties toward the distribution. However, there are members of society who are not independent, such as those who are disabled, orphaned, widowed, or unemployed; they need to be looked after collectively by the community at the local and international levels. The second subsystem is the property ownership system in Islam, which encourages private possessions but prohibits extreme consumption and conditions that could lead to exploitation. Although the ownership system is considered private, it is bound by social rights as prescribed by the Qur'an. Islam has ordained another dictum, which requires society at large to meet the public needs that the state should undertake: that is, social safety and security. This includes helping those who are unable to work or are unemployed with a legitimate excuse and have no one to depend on.

Social security has been further fortified and consolidated through the implementation of Islamic rules of inheritance. These rules underscore the interdependent dimensions and measurements among the members of a society by obligating them to apportion the inheritances and patrimonies of the deceased among the inheritors in accordance with the degrees or levels of kinship or relationship to the deceased. The notion of "neighborhood" is a firmly interdependent relationship that has been expanded to three categories: a neighbor who is a relative; a neighbor who is a stranger; and a casual or temporary neighbor with whom one interacts temporarily for a certain time. All of them deserve respect and kind treatment, regardless of their religion, race, or color. Islam requires showing consideration toward neighbors. Therefore, the responsibility for social safety and security that the Islamic state had undertaken in the past was not only restricted to its citizens, but also included all residents (even those living temporarily in the Islamic state).

The authors highlight application of two fundamental approaches that could become instrumental in expanding social security in the Islamic society: *Takaful* (cooperation and solidarity) and *ta'min* (a collective insurance contract based on *Takaful*). The *Takaful* system normally refers to social security in the Muslim world, but has a wider significance in Islam. Recently, the concept of *Takaful* has been applied as *ta'min* and is being operationalized quite similarly to a commercial insurance company. It is a collective insurance contract, whereby subscribers are committed to pay a specific amount of money as a donation to indemnify the victims on the basis of *Takaful* when the risk actually occurs. Its insurance operations are borne by a specialized company as a *wakil* (agency), *ajir* (employee), or *mudarib* (one who provides his time and skills) for a fixed fee. Such a company is ready to provide insurance services and manage the funds for the benefit of participants in a specific form of contract.

In *chapter 9*, Obiyathulla Ismath Bacha and Abbas Mirakhor examine Islamic capital markets in a global context and argue that since conventional capital markets that are heavily biased toward debt and debt-based instruments are inherently unstable, a risk-sharing friendly capital market as advocated by Islamic finance will lead to renewed stability. Risk-sharing financing, which is the basis of the Islamic capital market, promises inherent stability. Since risk is being shared and spread, the logic of this stability is clear. In a risk-sharing arrangement, there are self-correcting mechanisms that would ensure the avoidance of several excesses witnessed in the debt market. Risk-sharing finance raises the threshold of scrutiny, thereby avoiding bad/wasteful projects, which translates directly into improved resource allocation and economic efficiency. More importantly, the nature of risk-sharing finance in avoiding excessive leverage minimizes the vulnerability of economies to financial crises and the resulting boom-bust cycles. Development has a better chance of taking root when stability is prevalent.

The authors claim that implementing an Islamic capital market or a risk-sharing framework will require nothing extraordinary. Strengthening the rule of law, minimizing corruption, enhancing property rights, and similar steps would improve existing markets while also enabling increased risk-sharing. The easiest and least resistant means to increasing risk-sharing within an economy would be by expanding equity markets by deliberately reducing reliance on debt markets. Creating a level playing field for debt and equity by eliminating the tax shelter on interest rates would be a good beginning. Educating the public on the need to share rather than transfer risks would be necessary.

For risk-sharing systems to work, it is critical that investors be made to bear only the risks of the underlying asset/business. They should not also bear other risks, like political and regulatory risks. Failure to keep such risks in check would lead to an inevitable relapse to debt-based financing. One could make the case that fixed rate debt financing is popular not because investors want to avoid business risk but because of all the nonbusiness risks that are typically associated with the businesses. Once again, rule of law and sanctity of property rights and contracts as well as their enforcement would have to be paramount for a risk-sharing system to work.

In *chapter 10*, Andrew Sheng and Ajit Singh examine the problems of primary and secondary aspects of the conventional stock markets and their critiques of corporate governance, and explore how Islamic stock markets should avoid these defects. The relationship between the legal system and the stock market and the relationship between corporate finance and the stock market are salient to any assessment of the role of the stock market in economic development. The chapter presents a nuanced and balanced view of the feasibility and desirability of the Islamic stock market. It suggests that the Islamic stock market can compete effectively against conventional stock markets by improving on corporate controls and serving the real sector by helping SMEs raise capital. This requires the creation of a class of intermediaries that nurture SMEs before they access capital markets.

The authors argue that to be compatible with Shari'ah laws, an Islamic stock market will need to eliminate short-termism, speculation, and strategic pricing by stock market participants among other practices. The authors make reference to the famous U.K. Equity Market (Kay) Report, which recommends a fundamental change in the conduct of the stock markets and calls for long-term relationships among all participants in the equity chain: relationships that are based on respect and trust and involve notions of stewardship and mutual respect. The report also suggests that the entire ethos of the stock market should change to permit the exercise of appropriate values of trust, stewardship, and honesty. The authors further argue that the proponents of the Islamic stock markets will find it easier to implement Kay's reform program for the stock market than their U.K. counterparts. The strong ethical basis of the Islamic stock market gives it a decisive edge in meeting the requirements of the Kay review. The U.K. stock market may well learn from the experience of the Islamic stock market, with its strong ethical underpinnings.

Finally, the authors are of the view that the advocates of Islamic stock markets should regard the project of establishing Islamic stock markets a long-term commitment that may take two to three decades to complete. They should begin by concentrating on the financing needs of the excluded, particularly SMEs, and by implementing the spirit of the Kay Report, which is very much in accord with Islamic ethics.

In *chapter 11*, Hossein Askari and Scheherazade Rehman give a realistic view of the current state of affairs in OIC (Organization of Islamic Conference) countries and examine a very critical question: whether Islam has been supportive or detrimental to economic development and growth in Muslim countries. While it may be tempting to answer this question by simply assessing the performance of countries that are classified as Muslim, that would be a mistake. The impact of Islam on development and growth can be correctly determined if, and only if, countries are first classified by their adoption and adherence to Islamic teachings and only then assessed for the contribution of all factors in the context of a complete (not partial) model, including religion, to their development and growth.

Askari and Rehman examine the broad economic performance of OIC countries to see how they have adhered to, and fared in, the economic dimensions that are important in Islam. They assess the broad economic performance of OIC countries relative to other regional and country groupings and investigate whether the OIC countries have delivered broad-based and sustained development and growth. In addition to analyzing a 30-year trend of the United Nations Human Development Index as a broad-based measure for overall longitudinal development and growth, they also investigate the specific areas of education, gender, health, income (wealth), inequality, poverty, and environment/sustainability—important elements stressed in an Islamic economic system.

While these indicators confirm the generally held belief that the economic performance of OIC countries has been sub-par for the last 30 years, there is no credible correlation to Islamic teaching or any other religion. It is evident that these countries have not followed Islamic teachings, as these comparative results would indicate for economic dimensions stressed in Islam: human development, excellence in education, health care provision, economic prosperity, poverty eradication, equality and justice, and environmental preservation for future generations.

Results are preliminary, but they indicate that the majority of Islamic countries have not fully adhered to core Islamic principles. The average ranking of the 56 Islamic countries is 139, well below the average ranking of the 208 countries measured. If the Islamic countries (OIC) are compared with OECD (Organisation for Economic Co-operation and Development) countries, the disparities are even more pronounced. It could be argued that a fairer comparison would be to the group of non-OECD or middle-income countries. However, even then the Islamic countries do not perform well as a group.

The authors strongly conclude that there is little evidence to attribute the sub-par economic performance of Muslim countries to Islamic teachings. To the contrary, they note that Islamic teachings are fully supportive of sustained growth and prosperity: These teachings underscore the central role of efficient and sound institutions, free markets, market supervision, sound governance, equal opportunity, sanctity of honestly earned income and wealth, rule enforcement, transparency in all business dealings, the importance of education and good health, poverty eradication, financial stability (by embracing equity as opposed to debt financing), admonitions against corruption and hoarding, and so on. Islamic teachings on economic development and growth are similar to the foundational elements of capitalism as espoused by Adam Smith, which are the evolving recommendations of modern economic development theories, but with a strong dose of social justice.

In *chapter 12*, Azura Othman and Abbas Mirakhor address key economic policy challenges in the context of the Islamic economic and financial system. The recurrent financial and economic crises and the high incidence of poverty demonstrate the need for macroeconomic policies that strengthen economic fundamentals and stability of the financial system. The weaknesses in the current system can be pinned down to policies and practices that encourage excessive creation of debt and pay little attention to income disparity and the social and ethical aspects of market practices. The existence of "rentiers," which thrive on such policies, widens the divergence between the financial and real sectors of the economy. Therefore, policy tools that provide incentive structure for closing the gap between the financial and real sectors and at the same time enhance social solidarity through sharing of risks and return are needed to achieve economic justice. One of the main challenges to "reform" the current policy structure is steering out of the "path-dependency" (entrenched patterns and incentives) created by the element of interest ingrained in the financial system in the economy.

As a consequence of the recent crisis, there is renewed drive for governments around the world to strengthen their supervisory and regulatory roles to watch for imminent future crises. Policies must be put in place and regulations must be tightened to ensure that history does not repeat itself. The appropriate public policy must maintain a balance between self-interested behavior and moral assertions. Attention must be focused on ways and means of expanding collective risk sharing. The view toward risk has evolved from a perception that risk is mostly an individual responsibility to a view that envisions risk management as a collective, social, and moral opportunity to strengthen solidarity.

The role of the state through the institution of government has been shown to be no less important in achieving the desired justice and equity in economy and society. Challenges of implementation abound, but the solutions are practicable so long as everyone comes together in good faith to make them happen.

References

Al-Hasani, Baqir, and Abbas Mirakhor. 2003. *Iqtisad–The Islamic Approach to Economic Problems*. Global Scholarly Publications.

Deutsche Bank. 2011. *Global Islamic Banking Report* (November). London: Deutsche Bank.

Ernst & Young. 2012. *The World Islamic Banking Competitiveness Report 2012–13: Going Beyond DNA of Successful Transformation* (December). Bahrain: Ernst & Young.

Iqbal, Zamir, and Mirakhor, Abbas. 2011. *An Introduction to Islamic Finance: Theory and Practice*. 2nd ed. Singapore: John Wiley (Asia).

Mirakhor, Abbas. 2011. "Risk Sharing and Public Policy." 5th International Islamic Capital Market Forum, Securities Commission of Malaysia, November 10.

Mirakhor, Abbas, and Hossein Askari. 2010. *Islam and the Path to Human Economic Development*. Palgrave Macmillan.

Naqvi, Syed Nawab Haider. 2003. *Perspectives on Morality and Human Well-Being: A Contribution to Islamic Economics*. Markfield, Leicestershire, U.K.: The Islamic Foundation.

PART 1

Theoretical Foundation

CHAPTER 1

Epistemological Foundation of Finance: Islamic and Conventional

Abbas Mirakhor and Wang Yong Bao

Simply stated, epistemology deals with the question of what we know about a phenomenon and how do we know it. For precision, it is helpful to clarify terms used currently in discussions of Islamic finance. Practitioners use the term "Islamic finance industry" to refer to their activities in designing and trading ways and means of financing acceptable to Muslims. Taxonomically, industries in an economy belong to a sector, and sectors belong to subsystems that in turn belong to a larger system. For example, airplane manufacturing firms belong to the airline industry, which in turn belongs to the transportation subsystem, within an overall economic system. Similarly, a bank belongs to the banking industry, which belongs to the financial sector, which belongs to the financial subsystem, which belongs to the larger economic system, which, finally, belongs to an overall socio-political-economic system. What then of the Islamic finance industry? It was the conventional finance subsystem that gave birth to the current "Islamic finance industry."

Before the inception of the Islamic finance industry, there was what could be called a "market failure" in the conventional financial system. There was substantial unmet demand for financial products in compliance with Islamic belief. The Islamic finance industry grew out of the conventional finance subsystem to meet this demand. Muslim scholars' writings since the 1970s on the theory of Islamic finance had envisioned a financial system based on risk sharing in which there would be no interest rate-based debt contracts. Practitioners, most of whom had been operating in the realm of conventional finance, however, were interested in developing ways and means of finance that, while avoiding the appearance of interest-based debt, would nevertheless be familiar to and accepted by market players in conventional finance. The former emphasized profit-loss sharing (PLS); the latter focused on traditional methods of conventional finance,

---

Abbas Mirakhor is professor at the International Centre for Education in Islamic Finance, Kuala Lumpur, Malaysia, and Wang Yong Bao is associate professor at Xi'an International Studies University, Xi'an City, Shaanxi Province, China.

centered on risk transfer and risk shifting. In doing so, all financial instruments of conventional finance became subject to replicating, retrofitting, and reverse engineering of conventional financial instruments.

This chapter argues that there are two ideal financial systems based on risk sharing, conventional and Islamic, and one actual conventional system focused on risk transfer. There are two industries within the actual system: the conventional and Islamic finance industries. The chapter then proceeds to discuss the epistemology and the main characteristics of each of the two ideal systems. Finally, the chapter discusses the current state of Islamic finance, challenges it faces, and prospects for the future.

An Ideal Conventional Financial System

An overall socio-political-economic system gives rise to an economic system out of which grows a system of financing to facilitate production, trade, and exchange. The idea of the contemporary conventional economic system is usually traced to Adam Smith's conception of an economy as envisioned in his book, the *Wealth of Nations* (1776). What has been ignored until recently, however, is the fact that, from an epistemological point of view, Smith's vision of the economy is embedded in his vision of a moral-ethical system that gives rise to the economy envisioned in the *Wealth of Nations*. That moral-ethical system was well described in Smith's book, *The Theory of Moral Sentiments* (1759), which preceded his *Wealth of Nations* by some 17 years.

Whereas conventional economics considered Smith's notion of the "invisible hand" as a coordinator of independent decisions of market participants, in both *The Theory of Moral Sentiments* and in the *Wealth of Nations*, the metaphor refers to the design of the Creator, "who arranged the connecting principles such that the actions of all those seeking their own advantage could produce the most efficient allocation of resources, and thus the greatest possible wealth for the nation. This is indeed a benevolent designer" (Evensky 1993, 9). Smith contended that the objective of the Divine Design must have been the happiness of humans "when he brought them into existence. No other end seems worthy of that supreme wisdom and divine benignity which we necessarily ascribe to him..." (Smith [1759] 2006, 186–89). Smith's major contribution in his *Theory of Moral Sentiments* is to envision a coherent moral-ethical social system consistent with the Creator's design and show how each member of society would enforce ethical principles. Recognition of human frailties led Smith to recognition of the need for an organic coevolution of individual and society in a stage-wise process of accumulation of ethical system of values from one generation to next. While it is possible for any given society to move forward or stagnate and even regress, the benevolence of the invisible hand of the "Author of nature" guides the totality of humanity in its movement toward the ideal human society. Compliance with and commitment to a set of values—virtues of prudence, concern for other people, justice, and benevolence—would insure social order and cohesion (Mirakhor and Askari 2010; Mirakhor and Hamid 2009; Smith [1759] 2006).

Adam Smith and Kenneth Arrow

It was not until the second half of the last century that attempts were made to present a particular conception of Smith's vision of the economy. This conception saw the economy as a market system guided by the "invisible hand" that led to smooth functioning, coordinating "autonomous individual choices in an interdependent world" (Evensky 1993). Two such attempts were the works of Arrow and Debreu (1954) and Arrow and Hahn (1971), which sought to show "that a decentralized economy motivated by self-interest" would allocate resources such that it "could be regarded, in a well-defined sense, as superior to a large class of possible alternative dispositions ..." (Arrow and Hahn 1971, vi–vii). These attempts focused primarily on Smith's idea of a decentralized market economy, but in the process they abstracted from the well-spring of his thoughts, represented by the societal framework emphasizing moral-ethical values envisioned in *The Theory of Moral Sentiments*.

The work of Arrow and Debreu (1954) is fundamentally about optimal risk sharing in a decentralized market economy. It addresses the question of how best to allocate risk in an economy. The answer is that risk should be allocated to those who can best bear it. The work abstracted from the underlying institutional structure envisioned by Adam Smith in *The Theory of Moral Sentiments* and the *Wealth of Nations*. It appears that Arrow-Debreu took for granted the existence of such institutions as property rights, contracts, trust, rule of law, and moral-ethical values. Two key assumptions of this work were complete contracts and complete markets. By "complete contracts," it was meant that it was possible to design contracts such that all contingencies were covered. By "complete markets," it was meant that there was a market for every conceivable risk. Crucially, all future payoffs were contingent on specific outcomes. The Arrow-Debreu model did not include fixed, predetermined rates of interest as payoffs to debt contracts.

Following his seminal work with Debreu, Arrow made it clear that, while not stated explicitly in his work with Debreu and with Hahn, he envisioned it was "possible that the process of exchange requires or at least is greatly facilitated by the presence of several ... virtues (not only truth, but also trust, loyalty and justice in future dealings).... The virtue of truthfulness in fact contributes in a very significant way to the efficiency of the economic system ... ethical behavior can be regarded as a socially desirable institution which facilitates the achievement of economic efficiency in a broad sense" (Arrow 1971, 345–46). For example, if the institution of trust is strong in an economy, the universe of complete contracts can be replicated by simple contracts entered into by parties stipulating that terms and conditions of the contracts would be revised as contingencies arise. Arrow himself was to place emphasis on trust as the lubricant of the economy (Arrow 1974). Despite Arrow's attention to some important elements of the institutional structure that were integral to Smith's vision of an economy, such as its value system, the economics profession developed its own vision of that economy, focusing primarily on two concepts of "invisible hand" and "self-interest." The first was mentioned only once in the *Wealth of Nations* (see Smith [1776] 1976, 456) and the manner in which the second was used by economists has been referred to by Vivian Walsh (2000, 6) as a "vulgar ... misunderstanding" of what Smith meant by "self-interest." This narrowing of Smith's view has been subject to rather sharp criticism by Amartya Sen (1982, 1987), who suggests that ignoring much of Smith's views of humans, as expounded in *The Theory of Moral Sentiments*, led to a substantive deficiency in the formation of contemporary economic theory.

A careful reading of *The Theory of Moral Sentiments* and the *Wealth of Nations* provides immense support for Sen's position. Even beyond Sen's spirited criticism of economists' misunderstanding of Smith's self-interest motive is Smith's own insistence on the need to comply with "general rules of conduct." Smith explains, these rules "are the commands and laws of the Deity, who will finally reward the obedient, and punish the transgressor of their duty."

> When the general rules which determine the merit and demerit of actions comes thus to be regarded as the laws of an all-powerful being, who watches over our conduct, and who, in a life to come, will reward the observance and punish the breach of them—they necessarily acquire a new sacredness from this consideration. That our regard to the will of Deity ought to be the supreme rule of our conduct can be doubted of by nobody who believes his existence. The very thought of disobedience appears to involve in it the most shocking impropriety. How vain, how absurd would it be for man, either to oppose or to neglect the commands that were laid upon him by infinite wisdom and infinite power. How unnatural, how impiously ungrateful not to reverence the precepts that were prescribed to him by the infinite goodness of his Creator, even though no punishment was to follow their violation! The sense of propriety, too, is here well supported by the strongest motive of self-interest. The idea that, however, we may escape the observation of man, or be placed above the reach of human punishment, yet we are always acting under the eye and exposed to the punishment of God, the greatest avenger of injustice, is a motive capable of restraining the most headstrong passions, with those at least who, by constant reflection, have rendered it familiar to them. (Smith [1759] 2006, 186–89)

Consideration of the above quotation, as well as the rest of *The Theory of Moral Sentiments*, leads to at least three observations. First, this is the Smith that has been ignored by the economics profession. The Smith of economics is the author of the self-interest motive that is the basis of utility and profit maximization at any cost to society, including the impoverishment and exploitation of fellow human beings. Even his most ardent of supporters, Amartya Sen, has ignored the Smith of the quotation above. Second, Smith makes clear in his *Theory of Moral Sentiments* that compliance with the rules prescribed by the Creator and with the rules of the market was essential to his vision. Third, it is also clear that Smith considers the internalization of rules—being consciously aware of the ever-presence of the Creator and acting accordingly—as crucial to all human conduct, including economics. Smith succinctly and clearly shares some of the fundamental institutional scaffolding of Islam: belief in One and Only Creator; belief in accountability of the Day of Judgement; belief in the necessity of compliance with the rules prescribed by the Creator; and belief that justice is achieved with full compliance with rules. To paraphrase Sen, no space need be made artificially for justice and fairness; it already exists in the rules prescribed by the Law Giver.

The Arrow-Debreu Economy

An economy in which there are contingent markets for all commodities—meaning that there are buyers and sellers who promise to buy or sell given commodities "if any only if" a specified state of the world occurs—is called an Arrow-Debreu economy. In such an economy, it is the budget constraint of the participants that determines how much of each contingent commodity at prices prevailing in the market they can buy. Since these commodities are contingent on future states, they are risky. Therefore, the budget constraint of individuals determines the risk-bearing ability of each market participant. Arrow himself recognized that requiring such a market is unrealistic, as the extensive spectrum of securities required for such a market does not exist. But he suggested that in contemporary market economies there are instruments or securities that can be used as substitutes (Arrow 1971). Such securities, referred to as Arrow Securities, whose payoffs could be used to purchase commodities, would reduce the number of markets required while replicating the efficiency of risk allocation of complete contingent markets. Associated with complete markets are complete contracts. These are agreements contingent on all states of nature. In the real world, not all contracts can cover all future contingencies. Therefore, they are said to be incomplete contracts and may indicate inefficiencies in exchange. However, as suggested above, optimal contracts can be devised provided there is mutual trust between the parties to the contract. This could be a simple contract with provisions for modification of terms and conditions should contingencies necessitate change.

A compelling case can be made that insofar as the financial instruments are Arrow Securities (their payoff is contingent on the "state of nature"—that is, dependent on the outcome, not fixed or predetermined—and represents the reward to risk sharing), this ideal system would share many characteristics of an ideal Islamic system (Mirakhor 1993). However, not all Arrow Securities would satisfy Islamic requirements, as some may well represent contingent debt contracts to deliver a fixed predetermined amount of money if a given state of world occurs. Thus these may not represent an ownership claim, either. Shares of common stock of open corporations do meet these requirements. They are residual ownership claims and receive a return contingent on future outcomes; they are "proportionate claims on the payoffs of all future states" (Fama and Jensen 1983, 328). These payoffs are contingent on future outcomes. Stock markets that are well organized, regulated, and supervised are efficient from an economic point of view because they allocate risks according to the risk-bearing ability of the participants. In essence, this is the contribution of the Arrow-Debreu model of competitive equilibrium (1954; see also Arrow 1971), according to which, efficient risk sharing requires that the risks of the economy are allocated to market participants in accordance with their "respective degree of risk tolerance" (Hellwig 1998, 607–611).

From Ideal to Actual: Conventional Finance

As mentioned, what Arrow-Hahn and Arrow-Debreu set out to do was analytically and rigorously demonstrate the proposition that an "imposing line of economists from Adam Smith to the present have sought to show that a decentralized economy motivated by self-interest...would be compatible with a coherent disposition of economic resources that could be regarded, in a well-defined sense, as superior to a large class of possible alternative disposition..." (Arrow and Hahn 1971, vi–vii). But, as Evensky suggests, "the Smithian story told by Arrow and Hahn—and they are representative of modern economists—is an abridged edition. The spring that motivates action in Smith's story has been carried forward, but much of the rest of his tale has been forgotten" (Evensky 1987, 12). It can be argued, as Arrow himself seems to imply (1971), that the "rest of [Smith's] tale" would have been his vision of the institutional infrastructure (rules of behavior) that is envisioned in *The Theory of Moral Sentiments*. As such, abstracting from them would be unlikely to change the outcome of the mathematical analysis of Arrow-Debreu or Arrow-Hahn or both. Furthermore, had actual finance developed along the trajectory discernible from these works—steps taken toward completion of markets and of contracts, keeping in mind the overall institutional framework for the economy as envisioned by Adam Smith—the result might have been emergence of conventional finance different from the contemporary system. That system would instead be dominated by contingent, equity, risk-sharing financial instruments.

Perhaps the most influential factor in derailing that trajectory is the existence and the staying power of a fixed, predetermined rate of interest, for which there has never been a rigorous theoretical explanation. All so-called theories of interest from the classical economists to contemporary finance theories explain interest rate as the price that brings demand for and supply of finance into equilibrium. This implies that interest rates emerge only after demand and supply forces have interacted in the market, and are not ex ante prices. In fact, in some theoretical models, there is no room for a fixed, ex ante predetermined rate of interest. For example, introducing such a price into the Walrasian or Arrow-Debreu-Hahn models of general equilibrium (GE) leads to the collapse of the models, as they become over-determined (Cowen 1983, 609–611).

Even though no satisfactory theory of a positive, ex ante fixed rate of interest exists, all financial theory development following Arrow-Debreu-Hahn assumed its existence in the form of a risk-free asset, usually Treasury bills, as a benchmark against which the rates of return of all other assets—importantly, equity returns—were measured. These include theories such as the capital asset pricing model (CAPM), modern portfolio theory (MPT), and the Black-Scholes option pricing formula for valuing options contracts and assessing risk. For all practical purposes, the assumption of a risk-free rate introduced an artificial floor into the pricing structure of the real sector of the economy, and into all financial decisions. It can be argued that it is the existence of this exogenously imposed rate on the economy that transformed the Arrow-Debreu vision of a risk-sharing economy and finance. The resulting system became one focused on transferring or shifting risk, rather than sharing it. Such a system needed strong regulation to limit the extent of both. However, further developments in finance theory provided analytic rationale for an ideologically aggressive deregulation. One such rationale was the Modigliani-Miller Theorem of neutrality of capital structure of firms. In essence this theorem asserted that the value of a firm is independent of its capital structure. This implied that since firms want to maximize their value and since Modigliani-Miller showed that the value of the firm is indifferent to whether the firm debt finances or equity finances its capital structure, firms would prefer to incur higher debt levels for the firm rather than issue additional equity. Hence, the risk of additional debt would be shifted to other stakeholders (Jensen and Meckling 1976).

Another rationale was the development of the efficient market hypothesis (EMH), which claimed that in an economy similar to that of Arrow-Debreu, prices prevailing in the market contained all relevant information, such that there would be no opportunity for arbitrage. The implication was that if market efficiency is desirable, then markets should be allowed to move toward completion, through innovation and financial engineering, in order to create a financial instrument to allow insurance against all risks. For this to happen, it had to be demonstrated that it is possible to develop such a wide array of instruments, and that regulation had to become passive or even regressive to allow an incentive structure to induce innovation. Such a regulatory stance was initiated in almost all industrial countries in the 1980s and continued with an accelerated pace until the 2007–09 crisis. The former had already been demonstrated by the theory of spanning developed in late 1960s and early 1970s showing that one basic financial instrument could be spanned potentially into an infinite number of instruments (see Askari and others 2009). These developments, coupled with the high magnitude of leverage available from a money-credit creation process characteristic of a fractional reserve banking system, represented an explosive mix that reduced the vision of Adam Smith to the rubble of post-crisis 2007–08. The Arrow-Debreu vision of an economy in which risk was shared was first transformed into an economy in which the focus became risk transfer but that quickly transformed into one in which risks were shifted, ultimately, to taxpayers (Mirakhor and Krichene 2009).

An Ideal Islamic Finance System

The ideal Islamic finance system points to a full-spectrum menu of instruments serving a financial sector embedded in an Islamic economy in which the institutional "scaffolding" (rules of behavior as prescribed by Allah (swt) and operationalized by the Noble Messenger, including rules of market behavior prescribed by Islam) is fully operational (Chapra 2000; Iqbal and Mirakhor 2012). The essential function of that spectrum would be spreading and allocating risk among market participants rather than allowing it to concentrate among the borrowing class. Islam proposes three sets of risk-sharing instruments:

- *Mu'amelat* (transactions) risk-sharing instruments in the financial sector;
- Redistributive risk-sharing instruments through which the risks facing the less able segment of the population are shared by the economically more able segment of the society; and
- The inheritance rules specified in the Qur'an, through which the wealth of a person at the time of passing is distributed among present and future generations of inheritors.

As will be argued here, the second set of instruments is used to redeem the rights of the less able through the income and wealth of the more able. These are not instruments of charity, altruism, or beneficence. They are instruments of redemption of rights and repayment of obligations.

The spectrum of ideal Islamic finance instruments would run the gamut between short-term liquid, low-risk financing of trade contracts to long-term financing of real sector investment. The essence of the spectrum is risk sharing. At one end, the spectrum provides financing for purchase and sale of what has already been produced in order to allow further production. At the other end, it provides financing for what is intended or planned to be produced. In this spectrum, there does not seem to be room provided for making money out of pure finance, where instruments are developed that use real sector activity only as a veil to accommodate what amount to pure financial transactions. There are *dayn* (debt) and *Qard-al-hassan* (no-interest-based loan) used to facilitate real sector transactions in terms of consumption smoothing for those who have experienced liquidity shock. This is a case when a financier shares liquidity risk with the firms or consumers for whom an idiosyncratic risk has materialized or who use non-interest borrowing as an insurance against liquidity shocks.

It may be argued plausibly that in a modern complex economy, there is need for a variety of ready-to-use means of liquidity, and so long as instruments are deemed permissible, where is the harm? Usually, this argument starts with the reasoning that financial instruments that serve short-term, trade-oriented transaction contracts, such as *murabahah* (short-term, risk-sharing instruments), are permissible. From there, the argument goes that any instrument with a connection, no matter how tenuous, to the real sector transactions is also permissible. It is worth noting that transaction contracts permissible in Islam and the financial instruments intended to facilitate them are not the same thing. Islamic real sector transactions contracts (*Uqud*) that have reached us historically are all permissible. However, it is possible that a financial instrument designed to facilitate a given permissible contract may itself be judged nonpermissible. As the proliferation of derivative instruments in the period of run-up to the global financial crisis demonstrated, the number of financial instruments that have some relation, even if only nominal, to a real sector transaction is limited only by the imagination of financial engineers. This is the essence of the theory of spanning developed in finance in the late 1960s and early 1970s, which led to the design and development of derivatives (see Askari and others 2009). It is possible that a financial instrument may have weaker risk-sharing characteristics than the Islamic transaction contract it intends to serve.

Since Islamic finance is all about risk sharing, then the risk characteristics of a given instrument need to become paramount in decisions. One reason, among others, for nonpermissibility of interest-based debt contracts is surely due to the fact that this sort of contract transfers all, or at least a major portion, of risk to the borrower. It is possible to imagine instruments that on their face are compatible with the non-interest rate–based debt requirement, but are instruments of risk transfer and, ultimately, of shifting risk to taxpayers. An example would be a sovereign *ijarah sukuk* (rent-based financial instruments either backed or based on real assets) based on the assets subject to *ijarah* but credit-enhanced by other means, say collateral. All costs taken into account, such a *sukuk* may well be more expensive and involve stronger risk transfer characteristics than a direct sovereign bond (see Mirakhor and Zaidi 2007). Clearly, a judgment call needs to be made by the financiers and financial engineers when they design and develop an instrument to consider its risk-sharing characteristic. This is a call with which religious scholars alone should not be overburdened. Financiers and financial engineers should specify the risk-sharing characteristics of instruments they present to scholars for approval. In the long run, however, religious scholars' knowledge will have to catch up with modern finance as well as with the intricacies of risk and uncertainty.

It appears that at the present, the energies of financiers and financial engineers are focused on the design and development of instruments to accommodate the low end of risk-return, liquid transactions. Without effort at developing long-term investment instruments with appropriate risk-return characteristics, there is a danger of path-dependency, by which the market will continue to see more of the same: that is, more short-term, liquid, and safe instruments—albeit in greater variety. This possibility should not be taken lightly. As mentioned, since the early 1970s, finance has been quite familiar with the theory of spanning. According to this idea, an infinite number of instruments can be "spanned" out of a basic instrument. This is what led to the explosion of derivatives, which played an influential role in the recent global financial disaster. It has been estimated that in 2007, the total financial instruments, mostly derivatives, in the world was 12.5 times larger than the total global gross domestic product (GDP) (Mirakhor 2002). Recently, Rogoff (2011) has suggested that there is roughly $200 trillion of financial paper in the international system, of which $150 trillion is in interest-based debt instruments. At the same time, the global GDP that must validate this debt is at most $63 trillion. Given the differential rates at which these two sums are growing, it is difficult to see how the underlying global GDP can ever grow at a rapid enough pace to validate the debt. Similar developments could be awaiting Islamic finance if the ingenuity of financial engineers and the creative imagination of religious scholars continue to serve the demand-driven appetite for liquid, low-risk, and short-term instruments. In that case, the configuration of Islamic finance would have failed to achieve the hopes and aspirations evoked by the potential of the ideal Islamic financial system.

Epistemology of an Ideal Islamic Finance System
The fountainhead of all Islamic thought is the Qur'an. Whatever the theory of Islamic knowledge may be, any epistemology, including that of finance, must find its roots in the Qur'an.

The starting point of this discussion is therefore verse 275 of chapter 2 of the Qur'an, particularly the part of the verse that declares contracts of *Al-Bay'* (risk-sharing–based transactions) permissible and contracts of *Al-Riba* (interest-rate-based debt contracts) nonpermissible. Arguably, these few words can be considered as constituting the organizing principle—the fundamental theorem, as it were—of the Islamic economy. Most translations of the Qur'an render *Al-Bay'* as "commerce" or "trade." They also translate *Al-Tijarah* as "commerce" or "trade." However, there is substantive difference between *Al-Bay'* and *Al-Tijarah*, according to major lexicons of Arabic (such as *Lisan Al-Arab*, *Mufradat Alfaz Al-Qur'an*, Lane's *Arabic Lexicon*, and *Al-Tahquiq fi Kalamat Al-Qur'an Karim*, among others). Relying on various verses of the Qur'an (such as 2:111, 2:254, 35:29–20, 61:10–13), these sources suggest that trade contracts (*Al-Tijarah*) are entered into in the expectation of profit (*riba*). On the other hand, *Al-Bay'* contracts are defined as "*Mubadilah Al-Maal Bi Al-Maal*": exchange of property with property. In terms of contemporary economics, this phrase would be rendered as exchange of a property rights claim. These sources suggest a further difference in that those who enter into a contract of exchange expect gains but are cognizant of probability of loss (*Khisarah*).

It is also worth noting that all Islamic contractual forms, except spot exchange, involve time. From an economic point of view, time transactions involve a commitment to do something today in exchange for a promise of a commitment to do something in the future. All transactions involving time are subject to uncertainty, and uncertainty involves risk. Risk exists whenever more than one outcome is possible. Consider, for example, a contract in which a seller commits to deliver a product in the future against payments today. There are a number of risks involved. First, there is a price risk for both sides of the exchange; the price may be higher or lower in the future. In that case, the two sides are at risk, which they share once they enter into the contract agreement. If the price in the future is higher, the buyer would be better off and the price risk has been shed to the seller. The converse is true if the price is lower. Under uncertainty, the buyer and seller have, through the contract, shared the price risk. There are other risks that the buyer takes, including the risks of nondelivery and substandard quality. The seller faces additional risks, including the risk that the price of raw material, and cost of transportation and delivery, may be higher in the future. These risks may also be lower. Again, these risks have been shared through the contract. The same argument applies to deferred payment contracts.

Second, it may appear that spot exchange or cash sale involves no risk. But price changes can change after the completion of spot exchange is completed.

The two sides of a spot exchange share this risk. Moreover, from the time of the classical economists, it has been recognized that specialization through comparative advantage provides the basis for gains from trade. But in specializing, a producer takes the risk of becoming dependent on other producers specialized in production of what he needs. Again, through exchange, the two sides to a transaction share the risk of specialization. Additionally, there are pre-exchange risks of production and transportation that are shared through the exchange. It is clear that the contracts at the other end of the spectrum—*mudarabah* and *musharakah*—are risk-sharing transactions. Therefore, it can be inferred that by mandating *Al-Bay'*, Allah (swt) ordained risk sharing in all exchange activities.

Third, it appears that the reason for the prohibition of *Al-Riba* contracts is the fact that opportunities for risk sharing do not exist in this type of contract. It may be argued that the creditor does take on risk—the risk of default. But it is not risk taking per se that makes a transaction permissible. A gambler takes risk as well, but gambling is not permitted. Instead, what seems to matter is opportunity for risk sharing. *Al-Riba* is a contract of risk transfer. As John Maynard Keynes emphasized in his writings, if the interest rate did not exist, the financier would have to share in all the risks that the entrepreneur faces in producing, marketing, and selling a product (see Mirakhor and Krichene 2009). But by decoupling his or her future gains, by loaning money today for more money in the future, the financier transfers all risks to the entrepreneur.

Fourth, it is clear that by declaring the contract of *Al-Riba* nonpermissible, the Qur'an intends for humans to shift their focus to risk-sharing contracts of exchange.

It can be inferred from the preceding discussion that there are two types of contracts involving time:

- Contracts over time (or on the spot) involving trade in which there is expectation of gain (*riba*); and
- Contracts over time involving exchange in which there is expectation of gain or loss (*Khisarah*).

The latter must also refer to contracts of investment with uncertain outcome in terms of gain or loss. This, of course, does not mean that *mudarabah* and *musharakah* could not be used for longer-term trade in expectations of profits to be shared and for long-term investment, as was the case for centuries in the Muslim world, as well as in Europe, in the Middle Ages. Borrowed from Muslims and known as *commenda* in western Europe, *mudarabah* became quite popular as a means of financing long-term trade and investment (Brouwer 2005; Mirakhor 1983; Fischel 1933; Udovitch 1967, 1970a). Lopez (1976) suggests that there is a consensus among medieval historians that the *commenda* was of the highest importance and contributed greatly to the rapid growth of trade and investment, which led to great economic change and growth in Europe. The contribution of *commenda* to the industrial development of the Ruhr Valley in Germany and in building railroads throughout Europe were particularly pronounced (see Mirakhor 1983).

Therefore, the distinction that needs emphasis is that *Al-Bay'* covers long-term investment contracts that allow the growth of employment, income, and expansion of the economy. The focus of *Al-Tijarah* and all its financing instruments is trade of commodities already produced. In effect, Islam meets the financing needs of trade, as well as the requirements of resource allocation, investment, production, employment, income creation, and risk management.

Major economic implications follow from the points discussed. First, as the definition of *Al-Bay'* indicates, it is a contract of exchange of property. This means that the parties to the exchange must have property rights over the subjects of any contract that preceded the exchange. Second, parties must have the freedom not only to produce what they wish but also the freedom to exchange those products (goods and services) with whom they wish. Third, parties must have freedom to contract. Fourth, there must be means of enforcing contracts. Fifth, exchange requires a place for the parties to complete their transactions, meaning a market. Sixth, markets need rules of behavior to ensure their orderly and efficient operation. Seventh, the contract of exchange requires trust among the parties as to their commitments to perform according to the terms and conditions of exchange. Eighth, there must be rules governing the distribution of proceeds. Ninth, there must be redistributive rules and mechanisms to correct for inequitable patterns of distribution that emerge out of market performance. These are rules that govern the redemption of the rights of those who are not parties to the contract directly but who have acquired rights in the proceeds because, one way or another, they or their properties have contributed to the production of what is the subject of exchange. These implications are discussed below.

Property Rights
Briefly, the principles of property rights in Islam include the following:

- Allah (swt) has created all property and Allah (swt) is the ultimate owner.
- Resources created by Allah (swt) are at the disposal of all humans to empower them to perform duties prescribed by the Creator.
- While the ultimate ownership is preserved for the Creator, humans are allowed to combine their physical and intellectual abilities with the created resources to produce means of sustenance for themselves and others.
- The right of access to resources belongs to all of humankind universally.
- Humans can claim property rights over what is produced through their own labor or transfers through gift giving, exchange, contracts, inheritance, or redemption of rights in the produced property.
- Since created resources belong to all humans, the inability of a person (because of physical or mental limitations or other circumstances) to access these resources does not negate the individual's right to these resources.

- These rights must be redeemed; this establishes the rule of sharing with the less able.
- Sharing is implemented through redistributive mechanisms, such as *zakat*, which are redemption of rights and not charity.
- Since work and transfers are the only legitimate sources of property rights claims, all sources of instantaneous creation of property rights, such as theft, bribery, gambling, and *riba*, are prohibited.
- Unlike the conventional system of property rights, Islam imposes strict limits on the freedom of disposing of property; there is no absolute freedom for the owner to dispose of property, as there are rules against extravagance, waste, destruction of property, or its use in prohibited transactions.
- Property rights must not lead to accumulation of excessive personal wealth, as wealth is considered the life blood of the society, which must constantly circulate to create investment, employment, income, and opportunities for economic growth.
- Once the principles governing property rights are observed, particularly the rule of sharing, the owner's right to the remaining property, cleansed of others' rights, is inviolate.

It is through its rules of property rights that Islam envisions economic growth and poverty alleviation in human societies. The task of reducing poverty is accomplished through the discharge of the obligation of sharing derived from the property rights principles of Islam, which envision the economically less able as the silent partners of the more able. In effect, the more able members of society are trustee-agents in using resources created by Allah (swt) on behalf of themselves and the less able. In contrast to the property rights principles of the conventional system, property rights in Islam are not means of exclusion but of inclusion of the less able in the income and wealth of the more able, as a matter of rights that must be redeemed. In the conventional system, the rich help the poor as a demonstration of sympathy, beneficence, benevolence, and charity. In Islam, the more able are required to share the consequences of the materialization (incidence) of idiosyncratic risks—illness, bankruptcy, disability, accidents, and socio-economic disadvantages—for those who are unable to provide for themselves. The more able members of society diversify away a good portion of their own idiosyncratic risks, using risk-sharing instruments of Islamic finance. The economically well-off are commanded to share the risks of those who are economically unable to use the instruments of Islamic finance. It can be plausibly argued that unemployment, misery, poverty, and destitution in any society are prima facie evidence of violation of property right rules of Islam, or nonimplementation of Islamic instruments of risk sharing, or both. In Islam, the risks that would face the future generations are shared by the current generation through the rules of inheritance. These rules break up accumulated wealth as it passes from one generation to another to enable the risks of a larger number of people to be shared.

Contracts and Trust

Basically, a contract is an enforceable agreement. Its essence is commitment. Islam anchors all socio-political-economic relations on contracts. The Shari'ah itself is contractual in its conceptualization, content, and application. Its very foundation is the primordial covenant between the Creator and humans (see 7:172–173). In an unambiguous verse (6:152), the Qur'an urges the believers to fulfill the covenant of Allah. This is extended to the terms and conditions of all contracts through another clear verse (5:1) in which believers are ordered to be faithful to their contracts. They are ordered to protect faithfulness to their covenants and what has been placed in trust with them as a shepherd protects sheep (32:8; also 2:172, 16:91–92, 17:34). Thus, believers do not treat obligations of contracts lightly; they will take on contractual obligations only if they intend fully to fulfill them. Hence, their commitments are credible.

Contracts are means of coming to terms with future risks and uncertainty. They allocate risks by providing for future contingencies and set obligations for each party and each state in the future, as well as remedies for breach of contracts. Generally, there are four motives for entering into a contract: sharing of risk; transfer of risk; alignment of incentives; or minimization of transaction costs. *Mudarabah*, *musharakah*, and the purchase of equity shares are examples of risk sharing. Entering into an insurance contract is an example of transferring risks for a fee to those who can better bear them. Risk shifting occurs when the risks of a transaction or a contract between two parties are shifted to a third party. This concept was discussed by Jensen and Meckling (1976) in the context of corporate managers resorting to debt finance instead of issuing additional equity, thus shifting the risk of debt burden to other stakeholders. To align incentives, one party (usually the principle) enters into a contract with another (an agent), through which incentives are created for the latter to take actions that serve their objective to maximize joint surplus (Hart and Holstrom 1987). Contracts that are designed to reduce transaction costs are usually aimed at establishing stable, long-term relationships between parties in order to avoid ex ante information, search, and sorting costs, as well as ex post bargaining costs.

There is an organic relationship between contract and trust. Without trust, contracts become difficult to negotiate and conclude and costly to monitor and enforce. When and where trust is weak, complicated and costly administrative devices are needed to enforce contracts. Problems are exacerbated when, in addition to lack of trust, property rights are poorly defined and protected (Sheng 2009). Under these circumstances, it becomes difficult to specify clearly the terms of contract since transaction costs—that is, search and information costs, bargaining and decision costs, contract negotiations, and enforcement costs—are high. Consequently, there is less trade, fewer market participants, less long-term investment, lower productivity, and slower economic growth. Weakness of trust creates the problem of lack of credible commitment, which arises when parties to an exchange cannot commit themselves or do not trust that others can commit themselves to performing contractual obligations.

Empirical research has shown that where the problem of lack of commitment exists and is significant, it leads to disruption in economic, political, and social interaction among people. Long-term contracting will not be possible and parties to exchange opt for spot market or very short-term transactions (see, for example, Keefer and Knack 2005).

Considering these issues, one can appreciate the strong emphasis that the Qur'an—as well as the Messenger (pbuh)—has placed on trust, trustworthiness (see 4:57; 8:27), and the need to fulfill terms and conditions of contracts, covenants, and the promises one makes. These rules solve the problem of credible commitment and trust, and thus facilitate long-term contracts.

To illustrate the importance of trust, consider the role of complete contracts in the neoclassical theory of competitive equilibrium (Arrow 1971). A complete contract fully specifies all future contingencies relevant to the exchange. In the real world, a vast majority of contracts are incomplete. This requirement, therefore, is considered too stringent and unrealistic. Not only ignorance about all future contingencies make writing complete contracts impossible, even if all future contingencies are known, but it would be nearly impossible to write a contract that can accommodate them all. However, if the parties to a contract trust each other, they can agree to enter into a simple contract and commit to revising its terms and conditions as contingencies arise.

Markets

A major reason for contract of exchange is that the parties to the contract wish to improve their own welfare. For this to happen, parties must have the freedom to contract. This, in turn implies freedom to produce, which calls for clear and well-protected property rights to permit production and sale. To freely and conveniently exchange, the parties need a place to do so: that is, a market. To operate efficiently, markets need rules of behavior and clear, unambiguous rule-enforcement mechanisms to reduce uncertainty in transaction. Markets also need free flow of information. To reinforce the efficiency of market operations, trust must be established among participants, transaction costs must be minimized, and rules must be established to internalize externalities of two-party transactions. Andrew Sheng (2009, 9) suggests that "successful markets all share three key attributes: the protection of property rights, the lowering of transaction costs and high transparency." To achieve these attributes, preconditions and infrastructures are needed, including:

- Freedom of market participants to enter and exit the market, to set their own objectives within the prescribed rules, to employ ways and means of their own choosing to achieve their goals, and to choose whomever they wish as their exchange partner;
- An infrastructure for participants to access, organize and use information;
- Institutions that permit coordination of market activities;
- Institutions to regulate and supervise the behavior of market participants; and
- Legal and administrative institutions to enforce contracts at reasonable costs.

Both the Qur'an and *Sunnah* (body of knowledge based on the Messenger's words and deeds) place considerable emphasis on the rules of behavior. Once instated in Medina as the spiritual and temporal authority, the Messenger (pbuh) exerted considerable energy in operationalizing and implementing the property rights rules, the institutions of the market, and the rules of exchange and contracts, as well as rules governing production, consumption, distribution, and redistribution. He also implemented rules regarding the fiscal operations of the newly formed state, as well as governance rules. Specifically regarding markets, before the advent of Islam, trade had been the most important economic activity in the Arabian Peninsula. A number of dynamic and thriving markets had developed throughout the area. Upon arrival in Medina, the Messenger of Allah organized a market for Muslims structured and governed by rules prescribed by the Qur'an, and implemented a number of policies to encourage the expansion of trade and strengthen the market. Unlike the existing markets in Medina and elsewhere in Arabia, the Prophet prohibited imposition of taxes on individual merchants, as well as on transactions. He also implemented policies to encourage trade among Muslims and non-Muslims by creating incentives for non-Muslim merchants in and out of Medina. For example, traveling non-Muslim merchants were considered guests of the Muslims, and their merchandise was guaranteed by the Prophet against (nonmarket) losses. The market was the only authorized place of trade. Its construction and maintenance was made a duty of state. As long as space was available in the existing market, no other markets were constructed. The Prophet designated a protective area around the market. No other construction or facility was allowed in the protective area. While trade was permitted in the area surrounding the market in case of overcrowding, the location of each merchant was assigned on a first-come, first-served basis, but only for the duration of the trading day (Mirakhor and Hamid 2009).

After the conquest of Mecca, rules governing the market and the behavior of participants were institutionalized and generalized to all markets in Arabia. These rules included no restriction on interregional or international trade, including no taxation on entering into or exiting out of markets, and on imports and exports; free movement of inputs and outputs between markets and regions; and no barrier to entry to or exit from the market. Information regarding prices, quantities, and qualities were to be known with full transparency. Every contract had to fully specify the property being exchanged, the rights and obligations of each party to the contract, and all other terms and conditions. The state and its legal apparatus guaranteed contract enforcement. Hoarding of commodities was prohibited, as were price controls. No seller or buyer was permitted to harm the interests of other market participants: for example, no third party could interrupt negotiations between two parties in order to influence the outcome in favor of one or the other party. Short-changing—not giving full weights and measure—was prohibited. Sellers and buyers were given the right of annulment, depending on circumstances. These rights protected consumers against moral hazard of incomplete, faulty, or fraudulent information. Interference with supply before market entrance was prohibited, as it would harm the interests of the original seller and the final buyer. These and other rules—such as trust and trustworthiness, as well as faithfulness to the terms and conditions of contracts—substantially reduced transaction costs and protected market participants against risks of transactions (Mirakhor and Hamid 2009).

Achieving the Ideal: Uncertainty, Risk, and Equity Markets

Uncertainty is a fact of human existence. Humans live on the brink of an uncertain future. Uncertainty stems from the fact that the future is unknown and therefore unpredictable. If severe enough, uncertainty can lead to anxiety, decision paralysis, and inaction. Lack of certainty for an individual about the future is exacerbated by ignorance of how others behave in response to uncertainty. Yet individuals must make decisions and take actions that affect their own as well as others' lives. Making decisions is one of the most fundamental capabilities of humans; it is inexorably bound up with uncertainty. Facing an unknown, and generally unknowable future, individuals make decisions by forming expectations about payoffs to alternative courses of action. They can do so using subjective estimates of payoffs to actions based on personal experiences. Alternatively, individuals can use known probability techniques to form an expectation of returns to an action. Either way, the expected outcomes will form an expression in terms of probability of occurrence of consequences to an action. In other words, uncertainty is converted into risk.

Risk, therefore, is a consequence of choice under uncertainty. Generally, "even in the most orderly societies the future is by no means certain. Even if an individual or organization has defined goals they must reflect their attitude toward risk. In some cases risk may be evaluated statistically … [When] a population is large enough, some odds can be calculated with fair accuracy as is exemplified by some calculations in life insurance area. In general, however, many of the aspects of uncertainty involve low probability or infrequent events" (Shubik 1978, 124). This makes decisions difficult and actions risky. Risk exists when more than one outcome is possible. It is uncertainty about the future that makes human lives full of risks.

Risk can arise because the decision maker has little or no information regarding which state of affairs will prevail in the future; he or she, nevertheless, makes a decision and takes action based on expectations. Risk can also arise because the decision maker does not or cannot consider all possible states that can prevail in the future. In this case, even if the decision maker wants to consider all possible states of the future, there is so much missing information that it is impossible to form expectations about payoffs to various courses of action. This situation is referred to as "ambiguity." If severe enough, this type of uncertainty also leads to reluctance or even paralysis in making decisions. People adopt various strategies of "ambiguity aversion." One strategy is to exercise patience and postpone making decisions until passage of time makes additional "missing" information available. The Qur'an has many references to the need for patience: so much so that in a number of verses it is said that, "Allah is with those who are patient," and "Allah loves those who are patient."

Questions may arise as to how the existence of uncertainty and its overwhelming influence in human life can be explained within the context of Islamic thought. Why is life subject to so much uncertainty, necessitating risk taking? Since Allah (swt) is the Creator of all things, why create uncertainty? A full discussion of possible answers is beyond the task of this chapter. Suffice it to say that in a number of verses, the Qur'an makes reference to the fact that this temporary existence is a crucible of constant testing, trials, and tribulations (see, for example, 2:155 and 2:76). Not even the believers are spared. In verse 2 of chapter 29, the Qur'an asks: "Do humans think that they will be left alone when they say, 'We believe,' and they therefore will not be tested?" The fact that this testing is a continuous process is reflected in verse 126 of chapter 9: "Do they not see that they are tried every year once or twice? Even then they do to turn repentant to Allah, not do they remember" (see also chapter 2, verse 155). To every test, trial, and tribulation in their lives, humans respond, and in doing so, they demonstrate their measure of self-awareness and consciousness of Allah. If the response-action is in compliance with the rules of behavior prescribed by the Supreme Creator, that is, it is "*Ahsanu 'Amala*," the "best action" (11:7), meaning it is completely rule-compliant; then the trial becomes an occasion for self-development and strengthened awareness of Allah (swt). Even then, uncertainty remains. No one can be fully certain of the total payoff to one's life within the horizon of birth to eternity. It is recommended that Muslims never assume they are absolutely certain of the consequences of their actions. They are to live in a state of mind and heart suspended between fear (*khawf*) of consequences of their actions and thoughts, and the hope (*raja'*) in the Mercy of the All-merciful Lord Creator. All actions are risky because the full spectrum of future consequences of action is not known. The Qur'an refers to this idea of uncertainty by suggesting that "at times you may dislike a thing when it is good for you and at times you like a thing and it is bad for you. Allah knows and you do not" (2:216).

Risk Sharing

It follows from the preceding discussion that it would be difficult to imagine that the crucible of testing can proceed without uncertainty and risk. Statistician David Bartholomew, in his book, *God, Chance, and Purpose* (2008), asserts that "it could be plausibly argued that risk is a necessary ingredient for full human development. It provides the richness and diversity of experience necessary to develop our skills and personalities" (Bartholomew 2008, 230). He speculates that "the development of human freedom requires that there be sufficient space for that freedom to be exercised. Chance seems to provide just the flexibility required and therefore to be a precondition of free will" (Bartholomew 2008, 200). Further, he suggests that "we value our free will above almost everything; our human dignity depends upon it and it is that which sets us apart from the rest of the creation. But if we are all individuals free, then so is everyone else, and that means the risks created by their behavior, foolish or otherwise, are unavoidable. To forgo risk is to forgo freedom; risk is the price we pay for freedom" (Bartholomew 2008, 239–40).

While life and freedom are gifts of the Supreme Creator to humans, and uncertainty and risk are there to test and try humans to facilitate their growth and development, humans are not left unaided to face the uncertainty of life to suffer its consequences. Books, prophets, and Messengers have brought guidance as to how to best make decisions and take actions to mitigate the risks of this life and to improve the chances of a felicitous everlasting life. Islam, in particular, has provided the ways and means by which uncertainties of life can be mitigated. First, it has provided rules of behavior and a taxonomy of decisions—actions and their commensurate payoffs—as stated in the Qur'an. Complying with these rules reduces uncertainty. Clearly, individuals exercise their freedom in choosing to comply with these rules or not to comply.

That rules of behavior and compliance with them reduce uncertainty is an important insight of the new institutional economics. Rules reduce the burden on human cognitive capacity, particularly in the process of decision making under uncertainty. Rules also promote cooperation and coordination (Mirakhor 2009). In particular, Islam has provided ways and means by which those who are able to do so mitigate uncertainty by sharing the risks they face by engaging in economic activities with fellow human beings through exchange. Sharing allows risk to be spread and thus lowered for individual participants. However, if a person is unable to use any of the market means of risk sharing because of poverty, Allah (swt) has ordered a solution here as well: the rich are commanded to share the risks of the life of the poor by redeeming their rights derived from the Islamic principles of property rights. Islam's laws of inheritance provide further mechanism of risk sharing.

Individuals in a society face two types of risks. The first is the result of the exposure of the economy to uncertainty and risk due to external and internal economic circumstances of the society and its vulnerabilities to shocks. How well the economy will absorb shocks depends on its resilience, which will in turn depend on the institutional and policy infrastructure of the society. How flexibly these will respond to shocks will determine how much these risks impact individual lives when they materialize.

The second type of risk that individuals face relates to the circumstances of their personal lives. These include risks of injuries, illness, accidents, bankruptcy, or even change of tastes and preferences. This kind of risk is referred to as idiosyncratic. When idiosyncratic risks materialize, they play havoc with people's livelihood. This is because often the level of consumption that sustains them is directly dependent on their income. If their income becomes volatile, so will their livelihood and consumption. Engaging in risk sharing can mitigate idiosyncratic risk and allow consumption smoothing by weakening the correlation between income and consumption such that should these risks materialize, and the shock reduce income, consumption and livelihood of the individual do not suffer correspondingly.

It is important to note a nuanced difference between risk taking and risk sharing. Risk taking is an antecedent of risk sharing. The decision to take risk to produce a product precedes the decision about what to do about the risk in financing the project. The decision to share the risk in financing does not increase the inherent risks of the project, but it does reduce the risks for individuals involved in financing it, as it is spread over a larger number of participants.

It should also be noted that the Islamic contract modes that have reached us are all bilateral real sector contracts. Contemporary Islamic finance industry has made two big contributions. First, it has made bilateral contracts multilateral, as the contracts move from the real sector to the finance sector. Second, it has employed instruments of risk transfer available in conventional finance, but made them compatible with Shari'ah.

Instruments of Islamic finance allow risk sharing and risk diversification, through which individuals can mitigate their idiosyncratic risks. On the other hand, mandated levies, such as *zakat*, are means through which the idiosyncratic risks of the poor are shared by the rich as an act of redemption of the former's property rights in the income and wealth of the latter. Other recommended levies, beyond those mandated, such as *sadaqat* (plural of *sadaqah*) and *Qard-al-Hassan*, play the same role. They help reduce the poor's income-consumption correlation. In other words, the poor are not forced to rely on their meager income (if they even have an income) to maintain a decent level of subsistence living for themselves and their families.

It is possible that at some point in time, even these levies can be instrumentalized to be included in the full-spectrum menu of instruments of Islamic finance for risk sharing. In the face of risk, Islamic finance functions as a risk manager of society. Its instruments of risk sharing will help blunt the impact of economic shocks, disappointments, and suffering on individuals by dispersing their effects among a large number of people. Islamic finance will have instruments available for all classes of people to allow them to reduce their idiosyncratic risks and smooth their consumption. It will ensure that innovators, entrepreneurs, and small and medium size firms have access to financial resources without the need to take all risks on themselves, or abandon productive projects altogether. It will have instruments of insurance that not only provide protection against health and accident risks but also insure against risks to livelihood and home values to protect people's long-term income and livelihood. Such a full-spectrum Islamic finance can then truly be said to have "democratized finance" without transferring risks of any venture to a particular class or to the whole society. This would be in sharp contrast to the results of the "democratization of finance" project which led to the recent global financial crisis of the conventional system, in which the risks of financial innovations were shifted away from financiers. While the gains of this "democratization of finance" project were privatized, its pain was socialized (Sheng 2009).

The Stock Market

If there is validity to the conclusion that Islamic finance is all about risk sharing, then the "first-best" instrument of risk sharing is a stock market, "which is arguably the most sophisticated market-based risk-sharing mechanism" (Brav, Constantinides, and Geczy 2002). Developing an efficient stock market can effectively complement and supplement the existing array of other Islamic finance instruments, as well as those to be developed. It would provide the means for business and industry to raise long-term capital. A vibrant stock market would allow risk diversification necessary for managing aggregate and idiosyncratic risks. Such an active market would reduce the dominance of banks and debt financing, where risks become concentrated, making the financial system more fragile (Sheng 2009).

Idiosyncratic risks impact the liquidity of individuals and firms when they materialize. With an active stock market, individuals can buffer idiosyncratic liquidity shocks by selling equity shares they own on the stock market. Firms can also reduce their own idiosyncratic and liquidity risk through active participation in the stock market. They can reduce risk to the rate of return to their own operation, such as productivity risk, by holding a well-diversified portfolio of shares of stocks. Thus incentives are created for investment in more long-term, productive projects. Importantly, by actively participating in the stock market, individuals and firms can mitigate the risk of unnecessary and premature liquidation of their assets due to liquidity and productivity shocks (Pagano 1993). Moreover, an active and vibrant stock market creates strong incentives for higher degrees of technological specialization, through which the overall productivity of the economy is increased. This happens because without sufficiently strong risk sharing in the financial system through the stock market, firms avoid deeper specialization, fearing the risk from sectoral demand shocks (Saint-Paul 1992). The reason stock markets are such effective tools of risk sharing is because each share represents a contingent residual equity claim.

It can be argued that the actual operation of the Islamic finance market differs from its ideal. It essence, there is a market failure: missing markets in equity sharing. Strong government policy action can create an incentive structure for the Islamic finance market to complete the spectrum of its instruments. The market has developed an array of short-term, liquid, and reasonably safe instruments that are considered compatible with the teachings of Islam. This was not the case some 30 years ago. Then too, there was a missing market for Islamic instruments for which there was substantial demand. It took considerable commitment of resources and credibility on the part of governments, notably the government of Malaysia, to organize this missing market to meet existing demand.

The late 1970s and early 1980s represent the beginning of the age of Muslim awakening to the possibilities of applicability of Islam finance in contemporary economy. Perhaps with the passage of time, the private sector would have organized the missing market of Islamic finance on its own. It appears likely, however, that progress may not have been as rapid as it has been with government intervention. By far the most successful has been the Malaysian paradigm. This paradigm was characterized not only by the top-down push by the government, but also other ingredients that had to be put in place for the venture's success. The most important of these ingredients were human capital, a regulatory structure, and a financial infrastructure to allow the emergence of Islamic banks. One of the most important regulatory devices that encouraged the development of Islamic finance in Malaysia was the "no leakage rule." This rule required that the financial resources mobilized by the Islamic banking window had to be utilized solely to finance Islamic contracts.

The success of the Malaysian paradigm in a relatively short span of three decades recommends it strongly as an appropriate framework for future progress. Specifically, this paradigm would suggest that the same kind of intense dedication and commitment could successfully generate the ways and means of pushing the agenda of Islamic finance forward in terms of developing medium- to long-term instruments of risk sharing. In this way, governments' commitment of resources and credibility could energize innovations and development of the needed instruments. In this context, one strategy would be for governments to develop the long-term, high-return, riskier end of the spectrum of instruments of risk sharing: specifically, the stock market. This would create the needed incentive for the private sector to design and develop instruments in between the short-term, liquid end of the market and the stock market.

Advantages and Disadvantages of Stock Markets

A large number of theoretical and empirical studies in recent decades have focused on the investment-employment-growth benefits of stock markets (see the reference list in Askari and others 2010). When risk is spread among a large number of participants through an efficient stock market, closer coordination between the financial and real sectors is promoted, and the benefits of economic growth and financial system stability are better shared. Risk transfer through debt instruments, in contrast, along with high leverage, weakens the link between the financial and real sectors, thus posing a threat to the stability of the financial sector. As the growth of pure financial instruments—those with little connection to real assets—far outpaces the growth of the real sector activities, a phenomenon called decoupling (Menkoff and Tolksdorf 2001) or financialization (Epstein 2006; Palley 2007) emerges, whereby finance no longer is anchored in the real sector. The result is financial instability, leading to frequent bouts with crises. Reinhart and Rogoff, in their book *This Time Is Different: Eight Centuries of Financial Folly* (2009), have recently demonstrated the high frequency of crises in the history of the conventional system. Aside from the fact that all crises have been debt crises, all too often financial sector crises have required large government interventions and massive bailouts. Thus, while private financiers enjoy the gains of robust pure financial innovations that ultimately lead to decoupling, society at large suffers the pain of saving the real sector from the vagaries of financial sector crises. This is what Andrew Sheng (2009) called privatizing the gain, socializing the pain.

Aside from the fact that through risk sharing, stock markets become an effective instrument of financing long-term investments, they have an added benefit of being an instrument that individuals and firms can use to insure against liquidity and productivity shocks. While some individual idiosyncratic risks can be mitigated through the purchase of insurance policies, such as health, life, and accident insurance, there are potentially a large number of unforeseen, and therefore unpredictable, personal or family risks that are not as of yet insurable and for which no insurance policy can be purchased, such as risks to a person's livelihood. An individual can buffer against uninsurable risks by buying shares of stocks in good times and selling them when and if he or she experiences a liquidity shock. Similarly, stock markets can be used to diversify the risk of shock to asset returns. Firms can also use the stock market as a buffer against liquidity and productivity risks. These insurance functions of stock markets create motivation and incentives for investing in projects that have higher returns (are more productive) but lower liquidity.

Empirical studies have demonstrated that countries with robust stock markets rely more on equity and long-term financing and less on banks and short-term debt. Firms place greater reliance on external capital than on internal funds. With a strong stock market, venture capitalists can recoup their capital investment in a project through initial public offerings, thus promoting faster rollover of venture capital to make it available more frequently to finance other productive real sector projects. Not only can individuals and firms benefit from the existence of a vibrant and robust stock market that provides opportunities to share risk, but countries can benefit from risk sharing with one another. A large body of empirical research in recent years in the area of international risk sharing has demonstrated that there are gains to be made by countries when they trade in one another's securities. For example, a 2005 study shows the welfare gains to be made by the ten East Asian countries by sharing risk among themselves, and separately with the member-countries of the Organisation for Economic Co-operation and Development (OECD). The study (Kim, Kim, and Wang 2005) considered risk sharing in the case of these countries between 1970 and 2000 and found low levels of risk sharing among the countries themselves and between them and the OECD. Indonesia and Malaysia had the lowest level of risk sharing and therefore the largest potential welfare gains from improving the sharing of risk between them and other East Asian countries. The magnitude of gains was even higher through increased risk sharing with OECD member-countries. These results could likely be replicated in other areas and regions.

Given these advantages, the question arises as to why international risk sharing is so low. This question is one researchers have been trying to explain in recent years, along with another related puzzle called the equity premium puzzle that has been attracting attention since it was first formulated in 1985 by two researchers, Mehra and Prescott. It refers to a significant differential existing between stock market returns and the rate of interest paid on a safe bond (U.S. Treasury bonds) over an extended period of time. Economic theory would assert that the differential should not exist. Capital should have left debt instruments and moved into equities until the rates equalized. Hence, the puzzle to be explained is: why does this high differential persist? Over the years, the study, originally using U.S. data, has been replicated in a number of countries with the same results (Mehra 2003, 2006). The differential cannot be explained by the existing theory of behavior under risk. Researchers have used varieties of utility functions and risk characteristics, but the puzzle remains largely unexplained. Similarly, there have been attempts to explain the low international risk-sharing puzzle, but formal modeling has not been fruitful. It is suspected that the reasons that explain low participation in the domestic equity market—and hence the emergence of the equity premium puzzle—are the same factors that could explain the low international risk-sharing puzzle. The prime candidates are the low level of trust, and a related factor, the cost of entering the market.

Equity markets that are shallow also have limited participation. Empirical evidence (Erbaş and Mirakhor 2007; Guiso, Sapienza, and Zingales 2005) suggests one reason for low participation of the population in the stock market is the fact that people generally do not trust stock markets. The low level of trust, in turn, is explained by institutional factors and education. Moreover, high transaction costs—especially information and search costs, as well as the high cost of contract enforcement—are crucial factors inhibiting stock market participation. These factors also stem from the institutional framework in the economy (rules of behavior). Stiglitz (1989) suggests that disadvantages of equity finance stem from two informational problems:

- An adverse signaling effect, which leads good companies not to issue as many equity shares for fear that it may signal poor quality; and
- An adverse incentive effect problem, which suggests that equity finance weakens the incentive for the entrepreneurs to exert their maximum effort for the highest possible joint return.

This happens because once the project is financed, the entrepreneur knows that net returns must be shared with the financier and therefore may not be motivated to work as hard as when the returns would not have to be shared. While the idea has intuitive appeal, empirical evidence does not support it.

Allen and Gale (2007), on the other hand, suggest a more plausible and empirically stronger reason why stock market participation is limited. They argue that it is because of the costs involved. These include information costs; enforcement costs; and costs due to the weak governance structure of firms and markets. Their analysis concludes that if these costs are prohibitively high, firms leave the equity market and resort to debt financing through banks (101–15). But banks are highly leveraged institutions that borrow short (deposits) and lend long. This maturity mismatch creates potential for liquidity shocks and instability. And perhaps to different degrees, even in the case of banks, there are information problems that lead to market failures, such as credit rationing, which paralyzes the opportunity for risky but potentially highly productive projects because they are rationed out of the market.

There are two conflicting views of the behavior of banks in financing of projects. Stiglitz (1989) suggests that to protect their financial resources, banks generally discourage risk taking. Therefore, there is an inherent agency conflict.

The entrepreneur (agent) is interested in the high end of the risk-return distribution. By contrast, the bank (principle) is interested in safety, and thus is concerned with the low end of the risk-return distribution. This, Stiglitz asserts, "has deleterious consequences for the economy" (1989, 57). He further suggests that "from a social point of view, equity has a distinct advantage: because risks are shared between the entrepreneur and the capital provider the firm will not cut back production as much as it would with debt financing if there is down turn in the economy" (1989, 57). In contrast to Stiglitz's assertion that banks concentrate on the lower end of the risk-return distribution for reasons of safety, Hellwig argues that there is an oft-neglected informational problem of banks, which he refers to as "negative incentive effects on the choice of risk inherent in the moral hazard of riskiness of the lend strategy of banks" (1998, 335). This risk materialized dramatically in the period leading up to the recent financial crisis (see Askari and others 2010; Sheng 2009).

Conditions for a Vibrant, Robust Stock Market

Allen and Gale (2007) suggest that a successful, deep, and active stock market requires that information, enforcement, and governance costs be eliminated or at least minimized. Once this happens, the cost of entry into equity market becomes low and "there is full participation in the market. All investors enter the market, the average amount of liquidity in the market is high, and asset prices are not excessively high" (115). As mentioned, if the Islamic rules of market behavior—such as faithfulness to the terms and conditions of contracts, trust, and trustworthiness—are in place in a society, the informational problems and transaction costs, governance, and enforcement issues either would not exist or would be at such low levels as not to deter stock market entry.

There is, however, a paradigm gap between what Islam teaches and the actual behavior in the market. For this reason, actions governments take and the institutions they create to remedy the deficit in informational, enforcement, and governance behavior to reduce the cost of participation in stock markets must be stronger and more comprehensive than exist today. These policies, actions, and institutions should have the competence, efficiency, and enforcement capabilities to elicit the kind of behavior and results that replicate or closely approximate those expected if market participants behaved in compliance with Islamic rules. These would include:

- Policies to create a level playing field for equities to compete fairly with debt-based instruments; this means removing all legal, administrative, economic, financial, and regulatory biases that favor debt and put equity holding at a disadvantage;
- Creating positive incentives for risk sharing through the stock market;
- Investing in massive public education campaigns to familiarize the population with the benefits of stock market participation: the kind of campaign that Prime Minister Thatcher's government ran in the United Kingdom, which substantially increased stock market participation in a short span of time;

- Investing in human capital to produce competent, well-educated, and trained reputational intermediaries—lawyers, accountants, financial journalists, and religious scholars—which means investing in the creation of world class business and law schools;
- Limiting short sales and leverage (including margin operations) of nonbank financial institutions and the credit-creation ability of banks through prudential rules that effectively cap the total credit the banking system can create;
- Developing a strong and dynamic regulatory and supervisory system for stock exchanges that not only continuously monitors the behavior of markets and participants but stays a few steps ahead of those with a penchant and motivation to use regulatory arbitrage to get around rules and regulations;
- Finding ways and means of regulating and supervising reputational intermediaries, or at least mandating that they become self-regulating to ensure that false reporting or misreporting, or both, are minimized, under threat of liability to market participants;
- Ensuring completely transparent and accurate reporting of the day's trade by all exchanges; and
- Instituting legal requirements for the protection of the rights of minority shareholders.

These policies and actions are by no means exhaustive, but even this incomplete list would help reduce the cost of market participation, invest the market with credibility, and reduce reliance on debt financing. Black (2000) asserts that just one element of the above list, legal protection of minority shareholders' rights, gives countries large stock market capitalization, larger minority shareholder participation in the stock market, more publicly listed forms relative to the total population, less concentrated ownership, higher dividend payout, and lower cost of capital. Black also believes that a country will have the potential to develop a vibrant stock market if it can assure minority shareholders that they can obtain good information about the true value of businesses the listing companies are engaged in, and that there is sufficient legal, regulatory, and supervisory protection against company self-dealing transactions, such as insider trading.

Lack of good information about a firm's true value and the possibility of company self-dealing create the problems of moral hazard and adverse selection. Both problems can be addressed by legal rules and procedures, as well as by the existence of efficient and credible public and private institutions that monitor the stock market and companies listed on the stock exchange. These laws and institutions can assure investors of the honesty of dealings by firms and of the full transparency and accuracy of reporting and information. Extensive laws regarding financial disclosure—along with securities laws with strong sanctions for imposing the risk of liability (to investors) on accountants, lawyers, firms' insiders, and investment bankers in retaliation for false reporting, fraudulent misleading information, or faulty endorsements—can be powerful tools of dissuading all concerned from the temptation of defrauding investors with false reporting and misleading information. Requiring reputational intermediaries to be licensed by regulators, and revoking licenses or imposing heavy fines and initiating criminal proceedings against misbehavior, weakens the incentive structure for abuse of reporting, endorsing, and information processes. Strong listing standards that stock exchanges enforce fully through imposition of heavy fines or even delisting of companies that violate disclosure rules would discourage false information from reaching investors. Existence of an active, dynamic, well-informed financial press can be valuable in creating a culture of disclosure. A strong, independent, and dynamic regulatory agency is needed to monitor and supervise the stock market and behavior of its participants and aggressively promote a culture of transparency by requiring prompt and accurate reporting on all trades in the market. Finally, it bears repeating that government must invest considerable resources in developing world class business and law schools to ensure a competent source of supply of human capital to act as reputational intermediaries.

While these policies and institutions are crucial for reducing the cost of participation in stock markets and thus promoting widespread risk sharing, governments need to do more; they must lead by example. They could become active in markets for risk sharing. Generally, governments do share risks with their citizens and organizations. They share risks with individuals, firms, and corporations through tax and spending policies; they are silent partners. They also share the risk of the poor and disadvantaged through social expenditure policies. They share the risk of the financial system through monetary policy and deposit guarantees. They could choose to finance part of their budget, at least development spending, through risk sharing and direct ownership of development projects with their citizens. In this way, they would reduce the debt burden on the budget. This reduction in government borrowing would reduce the burden on monetary policy as well. Governments undertake public goods projects because the characteristics of these goods—notably, indivisibility and nonexclusivability—prohibit their production by the private sector. However, their social rate of return is substantial, and much higher than private rates of return. These projects could be undertaken jointly with the private sector through public-private partnerships. The proposal has a number of problems that must be resolved: market distortion, informational, and governance problems are just three of these (see Choudhry and Mirakhor 1997).

Government Finance and Risk Sharing

Financing a portion of government's budget through the stock market has many advantages, fifteen of which are summarized here. First, it can energize a stock market—provided that all preconditions, in terms of human capital, and the legal, administrative, and regulatory framework are met—and help strengthen the credibility of the market. Second, it can deepen and broaden the stock market. Third, it can demonstrate that stock markets can be used as a tool of risk and financial management. Fourth, it can reduce reliance of the budget on borrowing, thereby imparting greater stability to the budget, and mitigate the risk of "sudden stops." Fifth, it can have positive distributional effects because the financial resources that would normally go to servicing public debt can now be spread more widely among the public as returns to the shares of government projects. Sixth, it can enhance the potential for financing a larger portfolio of public goods projects without the fear of creating an undue burden on the budget. Seventh, it can make the task of monetary management simpler by limiting the amount of new money creation and limiting the number of objectives of monetary policy. Eighth, it can promote ownership of public goods by citizens, and thus have a salutary effect on maintaining public goods, as it can create an ownership concern among the public, and to some extent mitigate "the tragedy of commons." Ninth, it can have the potential to strengthen social solidarity. Tenth, it can also have the potential to promote better governance by involving citizens as shareholder-owners of public projects. Eleventh, it can provide an excellent risk-sharing instrument for financing of long-term private sector investment. Twelfth, it can also be an effective instrument for firms and individuals to use to mitigate liquidity and productivity risks. Thirteenth, by providing greater depth and breadth to the market and minimizing the cost of market participation, governments can convert the stock market into an instrument of international risk sharing, as other countries and their citizens and other investors can invest in the domestic stock market. Fourteenth, it can change the basis of monetary expansion from credit to equity as economic expansion in the real sector maps onto the financial sector. Finally, it can help demystify Islamic finance and create an environment of cooperation and coordination with international finance.

The design of risk-sharing instruments to be issued by governments is not difficult. These instruments can be traded in the secondary market if the shareholders experience a liquidity shock. Their rate of return can be structured as an index of return tied to the rate of return to the stock market. If the domestic stock market is not deep, then an index of regional or international stock market returns, or both, can be included. The argument is that since the social rate of return to public goods is much higher than the return to privately produced goods and services, the investment in public goods should have a rate of return at least as high as the return to the stock market to promote efficient resource allocation. Of course, since governments are usually less risky, the rate of return to government-issued shares must be adjusted downward to take account of governments' risk premiums. Depending on the country and the interest rate its government pays on borrowed money, it is not likely that the rate of return it would pay to holders of equity shares it issues—adjusted for the credit rating of the government reflected in lower risk—would be any higher than the interest rate it would pay to borrow. Even in the unlikely event that a few more basis points higher must be paid, the tradeoff is worthwhile, considering the positive contributions the instrument would make to the economy and the society (see Choudhry and Mirakhor 1997; Ul Haque and Mirakhor 1999).

Summary and Conclusion

This chapter has sought to trace the epistemological roots of conventional and Islamic finance. The reason for interest in the two fields is that the current Islamic finance industry evolved over the past three decades from conventional finance to address a market failure in conventional finance in terms of unmet market demand for Islamic finance products. Most practitioners of Islamic finance were bankers and market players well-versed and often well-established in the conventional finance sector. Their focus was, and is, to develop financial instruments familiar to the conventional finance market, albeit with religious compatibility as an objective. Their ingenuity, combined with the active and creative imagination of leading religious scholars, has led to the development of a rich array of synthetic and structured products, all of which, in one form or another, are replicated, retrofitted, or reverse engineered from conventional finance. This vast array—ranging from simple instruments such as lease-purchase to exchange traded funds (ETFs) to leveraged buyouts (LBOs)—are Islamic insofar as an attempt is made to ensure that fixed interest rates are avoided.

This chapter contends, however, that this, at best, is only meeting the second half of the part of verse 275 of chapter 2 of the Qur'an, in which Allah (swt) first ordains exchange contracts and then prohibits *Al-Riba* contracts. The chapter argues that this approach has further entrenched the current Islamic finance industry within the conventional financial system, rendering the Islamic finance industry a new asset class within the conventional system. The Islamic finance industry could have taken a different course, as a number of pioneering scholars had defined a trajectory for its development based on risk sharing (profit-loss sharing, or PLS). In any event, it was conventional finance that gave Islamic finance industry its take-off platform, thus making the study of the epistemology of conventional finance relevant.

This chapter has argued that it is an economic system that gives rise to a financial system. Therefore, to understand the origin of a financial system, one needs to understand the epistemology of its underlying economic system. Economists trace the epistemology of the conventional economy to Adam Smith. It was the genius of Kenneth Arrow and his principle co-authors, Gérard Debreu and Frank Hahn, to attempt to provide an analytically rigorous proof of what they saw as the vision of Smith for an economy. However, a number of contemporary scholars, including Amartya Sen, consider the neoclassical understanding of Smith's vision as distorted and an inadequate representation of Smith's works. This chapter argued that Smith's vision of the institutional infrastructure of the economy—that is, the moral-ethical rules governing behavior prescribed by "the Author of nature"—echoes some of the important rules prescribed by Allah (swt) in the Qur'an and operationalized by His Beloved Messenger. There is some tantalizing evidence from Arrow in the mid-1970s that suggests that he thought that those ethical-moral rules are crucial to the efficient operation of the economy.

The economy-finance nexus defined by Arrow-Debreu-Hahn GE models were risk-sharing conceptualizations in which securities represented contingent financial claims on the real sector. Equity share claims represent first-best instruments of risk sharing and satisfy characteristics required of Arrow Securities. It would appear that had the financial markets in industrial countries developed their financial sector along the lines suggested by the Arrow-Debreu-Hahn model, they could have had much more efficient risk sharing, and perhaps avoided the crises that have plagued the conventional financial system.

A number of post-mortem analyses of the recent crisis have developed constructive insights that may help steer the conventional system away from high credit, high leverage, and high debt, which are the ultimate causes of all financial crises (Reinhart and Rogoff 2009). Almost all of the many recommendations for reform of the conventional system—from *The Stiglitz Report* (Stiglitz 2010), at one end of the spectrum of thought among financial-economic scholars and practitioners, to *The Squam Lake Report* (French and others 2010), at the other end—include some form of control, whether direct or indirect, on credit, debt, and leverage within the financial system, including higher capital adequacy requirements. Some analysts have gone beyond these recommendations and have suggested reform of the fractional reserve banking system and deposit insurance (Kotlikoff 2010). It is likely that if such reforms are implemented, reliance on debt-creating flows within the conventional system would decline in favor of greater equity. Basil III has already taken steps—although not as significant as scholars such as Stiglitz or Hellwig have demanded—to enhance capital adequacy requirements, impose limits on leverage, and curtail proprietary trading of the banks. Whether these changes will be sufficient to induce the conventional system to move away from its overwhelming dominance on interest-based debt contracts, risk transfer, and risk shifting or whether it will take more severe bouts with crises before it does so remains to be seen.

A healthy debate is in progress regarding the future direction of Islamic finance. This chapter suggests a way forward that all countries would have to follow in any event to develop an effective financial system. The chapter has argued that risk sharing is the objective of Islamic finance. Theoretical and empirical research has shown a robust link between the strength of the financial system and economic growth (Askari and others 2010). This research has also demonstrated the crucial role that stock markets play in underpinning the strength of the financial system. Stock markets are also an effective instrument of international risk sharing, as well as a tool of individual and firm risk management. Therefore, developing countries are working toward organizing stock markets as part of their effort at financial development. This chapter argues that active involvement of governments in creating a vibrant and efficient stock market, and their participation in that market by financing a portion of their budget with equity, can create the incentives and motivation for further development of more effective risk-sharing instruments of Islamic finance.

The progress of Islamic finance over the last three decades is well recognized. In the course of its evolution thus far, the market has developed an array of short-term, liquid, low-risk instruments. While instruments of liquidity are needed in the market, so are instruments of long-term investment. What is of concern is that very little or no effort is being spent in developing instruments that can serve the long-term, less liquid, higher-return investments that have greater potential for generating employment, income, and economic growth. There is a strong perception that Islamic finance is focusing on developments of relatively safe instruments with debt-like characteristics promising maximum return with minimal risk in the shortest possible time. It is thought that this is what is driving Islamic finance. Currently, this is a major apprehension. Concentrating market energies on these types of instruments has possible detrimental effects. There is the possibility of repeatedly reinventing the same short-term, liquid, safe instruments, with only a small difference in finetuning, slicing, and dicing risk for purposes of product differentiation. The theory of spanning, which provided the analytic basis for the development of the derivatives market, assures that this process can be never-ending. The theory argues that one basic instrument can be spanned into an infinite number of derivatives. If the resources of the market are taken up by investment in these types of instruments, the economy will be deprived of financing for long-term investment on a risk-sharing basis.

There is a perception that the demand-driven market values safety and this is the reason why longer-term riskier Islamic finance instruments are not being developed. While the market should have instruments to meet the demand for short-term, low risk, and liquid trade financing, it would be unfortunate if the future evolution of Islamic finance focuses only on short-termism at the cost of neglecting the longer-term investment needs of the real sector. While instruments developed so far emphasize safety, the recent crisis in the conventional system, as well as the turmoil in the *sukuk* market, demonstrate that no one instrument is immune to risk and that it is unrealistic to perpetuate a myth that safety with high returns in financial markets is possible. There is always risk. The question is how to allocate it to those who are in the best position to bear it and how to build a system resilient enough to absorb shocks emanating from the materialization of risk. The answer must surely lie in a system that provides a full-spectrum menu of risk-sharing instruments.

A related concern is that by focusing solely on short-termism, there is the possibility of encouraging the emergence of path-dependency. Economic changes generally occur in increments. Growth of markets and capital formation are path-dependent. That is, later outcomes are partly a function of what has inspired the earlier rounds of economic and financial exchange (Sheng 2009). Once path-dependency sets in, change becomes difficult. At times, path-dependency is exacerbated by the insularity and silo mentality generated by a perception that all is well with established ways of doing things, and therefore no change is required. There is a concern that such path-dependency may well emerge that conveys a message that short-termism, safety, and liquidity, as well as no *riba*, are all there is to Islamic finance. The thrust of this chapter is that this is not so.

Islamic finance is more about risk spreading and risk sharing. This chapter suggests that, for those who are able to participate in the financial sector, Islamic finance provides risk sharing through transactions. For those unable to utilize instruments of Islamic finance to mitigate risk because of poverty, the financially able are commanded to share the risks of the less able through the redistributive instruments prescribed by Islam. Thus the financially more able must share the risks to the life of the poor—not as an act of charity but as a duty of redeeming a right of the less able: a right that is a direct result of the property rights principles of Islam. Inheritance laws are also a means of risk sharing.

One must not lose sight of the fact that Islamic finance is a new industry. After centuries of atrophy, it has begun operating at a noticeable level of commercial significance only recently. In the process, it is competing against a path-dependent financial system that is centuries old. It is making a serious attempt to return to its roots, but systematically and within the framework of the current economic, social, and financial reality. This would suggest that in time, Islamic finance can and will develop a full-spectrum menu of instruments to serve all risk-return appetites. This chapter, without contradicting this argument, suggests a way forward by arguing for government intervention to develop a vibrant and active stock market that can energize and accelerate progress. This can be justified on many grounds. Among the most compelling, empirical evidence has shown a strong and robust relationship between financial development, including an active stock market, and economic growth.

Arguably, the stock market is the first-best instrument of risk sharing. Developing an active and efficient stock market can promote international as well as domestic risk sharing that can make the economy and its financial system more resilient to shocks. Moreover, this chapter suggests that lack of available equity instruments within the menu of Islamic finance instruments is akin to a market failure, creating a strong ground for government intervention. Additionally, the chapter suggests that the introduction of Islamic finance at the global level represents a remedy for the failure of financial markets to meet a strong demand for Islamic instruments. It took a top-down, government commitment, dedication, and investment of resources, particularly in the case of the government of Malaysia, to correct this market failure.

Government intervention can remedy the current failure of the market to develop long-term, riskier, higher-return equity instruments. Some 65 years ago, Domar and Musgrave (1944) suggested that fuller participation of government in sharing the private sector's gains and losses would encourage a greater amount of risky investment (see also Stiglitz 1989). This governments could do by developing a stock market with low costs of entry to ensure the widest possible participation by investors. In doing so, governments could also ensure that stock markets would have limitations on short selling and leverage operations by establishing market-based regulatory measures. Creating such a stock market would represent a leap forward by providing an effective instrument for domestic and international risk sharing and long-term equity investment. This chapter suggests that governments can enhance the credibility and appeal of the stock market by financing part of their budgets by issuing equity shares that would be traded in the market. Government could also mount public information campaigns to educate the population regarding the risk-sharing characteristics of the stock market. This strategy was adopted in the United Kingdom, with considerable success. Islamic finance has developed instruments to serve the low end of the time-risk-return profile of its transactions menu. Such a stock market would serve the high end. The intermediate space of the menu could then be left for the private sector to complete.

References

Allen, F., and D. Gale. 2007. *Understanding Financial Crises*. New York: Oxford University Press.

Arrow, K. J. 1971. *Essays in the Theory of Risk-Bearing*. Amsterdam: North-Holland Publishing Company.

———. 1974. *The Limits of Organizations*. New York: Norton.

Arrow, K. J., and G. Debreu. 1954. "The Existence of an Equilibrium for a Competitive Economy." *Econometrica* XXII: 265–90.

Arrow, K. J., and F. Hahn. 1971. *General Competitive Analysis*. San Francisco: Holder Day.

Askari, H., Z. Iqbal, and A. Mirakhor. 2009. *Globalization and Islamic Finance*. Singapore: John Wiley and Sons (Asia).

Askari, H., Z. Iqbal, N. Krichene, and A. Mirakhor. 2010. *The Stability of Islamic Finance*. Singapore: John Wiley and Sons (Asia).

Bartholomew, D. J. 2008. *God, Chance and Purpose*. Cambridge, U.K.: Cambridge University Press.

Black, B. S. 2000. "The Core Institutions that Support Strong Securities Markets." *The Business Lawyer* 55: 1565–607.

Brav, A., G. M. Constantinides, and C. C. Geczy. 2002. "Asset Pricing with Heterogeneous Consumers and Limited Participation: Empirical Evidence." *Journal of Political Economy* 110 (4): 793–824.

Brouwer, M. 2005. "Managing Uncertainty through Profit Sharing Contracts from Medieval Italy to Silicon Valley." *Journal of Management and Governance* 9: 237–55.

Chapra, M. U. 2000. *The Future of Economics: An Islamic Perspective*. Leicester, U.K.: The Islamic Foundation.

Choudhry, N. N., and A. Mirakhor. 1997. "Indirect Instruments of Monetary Control in an Islamic Financial System." *Islamic Economic Studies* 4 (2).

Cowen, T. 1983. "The Rate of Return in General Equilibrium: A Critique." *Journal of Post Keyensian Economics* (Summer): 608–17.

Domar, E. D., and R. A. Musgrave. 1944. "Proportional Income Taxation and Risk Taking." *Quarterly Journal of Economics* LVI (May).

Epstein, G. 2006. *Financializaton and the World Economy*. Cheltenham, U.K.: Edward Elgar.

Erbaş, N., and A. Mirakhor. 2007. "The Equity Premium Puzzle, Ambiguity Aversion and Institutional Quality." IMF Working Paper, International Monetary Fund, Washington, DC.

Evensky, J. 1987. "The Two Voices of Adam Smith: Moral Philosopher and Social Critic." *History of Political Economy* 19 (1): 123–44.

———. 1993. "Ethics and the Invisible Hand." *Journal of Economic Perspectives* 7 (2): 197–205.

Fama, E. F., and M. C. Jensen. 1983. "The Agency Problems and Residual Claims." *Journal of Law and Economics* XXVI: 327–49.

Fischel, W. 1933. "The Origin of Banking in Medieval Islam." *Journal of the Royal Asiatic Society* 65 (20): 339–52.

French, K. R., M. N. Baily, J. Y. Campbell, J. H. Cochrane, D. W. Diamond, D. Duffie, A. K. Kashyap, F. S. Mishkin, R. G. Rajan, D. S. Scharfstein, R. J. Shiller, H. S. Shin, M. J. Slaughter, J. C. Stein, and R. M. Stulz. 2010. *The Squam Lake Report: Fixing the Financial System*. Princeton, NJ: Princeton University Press.

Guiso, L., P. Sapienza, and L. Zingales. 2005. "Trusting the Stock Market." NBER Working Paper 11648, National Bureau of Economic Research, Cambridge, MA.

Hart, O., and B. Holstrom. 1987. "The Theory of Contracts." In *Advances in Economic Theory, Fifth World Congress*, edited by T. Bewley. Cambridge, U.K.: Cambridge University Press.

Hellwig, M. 1998. "Banks, Markets, and Allocation of Risks in an Economy." *Journal of Institutional and Theoretical Economics* 154 (1): 328–45.

Iqbal, Z., and A. Mirakhor. 2012. *An Introduction to Islamic Finance: Theory and Practice*. Singapore: John Wiley and Sons.

Jensen, M. C., and W. H. Meckling. 1976. "Theory of the Firm: Managerial Behavior, Agency Costs and Ownership Structure." *Journal of Financial Economics* 3 (4): 305–60.

Keefer, P., and S. Knack. 2005. "Social Capital, Social Norms and the New Institutional Economics." In *Handbook of New Institutional Economics*, edited by C. Menard and M. Shirley, 701–75. Amsterdam: Springer.

Kim, S., H. Kim, and Y. Wang. 2005. "Regional versus Global Risk Sharing in East Asia." *Asian Economic Papers* 3 (3): 195–201.

Kotlikoff, L. 2010. *Jimmy Stewart is Dead: Ending the World's Ongoing Financial Plague with Limited Purpose Banking*. Hoboken, NJ: John Wiley and Sons, Inc.

Lopez, R. S. 1976. *The Commercial Revolution of the Middle Ages, 950–1350*. Cambridge, U.K.: Cambridge University Press.

Mehra, R. 2003. "The Equity Premium: Why Is It a Puzzle?" *Financial Analysts Journal* 59 (January/February): 54–69.

———. 2006. "The Equity Premium in India." NBER Working Paper 12434, National Bureau of Economic Research, Cambridge, MA.

Mehra, R., and E. C. Prescott. 1985. "The Equity Premium: A Puzzle." *Journal of Monetary Economics* 15: 145–61.

Menkoff, L., and N. Tolksdorf. 2001. *Financial Market Drift: Decoupling of the Financial Sector from the Real Economy?* Heidelberg-Berlin: Springer-Verlag.

Mirakhor, A. 1983. "Muslim Contribution to Economics." Presented at the Midwest Economic Association Meeting, April 9–7. Reprinted in *Essays on Iquistad*, edited by B. Al-Hassani and A. Mirakhor, 2003. New York: Global Scholarly Publications.

———. 1993. "Equilibrium in a Non-Interest Open Economy." *Journal of King Abdulaziz University: Islamic Economics* 5: 3–23.

———. 2002. "Hopes for the Future of Islamic Finance." *New Horizon* 121 (July–August): 5–8.

———. 2009. "Islamic Economics and Finance: An Institutional Perspective." *IIUM Journal of Economics and Management* 17 (1): 31–72.

Mirakhor, A., and H. Askari. 2010. *Islam and the Path to Human and Economic Development*. New York: Palgrave.

Mirakhor, A., and I. S. Hamid. 2009. *Islam and Development: The Institutional Framework*. New York: Global Publications.

Mirakhor, A., and N. Krichene. 2009. "The Recent Crisis: Lessons for Islamic Finance." IFSB 2nd Public Lecture on Financial Policy and Stability, Islamic Financial Services Board, Kuala Lumpur, Malaysia.

Mirakhor, A. and I. Zaidi. 2007. "Profit-and-Loss Sharing Contracts in Islamic Finance." In *Handbook of Islamic Banking*, edited by K. Hassan and M. Lewis. Cheltenham, U.K.: Edward Elgar.

Pagano, M. 1993. "Financial Markets and Growth: An Overview." *European Economic Review* 37: 613–22.

Palley, T. J. 2007. "Financialization: What It Is and Why It Matters." Working Paper 252, The Levy Economics Institute, Annandale-on-Hudson, NY.

Reinhart, C., and K. Rogoff. 2009. *This Time Is Different: Eight Centuries of Financial Folly*. Princeton, NJ: Princeton University Press.

Rogoff, K. 2011. "Global Imbalances without Tears." Project Syndicate, 2011-03-01.

Saint-Paul, G. 1992. "Technological Choice, Financial Markets and Economic Development." *European Economic Review* 36: 763–81.

Sen, A. K. 1982. "Rational Fools." In *Choice, Welfare and Measurement*, edited by A. K. Sen. Cambridge, MA: MIT Press.

———. 1987. *On Ethics and Economics*. Oxford, U.K.: Blackwell.

Sheng, A. 2009. *From Asian to Global Financial Crisis*. New York: Cambridge University Press.

Shubik, M. 1978. "On the Concept of Efficiency." *Policy Science* 9: 121–29.

Smith, A. (1759) 2006. *The Theory of Moral Sentiments*. London: A. Milar. Reprint, Courier Dover Publications. Citations refer to the 2006 edition.

———. (1776) 1976. *An Inquiry into the Nature and Causes of the Wealth of Nations*. Reprint, edited in two volumes by W. B. Todd. Citations are to vol. 2 of the Glasgow Edition of *The Works and Correspondence of Adam Smith*. Oxford, U.K.: Clarendon Press.

Stiglitz, J. E. 1989. "Financial Markets and Development." *Oxford Review of Economic Policy* 5 (4): 55–68.

———. 2010. *The Stiglitz Report*. New York: The New Press.

Udovitch, A. L. 1970a. "Commercial Techniques in Early Medieval Islamic Trade." In *Islam and the Trade of Asia*, edited by D. Richards, 37–62. Oxford, U.K.: Bruno Cassirer; Philadelphia: University of Pennsylvania Press.

———. 1970b. *Partnership and Profit in Medieval Islam*. Princeton, NJ: Princeton University Press.

Ul Haque, N., and A. Mirakhor. 1999. "The Design of Instruments for Government Finance in an Islamic Economy." *Islamic Economic Studies* 6 (2): 27–43.

Walsh, V. 2000. "Smith after Sen." *Review of Political Economy* 12 (1): 5–25.

Background Reading

Adrian, T., and H. S. Shin. 2008. "Liquidity and Leverage." Staff Report 328, Federal Reserve Bank of New York.

Aiyagari, S. R. 1994. "Uninsured Idiosyncratic Shock and Aggregate Saving." *Quarterly Journal of Economics* 109 (3): 659–84.

Albuquerque, R. 2003. "The Composition of International Capital Flows: Risk Sharing through Foreign Direct Investment." *Journal of International Economics* 1 (2): 353–83.

Alesina, A., and E. La Ferrara. 2002. "Who Trusts Others?" *Journal of Public Economics* 85: 207–34.

Alfaro, L., A. Chanda, S. Kalemli-Ozcan, and S. Sayek. 2005. "How Does Foreign Direct Investment Promote Economic Growth: Exploring the Effects of Financial Markets on Linkages." NBER Working Paper 12522, National Bureau of Economic Research, Cambridge, MA.

Al-Hassani, B., and A. Mirakhor, eds. 2003. *Essays on Iqtisad*. New York: Global Scholarly Publications.

Al-Isfahani, A. 1992. *"Mufradat Alfaz Al Quran."* Dar Al-Qalam, Damascus.

Al-Liban, I. 1967. "Islam Is the First Religious System to Recognize the Right of the Poor to the Wealth of the Rich." *The Islamic Review*, August: 14–19.

Al-Mustafaoui, S. H. 1995. *Al-Tahquiq Fi Kalamat Al-Quran Al-Karim*. Tehran: Ministry of Islamic Culture and Guidance.

Allen, F., and D. Gale. 1994. *Financial Innovations and Risk Sharing*. Cambridge, MA: The MIT Press.

Anderson, J. N. D., and J. J. Coulson. 1958, "The Moslem Ruler and Contractual Obligations." *New York University Law Review* 33 (7).

Arndt, H. W. 1998. "'Market Failure' and Underdevelopment." *World Development* 16 (2): 219–29.

Ashraf, N., B. Iris, and P. Nikita. 2005. "Decomposing Trust and Trustworthiness." Working Paper, Department of Economics, Harvard University, Cambridge, MA.

Askari, H., Z. Iqbal, and A. Mirakhor. 2009. *New Issues in Islamic Finance and Economics*. Singapore: John Wiley and Sons (Asia).

Bailey, W., C. X. Mao, and K. Sirodom. 2007. "Investment Restrictions and the Cross-Border Flow of Information: Some Empirical Evidence." *Journal of International Money and Finance* 26: 1–15.

Balgati, B., P. Demitriades, and S. H. Law. 2007. "Financial Openness and Institution: Evidence from Panel Date." Paper presented at the Conference on New Perspectives on Financial Globalisation, sponsored by the Research Department, International Monetary Fund, Washington, DC.

Baltensperger, E. 1978. "Credit Rationing: Issues and Questions." *Journal of Money, Credit and Banking* 10 (2): 170–83.

Bar, A., M. Dekker, and M. Fafchamps. 2008. "Risk Sharing Relations and Enforcement Mechanisms." CSAE WPS/2008-14, Centre for the Study of African Economies, Oxford University.

Beck, T., A. Demirgüç-Kunt, and R. Levine. 2007. "Finance, Inequality and the Poor." *Journal of Economic Growth* 12 (1): 27–49.

Beck, T., and R. Levine. 2004. "Legal Institutions and Financial Development." In *Handbook of New Institutional Economics*, edited by C. Menard and M. Shirley. Dordrech, The Netherlands: Kluwer.

Bekaert, G., C. R. Harvey, and C. T. Lundblad. 2001. "Emerging Equity Markets and Economic Development." *Journal of Development Economics* 66: 465–504.

Beugelsdijk, S., H. de Groot, and A. van Schaik. 2004. "Trust and Economic Growth: A Robustness Analysis." *Oxford Economic Papers* 56: 118–34.

Bionski, M., and D. Probst. 2001. "The Emergence of Trust." University of Mannheim. Unpublished.

Black, B. S. 2000. "The Legal and Institutional Preconditions for Strong Securities Markets." *UCLA Law Review* 49: 781–855.

Bockelmann, H., and C. Borio. 1990. "Stability Properties of an Equity-Based Financial System." *De Economist* 138 (4).

Broner, F. A., and J. Ventura. 2006. "Globalisation and Risk Sharing." NBER Working Paper 12482, National Bureau of Economic Research, Cambridge, MA.

Bushman, R. M., and J. D. Piotroski. 2005. "Financial Reporting Incentives for Conservative Accounting: The Influence of Legal and Political Institutions." *Journal of Accounting and Economics* 42 (1–2): 107–48.

Calderon, C., A. Chong, and A. Galindo. 2002. "Development and Efficiency of the Financial Sector and Links with Trust: Cross-Country Evidence." *Economic Development and Cultural Change* 51 (1): 189–204.

Chapra, M. U. 2006. "Financial Stability: The Role of Paradigm and Support Institutions." In *Islamic Financial Architecture: Risk Management and Financial Stability*, edited by T. Khan and D. Muljawan. Jeddah, Saudi Arabia: Islamic Research and Training Institute (IRTI).

———. 2007. "Challenges Facing the Islamic Financial Industry." In *Handbook of Islamic Banking*, edited by M. K. Hassan and M. K. Lewis, 325–60. Cheltenham, U.K.: Edward Elgar.

Cho, Y. J. 1986. "Inefficiencies from Financial Liberalisation in the Absence of Well-Functioning Equity Markets." *Journal of Money, Credit and Banking* 17 (2): 191–200.

Cizakca, M. 1996. *A Comparative Evolution on Business Partnerships. The Islamic World and Europe, with Specific Reference to the Ottoman Archives*. Leiden, The Netherlands: Brill.

———. 2000. *A History of Philanthropic Foundations*. Istanbul, Turkey: Bogazici University Press.

———. 2011. *Islamic Capitalism and Finance: Origins, Evolution and the Future*. Cheltenham, U.K.: Edward Elgar.

Claessens, S. 1995. "The Emergence of Equity Investment in Developing Countries–Overview." *The World Bank Economic Review* 9: 1–17.

Claessens, S., and E. Perotti. 2006. "The Links between Finance and Inequality: Channels and Evidence." Background paper for the *World Development Report 2006*, World Bank, Washington, DC.

Clementi, G. L., and G. MacDonald. 2004. "Investor Protection, Optimal Incentives, and Economic Growth." *Journal of Economics* 119 (3): 1131–75.

Dollar, D., and A. Kraay. 2002. "Growth Is Good for the Poor." *Journal of Economic Growth* 7 (3): 195–225.

Epstein, G. 2002. "Financialization, Rentier Interests, and Central Bank Policy." University of Massachusetts Amherst, Amherst, MA. www.umass.edu/per/finagenda.html#alphalist.

Fergusson, L. 2006. "Institutions for Financial Development: What Are They and Where Do They Come From?" *Journal of Economic Surveys* 20 (1): 27–69.

French, K. R., and J. M. Poterba. 1991. "Investor Diversification and International Equity Markets." *American Economic Review* 81 (1): 222–26.

Frisch, D., and J. Baron. 1988. "Ambiguity and Rationality." *Journal of Behavioral Decision Making* 1: 149–57.

Fukuyama, F. 1996. *Trust, the Social Virtues and the Creation of Prosperity*. Free Press Paperbacks.

Geertz, C. 1978. "The Bazaar Economy: Information and Searching Peasant Marketing." *American Economic Review* 68 (2).

Gelos, R. G., and S-J. Wei. 2002. "Transparency and International Investor Behavior." NBER Working Paper 9260, National Bureau of Economic Research, Cambridge, MA.

Goitein, S. D. 1955. "The Cairo Geniza as a Source of the History of Muslim Civilization." *Studia Islamica* 3: 75–91.

———. 1964. "Commercial and Family Partnerships in the Countries of Medieval Islam." *Islamic Studies* 3 (3): 315–37.

Goldberg, V. P. 1985. "Price Adjustment in Long-Term Contracts." *Wisconsin Law Review* 483 (1985): 527–43.

Goodhart, C. 2004. *Financial Development and Economic Growth: Explaining the Links*. New York: Palgrave Macmillan and British Association for the Advancement of Science Books.

Guiso, L., P. Sapienza, and L. Zingales. 2004. "The Role of Social Capital in Financial Development." *American Economic Review* 94 (3).

Habachy, S. 1962. "Property, Right, and Contract in Muslim Law." *Columbia Law Review* 62 (3): 450–73.

Halaissos, M., and C. Bertaut. 1995. "Why Do So Few Hold Stocks?" *The Economic Journal* 105 (432): 1110–29.

Hassan, M. K., and M. K. Lewis, eds. 2007. *Handbook of Islamic Banking*. Cheltenham, U.K.: Edward Elgar.

Heiner, R. A. 1983. "The Origin of Predictable Behavior." *American Economic Review* 73: 560–95.

Henisz, W. J. 2000. "The Institutional Environment for Economic Growth." *Economics and Politics* 12: 1–31.

Henry, J. E. 1997. "Property Rights: Markets and Economic Theory." *Review of Political Economy* 11 (2).

Henry, P. B. 2000. "Stock Market Liberalization, Economic Reform, and Emerging Market Equity Prices." *Journal of Finance* 55 (2): 529–64.

Hoff, K., and J. Stiglitz, 2001. "Modern Economic Theory and Development." In *Frontiers of Development Economics: The Future in Perspective*, edited by Gerald M. Meier and J. Stiglitz, 389–459. Washington, DC: World Bank and Oxford University Press.

Hong, H., J. D. Kubik, and J. C. Stein. 2004. "Social Interaction and Stock-Market Participation." *Journal of Finance* 54 (1): 137–63.

Honohan, P. 2004. "Financial Sector Policy and the Poor: Selected Findings and Issues." World Bank Working Paper 43, World Bank, Washington, DC.

Huberman, G., and S. Kandel. 1987. "Mean-Variance Spanning." *Journal of Finance* 42 (4): 873–88.

Huberman, G., S. Kandel, and R. F. Strambaugh. 1987. "Mimicking Portfolios and Exact Arbitrage Pricing." *Journal of Finance* 42 (1): 1–9.

Ibn Mandhoor. 1984. *Lisaan al-'Arab*. Qom, Iran: Nashr Adab.

Ibn Umar, Y. 1975. *Ahkam al-Suq. Al-Sharikah al-Tunisiyyah li al-Tawzi*. Tunisia.

Imamuddin, S. M. 1960. "Bayt Al-Mal and Banks in the Medieval Muslim World." *Islamic Culture*, January.

Iqbal, Z., A. Mirakhor, H. Askari, and N. Krichene. 2012. *Risk Sharing in Finance*. Singapore: John Wiley and Sons (Asia).

Ju, J., and S-J. Wei. 2006. "A Solution to Two Paradoxes of International Capital Flows." IMF Occasional Paper 178, International Monetary Fund, Washington, DC.

Kamali, M. H. 2002a. *Islamic Commercial Law*. Kuala Lumpur: Islamiah Publishers.

———. 2002b. *The Dignity of Man: An Islamic Perspective*. Kuala Lumpur: Ilmiyah Publishers.

Kenny, R. W., and B. Klein. 1983. "The Economics of Block Booking." *Journal of Law and Economics* 20 (October): 497–540.

Khadduri, M. 1977. "Property: Its Relation to Equality and Freedom in Accordance with Islamic Law." In *Equality and Freedom: Past, Present, and Future*, edited by C. Wellman. Wiesbaden, Germany: Franz Steiner, Verlag GmBH.

King, R. G., and L. Ross. 1993. "Finance and Growth: Schumpeter Might Be Right." *Quarterly Journal of Economics* 108 (3): 717–38.

Kister, M. J. 1965. "The Market of the Prophet." *Journal of the Economic and Social History of the Orient* (January).

Klir, G. J. 2006. *Uncertainty and Information*. Hoboken, NJ: John Wiley and Sons.

Knack, S., and P. Keefer. 1997. "Does Social Capital Have an Economic Payoff: A Cross-Country Investigation." *The Quarterly Journal of Economics* 112 (4): 1251–88.

Kose, A., E. Prasad, and M. Terrones. 2007. "How Does Financial Globalization Affect Risk Sharing? Patterns and Channels?" IMF Working Paper WP/07/238, International Monetary Fund, Washington, DC.

Lane, E. W. 2003. *An Arabic-English Lexicon*. Lahore, Pakistan: Suhail Academy.

Levine, D. P. 1997. "Knowing and Acting: On Uncertainty in Economics." *Review of Political Economy* 9 (1): 5–7.

Levine, R., and S. Zervos. 1998. "Stock Market, Banks and Economic Growth." *American Economic Review* 88: 537–58.

Lewis, K. K. 1996. "Consumption, Stock Returns, and the Gains from International Risk-Sharing." NBER Working Paper 5410, National Bureau of Economic Research, Cambridge, MA.

Lieber, A. E. 1968. "Eastern Business Practice and Medieval European Commerce." *Economic History Review*, 2nd Series 21: 230–43.

Lorenz, E. 1999. "Trust, Contract and Economic Cooperation." *Cambridge Journal of Economics* 23: 301–51.

Magill, M., and M. Quinzii. 1988. "Incentive and Risk Sharing in a Stock Market Economy." Working Paper, University of Southern California.

Mazzoli, M. 1998. *Credit, Investment and the Macroeconomy*. New York: Cambridge University Press.

McMillan, J. 2002. *Reinventing the Bazaar: A Natural History of Markets*. London: W. W. Norton.

Mirakhor, A. 2003. "Muslim Contribution to Economics." Paper presented at the Annual Meeting of the South-Western Economic Association, March. *Essays on Iqtisad*, edited by B. Al-Haasani and A. Mirkakhor, Reprint, New York: Global Scholarly Publications.

———. 2010. "Whither Islamic Finance?" Presented at the Securities Commission of Malaysia, March.

Mirakhor, A., and Z. Iqbal. 1988. "Stabilization and Growth in an Open Islamic Economy." IMF Working Paper 22, International Monetary Fund, Washington, DC.

Musa, M. Y. 1955. "The Liberty of the Individual in Contracts and Conditions According to Islamic Law." *Islamic Quarterly* 2: 79–85.

Power, D., and G. Epstein. 2003. "Rentier Income and Financial Crises." Working Paper 57, Political Economy Research Institute, University of Massachusetts, Amherst, MA.

Rayner, S. E. 1991. *The Theory of Contracts in Islamic Law*. London: Graham and Trotman.

Saltuk, O. 2002. "Risk Sharing, Risk Shifting and Optimality of Convertible Debt in Venture Capital." Department of Economics, Southern Methodist University, Texas.

Shiller, R. J. 1993. *Macro Markets*. Oxford, U.K.: Clarendon Press.

———. 2003. *The New Financial Order: Risk in the 21st Century*. Princeton, NJ: Princeton University Press.

Shleifer, A., and D. Wolfenson. 2002. "Investor Protection and Equity Markets." *Journal of Financial Economics* 66: 3–27.

Siddiqi, M. N. 1985. *Partnership and Profit-Sharing in Islamic Law*. Leicester, U.K.: The Islamic Foundation.

———. 2001. *Economics, An Islamic Approach*. Islamabad: Institute of Policy Studies; Leicester, U.K.: The Islamic Foundation.

———. 2006 "Shariah, Economics and the Progress of Islamic Finance: The Role of Shariah Experts." Seventh Harvard Forum on Islamic Finance, Cambridge, MA, April 21.

Smith, S. C. 1988. "On the Incidence of Profit and Equity Sharing." *Journal of Economic Behavior and Organisation* 9: 45–58.

Smithson, M. 1989. *Ignorance and Uncertainty: Emerging Paradigms*. New York: Springer-Verlag.

Stiglitz, J. E., and A. Weiss. 1981. "Credit Rationing in Markets with Imperfect Information." *American Economic Review* 71 (3): 333–421.

Stultz, R. 1999a. "International Portfolio Flows and Security Markets." In *International Capital Flows*, edited by M. Feldstein. Chicago, IL: Chicago University Press.

———. 1999b. "Globalization, Corporate Finance, and the Cost of Capital." *Journal of Applied Corporate Finance* 12 (3): 8–25.

Tesar, L. L. 1995. "Evaluating the Gains from International Risk-Sharing." *Carnegie-Rochester Conference Series on Public Policy* 42 (June): 95–143.

Tobin, J. 1984. "On the Efficiency of the Financial System." *Lloyds Bank Review* 153: 14–15.

Udovitch, A. L. 1962. "At the Origins of the Western Commenda: Islam, Israel, Byzantium?" *Speculum* 37 (2): 198–207.

Uslaner, E. M. 2008. "The Moral Foundations of Trust." University of Maryland, College Park, MD.

van Wincoop, E. 1994. "Welfare Gains from International Risk Sharing." *Journal of Monetary Economics* 34 (October): 175–200.

———. 1999. "How Big Are Potential Welfare Gains from International Risk Sharing?" *Journal of International Economics* 47 (1): 109–235.

Weiss, W. M. 1989. *The Bazaar: Markets and Merchants of the Islamic World*. London: Thames and Hudson.

Zak, P., and S. Knack. 2001. "Trust and Growth." *The Economic Journal* 111 (April): 295–321.

Zarqa, M. A. 1984. "Islamic Distributive System." *Journal of Research in Islamic Economics* 2 (1).

———. 1991. "Rules of Exchange in Islamic Fiqh: An Introduction for Economics." *Journal of Research in Islamic Economics* 3: 35–70.

CHAPTER 2

Islamic Finance Revisited: Conceptual and Analytical Issues from the Perspective of Conventional Economics

Andrew Sheng and Ajit Singh

Introduction

Islamic finance has come of age. Islamic banking and finance have been growing at a very fast rate, despite apparent serious setbacks (such as interruption of payments in Abu Dhabi in 2009, the Great Recession in Western countries between 2008 and 2010, and the recent turmoil in Middle Eastern countries). The industry, which was valued at a mere $150 million in the 1990s, has increased to nearly $1 trillion. Although it is still a niche market and its share in world finance is quite small, it is nevertheless poised for further rapid expansion as economic development proceeds, particularly in the Muslim world. The current composition of Islamic finance consists of roughly $800 billion in Islamic banking funds; $100 billion in the *sukuk* (Islamic bonds), and another $100 billion in *Takaful* (Islamic insurance), Sheng (2011) estimates. According to data recently released by Standard & Poor's, in the first quarter of 2011, $32.4 billion of *sukuk*, were issued, compared with $51.2 billion raised in all of 2010. The engine of the global market up to now has been Malaysia, which accounted for 58 percent of funds raised in the first quarter.

However, the situation may be changing, with the big Western banks such as Goldman Sachs and HSBC deciding to enter the Islamic bond market. This is partly due to the current financial difficulties of the Euro Area banks and conventional debt markets. HSBC's Middle East unit became the first Western bank

---

Andrew Sheng is President, Fung Global Institute, Hong Kong, and the Third Holder of the Tun Ismail Ali Chair, University of Malaya, Malaysia. Ajit Singh is Emeritus Professor of Economics, University of Cambridge; Life Fellow, Queens' College, Cambridge, the United Kingdom; and the Fifth Holder of the Tun Ismail Ali Chair, University of Malaya, Malaysia. In 2012, he was appointed to the Dr. Manmohan Singh Chair at Punjab University, Chandigarh, a newly created professorship to honor the Indian Prime Minister.

to issue a *sukuk* in May 2012; it was worth $500 million and carried a maturity of five years. The French Bank Credit Agricole has said it is considering issuing an Islamic bond or creating a wider *sukuk* program that could lead to several issues. However, the big recent event in the Islamic bond market has been the controversial decision of Goldman Sachs to raise $2 billion from this market. The controversy is due to the fact that several Shari'ah law scholars have argued that the Goldman Sachs' *sukuk* does not meet requirements of Shari'ah law. However, the merchant bank denies the charge of noncompliance and appears to be sticking to its decision to go ahead with the *sukuk* (Reuters 2012).

The rapid growth of Islamic finance, however, has not been a spontaneous event but one carefully prepared and helped by Islamic governments and their central banks. The Central Bank of Malaysia (Bank Negara Malaysia) has been in the forefront of these efforts, and has assisted the growth of Islamic finance by establishing an institutional framework for a clear understanding and propagation of the laws of Islamic finance (see Mirakhor 2010). This is no mean achievement, as Islamic scholars disagree on many crucial aspects of Shari'ah laws. The Malaysian government's chief objective has been to help establish regulatory and monitoring institutions that will provide an internationally accepted and unambiguous conception of laws relating to Islamic banking and financial organizations. The International Monetary Fund (IMF) has also been helpful in these and other respects, together with a number of other Islamic governments (including those of Bahrain, Pakistan, and Sudan). Apart from the IMF, a number of non-Islamic financial centers have also recently taken steps to encourage Islamic banking and finance. Tax laws have been revised to facilitate Shari'ah-compliant financial instruments, such as the long-term *sukuk* bonds mentioned above. A notable recent entrant in this field has been the non-Islamic center of Singapore, which has started doing business in Islamic finance. A number of non-Islamic countries in Europe, including the United Kingdom, have also taken legal action to facilitate Islamic banking, as these countries want a slice of this fast-growing market. By contrast, there are other jurisdictions where many people would like to ban Shari'ah law. A recent example is Oklahoma. But the U.S. courts have ruled out anti-Shari'ah law legislation on constitutional grounds.

The reasons for expecting rapid expansion of Islamic finance lie not only in the increasing incomes of Islamic populations, but also in the fact that the basic infrastructure for Islamic finance has now been laid with the establishment of the Accounting and Auditing Organisation for Islamic Financial Institutions (AAOIFI) and the Islamic accounting standards authority, the Islamic Financial Services Board (IFSB), the international Islamic financial regulatory standard-setting organization. The Institute for Education in Islamic Finance (ISRA) also provides an invaluable website that is increasingly the transparent source for Shari'ah interpretations on what is considered acceptable under Islamic law (Sheng 2011).

The *Islamic Finance Global Stability Report*, which was jointly produced by a number of organizations in 2010, presents a comprehensive overview of the global financial architecture—and the cooperation and collaboration mechanisms among IFSB members—needed to promote a competitive, resilient, and stable

Islamic finance industry (IFSB, IDB, and ITRI 2010). The Islamic Financial Stability Forum that has resulted from this report, and the International Islamic Liquidity Management (IILM), provide Islamic finance with a wider range of tools and instruments, as well as a road map leading toward a vision of an integrated and sound global Islamic financial industry (Ahmed and Kohli 2011, xxvii).

Against this empirical background, this study now turns to its main purpose, which is theoretical and conceptual. It seeks to relate the concepts of Islamic finance to those of conventional finance and to examine certain important economic questions that arise from the interactions between the two kinds of theories. The study is written self-consciously from the perspective of conventional (or modern) economics.[1] It identifies similarities and dissimilarities between these two systems of thought and speculates on the extent to which the differences can be resolved. The central conclusion of the study is an optimistic one: namely, that each of the two paradigms of thought has its own strengths and weaknesses, but can nevertheless coexist with the other without any serious difficulties.

World Bank economists Thorsten Beck, Asli Demirgüç-Kunt, and Ouarda Merrouche (2010) have recently observed that while there is a large literature for practitioners on Islamic finance in general, and specifically Islamic banking, there are few academic papers. This study is intended to help fill that gap.

The Central Tenet of Islamic Finance: Absolute Prohibition against Interest Rates

In the 1970s when the subject of Islamic finance was first raised in a serious way, its central tenet of the absolute prohibition of interest payments on debt was severely criticized by mainstream economists. It was alleged that such a prohibition was incompatible with modern economic analysis and would result in a gross misallocation of resources. It was dubbed as a zero interest system in which there was no return to capital. Professor Abbas Mirakhor (2009) reports that the BBC and the *Wall Street Journal* regarded the system as being totally nonviable and derived from "voodoo" economics.

Apart from these popular criticisms of Islamic injunctions against any interest payments, there were also serious academic objections. Professor Mirakhor (2010) summarizes the main points of these criticisms:

- Zero interest meant infinite demand for loanable funds and zero supply.
- Such a system would be incapable of equilibrating demand for and supply of loanable funds.
- With a zero interest rate, there would be no savings.
- This meant no investment and no growth.
- In this system, there could be no monetary policy, since no instruments of liquidity management could exist without a fixed predetermined rate of interest.
- This all meant that in countries adopting such a system, there would be one-way capital flight.

It should be noted that, ironically, all the above criticisms would also today apply to countries that practice zero interest rate policies under quantitative easing.

Cost-Benefit Analysis, Time Preference, and Shari'ah Law

In contrast with Islamic economic analysis, conventional economists widely use the notion of interest rates in their work. In terms of their paradigm, they have legitimate use of zero interest rates, negative interest rates, and positive interest rates in examining real world economies. To illustrate with a difficult case, one commonly used concept in both theoretical and applied conventional economics is that of the cost-benefit analysis of a project, or of a development policy, or the choice of a particular technique of production. To take a simple specific example of a project to build a bridge across a river, the cost-benefit analysis would involve estimating the time series of respective costs and benefits that would accrue during the time span of the project. The costs and benefits would normally differ not only in their magnitudes but more importantly in their respective time profiles. In order to assess whether the proposed project is viable, one needs to systematically compare the two time series. This is done in cost-benefit analysis by taking the net present value of each of the series—the latter being determined by deflation by a common rate of discount. This rate of discount, which is normally taken to be the market interest rate, is supposed to reflect society's preference between consumption or utility today and consumption or utility tomorrow. If the two are equally valued, this may be regarded as the case of Islamic finance, with a zero discount or interest rate.

Interestingly, in conventional economics in the classic work of Arthur Pigou (1920) and F. P. Ramsey (1928) on this subject, it is also strongly argued that this time preference should be zero, the purpose in this case being the achievement of intergenerational fairness. A positive discount rate or interest rate would greatly favor the current generation at the expense of future generations. Pigou considered it as ethically wrong to discount future consumption or utility just because it takes place in the future. He argued that discounting was basically due to myopic behavior. Pigou and Ramsey took the view that a zero rate of discount would promote equity by preventing the current generation from acting selfishly. They regarded a non-zero rate of discount as necessarily implying an unfair advantage for the current generation.

Thus Pigou and Ramsey's ethical judgments coincided with those of Islamic finance on this particular issue. However, there is a more significant argument in favor of a non-zero discount rate or a positive time preference, which is based on the fact that the society tomorrow is likely to be richer than it is today because of economic growth. In these circumstances, a social rate of time preference has a sound ethical justification. Summarizing a huge literature on optimal growth theory, Marini and Scaramozzino (2000, 644) rightly note, "Under endogenous productivity growth, the optimal social discount rate must be equal to the marginal social product of capital … Positive social time preference, far from discriminating against future generations, is essential for an equitable intertemporal allocation of resources."

It is a moot point whether a non-zero discount rate in cost-benefit analysis accords with Shari'ah law. Nevertheless, it may be useful to observe that the non-zero discount rate arises here entirely from the fact of greater production in the subsequent time periods. Therefore, it is different from the case of money earning interest without any effort. Here the non-zero rate is associated with economic growth.

Interest Rates, Savings, and Financial Liberalization

Another, more straightforward example of the use of positive interest rates in conventional economics is provided by the work of R. I. McKinnon (1973) and E. S. Shaw (1973), which has played a major role in financial liberalization in developing countries since the 1970s. In this research, high interest rates are viewed extremely positively. As this work of the so-called Stanford School has had a wide impact, it will be useful to examine it a little more fully. Writing in the 1970s, McKinnon and Shaw attributed the poor performance of investment and growth in developing countries to "financial repression," as expressed in interest rate ceilings, high reserve ratios, and directed credit programs.

The Stanford economists, therefore, argued strongly in favor of financial "derepression." They suggested that the liberalization of the financial system would lead to higher interest rates and thereby to greater savings, to greater quantity as well as quality of investments, and to growth. This work is controversial, however, and its conclusions are contrary to much of mainstream economics as well as the foundations of Islamic finance.[2] The main testable hypotheses of the Stanford economists were (a) high interest rates would yield higher savings; (b) higher savings would lead to higher investment; and (c) high interest rates will also improve the productivity of investment and thereby lead to faster growth.

All these assertions are debatable, at a theoretical level as well as empirically. It is not the purpose here to provide a detailed analysis of these propositions. Suffice it to say, very briefly, that mainstream modern economists—the Keynesian economists, in particular—contest the McKinnon and Shaw hypotheses on the ground that their underlying model assumes that savings determine investment. Savings are, however, done by one kind of economic agents (individuals and households), and investments are carried out by other groups, such as firms and entrepreneurs. The different kinds of agents have different motivations, and there is no reason why savings should determine investment.[3] Critics also point out that McKinnon and Shaw assume there is always full employment of resources. Moreover, they suggest that whether or not higher interest rates in the formal sector following liberalization will increase aggregate savings depends on the savings behavior of the losers and gainers from this process. To the extent that the personal sector (individuals and households) finances the investments of the corporate sector—which are often highly geared in developing countries—higher interest rates may reduce corporate profits and retained earnings. The central point is that, although the rise in interest rates will increase personal income, if the savings propensity of the personal sector is lower than that of the corporate sector (which is likely), it will lead to a decline in total savings (Akyuz 1991).

More importantly, whether for the above reasons or others, empirical evidence from many countries that liberalized their credit markets in the 1980s and 1990s and increased real interest rates—particularly Asian countries—shows that there was no systematic rise in aggregate savings in these countries. This was also the conclusion reached by Cho and Khatkhate (1989) in their influential analysis of Asian countries. Akyuz (1991) reached the same conclusion with respect to aggregate savings in relation to Turkey's liberalization experiment during the late 1970s and in the 1980s.

As for the effects of credit market liberalization on the efficiency of the investment allocation process, leaving aside the disastrous consequences of such liberalization in the Southern Cone countries in the 1970s, many successful economies have used subsidies—indeed, negative interest rates—for long periods of time as an important part of their industrial policies during the course of economic development. This has certainly been true of Japan, which provided negative real interest rates to its favored corporations for much of the postwar period of its most rapid industrialization (1950–73) (see Amsden and Singh 1994; Singh 1995). Subsidies and directed credit were also central features of the Republic of Korea's highly successful industrial policy during the previous two decades, as Amsden (1990) notes.

To sum up, there is enough evidence to indicate that, contrary to the Stanford School, a high-interest rate policy based on financial derepression was apparently not regarded as being suitable by many developing countries. The most successful economies in East Asia did not follow such policies. Policymakers in developing countries ordinarily try to maintain low interest rates in order to encourage investment and growth. In that sense, there is unlikely to be much difference at a practical level in the performance of Islamic and non-Islamic countries in the real world.

However, at a conceptual level, the difference between the two paradigms is huge. Islamic scholars do not find any justification for positive interest rates. Nevertheless, the fundamental flaw in the mainstream strictures against the zero interest rate policy of Islamic finance was that it failed to take into account the fact that although the policy did not reward financial investment with interest payments, profits on capital and enterprise were fully allowed, and indeed encouraged. Finally, in addition to zero and positive interest rates, conventional economics also employs negative interest rates. These often arise from the government's industrial policy, where the government wishes to encourage certain industries and is therefore willing to "socialize" the risks involved for the individual firm; in other words, the government subsidizes the relevant activities of the firm.

Keynes and Zero Interest Rates

As discussed, the Stanford School expectation that high interest rates would generate high savings and investments is not only incompatible with empirical evidence but is also regarded as being theoretically erroneous by many modern economists. Most significantly in the context of this study, John Maynard Keynes, in his magnum opus, *The General Theory of Employment, Interest, and Money* (1936), provided a powerful defense of zero interest rates and condemned usury, historic or contemporary. Usury was strongly opposed both by Islam and the Christian Church in medieval Europe and elsewhere. Although Keynes did not set out to do so, his analysis, in our view, provides the best rationale for some of the basic principles of Islamic finance. In *The General Theory*, Keynes wrote:

> There remains an allied, but distinct, matter where for centuries, indeed for several millennia, enlightened opinion held for certain and obvious a doctrine which the classical school has repudiated as childish, but which deserves rehabilitation and honour. I mean the doctrine that the rate of interest is not self-adjusting at a level best suited to the social advantage but constantly tends to rise too high, so that a wise Government is concerned to curb it by statute and custom and even by invoking the sanctions of the moral law. (351)

Keynes went on to observe:

> Provisions against usury are amongst the most ancient economic practices of which we have record. The destruction of the inducement to invest by an excessive liquidity-preference was the outstanding evil, the prime impediment to the growth of wealth, in the ancient and medieval worlds. And naturally so, since certain of the risks and hazards of economic life diminish the marginal efficiency of capital while others serve to increase the preference for liquidity. In a world, therefore, which no one reckoned to be safe, it was almost inevitable that the rate of interest, unless it was curbed by every instrument at the disposal of society, would rise too high to permit of an adequate inducement to invest. (351)

Thus, Keynes made common cause with Christian scholars and the medieval church in denouncing usury, and raised issues with those modern economists (the neo-classicals) who believed that free markets would automatically generate interest rates that would ensure full employment. In the context of the economic problems of his day, Keynes thought that it was evident that the market magic was not working. A nonmarket but low or zero interest rate was therefore the right policy stance.

Keynes believed that only a very low or zero interest rate could ensure continuous full employment in a modern economy. From a Keynesian perspective, there are two essential issues concerning the determination of interest rates and employment. The first is the question of the level of interest rates. The second is the issue of marginal efficiency of capital. It is important to note in the context of this study that Islamic finance addresses both these concerns. By religious injunction, interest rates are kept at zero. At the same time, Islamic laws encourage circulation of money, rather than keeping it locked up and unused. Islamic finance, indeed, encourages the union of capital and enterprise in order to meet society's needs.

Keynes also opposed high interest rates on the grounds of equity. He wrote:

> The justification for a moderately high rate of interest has been found hitherto in the necessity of providing a sufficient inducement to save. But we have shown that the extent of effective saving is necessarily determined by the scale of investment and that the scale of investment is promoted by a *low* rate of interest,

provided that we do not attempt to stimulate it in this way beyond the point which corresponds to full employment. (375, emphasis in the original)

Keynes further noted:

Interest today rewards no genuine sacrifice any more than does the rent of land. The owner of capital can obtain interest because capital is scarce, just as the owner of land can obtain rent because land is scarce. But whilst there may be intrinsic reasons for the scarcity of land there are no intrinsic reasons for the scarcity of capital. (376)

Minsky [1975] (2008) provides a valuable analysis of Keynes' thinking on these matters concerning full employment and more equal distribution of income. It is worth quoting in full the relevant passages:

Keynes' vision that the euthanasia of the rentier, as a necessary outgrowth of the accumulation process, will radically decrease, if not eliminate, income from the ownership of scarce capital resources requires the prior achievement of a state of disciplined wants, a stable population, and a lifting of the burdens of war. None of these conditions have been fully satisfied—and of these conditions, it may well be that the disciplined-wants requirement is furthest from sight.

Keynes advanced two reasons why capital income should and would decrease as a proportion of total income. There was no need for high incomes to decrease the propensity to consume. In fact, a low propensity to consume is counterproductive, for it decreases the inducement to invest. Furthermore, in a short space of time, full investment could be achieved if full employment were maintained and if wants were disciplined. Once such full investment had been achieved then a new social order could emerge, for (as Keynes himself argued), "All kinds of social customs and economic practices, affecting the distribution of wealth and of economic rewards and penalties, which we now maintain at all costs, however distasteful and unjust they may be in themselves, because they are tremendously useful in promoting the accumulation of capital, we shall then be free, at last, to discard." (Minsky 2008, 155–56, citing Keynes [1931, 1963], 329)

In order to put Keynes's analysis of usury in perspective, it may be interesting to see how modern economic historians view this phenomenon. Rubin (2011) provides an alternative interpretation to the conventional ones regarding the incidence and magnitude of usury over the ages and spells out its implications for underdevelopment of the Muslim world compared to the Christian world. Rubin's basic argument is that the political authorities of the Muslim world required more help from the religious authorities in order to legitimize their regime. He puts this forward as a main explanation of why the Islamic usury laws were more stringent than those of Christianity in the Middle Ages, although before 1,000 A.D. it was the other way around. Only time and further research will tell whether Rubin's analysis is valid. We note, however, that Rubin regards any freedom to practice usury as a positive aspect, without considering the negative aspects that Keynes outlined above. He does not call attention either to the question of marginal efficiency of investment or the relationship between the latter and interest rates. This brief historical perspective on Islamic finance raises important further questions, which will be discussed in the final session.

Economic System and Usury: A Summing-Up

Building on the historical perspective on usury, this study takes up further analytical issues concerning the role of interest rates and their abolition in diverse economic systems. An economic system where capital is rewarded according to its earning capacity could be entirely adequate for achieving sufficient savings and investments for economic growth, and for allocating them efficiently. The main proposition of Islamic finance is that the return to capital is determined after the investment (ex post) and would be based solely on the return to economic activity in which the capital was employed. Savings and investment would be determined by this ex post rate of return on capital. Indeed, subsequent research showed that the Islamic system can be based entirely on equity capital, without debt, and is therefore often more stable than the conventional system based on debt. This question will be discussed further in the fourth section, where the Modigliani and Miller (MM) theorems and their implications for optimal financial structure for firms will be analyzed. This discussion raises an important question for conventional economists: whether an economic system requires an ex ante interest rate to function efficiently. Here, Professor Mirakhor (2011) has reminded us that the Arrow-Debreu-Hahn system of general equilibrium, together with its welfare properties, does not have an ex ante interest rate in the analysis (see Arrow and Hahn 1971; and chapter 1, this volume). This system is totally viable and is indeed the crowning glory of modern economics. Adding an extra variable such as the interest rate would overdetermine the system and would be difficult to interpret.

It is also interesting to note that because there is competition between conventional investors and investors in Islamic banks, there is not likely to be much difference in the rates of return earned by the two groups: interest, in the case of conventional banks; and share of profits, in the case of retail Islamic profit-loss sharing (PLS) accounts. This hypothesis is confirmed by a recent IMF study that compares the rate of return from the two kinds of banking institutions in Malaysia and Turkey from January 1997 to August 2010 (Çevik and Charap 2011).

The data reveal, as expected, a high degree of correlation between conventional deposit rates and the rate of return on retail PLS accounts in Malaysia and Turkey. A correlation of one-year term conventional bank deposit rates and the rate of return for PLS accounts was 91 percent for Malaysia and 92 percent for Turkey for the study period. Further econometric analysis by these authors provides strong evidence of cointegration between conventional bank deposit rates and PLS returns over the long term. The authors then use Granger causality analysis and error correction methodology to explore the direction of causation between conventional deposit rates and the rate of return on PLS accounts, both with respect to the levels of the variables and first differences.[4]

An important result of the authors' analysis using this methodology indicates that the null hypothesis (that changes in PLS returns do not "Granger-cause" changes in conventional deposit rates) cannot be rejected for either Malaysia or Turkey. But the null hypothesis (that changes in conventional deposit rates do not Granger-cause changes in PLS returns) can be rejected (Çevik and Cherap 2011).

In broad terms, an Islamic banking system is essentially an equity-based system in which depositors are treated as if they are shareholders of the bank. There is thus no fixed payment to the depositors for their money, but they are entitled to a share of the profits of the bank. In this equity-based system, corporate governance is rather different than in the conventional system. It will be argued below that this leads to problems of moral hazard for the Islamic bank. It will be suggested further that the redistributive stance of Islamic laws leads to the problems of moral hazard for the depositor. This requires either strong ethics or very strong regulation, or both, for the resolution of these difficulties. In view of their significance for the theory and empirics of Islamic finance, these points will be examined more fully in the next section.

Ethical Foundations of Islamic Finance

The rejection of interest payments is an essential element of Islamic finance. These and other ethical principles contained in Islamic commercial jurisprudence are derived from the Qu'ran, *Sunnah* (sayings of the Prophet), and legal reasoning by Shari'ah scholars, and in their entirety constitute the basis for Islamic finance (Ahmed and Kohli 2011, 1). Ethical principles guiding Islamic finance emphasize the avoidance of *Gharar* in the sense of deliberate ambiguity. Principles of Islamic finance are implemented through contracts. Shari'ah law covers conditions of contracts and rights and freedoms of the contracting parties, among other matters.

Importantly, there is a strong redistributive element in Islamic finance. As Professor Mirakhor (2011) notes, in the conventional system:

> [The] rich help the poor as a demonstration of sympathy, beneficence, benevolence and charity. In Islam, the more able are required to share the consequences of the materialization of idiosyncratic risks—illness, bankruptcy, disability, accidents and socioeconomically disadvantaged—for those who are unable to provide for themselves. The economically well- off are commanded to share risks of those who are economically unable to use the instruments of Islamic finance. In Islamic finance, the risks that would face the future generations are shared by the present generation through the rules of inheritance. These rules break up the accumulated wealth as it passes from one generation to another to enable sharing risks of a larger number of people. (15)

To illustrate with a simple example from an element of the Islamic banking code, consider the case of a mortgagee with an Islamic bank. In Islamic finance, the normal mortgage contract carries an implicit and explicit assurance that if the mortgagee is unable to pay his mortgage, the contract will entitle him for help from the bank. Some economists argue that this will create a moral hazard for the mortgagee. However, opinions differ. Other scholars suggest that if the mortgagee does not obey the Islamic ethical code outlined above, he or she will be subject to severe sanctions from members of the community. Similarly, Khan and Mirakhor (1994) argue that the banks have direct and indirect control over the agent-entrepreneurs through both explicit and implicit contracts. This is the case because banks could refuse further credit or blacklist the agent-entrepreneur and put at stake his/her credibility and respectability. This brings in a strong deterrent to irresponsible behavior. However, V. Sundararajan observes that this argument does not change the fact that the bank has no legal means to intervene in the management of the current enterprise while it is done by the agent entrepreneur (see Ahmed and Kohli 2011, 56).

To the mainstream economist, it seems very unlikely that adherents of Islamic finance will be able to live up to such high moral standards. Conventional economics invariably assumes that human beings are selfish and analyzes their activities on the basis of that postulate. If the same assumption of selfishness is made in relation to the participants in Islamic finance, it will lead to a huge moral hazard problem on the side of the debtor.

There is also the possibility of moral hazard on the side of the bank. This arises from the unrestricted *mudarabah* contract, where the bank manages the deposits at its own discretion.[5] This increases the moral hazard for a bank, as it may indulge in more risk taking, without adequate capital. As Sundararajan notes, investment depositors in Islamic banks do not enjoy the same rights as equity investors in conventional investment companies but do share the same risks (see Ahmed and Kohli 2011).

For these reasons, Islamic finance poses considerable pressure on the Islamic finance management to manage their investment risks to avoid moral hazard. It also poses considerable pressure on financial regulators to monitor investment and agency (bank intermediary) behavior to avoid passing all risks ultimately to the depositor. A third unknown factor is the certainty of the Shari'ah bankruptcy courts to enforce disputes over contracts that show clear signs of moral hazard (or shirking by borrower/investee to avoid his repayments).

The most recent empirical research by World Bank economists Beck, Demirgüç-Kunt, and Merrouche (2010), referred to earlier, suggests that conventional and Islamic banking are more alike than previously thought. As they argue:

> Differences in business models—if they exist at all—do not show in standard indicators based on financial statements information. Other differences, such as cost efficiency, seem to be driven more by country differences than by bank type differences. Finally, the good performance of Islamic banks during the recent crisis appears to be driven by higher precaution in liquidity holdings and capitalization, but no inherent difference in asset quality between the two bank types .... (3)

Although based on rather different data and a different definition of the analytical problem, the World Bank economists' conclusions from their empirical study support the findings of the IMF economists, Çevik and Cherap (2011), as discussed in the previous section.

Although as noted in the first section, Islamic finance has expanded very fast, it still has a small share of world finance and is still in a niche market (Tan 2009). Some respected commentators argue that the market has concentrated on the development of safe, short-term financial instruments and ignored the long-term market. These scholars fear that because of path-dependency, which is characteristic of many economic events, the Islamic finance industry may simply continue to operate on the short end of the market. Indeed, these well-wishers of Islamic finance would like to take a major step forward and develop an Islamic stock market to meet the needs of the Islamic investors for investments with long-term horizons. This important question will be examined in detail in the fifth section.

Modigliani and Miller Theorems

Having examined the two basic tenets of Islamic finance, the discussion now moves on to consider a fundamental tenet of modern economics: the MM theorems concerning the optimal financial structure of firms. The discussion also analyzes the feasibility and desirability of establishing stock markets based on Islamic rules to assist the growth of Islamic finance.

Since the late 1950s and until recently, the modern neoclassical view of finance has been dominated by the so-called "irrelevance theorems" associated with Modigliani and Miller (1958, 1963). In seminal contributions, starting with their pioneering 1958 paper, Modigliani and Miller put forward two central propositions about the theory of finance. They showed that in fully developed capital markets, under fully idealized neoclassical assumptions of perfect competition, no transaction costs, no taxation, and no bankruptcy, even in a world of uncertainty, the stock market valuation of the firm is independent of its financing or dividend payout decisions. On the basis of certain further restrictive assumptions about expectations and the nature of uncertainty (such as uniformity in expectations held by all investors concerning the stock market), they established that the market would value the firm's shares entirely on the basis of its earnings prospects; share prices would be invariant to the capital structure of the firm or to the extent to which it resorts to internal or external sources to finance its investment plans.

Miller (1991, 269) provides an intuitive explanation for the MM theorems with the help of an analogy. "Think of the firm as a gigantic tub of whole milk. The farmer can sell the whole milk as it is. Or he can separate out the cream, and sell it at a considerably higher price than the whole milk would bring. The Modigliani-Miller proposition says that if there were no costs of separation, (and, of course, no government dairy support program), the cream plus the skim milk would bring the same price as the whole milk." Villamil (1992) elaborates on this explanation in the following terms:

> The essence of the argument is that increasing the amount of debt (cream) lowers the value of outstanding equity (skim milk)—selling of safe cash flows to debt-holders leaves the firm with more lower valued equity, keeping the total value

on the firm unchanged. Put differently, any gain from using more of what might seem to be cheaper debt is offset by the higher cost of now riskier equity. Hence, given a fixed amount of total capital, the allocation of capital between debt and equity is irrelevant because the weighted average of the two costs of capital to the firm is the same for all possible combinations of the two. (1)

At a deeper level, the MM theorems suggested a dichotomy between finance and the real economy: corporate growth and investment decisions were dictated completely by "real" variables such as productivity, demand for output, technical progress, and relative factor prices of capital and labor. Finance in this paradigm is always permissive and simply facilitates the investment process.

As in the case of neoclassical economics, the normal Keynesian perspective on the role of finance in investment and economic growth also assumes well-developed capital markets. However, this perspective does not postulate perfect capital markets in the sense that the relevant information on costs, reliability, and other aspects of the transaction is not available on equal terms to all the participants in the market. According to the Keynesian view, corporate investment is essentially determined by "animal spirits," by business people's confidence, by expected demand, and by the cost of capital. The latter variable in practice is regarded as being relatively insignificant compared with demand factors.

As they do not accept the assumption of perfect capital markets, Keynesian economists do not generally believe that the Modigliani and Miller propositions are operational in the real world. These neoclassical irrelevance theorems also run contrary to the traditional conception of a firm's investment and financing decisions. The traditional view was a so-called "pecking order" theory of finance (Donaldson 1961; Fazzari, Hubbard, and Peterson 1988; Myers 1984), which suggested that firms always preferred internal to external finance—and, if they had to use external finance, they would prefer to employ debt, and only as a last resort, equity finance. The firm's capital structure and its dividend payout decisions, in this analysis, were important variables that had an independent influence on its share price. More generally, the nonavailability of the appropriate kind of finance could constrain a firm's growth or investment plans: this suggestion was often incorporated in the postwar microeconomic investment models in the Keynesian spirit. Meyer and Kuh (1957) and Meyer and Glaüber (1964) are classic references. These issues have been carefully examined in Stiglitz (2005).

Paradoxically, the above traditional theory of finance has been resurrected and revalidated by a number of theoretical developments in the last two decades that attempt to relax some of the highly restrictive assumptions of the Modigliani and Miller propositions. With respect to the latter, it was noted at the simplest level that if taxation and the possibility of bankruptcy and financial distress are introduced into the analysis, this would produce an optimal capital structure for the firm and thus invalidate the Modigliani-Miller irrelevance theorems. Many corporate tax systems, for example, allow interest to be deducted as a cost, which provides a significant tax advantage to the use of debt finance. There is, however, a trade-off, since too high a level of debt increases the risks of bankruptcy or financial distress in an economic downturn. This simple trade-off model leads to an optimal debt-equity ratio for the firm, which maximizes its stock market valuation.

More complex considerations and theoretical developments involving asymmetric information between insiders (managers) and outsiders (creditors or shareholders), problems of adverse selection, moral hazard, agency costs, signaling, and transaction costs lead to different costs of the various forms of finance, but can be shown to be broadly compatible with the "pecking order"–type theory outlined above. (The classic reference here is Myers and Majluf 1984.) In general, this far richer and more complete analysis of the issues points to the significance of the corporate capital structures and the financial decisions for the real economy. At the very least, the new models of the firm suggest that "finance" is not simply a veil, but that there are very important interactions between corporate finance and the real economy. Thus, unlike the neoclassical investment models (see in particular the widely acknowledged and valued contributions by Jorgenson, Ho, and Stiroh [2005] that dominated the profession in the 1960s and 1970s), many economists subsequently in the light of the new interpretation of MM theorems, particularly the post-Keynesian ones, came to regard "cash flow" and corporate retained earnings as being a significant constraint on a firm's investment decisions.

However, the main concern in this study is not so much with corporate investment decisions, but with the question of the financial structures of Islamic and non-Islamic firms. Stiglitz (1988) establishes that under most conditions, if there is no bankruptcy, then the theorems would continue to hold. This suggests that under the neoclassical assumptions of MM theorems, any financial structure for Islamic firms is optimal, including that of all equity and no debt. However, if these strict assumptions are relaxed, particularly when there is a real possibility of bankruptcy, the firm valuation will depend on its debt-equity ratio. Thus, for any specific firm, there will be a corresponding optimal debt-equity ratio. There is no reason to believe that Islamic firms would attempt to achieve or would have achieved their respective optimum financial structures in terms of debt-equity ratios. Does this make Islamic firms less efficient? The answer is not necessarily so because the question of optimality in the above analysis is considered only from the perspective of an individual firm and not from that of society as a whole. Suppose all Islamic firms are 100 percent equity-financed. This may violate the results of the optimality tests of the MM theorems, but from the point of view of the society as a whole, such a capital structure may have considerable macroeconomic benefits, such as more stable GDP growth.

The fundamental point is that if all Islamic finance contracts are equity contracts, then it is vital for the banks to ensure that the investee/borrower is not too highly leveraged. The higher the leverage of the borrower, the higher the risks assumed by the Islamic finance investor. By definition, the lower the leverage of the borrower, the safer the financial system is on the whole.

Risk Sharing, Risk Shifting, and the Risks of Bankruptcy

From the perspective of conventional economics, there is another way of interpreting the differences between the Islamic and non-Islamic borrowing individuals and firms, as well as the lending banks. This involves the question of the relative costs and efficacy of bankruptcy in the two systems. So it is not just a matter of whether or not there is provision for bankruptcy or insolvency in a model of corporate finance, but what are its costs and who is expected to bear them, in law and in practice.

In terms of conventional finance, the real issues are those of information asymmetry, principal-agent (contract), and insolvency. Conventional finance assumes that one can shift the risks between two parties based upon contract. In Islamic finance, one starts with risk-sharing between the borrower and the bank. But in all contracts, there is an inherent information asymmetry when the borrower or investee does not know when they will enter economic insolvency (this being dependent on whether banks are willing to lend and the rate of interest). Most companies that are in trouble may still be solvent in terms of accounting, but economically insolvent, depending on the market-to-market price of assets, which also depends on the discount rate. In other words, the company may not know when it becomes insolvent (nor does the Islamic finance institution know). When the company becomes insolvent, the losses are automatically shared among its shareholders and holders of its obligations.

Hence, there is essentially no difference between the non-Islamic finance lender and the Islamic equity contract in these respects. Conventional lenders protect their own risks and shift these by contracting with the borrower, to include collateral and guarantees. If the real interest rate rises, however, the discounted cash flow value of the borrower's assets declines and the real value of liabilities increases, and the borrower may go into economic insolvency. At the same time, the collateral value of the lender's holdings of collateral also declines (especially if they are land or equity). Thus, at higher real rates of interest, especially during a crisis, the borrower moves into economic insolvency and therefore (nontransparently) transfers the insolvency risk to the lenders and holders of his or her paper. This risk-reversion is identical in form for Islamic finance or non-Islamic finance firms.

There is a further cost of bankruptcy (transactions cost in time, legal fees, and the like), which the borrower or investor may have to invest in so as to recoup his or her loan or investment. Thus, if both Islamic finance and non-Islamic finance contracts involve involuntary risk-sharing, then the only real distinguishing feature between the two systems is whether the bankruptcy laws are strong enough and efficient enough for enforcement.

In the Islamic finance contract, there is a moral or nontemporal sanction on the borrower, in the hopes that this "soft power" will be more effective than "hard power"—legal or other means of enforcement—to force the borrower to repay. The reason is that there is information asymmetry between the borrower's true solvency and the lender/investor. The borrower may engage in lying or hiding his or her true solvency in order to pass as much of the losses as possible to the lender and/or investor. It cannot be determined a priori whether the soft power of Islamic finance is necessarily better than the legal power of debt enforcement. This depends on the circumstances of the case, the legal powers in a country, the effectiveness of the courts, and the like.

To put it clearly, all debt or risk-sharing contracts suffer from moral hazard. If they are not enforced against cheating or free-riding, then risks will pass to the solvency holder/lender. In simple utility terms, when the marginal benefit to borrowers is higher than the cost of sanctions, then they will not pay. An important question is therefore whether sanctions are real enough for the borrowers to make the necessary adjustments so that if they cannot pay today, they shall at least pay tomorrow.

It is arguable that the costs of bankruptcy to the borrowers in terms of conventional finance are lower for the Islamic finance borrower than for the non-Islamic finance borrower. In the case of the latter, there are not only the laws relating to bankruptcy, but also daily court judgments implementing the law. This will tend to make the loan contract more transparent, and probably more painful in case of default. It is worth noting that the basic laws on bankruptcy differ greatly between advanced countries, notably the United States and the United Kingdom. In broad terms, the U.K. law is less user-friendly to the borrower than the U.S. law, which has Chapter 13 provisions allowing the firm to continue as a going concern for a longer period than would normally be permitted by English receivership arrangements. It may also be observed that because of the novelty of Islamic finance, there may be nonuniform implementation of the bankruptcy laws for Islamic firms. It is not clear how many cases of bankruptcy in Shari'ah law are ever settled by Shari'ah courts. It is also not clear whether the judgments of these courts are accepted more generally by the public and by non-Islamic courts.

The conclusion of this section is that whether Islamic or non-Islamic finance is more effective in avoiding moral hazard would depend on the entire financial infrastructure of risk management systems, regulatory systems, and court systems. If Islamic financial systems end up with lower debt/equity as a whole than non-Islamic systems, then the Islamic finance system is likely to be able to cushion shocks as a whole. However, this is a question of practice, not one of theory.

The Stock Market and Islamic Finance

Islamic economists greatly favor the establishment of a stock market based on Islamic principles in order to further the expansion of Islamic finance. Long ago, Professor Mokhtar Metwally (1984) observed:

In an Islamic economy where interest bearing loans are prohibited and where direct participation in business enterprise, with its attendant risks and profit sharing, is encouraged, the existence of a well-functioning Stock Exchange is very important. It would allow for the mobilization of savings for investment and provide means for liquidity to individual shareholders. However, existing Stock Exchanges in non-Islamic economies have many drawbacks. They generate practices such as speculation and fluctuations in share prices which are not related to the economic performance of enterprises. These practices are inconsistent with the teachings of Islam. (19)

Professor Abbas Mirakhor, a leading scholar of Islamic finance, has recently urged government intervention to develop stock markets in Islamic countries. In his view, the stock market is not only a principal means of risk sharing, but is probably the best available instrument. The establishment of stock markets on a sound basis can benefit international and national risk sharing and thereby make the whole system much more stable. The stock market would thus be a useful addition to complete the Islamic sequence of markets to enhance economic efficiency.

However, the merits and demerits of stock markets have long been the subject of acute controversy in mainstream economics, with John Maynard Keynes (1936) a leading critic of stock markets. This is a large controversial subject on which both authors of this study have written before (see Sheng 2009; Singh 1992, 1995, 1997, 2012). Nevertheless, in this context, we simply note that Islamic stock markets would be very helpful if they could be organized to obey the Islamic precepts. The main difficulty arises from the fact that since it is virtually impossible to distinguish between speculative and nonspeculative investment strategies, it would be difficult to establish a stock market in which Islamic ethics and nonspeculative strategies are followed by all players. In our next paper, we intend to explore how in the real world, the conventional and Islamic stock markets could deal with the fundamental problems of primary fund raising for corporations and the price discovery/valuation of secondary market listed stocks.

Interim Summary of the Main Findings and Two Further Questions

As this chapter has ranged over several fields of conventional and Islamic economics, it will be useful to summarize the main theoretical and empirical findings. The study first examined the central tenets of Islamic finance from the perspective of conventional economics. It started with the question of absolute prohibition under Islamic finance of interest payments in any form. The main conclusion is that it is possible to run an efficient economic system of the Islamic kind, which has no interest payments, but which allows profits on capital and enterprise. Such a system, based totally on equity finance, is completely viable and may, in fact, be more stable than a part-debt financed conventional system.

A salient finding of this study is that the best rationale for zero interest rates is provided by John Maynard Keynes in *The General Theory*. Keynes was not writing specifically about Islamic finance, but he endorsed the thinking of medieval Christian scholars and others who fundamentally objected to usury. Keynes sought to rehabilitate these scholars, whom the conventional economics of the nineteenth and twentieth century (for example, the Classical School) considered to be irrelevant and beyond the pale. He regarded high interest rates as the root cause of the problem of unemployment, and favored zero or low interest rates in order to achieve continuous full employment. He found no evidence, or any reasonable theory, that could show that the market system automatically generated interest rates that lead to full employment. He sought to lower interest rates, and to raise the marginal efficiency of investment (expected profitability) to achieve this important objective. Basic Keynesian doctrine fits in well with the Islamic emphasis on zero interest rates and the combination of capital and enterprise to produce social output.

However, it is generally recognized that conventional economics legitimately uses interest rates—zero, negative, and positive—for its analysis of various economic issues. There is little evidence, however, to support the McKinnon and Shaw hypotheses that financial liberalization necessarily leads to high interest rates, which in turn generate high savings, investment, and economic growth. The highly successful East Asian countries employed low, even negative, rates rather than high interest rates during their industrialization.

This study also considers from the perspective of Islamic finance the technique of cost-benefit analysis widely used in conventional economics. This involves the discussion of time preferences between generations and the rate of discount used in cost-benefit analysis: should it be zero or a positive number? There are reasonable arguments that suggest that both these discount rates may be compatible with Shari'ah law. It is up to Shari'ah scholars, however, to determine the merits of this argument.

As developing country policy makers are prone to use low but positive interest rates to encourage investment and growth, there is very little difference between conventional and Islamic (zero interest rate) paradigms in practical terms. The rates of return on deposits in conventional banks and those of profit-sharing accounts in Islamic finance tend to be highly correlated and broadly of similar magnitude.

An analysis of the second major tenet of Islamic finance—namely, its ethical system—indicates that if human beings strictly adhere to the requirements of Islamic ethics, there would be few moral hazard problems in Islamic banking. However, since total adherence to the Islamic ethical system is unlikely for most individuals and institutions, important moral hazard issues loom large, both on the side of the depositors in Islamic banks as well as on the side of the Islamic banks themselves. These would need to be resolved in the real world by extensive regulation. It is a moot point whether such far-reaching regulation of ethical behavior, particularly of individuals, is at all feasible or desirable.

Turning to the relevant chief tenets of conventional economics, we find that there is no straightforward application of MM theorems to Islamic firms and banks. This is because the assumptions underlying these theorems of no transactions costs, perfect markets, no taxation, and no bankruptcy have relevance to real world entities, whether Western or Islamic. If these assumptions are relaxed to conform more to the real world, then one would get an optimal capital structure: that is, some particular debt-equity ratio for a specific firm. However, this is looking at the question of optimality from the point of view of the firm rather than that of society as a whole. Further, it will be difficult to reach the judgment that Islamic firms have nonoptimal capital structures on the basis of MM theorems alone.

Although for MM theorems, the concept of bankruptcy is important, in the real world it is its costs and who pays these costs that are significant factors in distinguishing between the two systems. The real issues are information asymmetry, principal-agent problems, and insolvency costs—and whether or not the practical application of these concepts leads to a "hard" or "soft budget constraint" for the borrowing firms, which do not wish to pay and aim to shift the burden to the lender. In the Islamic finance contract, there is an additional implicit sanction against this type of moral hazard affecting the borrower, which may be called "soft power." In some instances, this may be more effective than the "hard power" of bankruptcy laws, but it is difficult to imagine that it will be so every time or in most cases.

This chapter also considers very briefly the desirability of establishing stock markets in Islamic finance systems, in order to further the completion of these systems and to help with their expansion. It concludes that a conventional stock market (that induces speculative behavior) would not be useful for Islamic economies because speculation is prohibited under Shari'ah law. Yet the search for an ethical stock market must continue.

In the light of the above findings on Islamic and non-Islamic finance, it would be useful to consider two further important and relevant issues at least briefly. The first is whether Islamic finance promotes economic development. The second is whether this type of finance poses a challenge to the current dominant theory and practice of finance.

Islamic Finance and Economic Development

Regarding the first question, this study has argued that Islamic finance, because of its rejection of interest rates and debt, is a force for stability in the national and international economy. However, this raises the question whether, apart from leading to stable economic development, this type of finance also promotes higher economic growth. This is where economic history becomes highly relevant. Important recent contributions by Kuran (2011) and Chaney (2011) bear on this issue. Kuran (2011) suggests that the reason for the success of Western Europe and the decline of Islam since the Middle Ages has been due to the Muslim world's inability to adopt institutions that facilitate the accumulation of capital and impersonal exchange. Capital accumulation was handicapped by the redistributive character of Islamic inheritance laws, for example. In contrast, Western Europe institutional development encouraged both impersonal markets and capital accumulation.

Although most economists would accept the basic idea that economic growth is facilitated by appropriate institutions and retarded by inappropriate ones, Kuran's analysis is not entirely helpful. In contrast to Kuran, Harvard economic historian Chaney (2011) argues that, in the final analysis, it was the long-standing political equilibrium in the Middle East rather than Islamic law that held back the region. He argues that "Islamic law as interpreted in each period by Muslim religious leaders may have been largely endogenous to the incentives and constraints this (the ruling) group faced. Had the Middle East's political equilibrium changed, the religious leaders' interpretation of Islamic law would have also changed. Alternatively, these leaders could have lost political power and Islamic law might have ceased to be enforced" (1469).

Turning from history to the current era, in many Muslim countries a fundamental change has occurred in the institutional arrangements that facilitate economic progress. Not only are banks, large and small, encouraged and other savings institutions allowed, but so are a number of new financial instruments that meet the requirements of Shari'ah law. Similarly, the traditional Islamic emphasis on profitability encourages investment that contributes to growth and full employment, as does its emphasis on redistribution of wealth. Interpersonal redistribution, rather than being a negative force for accumulation and economic development, becomes, in the current era, a positive force for maintaining aggregate demand for achieving full employment. It is therefore arguable that Islamic finance in general does not necessarily have negative consequences for economic growth, but rather quite the opposite.

The Real Challenge of Islamic Finance[6]

A second general question regarding Islamic finance relates to the issue of competition between Islamic and non-Islamic finance. Will fast-growing Islamic finance eventually seriously challenge the current Western approach of finance? As noted, from humble beginnings in the 1990s, Islamic finance has become a trillion-dollar activity. The global consensus is that Islamic finance has a bright future, owing to favorable demographics and rising incomes in Muslim communities.

The real challenge posed by Islamic finance for the Western world arises not so much from its prohibition on interest rates but rather from the second major tenet of Islamic finance, which holds that if people adhered strictly to its ethical requirements, there would be fewer moral hazard problems. Moral hazard exists, however, in all systems in which the state ultimately absorbs the risks of private citizens.

The extent to which any particular system is efficient in avoiding moral hazard is a matter of practice rather than of theory. Many would agree that, historically, Christian morality played an important role in the rise of Western capitalism. Secular capitalism, however, has recently experienced an erosion of values, whereby the financial sector has put its own interests above those of the rest of society. If the ethical values in Islamic finance—grounded in Shari'ah religious law—can further deter moral hazard and the abuse of fiduciary duties by financial institutions, Islamic finance could prove to be a serious alternative to current models of derivative finance.

Indeed, the basic tenets of Islamic finance force us to rethink the ethical basis of monetary arrangements under the current Western financial system, particularly financial and economic globalization in the context of an international reserve currency system founded on fiat money. In the past, gold was the anchor of monetary stability and financial discipline, though at times it was deflationary. The test of any alternative financial system depends ultimately on whether it is—or can be—more efficient, ethical, stable, and adaptable than the prevailing system. For now, there is no Islamic global reserve currency, no Islamic central bank, and hence no Islamic lender of last resort. But the Islamic world is the custodian of huge natural resources that back its trading and financial activities.

As the Islamic world grows in stature and influence, Islamic finance could become a formidable competitor to the current dominant financial system. The world would have much to gain if the two systems were to compete fairly and constructively to meet people's needs for different types of finance.

Conclusion

The Western system has been dominant until now, but of late it has shown itself to be less than perfect. In these circumstances, it would be eminently sensible if there were an alternative economic and financial system.

In the last two decades, because of the excesses of the IMF (Washington Consensus policies, structural adjustment policies in Africa, and the IMF's neoliberal agenda for much of the period), demand has been growing around the world for an alternative to the IMF, including the important function of lender of last resort.

In the context of the Asian crisis, for example, there were serious demands for regional financial systems that would better serve local needs for national and international finance to promote regional development. In Latin America, there was strong support for the establishment of a regional central bank.

Islamic finance has long represented a distinct approach to economic thinking and financial practice and provides a potentially complete system. One can envisage a future in which the two systems—the Western and the Islamic—each with its distinct characteristics, run in parallel, offering individuals and businesses open choices between the two.

Cooperation between these two systems is eminently desirable and feasible. The conventional and Islamic finance could cooperate and even compete to produce the best outcome for common projects, such as the provision of cheap banking for the world's poor or for investment in environmental undertakings. There is wide consensus that the world's poor should have wider access to finance. This may be more appropriate under the Islamic finance system because of its more ethical basis.

Notes

1. The words conventional and modern economics are used interchangeably throughout this chapter.
2. The second and fourth sections draw on and update the material in Singh and Hamid (1992) and Singh (1995). See also Singh (1997).
3. In advanced countries, despite the stock markets, most firms finance their investment from their retained earnings. There is relatively little resort to the stock markets. However, the corporate motivation for increasing or decreasing retained earnings, is not the same as that of individual households. In developing countries, the motivation for savings and investment are somewhat different. Strangely enough, despite the relatively low development of stock markets in developing countries, these countries rely more on the stock market than the advanced countries. This is known in technical literature as the Singh-paradox. See Singh (2003); Gugler, Mueller, and Yurtoglu (2003).
4. The question of causation is an extremely complex one in all social sciences. One cannot assume that if an event A takes place after another event B, that B cannot cause A. The economists have provided a definition of causality based on this idea. But it is accepted that not everybody will accept this idea of causation. In order to make clear the specific way in which the economists use the notion of causation, the term Granger-causality is used.
5. *Mudarabah* is a "partnership where one provides the capital and the other the entrepreneurial expertise with the profits being shared" (UBS web definition; see also Ahmed and Kohli 2011, 275).
6. This section is based on the authors' op-ed column published in April 2012 by Project Syndicate (Sheng and Singh 2012). See also Sheng (2010).

References

Ahmed, J., and H. S. Kohli, eds. 2011. *Islamic Finance: Writings of V. Sundararajan*. New Delhi: Sage Publications India Pvt. Ltd.

Akyuz, Y. 1991. "Financial Liberalisation in Developing Countries: A Neo-Keynesian Approach." UNCTAD Discussion Paper 36, United Nations Conference on Trade and Development (UNCTAD), Geneva.

Amsden, A. H. 1990. "Why Isn't the Whole World Experimenting with the East Asian Model to Develop? Review of the East Asian Miracle." *World Development* 22 (4): 627–33.

Amsden, A., and A. Singh. 1994. "The Optimal Degree of Competition and Dynamic Efficiency in Japan and Korea." *European Economic Review*, Elsevier 38 (3–4): 941–51.

Arrow, K. J., and F. Hahn. 1971. *General Competitive Analysis*. San Francisco, CA: Holden-Day.

Beck, T., A. Demirgüç-Kunt, and O. Merrouche. 2010. "Islamic vs. Conventional Banking: Business Model, Efficiency and Stability." Policy Research Paper 5446, World Bank, Washington, DC.

Çevik, S., and J. Charap. 2011. "The Behaviour of Conventional and Islamic Bank Deposit Returns in Malaysia and Turkey." IMF Working Paper WP/11/56, International Monetary Fund, Washington, DC.

Chaney, E. 2011. "Islamic Law, Institutions and Economic Development in the Middle East, Review Essay." *Development and Change* 42 (6): 1465–72.

Cho, Y.-J., and D. Khatkhate. 1989. "Lessons of Financial Liberalization in Asia: A Comparative Study." World Bank Discussion Paper 50, World Bank, Washington, DC.

Donaldson, G. 1961. *Corporate Debt Capacity*. Cambridge, MA: Harvard University Press.

Fazzari, S. M., R. G. Hubbard, and B. C. Peterson. 1988. "Financing Constraints and Corporate Investment." *Brookings Paper on Economic Activity* 1 (1): 141–206.

Gugler, K., D. Mueller, and B. Yurtoglu. 2003. "The Impact of Corporate Governance on Investment Returns in Developed and Developing Countries." *Economic Journal*, Royal Economic Society 113 (491): F511–39.

IFSB, IDB, and ITRI (Islamic Financial Services Board, Islamic Development Bank, and Islamic Training and Research Institute). 2010. *Islamic Finance Global Stability Report*. http://www.ifsb.org/docs/IFSB-IRTI-IDB2010.pdf.

Jorgenson, D., M. S. Ho, and K. J. Stiroh. 2005. "Growth of U.S Industries and Investments in Information Technology and Higher Education." In *Measuring Capital in the New Economy*, 403–78. Cambridge, MA: National Bureau of Economic Research.

Keynes, J. M. (1931) 1963. *Essays in Persuasion*. New York: W. W. Norton & Co. Citations are to the 1963 edition.

———. 1936. *The General Theory of Employment, Interest, and Money*. New York: Harcourt, Brace and Company.

Khan, S. M., and A. Mirakhor. 1994. "Monetary Management in an Islamic Economy." *Journal of King Abdulaziz University: Islamic Economics* 6: 3–21 (1414 A.H./1994 A.D.).

Kuran, T. 2011. *The Long Divergence: How Islamic Law Held Back the Middle East*. Princeton, NJ: Princeton University Press.

Marini, G., and P. Scaramozzino. 2000. "Social Time Preference." *Journal of Population Economics* 13 (4): 639–45.

McKinnon, R. I. 1973. *Money and Capital in Economic Development*. Washington, DC: Brookings Institution Press.

Metwally, M. M. 1984. "The Role of the Stock Exchange in an Islamic Economy." *Journal of Research in Islamic Economics* 2 (1): 19–28.

Meyer, J. R. and R. R. Glaüber. 1964. "Investment Decisions, Economic Forecasting and Public Policy." Research Division, Department of Business Administration, Harvard University, Cambridge, MA.

Meyer, J. R., and E. Kuh. 1957. *Investment Decision: An Empirical Study*. Cambridge, MA: Harvard University Press.

Miller, M. H. 1991. *Financial Innovations and Market Volatility*. Cambridge, MA: Blackwell Publishers.

Minsky, H. P. (1975) 2008. *John Maynard Keynes*. New York: Columbia University Press. Reprint, McGraw-Hill Professional. Citations refer to the McGraw-Hill edition.

Mirakhor, A. 2009. "Recent Crisis: Lessons for Islamic Finance." SC-UM Visiting Scholar Programme Public Lecture, Suruhanjaya Sekuriti, Malaysia, September 29.

———. 2010. "Hopes for the Future of Islamic Finance." Presentation to the Institute of Islamic Banking and Insurance, London.

———. 2011. "Keynote Address." Foundations of Islamic Finance Conference Series, Epistemological Foundation of Finance: Islamic and Conventional, March 8–10.

Modigliani, F., and M. Miller. 1958. "The Cost of Capital, Corporate Finance and the Theory of Investment." *American Economic Review* 48: 261–97.

———. 1963. "Corporate Income Taxes and the Cost of Capital: A Correction." *American Economic Review* 53: 433–43.

Myers, S. C. 1984. "The Capital Structure Puzzle." *Journal of Finance* 39 (3): 575–92.

Myers, S. C., and N. S. Majluf. 1984. "Corporate Financing and Investment Decisions When Firms Have Information That Investors Do Not Have." *Journal of Financial Economics* 13 (2): 187–221.

Pigou, A. C. 1920. *The Economics of Welfare*. London: Macmillan.

Ramsey, F. P. 1928. "A Mathematical Theory of Saving." *Economic Journal* 38: 543–59.

Reuters. 2012. "Goldman Sachs in New Flap over Islamic Bond." January 11. http://blogs.reuters.com/faithworld/2012/01/11/goldman-sachs-in-new-flap-over-islamic-bond-suspected-to-be-not-100-halal/.

Rubin, J. 2011. "Institutions, the Rise of Commerce and the Persistence of Laws: Interest Restrictions in Islam and Christianity." *The Economic Journal*, Royal Economic Society 121 (557): 1310–39.

Shaw, E. S. 1973. "Financial Deepening in Economic Development." Working Paper 233, The Hebrew University of Jerusalem.

Sheng, A. 2009. *From Asian to Global Financial Crisis*. New York: Cambridge University Press.

———. 2010. "Is Islamic Finance the New Challenge to Wall Street?" Commentary, *The China Post*, November 7.

———. 2011. "Finance Cannot Be Left to Free Markets: An Asian Tribute to Minsky." 20th Hyman P. Minsky Conference, Levy Institute, Bard College, New York, April 15.

Sheng, A., and A. Singh. 2012. "The Challenge of Islamic Finance." *Project Syndicate*, Op-Ed column, April 17.

Singh, A. 1992. "Corporate Takeovers." In *The New Palgrave Dictionary of Money and Finance*, edited by J. Eatwell, M. Milgate, and P. Newman, 448–86. London: Macmillan.

———. 1995. "Corporate Financial Patterns in Industrialising Economies: A Comparative International Study." IFC Technical Paper 2, International Finance Corporation, Washington, DC.

———. 1997. "Financial Liberalisation, the Stock Market and Economic Development." *Economic Journal* 107 (442): 771–82.

———. 2003. "Corporate Governance, Corporate Finance and Stock Markets in Emerging Countries." Working Paper 258, Working Paper Series, Centre for Business Research, University of Cambridge. A revised version of this paper was published in the *Journal of Corporate Law Studies* 3 (1): 41–72.

———. 2012. "Financial Globalisation and Human Development." *Journal of Human Development and Capabilities*, Taylor and Francis Journals, 13 (1): 135–51.

Singh, A., and J. Hamid. 1992. "Corporate Financial Structures in Developing Countries." IFC Technical Paper 1, International Finance Corporation, Washington, DC.

Stiglitz, J. E. 1988. "Why Financial Structure Matters." *Journal of Economic Perspectives* 2 (4): 121–26.

———. 2005. "Modigliani, the Modigliani-Miller Theorem and Macroeconomics." Paper presented at the Franco Modigliani and Keynesian Legacy Conference, New School University, April 14–15.

Tan, E. C. 2009. "Review of *Islamic Finance Principles and Practice*, by Hans Visser." University of Malaya, Kuala Lumpur.

Villamil, A. P. 1992. "The Modigliani-Miller Theorem." In *The New Palgrave Dictionary of Money and Finance*, edited by P. Newman. Palgrave Macmillan.

CHAPTER 3

The Foundational Market Principles of Islam, Knightian Uncertainty, and Economic Justice

S. Nuri Erbaş and Abbas Mirakhor

Introduction

> *For whoever would profess, as I have heard at one time or another, that religion is merely 'an aspect of economics' would do well to close these pages without further ado and devote himself exclusively to the study of economics.*
>
> <div align="right">Jean Bottéro (<i>Birth of God</i>, 2000, 161)</div>

There are two main approaches to the possible correlation between religion and economic development.[1] The secularization hypothesis tests whether economic development and improvement in living and education standards results in less religiosity. The second approach explores whether religion has an impact on economic development. The latter is along the lines of Max Weber's insight that the Protestant Ethic—exhorting honesty, trust, a work ethic, and thrift—has promoted development of entrepreneurial capitalism and industrialization in the West. Some studies also note that nonmarket activities, including social networking through religious channels, have market value because they create positive externalities by enhancing information, relationships, and solidarity, such as finding employment or getting business through friends and acquaintances who belong to a network. Moreover, such activities have hedonic value because they increase life satisfaction. Underlining the importance of faith relative to networking through religious channels, McCleary and Barro (2006, 51) subscribe to the

---

S. Nuri Erbaş was a visiting professor at the International Centre for Education in Islamic Finance (INCEIF), Kuala Lumpur, Malaysia. Abbas Mirakhor is a professor at INCEIF. We thank INCEIF for funding and our colleagues there for the collegial research environment they provided. We thank Mr. Hew Dundas (Arbitration International, the United Kingdom) for his guidance on arbitration data and interpretation, Mr. Peter Clark (IMF Research Department, retired) for his insightful questions and comments, Prof. John Wallis (Department of Economics, University of Maryland College Park) for an inspiring discussion, and Dr. David Eddy for his steadfast encouragement. Without implications, their input greatly improved this paper. The authors are solely responsible for all views expressed and any remaining errors.

view that "believing in religion relative to belonging to a religion is the main channel through which religion matters for economic and other outcomes." If so, then faithful adherence to market principles exhorted by religion has economic significance. This is the main point that motivates this study in relation to the foundational Islamic market principles.

There is an absence of expository discussion in the literature of the scriptural predisposition of a religion toward investment and growth. This scriptural dislocation is the reason why quantitative investigations (based on rather tentative indicators) of the correlation between religion and religiosity and economic performance appear to be disjointed and somewhat ad hoc trial runs to be taken only at face value (see Mitchell's similar observations in Barro and Mitchell 2003). Regression analysis may also be misleading because the selection of some quantifiable indicators of religiosity is not substantiated in the scriptural context of a religion. Among the indicators based on survey results, spiritual incentives and disincentives appear to be significant. McCleary and Barro (2006) find that fear of damnation is more significantly correlated with economic performance than belief in salvation. As McCleary (2007) observes in the Islamic context, indeed there are graphic and corporeal descriptions of heaven and hell in the Qur'an. However, in Islam how and why one merits salvation in heaven or deserves damnation to hell is at the ineffable judgment and mercy of Allah. The Qur'an excoriates rote belief. It is not sufficient to believe in salvation or damnation. Humans do not easily understand the path to salvation or damnation, but exercising free will in obeying or disobeying the ordained rules of Islam shows that path at the final judgment of the merciful Allah. As for mosque attendance as an indicator of religiosity, collective prayer is exhorted to reinforce social bonding among the faithful. Individual observance is flexible: for example, it is possible to make up for missed prayers in private and out of the time schedule punctuated by the call to prayer five times a day. Even a bed-ridden invalid, if he were conscious, could do his prayers with his eyes or in his mind and fulfill one of the ordained Five Pillars of Islam, and he would be judged as observant toward salvation. If covering of women were taken as an indicator of religiosity, it might be vulnerable to the possibility that such behavior could be the result of cultural orthopraxy rather than religious orthodoxy, and it might not have much to do with the foundational principles of Islam.[2]

Furthermore, many studies exhibit a contextual vacuum because they exclude, or address only in passing, the insights from institutional and behavioral economics. The discussion is not placed within the analytical framework of those disciplines. This seems most conspicuous where there is no historical perspective on institutional change. Happenstance and its unpredictable effects on economic performance need not be significantly correlated with religiosity or the foundational principles of a given faith. Historical factors also twist and turn economic performance over time. Historical evolution of market institutions originating from religion (Kuran 2011, with Cizakça 2011 providing a counterpoint), institutional strengths and weaknesses (Rodrik, Subramanian, and Trebbi 2002), culture (Harrison and Huntington 2000; Harrison 2006), and identity (Akerlof and Kranton 2010) are as fundamental as faith in determining economic performance—if not more so.

For example, we examined the correlation between equity premium and social trust using a confidence index we constructed based on World Values Survey data on the degree of confidence in various social and political categories (Erbaş and Mirakhor 2010).[3] For a sample of 45 countries, including 7 countries where Islam is the predominant religion, we found a statistically significant positive correlation between the equity premium and trust, including religion (confidence in church), whereas we had expected a negative correlation.[4] But excluding religion, the equity premium was not significantly correlated with our confidence index. However, selective World Bank Worldwide Governance Indicators (World Bank 2008) and some indicators of financial development were statistically significant and negatively correlated with the equity premium, as expected. For the Muslim countries, our confidence index indicated significantly higher trust, including religion, but equity premiums were also significantly higher than in the non-Muslim countries. But when we excluded the factor of religion from our index, the average index value (higher value indicating higher confidence) for the Muslim countries dropped by 21 percent.[5] On the other hand, according to the Governance Indicators, on average, the Muslim countries ranked significantly below the average for industrial countries. The same was true for selective indicators of financial development. Evidently, other factors (such as government effectiveness, credit to the private sector, and equity and bond market capitalization) are more significant than religion in explaining the high equity premium in both Muslim and non-Muslim countries.

Therefore, we think that the analysis of the impact of religion on economic performance begs for an analytical context in which it can be substantiated. Religion being as old as human history and so intricately intertwined with it, it is no doubt a daunting task to control for historical factors while testing for statistically significant correlations between economic performance and religion. However, institutional and behavioral economics provide a rich and manageably focused context for analyzing the possible impact of religion on economic development.[6] The core insight of new institutional economics is that rules and compliance with them provide economic incentives (protection of property rights, contract enforcement) and reduce uncertainty (predictable rules responses).

Concerning incentives, religion as an institution may have a scriptural predisposition to incentivizing market-based enterprise and wealth accumulation. This appears to be the crux of Weber's point about the Protestant Ethic. Barro (2006) and Harrison (2006) observe such a predisposition in the various evangelical denominations in the United States, which also seem to be taking a hold in mostly Catholic Central and South American countries.

Concerning uncertainty, as far as we know, the literature has not paid enough attention to the role of secular institutions or of religion as an institution in reducing economic uncertainty. Here, we mean Knightian uncertainty (discussed further below). Human economic behavior, rational and moral, cannot be reduced to prespecified probability distributions that trivialize uncertainty as a random walk. With perfect information and foresight, errant or immoral intent can be terminated and sanctioned before it becomes behavior. But humans must submit that capacity to the highest authority. The economic function of moral behavior and the social trust it engenders is analytically meaningful in the context of substantive uncertainty emanating from unknown and unknowable contingencies and human responses to them over space and time. It is in the context of Knightian uncertainty that the economic function of beliefs, norms, rules, institutions, and their inheritance from generation to generation becomes substantiated. Faith-based rules may also reduce economic uncertainty by establishing behavioral reference points and by promoting social trust, cooperation, and solidarity, and thus generating positive externalities. We propose that a fundamental analytical context in which to explore the correlation between religion and economic progress is human decision behavior in substantive uncertainty and the scriptural guidance that religion provides to reduce it.

We further observe that social trust is built on society's belief in justice in general and economic justice in particular. Lack of economic justice—in the form of predatory competition; corruption; risk of expropriation; ascription-based as opposed to achievement-based upward mobility; restricted access to markets, financing, and education; and widespread poverty—undermines trust and incentives to invest in human and physical capital. Economic justice is a fundamental moral issue that emanates from uneven wealth accumulation through market-based economic progress, even though progress may improve welfare of nearly all income classes. Emergence of social safety net schemes in industrial countries cannot be attributed only to self-serving efforts of the rich to co-opt and pacify the threat of class warfare, although history has born witness to such conflicts frequently enough. The undeniable success of market economies inevitably brings with it the moral dilemma between economic progress and income inequality reflecting the innate human predisposition to justice for all fellow humans. Religion may provide scriptural guidance to achieve a measure of economic justice, in line with the Abrahamic traditions that exhort moral market behavior, fairness, and charity.

Thus, a robust analytical context emerges in which we can analyze the economic impact of religion on the basis of three fundamental factors that play a role in economic development: *incentives, uncertainty,* and *justice*. It appears this is the missing context underlying the search for a testable causality going from religion to economic development. There is a need to examine the market principles embedded in a specific religion and their particular influence on *preferred* economic behavior.[7] Among the Abrahamic traditions, an example *par excellence* is Islam because the Qur'an and the Traditions of the Messenger specify a comprehensive set of rules relating to economic incentives, uncertainty, and justice. Those rules cover contracts, property rights, market organization, moral behavior in uncertainty, and redistribution of wealth (Mirakhor 2010). Among them, the ordained fulfillment of contracts and proscription of interest-based contracts are fundamentally central as the defining characteristics of an economy based on Islamic principles.

For much of their economic history, Muslims structured their markets in accordance with the rich legacy of the market institutions in the traditions of the Qur'an and the Messenger. Those institutions were rule-based, market-oriented, and innovative. History gives proof that Islamic societies thrived and some grew into global economic powers. That rich legacy was not sustained, resulting in a state of underdevelopment relative to the West in the last two centuries and relative to other countries that have made great strides in economic development more recently. The historical reasons for the decline are complex, including warfare, devastating invasions, geography, decline of scientific thought (Reilly 2010), moral and institutional decay resulting in erosion of social trust, internecine power struggles and despotic rule, and predatory taxation to finance wars and indulgence (Chapra 2010). In addition, Kuran (2011) argues that Islamic law may have played an unintended but incrementally determining role as a hindrance to adaptation of Islamic economic institutions and contractual forms, in contrast to the innovations in the West that facilitated large-scale industrial organization and unprecedented growth and prosperity. Any one of those factors is a *bona fide* topic of voluminous analysis. For the purposes of this chapter, a more limited focus is necessary. Our specific focus is the broad *foundational* principles of Islam that guide economic behavior and market organization. This might put to rest at the outset possible impatience arising out of justified questions about the reasons behind the decline and the current state of the economies of the predominantly Muslim countries. Our narrow focus is not a nostalgic harkening back to a real or imagined past that most Muslims indelibly remember as a golden age. It is an attempt—perhaps a rather impossible one—at abstracting our analysis from the twists and turns of history that ineluctably have had a major impact on the economic decline, regardless of the foundational economic principles of Islam.

The Foundational Islamic Market Principles

Property Rights

The Qur'an sanctifies private property (2:275). Central to the functioning of Islamic finance, the Qur'an proscribes interest-based contracts, borrowing, and lending. The implications of this fundamental Islamic tenet will be discussed at length later.

The parties to exchange must have property rights for the goods and services being exchanged. The Islamic principles governing property rights are the following:

- Allah has created all things in the universe and the Creator is the ultimate owner of property. Resources created are placed at the disposal of all humans. While ultimate ownership is reserved for the Creator, humans are to combine

their abilities with created resources to develop the earth and produce means of sustenance for themselves and others.
- Property rights must not lead to wealth accumulation in the form of hoarding, as wealth is considered the life-blood of the economy, which must constantly circulate to create investment, employment, income, and economic growth opportunities. Property must not be wasted.
- Right of access to all created resources belongs to all humankind. Humans can claim property rights over what they produce through their own labor and voluntary transfers.
- Since all humans are entitled to all created resources, the inability to access resources does not negate the individual's initial rights to resources. These rights must be redeemed through a rule that ordains sharing, which cleanses the property of the rights of others and renders the property claims of the owner inviolate and sacred.
- Post-exchange sharing and distribution of property claims must be implemented in line with contractual commitments. Such transfers are not charity, but redemption of an original right.
- Unlike the conventional system of property rights, Islam imposes limits on the freedom to dispose of property. There is no absolute freedom for owners to dispose of property as they choose, and the impact of disposing of property on third parties must be considered, among other things. There are rules against waste, such as destruction of property and its use in prohibited transactions.
- Since work and voluntary transfers are the only legitimate source of creation of property rights, all sources of windfall property rights, such as theft, bribery, gambling, and usury are prohibited.
- Property rights of a person terminate at the point of death. Property is then divided among the network of survivors according to strict rules prescribed by the Qur'an. This rule then becomes an instrument of redistribution to affect intergenerational justice.

Market Rules and the Messenger's Implementations

Trade was the most important economic activity in the Arabian Peninsula before Islam. A number of dynamic and thriving markets had developed throughout the area. The Messenger was no stranger to markets. Being a trader for decades from childhood until he received the Revelation, he had an intimate familiarity with markets.[8] That experience reflected on the market principles and institutions he established with the guidance of the Qur'an. Once installed in Medina in 622 as the spiritual and temporal authority, the Messenger organized a market and implemented a number of policies to strengthen markets and encourage the expansion of trade. The rules governing market operations the Messenger implemented included the following:

- Freedom of exchange: Freedom for agents to set their own objectives and choose partners for exchange under the prescribed market rules, employing ways and means of their own choosing to achieve their economic goals.

- The market as the venue of exchange: Infrastructure was created for market participants to access information and coordinate economic activity. Information regarding quantities, qualities, and prices of products was to be made available to market participants with full transparency. Shortchanging—that is, not complying with full weights and measures—was prohibited.
- Free markets: Unrestricted interregional or international trade, with no taxation of imports and exports; free movement of inputs and outputs between markets and regions; no barriers to market entry and exit; price controls and speculative hoarding of commodities were prohibited.
- Contract rules: Every contract had to specify fully the property claims being exchanged and the rights and obligations of each party under the contract. All other terms and conditions had to be registered transparently. Depending on the circumstances, sellers and buyers were given the right of annulment of contract.
- Fairness in exchange: No buyer or seller was allowed to harm the interests of other market participants. For example, no third party could interrupt negotiations between two parties to an exchange in order to influence the outcome in favor of one or the other party to the negotiations. Interference with supplies before market entrance was prohibited to protect the interests of the original suppliers and the final consumers.
- Distribution of profit and loss according to the stipulations of contract and its performance: The distribution of proceeds between parties to exchange must honor *pre*-contract commitments *and post*-contract performance. These rules also cover the redemption of the rights of those who may not have been directly parties to exchange but who have acquired rights in the proceeds because, one way or another, they or their properties have contributed to the production of the products subject to exchange.
- The role of the state and the legal apparatus was defined to guarantee contract enforcement: Market supervisors were appointed and charged with the duty of ensuring compliance with rules.

These rules, known as the Medina market rules, evidently served as strong incentives for trade and growth in and outside Arabia with the advent of Islam (Sadr 1996). The foundational rules protect property rights and contracts, provide economic incentives, and reduce market uncertainty. They have universal and enduring qualities, so far as we understand the preconditions for a robust free-market economy today.

Knightian Uncertainty and the Islamic View of Uncertainty

Knightian Uncertainty

Rational expectations hypothesis has dominated the contemporary economics and finance literature in recent decades. It generally embraces the implicit assumption that economic structure is stationary over time, or possible structural changes are somehow anticipated. Economic agents not only anticipate the future values of economic variables subject to random errors with prespecified distributions, but they also anticipate the impact on economic variables of changes in the economic environment and structure, presumably also subject to other error terms. The implication is that there are errors on errors (probabilities on probabilities) in forming expectations. For the dynamic theory to be valid in essence, complex randomness of economic prospects over time needs to be reducible to simple error terms at the initial point in time.[9] This is the equivalent of the reduction axiom of expected utility theory.

As the time horizon is extended, the assumption that uncertainty is reducible to known distributions at present loses credibility. In reality, possible payoffs and associated probabilities to economic enterprise are *not* known with precision, especially over time. There is Knightian uncertainty, or, ambiguity, as distinct from measurable risk.[10] Frank Knight, who lends his name to distinguishing uncertainty from risk, is the first contemporary economist to substantively address the impact of uncertainty on economic decision-making, entrepreneurship, investment, and social progress. His landmark contribution is *Risk, Uncertainty, and Profit* ([1921] 2002).[11] Knight argues:

> Our dogma ... is the presupposition of knowledge ... that the world is made up of things, which, under the same circumstances, always behave in the same way ... but workable knowledge of the world requires much more than the assumption that the world is made up of units which maintain an unvarying identity in time ... In addition, we have to make the still more questionable assumption that the situation elements or fundamental kinds of object properties upon which we fall back for simplicity (practical finitude) in view of the unmanageable number of kinds of objects as wholes, are unvarying from one "combination" ... to another .... The ordinary decisions of life are made on the basis of "estimates" of a crude and superficial character. In general, the future situations in relation to which we act depend upon the behavior of an indefinitely large number of objects, and is influenced by so many factors that no real effort is made to take account of them all, much less estimate and summate their separate significance. (197–232)

The Islamic View of Substantive Uncertainty

Do humans think that they will be left alone when they say, 'We believe,' and they therefore will not be tested?

Qur'an 29:2

How is the existence of uncertainty and its overwhelming influence in human life explained by Islamic thought? For believers, Allah is the creator of all things. Why does the Creator subject life to so much uncertainty? The answer appears in the Qur'an under the concept of *testing*, also shared by the other Abrahamic traditions. The Creator tests humans by the decisions they make in uncertainty. The main reason is to motivate humans to use their free will for self-improvement and for spiritual growth (Mirakhor 2009, 2010).

Human growth is not possible without being tested by confrontation with uncertainty.[12]

The Qur'an makes clear that humans lack perfect information and they are cognitively limited in their understanding of Allah and the universe He created in its entirety. Consequences of human actions and their collateral influence on others now or over time are known fully by the Creator alone (2:30–33; 2:216; 7:89; 24:11; 49:16–18; 65:12). Humans are given free will in making decisions and taking actions, but they are not left unaided in facing life's uncertainties. There are ordained rules for decisions and actions in uncertainty. Compliance with the rules of the Law Giver is the only way to ensure that decisions and actions are beneficent and efficient and that they entail low costs (4:46; 4:59; 4:66; 4:77; 11:84; 17:35; 47:33; 48:16; 49:14). The rest of life is governed by human freedom to choose (called *'ibaha*, meaning permissibility). But with the ordained rules supporting limited human cognitive abilities, decision making in uncertainty becomes a less difficult task for the believer and the rules reduce anxiety in the face of life's ambiguities, inducing greater happiness.[13] The test becomes an occasion for self-development and strengthened consciousness of the Creator.

Risk sharing by rule adherence allows risks to be spread and reduced for market participants. Those who are able can mitigate uncertainty by sharing risks with fellow humans in market exchange. If some individuals are unable to participate in risk sharing through market exchange because of poverty, or, in general, for lack of sufficient resources for market access, the more able are ordained to share risks of the less able through compliance with the redistributive rules. Following the ordained rules reduces substantive (ontological and epistemological) uncertainty and enables humans to make rational as well as moral decisions. We interpret this "reduction" in the same sense as Frank Knight's and Herbert Simon's observations on economic decision-making in uncertainty within the "*practical finitude*" of available and utilized information and with "*procedural rationality*" of limited human cognition (Knight 2002; Simon 1976).

Institutional Development, Trust, and Uncertainty

Institutional Development, Behavioral References, and Uncertainty

Knight's examination of "Structures and Methods for Meeting Uncertainty" (2002, chapter VIII) can be summarized as increasing accumulation of data (sampling) and scientific knowledge (modeling), along with consolidation and specialization through large-scale organization of economic activity. Consolidation of economic activity in large corporations, in which hierarchical production decisions can be exercised more efficiently and effectively, reduces uncertainty and transforms it into measurable (and therefore, priceable) risk, so new markets are created. Similarly, uncertainty is consolidated and its costs are diversified through integrated (grouped) and specialized markets and business organizations (insurance, banking, financial investment markets); thus, decision makers "shift" uncertainty by transferring it to specialists. Central to this process of reducing uncertainty are legal guarantees for private property and contractual freedom that improve the prospects for control of resources (wealth) over time. Of course, consolidation, specialization, and systemic control of economic decisions and resources are the main underlying characteristics that define robust market institutions. Knight's main thesis is that such market institutions emerge mainly to deal with uncertainty. Reducing uncertainty through institutional grouping is at the core of social and economic development. It is progress.

Douglass North and others have posited that institutions serve two basic functions. First, they provide the right incentives to invest with appropriate protections (property rights). Second, institutions help reduce uncertainty in the Knightian sense by excluding many possible events, or by restricting their range (inconsistent and arbitrary rules responses). Oliver Williamson also underscores the role of institutions in shaping and regulating human behavior in uncertainty, implied by incomplete contractual situations. Nevertheless, substantive uncertainty persists, although reduced by institutional development. Martin Shubik (1978) emphasizes that uncertainty (especially about low probability events) is pervasive even in most orderly societies with strong institutions.

Robert Sugden (1989) stresses that human behavior, guided by norms and conventions, goes well beyond the predictions of game theory. Human behavior is the result of an evolutionary process that establishes successful common strategies, based on common experience for rules and conventions or moral, social, and institutional heuristics.[14] Psychological and behavioral evidence indicates that trust, reputation, cooperation, fairness, referencing, or anchoring to beliefs matter in decision making significantly, both at the reflexive and reflective levels.[15] As Herbert Simon (1976) suggests, "decision processes, like all other aspects of economic institutions, exist inside human heads" (146). On human cognition and rational behavior in uncertainty, the psychologist Gerd Gigerenzer (2007) argues: "Intelligence means taking bets, taking risks" (42). On the role of morals, Gigerenzer leans on the Chomskian interpretation: "Humans have an innate capacity for morals just as they do for language...Moral grammar... can be described by rules-of-thumb" (185). Along Sugden's lines, Gigerenzer (2007) underlines that "good intuitions must go beyond the information given, and therefore, beyond logic" (103). At this juncture, we suggest that a fundamental factor that lies beyond logic is faith.

In this light, a basic function of institutions and behavioral references is reducing uncertainty by instilling and preserving social trust. Cultural values and morals matter significantly in shaping institutions, market interactions, and economic performance.[16]

The Role of Rationality and Morals in Uncertainty

From the point of view of ethics, immoral economic behavior in an environment of certainty poses little philosophical challenge. With perfect foresight, economic circumstances and decision outcomes would be known perfectly, including intent for behavior deemed immoral by the standards of prevailing and enforced social mores. Immoral intent, now or in the future, would be caught and prevented before it would become immoral behavior. Thus, moral behavior would be ensured over time and, in the spirit of neoclassical dynamic optimization models with perfect foresight, it would be possible to attain an efficient *and* moral economic equilibrium. But in uncertainty, immoral intent is not known ahead of time to be corrected and sanctioned before intent becomes behavior. Economic agents' behavior cannot be known with precision or may even be unknowable. Information becomes a commodity that can be hoarded and not shared. It is therefore possible for immoral economic agents to acquire a competitive advantage to reap rents from imperfect knowledge and asymmetric information. The role of morals in economic interactions becomes analytically substantiated in uncertainty.

How do morals fit in the analysis of human economic behavior in uncertainty? It turns out that *homo economicus* is not only the self-serving robot, as usually assumed in neoclassical theory. Behavioral evidence about his or her nature is gaining increasing acceptance in economic analysis. She dislikes uncertainty, thinks in terms of narratives she constructs, and uses fallible heuristics to make decisions. She has passions; needs moral, social, and institutional references and guidance; and has a sense of justice.[17] In that light, *homo economicus* is also *homo ethicus*—but this is not a Dr. Jekyll and Mr. Hyde type of personality. The two aspects of her character coexist, but not to the detriment of each other: they are symbiotic; they complement each other. Axiomatically accepting only the *economicus* aspect of human economic behavior is the fundamental heuristic bias peculiar to neoclassical economics that renders the decision maker an inhuman robot. Her behavior is precisely defined in order to obtain precise equilibrium solutions, but at considerable expense of realism (Frydman and Goldberg 2007; Sargent 1993). The question is not whether the *economicus* aspect of human nature explains observed economic behavior and outcomes better than the *ethicus* aspect. It is whether both the *economicus* and *ethicus* aspects explain more—perhaps in that order.

The red line neoclassical economics draws between rationality and morality is often blurred in reality. Itzhak Gilboa, Andrew Postlewaite, and David Schmeidler (2009, 289–90) note: "One may adopt an a priori axiomatic approach, subscribing to a set of rules that by definition dictate the 'right' thing to do, moral or rational." But it is impossible for individuals to be consistent in adhering to those moral or rational rules in all circumstances. A given set of circumstances that has led to one decision or another is never replicated over time, so adherence to both moral and rational rules is compromised by sometimes violating them. Consequently, decision dilemmas may arise where "benevolence" might yield a code of behavior that is acceptable, "or at least a step in the right direction." We take the liberty of interpreting right as moral.

Compromising moral and rational rules of behavior is an inevitable consequence of limited human cognitive abilities, limited information, and substantive uncertainty. Faith-based rules cannot muster uncompromising moral economic behavior in obeying the rules and eliminate decision uncertainty in all circumstances. However, moral behavior that faith exhorts is not an altruistic reification of human behavior that guarantees complete commitment to rules. The Ten

Commandments are not in denial of human proclivity for immoral behavior but in recognition of it. But trust in moral behavior is a part of everyday life in exchange and contracts, no matter how simple or sophisticated markets may be. Thus, faith-based rules have a market function. We interpret the economic role of Islamic rules as rather a frame of reference that guides moral market behavior than one that can actually achieve it completely. But those rules have a claim to pointing the way to gains from moral economic behavior, to the extent that humans can stay committed to them, perhaps beyond logic.[18] Given human frailties and proclivity for temptation by greed, faith-based rules, with their millennia-old traditions and deep hold on the human mind, urge decision makers to pursue moral market behavior in the face of uncertainty. There is economic value to a moral frame of reference.

Evidence from behavioral economics is not entirely encouraging about the wisdom of economic decisions of average individuals. This appears to be especially true for decisions made in uncertainty over time (Tversky and Kahneman 1999). Humans display persistent biases in *not* making the "best" decisions over and over again. There are repeated decision patterns that are flawed, and they create negative externalities for the society as a whole (low savings, low health insurance coverage, excessive debt). As Thaler and Sunstein (2008) extensively document, some paternalistic "nudges" help in inducing better preferences with long-term consequences (such as a nudge to choose a higher savings plan for retirement, and higher health insurance coverage for old age). Nudges appear to reduce decision uncertainty by appropriately framing choice alternatives and steering decision makers away from errors in decision making when choices must be made with limited information and often in ignorance. Thaler has coined the term "libertarian paternalism" for policies that provide such guidance but also offer alternatives to give the individual freedom of choice. Ultimately, the determining factor for the individual's decision is his trust in the wisdom of paternalistic nudges made in good faith. Faith-based rules can be interpreted similarly, even though they often *urge* rather than nudge, and sometimes narrow down decision alternatives to *one*. This is not strictly in the libertarian spirit. But as for trust in the wisdom of guidance, the notion of God as a father or a mother figure or a shepherd is not without foundation in uncertainty.

Trust and Contacts in Uncertainty

Explicit contracts codified under the law guide economic behavior by defining the relationship and obligations of the parties involved, by enforcing commitments, and by sanctioning errant behavior. In addition, established goodwill and reputation play a fundamental role in structuring contracts. But in modern economies, contracts are generally impersonal, signed between parties who are not intimately familiar with each other, and they are executed on the faith that the governing contract law will treat possible disputes fairly under the impartial cloak of anonymity. It is not a coincidence that even third parties prefer committing to contracts and resolving disputes under the contract laws of countries that have a justified reputation for impartiality and for strong and expeditious enforcement that reduces uncertainty surrounding legal outcomes.[19]

Furthermore, economic agents, consciously or unconsciously, also rely on numerous implicit contracts on a daily basis—some as quotidian as buying food on the goodwill that it is uncontaminated or the scale is not rigged. From an institutional point of view, a strong regulatory environment reduces uncertainty about outcomes of implicit contracts, along with established good reputation. But implicit contracts, like explicit contracts, ultimately rest on trust in moral behavior of the parties engaged in economic exchange. In the final analysis, no contract is complete. Moral behavior and trust make the epoxy that fills the holes and makes contracts more complete.

It can be argued that social norms that serve as decision frames, faith-based or not, are malleable with respect to individual interpretation and opportunism. Norms do not provide a well-defined legal context that prescribes clearer—or at least less ambiguous—rules. However, the law is also an incomplete contract, and social norms and morals make it more complete. Rules codified by law are unambiguous to the extent they engender trust among those who are subject to it. Without well-functioning and trusted legal institutions, laws can be and are applied arbitrarily and opportunistically. Trust in independence of courts from political and other influence is a valued social asset, and lack of it creates great ambiguities. Contracts being incompletely defined and enforced by law, an established moral code—by norm, convention, and faith—that is shared by contracting parties is of paramount importance to urge preferred economic behavior.

Contracts, Islamic Market Principles, and Uncertainty

O you who truly believe! Fulfill all contracts!

Qur'an 5:1

Observing the ordained rules of moral market behavior embedded in the Abrahamic traditions can mitigate uncertainty. Moral market behavior is a fundamental exhortation of Islam. The fundamental prescriptions and exhortations in the tradition of the Qur'an and the Messenger serve to reduce uncertainty. Among them, commitment to contracts is central. The strong emphasis the Qur'an places on the need to fulfill the terms and conditions of covenants can be appreciated better when trust is viewed as social capital.

Contracts are procedural means of coming to terms with uncertainty. They allocate risks by specifying the obligations of each party in anticipated future states and remedies for breach of contract. Generally, there are three motives for entering into contracts: sharing of profit and risk, alignment of incentives, and minimizing transaction costs. To align incentives, one party (principal) enters into a contract with another (agent) through which incentives are created for the agent to take actions that serve to maximize the joint surplus of the contracting parties.[20] There is an organic economic relationship between contracts and trust. When and where trust is weak, complicated and costly administrative devices are needed to enforce contracts (cost associated with search for information, bargaining, contract negotiation and renegotiation, enforcement). Without trust, especially long-term contracting becomes limited, and parties to exchange opt for the spot market or short-term transactions and investments. Consequently, there is narrower market exchange, less market participation, less long-term investment, and lower economic growth (see Cizakça 2011 for a historical review in the Islamic context).

Islam anchors all social, political, and economic relations on contracts. The fabric of Islam's institutional structure is contractual in its conceptualization, content, and application. According to the Islamic law, the essence of a contract is commitment to its terms and conditions as prescribed by the Qur'an. The very foundation of contractual obligations is the primordial covenant between the Creator and humans (7:172–73). The Qur'an urges the believers to fulfill this covenant (6:152). The believers are ordered to be faithful to their covenants, contracts, and promises, and to what has been placed in trust with them as the shepherd protects his flock (2:172; 16:91–92; 17:34; 32:8). The believers are not to treat obligations of contracts lightly. They will take on contractual obligations if and only if they intend to fully honor them (Mirakhor and Hamid 2009). Moral hazard is addressed, as each and every party to a contract is ordained to remain faithful to the obligations assumed under the contract.

Islamic Contracts and Risk Sharing

The starting point of this discussion is the most important verse of the Qur'an from the economic point of view (2:275). It establishes what can be referred to as the fundamental principle of an Islamic economy. The verse ordains the prohibition of interest-based debt contracts, and instead prescribes exchange-based contracts.

Exchange-Based Contracts and Risk Sharing

Interest-based debt contracts do not involve exchange of full property claims. They create a property claim for the lender on the property claims of the borrower in the amount of principal and interest, whether or not repayable ex post. Exchange-based contracts create a property claim on the principal and a portion of profits of the borrower before and after profits or losses are realized. Thus, in exchange-based contracts, the contracting parties share the risks of the transaction not only ex ante but also ex post. This is the basic principle of Islamic finance.

The lender is affected by bad outcomes ex post in interest-based contracts, as well. In the event of default, the lender loses money ex post; however, the lender's initial claim on the borrower continues. Bad debts can be settled through renegotiation of the terms, as is often the case. But this is a costly process because it involves renegotiation and litigation costs and risk of bankruptcy for both the lender and the borrower. For example, as housing values plummeted in the United States during the recent financial crisis, many mortgagors (even wealthy ones) defaulted on purpose.[21] They had a strong economic incentive to do so because the collateral value of their property had fallen significantly below the discounted mortgage loan value. Post-contract events made forcing foreclosure by the borrower economically sensible. Contracts that would have incorporated ex post market conditions might have averted or reduced such collateral costs by enabling ex post risk sharing between lenders and borrowers: for example, by incorporating *as a rule* the terms of adjustment of the mortgage loan obligation (both in the principal and interest) in relation to the realized value of the property.[22]

In exchange-based contracts predicated on risk sharing ex ante and ex post, both the lender and the borrower are entitled to the realized profit or liable for the realized loss according to their shares specified in the contract. Islamic contracts are also in the realm of Knightian uncertainty ex ante, but contractual obligations for risk sharing continue after the outcomes are realized and uncertainty is resolved. Thus, risk sharing is not truncated at the point of contracting.

This arrangement may have some fundamental beneficial effects. First, it may reduce uncertainty aversion because benefits and costs of unanticipated outcomes are shared between parties after the resolution of uncertainty. Second, because of reduced uncertainty aversion, many new areas of investment may become profitable and new markets are created to the benefit of entrepreneurs and the society. Third, such contracts may reduce transactions costs involved in ex post contract enforcement. Fourth, economic volatility may be reduced because investments discontinued in the event of a shock may be continued; for example, many mortgagors may prefer servicing lower principle and interest payments, instead of opting for foreclosure, with beneficial collateral effects on housing maintenance and other household services, schools, and shops—and by and large, on happier neighborhoods and happier lives. Fifth, it may reduce predatory lending, observed amply in the case of subprime mortgages that triggered the 2008 crisis. Similarly, profligate consumer credit at rates verging on usurious in some cases—especially for the cash-constrained poor—may be curtailed.[23] Finally, such contracts may be more parsimonious because they reduce the need for creating complex instruments such as derivatives for ex ante and ex post risk sharing (hedging), which might increase risk exposure because of their complexity.

We see no reason that conventional financial instruments cannot be designed to accommodate to some extent ex post losses and gains that are unanticipated ex ante.[24] In general, such contracts would be Islamic in nature, provided that they are based on direct property claims. Derivatives, at least in theory, are contracts that facilitate broader risk diversification by hedging ex ante against possible outcomes ex post. The recent financial crisis teaches us that derivatives are vulnerable to speculation reflecting increasing complexity created by many generations of derivatives of derivatives and marketing to a fractal of counterparties. In the absence of a clearing house, it is difficult if not impossible to know who owes what to whom. Counterparties have little understanding of derivative asset values, much less knowing who owes what to whom. Thus, intrinsic values of derivatives become ambiguous, or at least hard to price. In the process—borrowing the term from Karl Marx—"*fictitious capital*" is created, representing only putative property claims far removed from the original direct claims on real goods and services. This results in a decoupling of the financial and real sectors and increases ambiguity of risk exposure. The chain reaction resulting from diminished trust in one link quickly cascades into financial panic and abruptly deflates derivative asset values. On the upside, derivatives diversify risk on a broader scale; on the downside, their complexity and the associated ambiguity of their market value increase risk exposure.

Complexity and Risk

Complexity is unavoidable in the modern economy, but simplification of contracts can make them less ambiguous, more transparent, and easier to understand and to act on. Vito Tanzi (2007) goes further to argue that there is a trade-off between progress through increased complexity and the cost of systemic failures arising out of complexity. For example, a nuclear reactor is a very complex system that produces energy at low cost but, even with a small probability, its systemic failure can create insufferable social costs. Complexity also facilitates obfuscation by insiders for self-gain and exploitation of asymmetric information to reap economic rents. As the old Turkish proverb goes, "The wolf likes murky weather." Asset managers can exploit complexity in the assessment of asset values. As manager compensation appears to be in increasing but not in decreasing proportion to asset values, the "it is what I say it is" approach to pricing complex assets seems to serve managers very well. Unsophisticated investors can take risks they do not understand because of their complexity. Simpler financial instruments are likely to reduce uncertainty, although at the cost of less risk diversification. But benefits from risk diversification by complex financial instruments need to be weighed against great costs of systemic failures they can cause.

The relative advantage of the parsimonious simplicity of Islamic risk-sharing contracts becomes clearer when they are juxtaposed against derivatives. A simple contract predicated on direct claims on real goods and services is less ambiguous for both the lender and the borrower because the parties know first-hand who owes what to whom and how claims and obligations will be adjusted to realized outcomes according to the rules. Islamic rules prohibit derivatives because they are not predicated on direct claims on real goods and services. If further risk sharing is desired, more parties may be involved directly in the contract subject to the same rules, and each party knows the claims and obligations of other parties. The clearinghouse is the contract.

The stock market is an example. While large and impersonal, the stock market pools adequate information about the distribution of direct claims on assets representing real goods and services. Listed companies, subject to shareholder approval, can issue more stock or reduce outstanding stock and adjust dividend payments as it suits their profitability and risk diversification purposes. Risks are directly shared ex ante and ex post. Participation in the stock market is not prohibited under the Islamic rules, and there are active markets in most predominantly Islamic countries.

Economic Development, Financial Stability, and Contractual Forms: A Historical Perspective

Kuran's (2011) remarkable thesis about the historical inadaptability of Islamic contractual forms deserves due attention. Kuran asserts that, following the maturation of Islamic contractual forms to accommodate large-scale exchange and trade along with the expanding global reach of Muslim countries, those forms exhibited little evolution for centuries. Islamic contractual forms remained personal in nature, unable to outlive the original investors, which deterred long-term capital accumulation on a large scale. Shari'ah-based inheritance laws, providing for division of accumulated capital between many heirs and claimants, became a hindrance to more permanent capital accumulation. In short, those contractual forms were unable to adapt to perform the basic function attributed to strong institutions of providing incentives for capital accumulation and investment. In contrast, in the West, new contractual forms (such as corporate law) and inheritance laws were developed to facilitate innovative techniques of industrial organization that accommodated and incentivized impersonal and large-scale risk pooling, long-term capital accumulation, and investment. This path-dependent "long divergence" led to the less developed state of Muslim economies relative to the West as an unintended but incrementally cascading consequence of Islamic law over many centuries.

Kuran's thesis invites a counterpoint. Impersonal contractual and organizational forms appear to be intrinsically prone to economic crises by creating informational requirements that cannot be resolved even by the most advanced information flows in modern markets. The history of Western economies based on contractual forms that have enabled growth is replete with frequent and disastrous crises. Kuran marks the beginning of modern economic growth around 1750. Accordingly, a reasonable conjecture is that industrialization in the West emerges as of the beginning of the nineteenth century and the economic rise of the West relative to the predominantly Muslim countries gains momentum around 1800, with that disparity growing well into the twentieth century. On the history of banking crises, Carmen Reinhart and Kenneth Rogoff (2009, appendix A.3, 344–47) report the data summarized in table 3.1.

From 1800 to 1914, all banking crises are in non-Muslim countries and mostly in those that now make up the top list of high-income Western industrial countries (others include the remaining Western European industrial countries of today and Canada). The top five high-income non-Muslim countries are the largest Western economies, where impersonal contractual forms and large-scale industrial organization were developed early on. The United States scores 10 crises (every 12 years), the United Kingdom scores 9 crises (every 13 years), and France scores 7 crises (every 16 years). Germany, a relatively late bloomer in industrialization, scores 3 crises (every 11 years) from 1880 to 1914. Another late bloomer, Japan, scores 3 crises (every five years) from 1901 to 1914. Including other high-income countries, there were 55 crises from 1800 to 1914. On average, that corresponds to a crisis about every two years (25 months).

Table 3.1 Banking Crises in Predominantly Muslim and Non-Muslim Countries, 1800–2008

Historical periods	Number of crises 1800–2008	Number of crises 1800–1979	Number of crises 1800–1914	Number of crises 1915–29	Number of crises 1930–69	Number of crises 1970–79	Number of crises[b] 1980–2008
Years in period	209	180	115	15	40	10	29
Total	285	137	73	23	32	9	148
Muslim[a]	25	1	0	0	1	0	24
High-income	0	0	0	0	0	0	0
Middle-income	14	1	0	0	1	0	13
Low-income	11	0	0	0	0	0	11
Non-Muslim	260	136	73	23	31	9	124
High-income	124	89	55	14	16	4	35
France	9	8	7	0	1	0	1
United Kingdom	15	11	9	0	1	1	4
United States	12	10	10	0	0	0	2
Germany	6	6	3	1	1	1	0
Italy	10	9	6	1	2	0	1
Japan	6	5	3	2	0	0	1
Other	66	40	17	10	11	2	26
Middle-income	100	41	16	7	14	4	59
Low-income	36	6	2	2	1	1	30

Average number of months between crises								
Historical periods	1800–2008	1800–1979	1800–1914	1915–29	1930–69	1970–79	1980–2008
Months in period	2,508	2,160	1,380	180	480	120	348
Total	9	16	19	8	15	13	2
Muslim[a]	100	–	–	–	–	–	15
High-income	–	–	–	–	–	–	–
Middle-income	179	–	–	–	–	–	27
Low-income	228	–	–	–	–	–	32
Non-Muslim	10	16	19	8	15	13	3
High-income	20	24	25	13	30	30	10
Middle-income	25	53	86	26	34	30	6
Low-income	70	360	690	90	480	120	12

In percent of total								
			1980–2008					
Historical periods	Number of crises 1800–2008	Number of crises 1800–1979	Number of crises	Number of countries	Number of crises	Number of countries	Average per capita income, 2008[c]	World Bank Governance Index, 2008[d]
Total	100	100	100	100			12,500	49
Muslim[a]	9	1	16	17	100	100	3,114	33
High-income	0	0	0	0	0	0	–	–
Middle-income	5	1	9	8	54	47	5,693	38
Low-income	4	0	7	9	46	53	793	28

table continues next page

The Foundational Market Principles of Islam, Knightian Uncertainty, and Economic Justice

Table 3.1 Banking Crises in Predominantly Muslim and Non-Muslim Countries, 1800–2008 *(continued)*

			In percent of total					
				1980–2008			Average per capita income, 2008[c]	World Bank Governance Index, 2008[d]
Historical periods	Number of crises 1800–2008	Number of crises 1800–1979	Number of crises	Number of countries	Number of crises	Number of countries		
Non-Muslim	91	99	84	83	100	100	14,439	52
High-income	44	65	24	27	28	33	36,895	83
Middle-income	35	30	40	32	48	38	5,527	45
Low-income	13	4	20	24	24	29	1,039	27

Sources: Reinhart and Rogoff 2009, appendix A.3, 344–47; World Bank; Organization of Islamic Cooperation for percentage of Muslim population in total; and authors' calculations.

a. Countries with a Muslim population of 60 percent or more in total. For both Muslim and non-Muslim countries high-, middle-, and low-income categories are based on the following World Bank definition: high income is greater than $12,276 per capita; middle income is between $1,006 and $12,275 per capita; and low income is less than $1,005 per capita. "–" indicates zero or near zero crises during the period.
b. Excludes two high-income countries (one Muslim, one non-Muslim) that are oil producers with small populations from the total number of crises; each had one crisis, so their exclusion does not appreciably bias the results.
c. In current U.S. dollars. "–" indicates that available data are not presented because no crisis is reported for a high-income Muslim country during the periods examined.
d. Higher number indicates better quality; simple average of six governance categories: voice and accountability; political stability; government effectiveness; regulatory quality; rule of law; and, control of corruption. "–" indicates that available data are not presented because no crisis is reported for a high-income Muslim country during the periods examined.

When the non-Muslim low- and middle-income countries that inherited or adopted Western contractual forms and market institutions (no doubt in varying degrees of effectiveness) are included, the number of crises rises to 73, corresponding to one crisis every 19 months. A predominantly Muslim country, Turkey (classified as middle-income then), makes its debut in 1931, after adopting most Western financial and contractual forms following the foundation of the Republic in 1923 and even earlier in the decades before by the Ottoman Empire. The picture is essentially the same during the 1800–1979 period. Nearly 100 percent of bank crises occur in non-Muslim countries, with high-income countries accounting for 65 percent of them.

But the picture changes dramatically from 1980 to 2008. There were 24 crises in low- and middle-income Muslim countries, which accounts for 16 percent of the total number of crises, corresponding to one crisis every 15 months. This is the period when banking sector reforms and liberalization were undertaken by Muslim countries through integration with the Western financial markets and consolidation of the Western banking standards and practices. During that period, non-Muslim low- and middle-income countries score 89 crises, which accounts for about 60 percent of crises, corresponding to one about every four months. For these countries as well, this was the period of financial sector reform and liberalization and integration with mature financial markets. Mature markets—high-income non-Muslim countries—also had their share of woes during this period. They score 35 crises, amounting to 24 percent of total, or one crisis every 10 months.

On the scale of World Bank Worldwide Governance Indicators, mature markets display by far the highest institutional quality compared to Muslim and non-Muslim middle-income countries from 1980 to 2008. The same is true for some indicators of financial development. Nevertheless, mature markets' share in crises is higher than the Muslim countries' share.[25] It appears that mature markets also have some reforming to do to improve financial stability, including reforms to correct some flaws in the prevalent contractual forms that govern modern financial markets, as observed in the course of the financial reforms undertaken in the United States following the 2007–09 financial crisis.

The data are not controlled for many important factors, such as the degree of banking sector liberalization, capital mobility, exchange rate stability, fiscal and external balances, oil-rich Muslim countries' ability to avert banking crises with their vast financial resources, and so on (Reinhart and Rogoff provide a brief background). But the data permit an informed judgment: The high frequency of banking crises points to a systemically crisis-prone nature in impersonal large-scale financial institutions and underlying contractual forms that have evolved in the West and have subsequently been adopted by Muslim countries. Living dangerously has its rewards and punishments, as Muslim countries learned later.

From 1980 to 2008, Muslim and non-Muslim countries' shares in crises and in the country count are not appreciably different. Again the caveat applies that this comparison is unrefined because it does not control for many other factors that underlie banking crises. But it strongly suggests that religion has *not* been a significant factor in banking crises in the last three decades. The cause of crises is institutional. Financial practices and institutions developed in the West have been adopted or inherited by both Muslim and non-Muslim low- and middle-income countries in varying degrees of effectiveness in the course of their economic development. In the last two to three decades, those countries have become much more integrated and consolidated their financial arrangements and instruments with mature markets. Consequently, active financial markets in both middle-income Muslim and non-Muslim countries have emerged, attracting significant financial capital from global markets. Many of the middle-income Muslim and non-Muslim countries in the sample are emerging markets. Evidently those countries have also inherited or adopted something else: financial instability. The impersonal nature of financial markets and underlying contractual forms that enable large-scale risk and capital pooling and hence economic development appear to be systemically prone to financial crises in both predominantly Muslim and non-Muslim countries.

Broadly, the data point to a trade-off between benefits from the development of complex financial instruments and underlying contractual forms and great costs of the systemic failures they can cause. Innovations in modern contractual forms based on Islamic principles that exhort ex ante and ex post risk sharing and personal liability—at least at the managerial level—may help improve financial stability and decrease moral hazard in making high-risk bets with other people's personal money entrusted in impersonal fiduciary responsibility and due diligence. Such innovations may have global economic value.

Risk Sharing Rules and Financial Crises

Predatory competition in financial markets is not a barbaric relic of the past. The financial crisis that erupted in 2007–09 shows how in various ways—previously unimagined, much less predicted—economic agents, and even regulators, were fooled by those who had asymmetric information. The belatedly well-known examples are creative bookkeeping to mask off-balance sheet liabilities; collusion between the rated and rating agencies; oblivious indifference of regulators to fulfilling their public fiduciary responsibilities and mandated duties; outright fraud; and, last but not least, the outright failure of market professionals and their sophisticated methodologies to assess derivative risks associated with complex financial products and their reckless marketing, taking advantage of investors' trust. A fundamental cause of the 2007–09 financial crisis is the negligent, immoral, even criminal behavior of some actors. This is a breach of fiduciary responsibility and trust, with obvious disastrous consequences. It is not compatible with the commonly shared morals that guide economic behavior across many cultures and faiths. A lot of valuable social capital was lost in that financial crisis.[26]

Industrial organization in the form of corporations shields shareholders and managers from personal liability under bankruptcy laws. In Knight's sense, "grouping" through corporate organization "shifts" uncertainty to specialists and promotes informed risk taking and investment. But most corporate shareholders are passive participants, and they are not knowledgeable in managing the large entity in which they are invested. Does the corporation also promote excessive risk taking by managers with other peoples' money?[27] Can a measure of ex ante and ex post personal liability for managers be an effective safeguard against crises and lower their frequency? There are compelling arguments for self-regulation in financial markets and against government regulation whose unintended consequence may be stifling financial innovation, apparently reflecting public regulators' inability to keep apace with market developments. If so, can contractual forms of ex ante and ex post risk sharing be more effective and less costly in ensuring economic stability than top-down regulation and ex post litigation?

Such questions have been widely debated following the recent crisis in the process of formulating the sadly ex post financial reform legislation in the United States. The fundamental themes include: letting financial firms bear the costs of bankruptcy and liquidation instead of bailing them out with taxpayer money, since taxpayers are not direct participants to failed investments; discouraging excessive (fictitious?) financial expansion before it becomes too big to fail; limiting the increasing complexity of financial instruments that obfuscates the value of direct claims on investment; transparency and accountability for derivative trading to prevent managers from making enormous bets with other peoples' money; claw-back of manager compensation in the event of egregious failure of judgment in risk taking in order to shift performance evaluation focus from short-term reward for short-term profit to long-term reward for long-term success in ensuring growth and stability; directly bearing at least a minimum margin of credit risk (5 percent or more) for marketing asset-backed securities to third parties; and prohibiting bank participation in third-party investments using the money of depositors who are not direct parties to such investments (the Volker Rule). The main thrust of those themes is urging direct ex post liability and accountability for risks taken ex ante.

Moral Commitment to Contracts and Arrow-Debreu Securities

If contracts could prespecify terms to mitigate all future contingencies by means of Arrow-Debreu type of risk-sharing securities (see chapter 1), then risks would be allocated efficiently among market participants in accordance to the risk-bearing ability or risk preference of each participant (Arrow 1971). We observe an interesting theoretical convergence between the economic function of moral commitment to contracts and Arrow-Debreu securities. Moral commitment provides a normative solution for resolving uncertainty, while the Arrow-Debreu conjecture provides a positivist solution to the satisfaction of the axioms of the utilitarian paradigm. It can be argued that derivative Arrow-Debreu securities can be created to eliminate risk on risk of breach of contract on contract, and so on, ad infinitum. We think such a conjecture of a fractal of contracts on contracts to cover risks on risks is *not* simply a technical matter that can be resolved by taking the limit to infinity in order to establish a theoretical equilibrium in uncertainty. In reality, Zeno makes it to the end of his run. Economic agents strike incomplete contracts, and the economy moves on within the practical finitude of assessing future contingencies in finite time. Ultimately, as incomplete as it may be, it is trust that reduces substantive uncertainty to a practical level that can be resolved by procedural rationality.[28]

Decision Flexibility and Uncertainty

The economic value of flexibility in investment decisions has been recognized in the literature. Koopmans (1964) notes that, in real life, a sequential decision problem is never realized in full detail as a completely spelled-out program. Future opportunity sets cannot be anticipated in full detail because of uncertainty. An early discussion of economically significant benefits from flexibility is by Marschak and Nelson (1962). They argue that flexibility comes at a cost, such as the cost of accepting lower payoffs or the cost of delaying some payoffs into the future. They propose a measure of flexibility in decision making according to which the more the decision maker expects to learn from each decision outcome, the more she values flexibility. Sequential decision programs are ambiguous over time, and more so as the time horizon becomes longer. Along those lines, Kreps (1992, 1999) points out that learning from the consequences of a particular decision may diminish ambiguity over time.

Dixit and Pyndick (1994) emphasize that most investments take considerable time to implement and investment decisions are often irreversible: at least, significant costs are associated with reversal that may exceed the cost of waiting. Furthermore, multistage investments cannot be implemented all at once, and such investments may stall at least for a time or even be abandoned. Investments are compound prospects. Splitting multistage investments, or implementing them as segmented decisions over time, as opposed to once-and-for-all decisions with an ex ante commitment for the entire time horizon, gives investors the option of continuing or halting or abandoning an investment to hedge against uncertainty over time, and decision makers may be willing to pay for such flexibility. Flexibility has option value. Those authors conclude with the provocative observation that investment may be much less sensitive to interest rates and taxes than to uncertainty in the economic environment over time. We take the liberty of extending that conclusion by emphasizing that investment may be much less sensitive to interest rates and tax policies than to trust.

We have already referred to Kuran's (2004a) observations on decision flexibility in business contracts under Islamic law. Islamic contractual forms with ex ante and ex post risk sharing allow for decision flexibility and a formal framework for renegotiation in the face of unanticipated outcomes, as uncertainty is resolved.

Economic Justice in the Islamic Context and Uncertainty

Environed as we are by risks and perils, which befall us misfortunes, no man of us is in a position to say: 'I…am sure… I shall never need aid and sympathy.' At the very best, one of us fails in one-way and another, if we do not fail altogether. Therefore the man under the (falling) tree is the one of us who for the moment is smitten. It may be you tomorrow, and I the next day. It is the common frailty in the midst of a common peril, which gives us a kind of solidarity of interest to rescue the one for whom the chances of life have turned out badly just now.

William Graham Sumner (*What Social Classes Owe Each Other*, 1883, 158)[29]

We observe an interconnection between Knightian uncertainty and the veil of ignorance conjecture advanced by John Rawls in his seminal work, *A Theory of Justice* (1972). Rawls's core argument is the following: Given an initial stratum of income distribution (the "*original position*") in which income is distributed unequally between members of the society, under the veil of ignorance—uncertainty about one's relative position in the original income stratum—rational self-seeking individuals will vote unanimously to establish the lexicographic redistribution rule. That rule stipulates that income of those at the highest rung of the stratum is to be distributed to those at the lowest rung until income of all individuals is equalized. Unanimous vote is the result of rational behavior, with freedom of choice to the satisfaction of the utilitarian paradigm.

Rawls's conjecture has been critiqued along three main lines.[30] First, some individuals might surmise to some extent that they are at the higher rungs of the initial income stratum even under the veil of ignorance. If a modicum of such information exists, real or imagined, those individuals must be extremely risk-averse to vote for the lexicographic rule. Second, the rule violates fundamental property rights on which the free enterprise system is based, and those rights cannot be subject to popular vote on moral and constitutional grounds. Finally, equalization of income according to the rule may create severe incentive effects that stifle economic growth and progress. Those critiques provide a framework for our discussion of the fundamental prescriptions of the Qur'an concerning economic justice.

Extreme Risk Aversion

The veil of ignorance conjecture should be evaluated not in the context of prespecified risk but in the context of Knightian uncertainty or even of complete ignorance (Hogarth and Kunreuther 1997). In the static sense, unless voters are somehow completely erased of the memory of their original relative income position, the veil of ignorance is an unrealistic conjecture. But in the dynamic sense, that conjecture gains credence because voters face ambiguity about their relative position in states that are far in the future. Theoretically, it seems immaterial how far the future is because the lexicographic rule will presumably apply forever, if adopted. The usual assumption in dynamic optimization models is that agents care as much for their descendents' welfare as theirs. Descendants of the aristocracy, even descendants of defunct royal dynasties, sometimes join the ranks of the working classes. Presumably, the extreme risk aversion critique is in reference to some knowable probability distribution of the relative income positions of voters, now and into an indefinite future. This is unrealistic in Knightian uncertainty. In the dynamic context, that critique is not well placed. The issue is not risk aversion but ambiguity aversion, which can explain some economic behavior without resorting to an extreme degree of risk aversion that is difficult to justify (such as the equity premium puzzle).[31] Therefore, the veil of ignorance conjecture can be better substantiated in reference to Knightian uncertainty.

The lexicographic rule is the fundamental and arguably the intemporal covenant of Rawls's theory of economic justice. But motivating the unanimous vote for that rule on the basis of self-seeking rational behavior puts a wedge between rational and moral aspects of human decision-making. If humans have an innate capacity for morals, as Gigerenzer (2007) argues, the evolution of that capacity likely reflects uncertainty about who might need whose charity and justice now or in the future. If this "moral grammar" can be described by rules-of-thumb, those rules-of-thumb can be described to a significant extent by rules-of-faith ordained by Islam and other religions. Islam ordains commitment to charity and justice. That is the intemporal covenant of economic justice accepted by the faithful. From their perspective, the individual's and his descendents' future economic positions are knowable only to Allah. But uncertainty is reduced by moral behavior in reference to the Islamic rules under the covenant that charity will meet with charity in this life or in the afterlife.

Redistribution of Wealth as a Violation of Basic Property Rights

According to the Islamic rules, a rather strong but flexible framework emerges to define economic justice in juxtaposition to property rights. All individuals are entitled to the resources and riches created by the Law Giver, who is the ultimate owner. Wealth and property must not be hoarded or wasted, but must be used in the service of society through investment and circulation in the market. Temporal wealth is to be shared through voluntary transfers (*sadaqah*) in general and the specifically ordained transfers (*zakat*). Compliance with the rules governing property rights, particularly sharing, cleanses the property of the rights of others and renders property claims inviolate and sacred. Thus, redistribution of wealth according to the prescribed rules does *not* violate property rights under Islamic law. The rules of property rights and redistribution are not negotiable and cannot be subject to vote by the faithful under Islamic prescriptions, much like Nozick's (1974) critique that fundamental property rights cannot be subject to vote on moral and constitutional grounds. Islam leaves free will in the hands of the individual to accept or decline the prescribed rules for redistribution of wealth at her own merit or peril at the final judgment of Allah.

Adverse Incentive Effects of Wealth Redistribution

The Qur'an implicitly exhorts that an economic system should generate growth and prosperity. In application, the Messenger's implementations were designed to facilitate that purpose. But the objective of an Islamic system is first and foremost social and economic justice served by full rule-compliance. The ordained rule for wealth redistribution is *zakat*, which is *not* charity but one of the Five Pillars of Islam that *must* be observed by all believers. *Zakat* prescribes that social insurance be extended to all members of society, regardless of familial, tribal, ethnic, or religious affiliation.[32] In this manner, the risk of reversals of fortune is more broadly shared. Paying for expenses that enable the needy to earn a living counts toward *zakat* (education of underprivileged children; medical expenses of those who cannot afford them; seed money to start a business for those who cannot access financing; paying for food for the needy; voluntary work). It bears repeating that wealth transfers through *sadaqah* in general and *zakat* in particular redeem the rights of the needy in the income and wealth of the economically more able as a corollary of the Islamic principles of property rights.

Prescribed for all faithful of means, *zakat* may well be the first of its kind as an institutionalized form of social insurance at a time when none other than familial and tribal association provided security for the individual, excluding charity at the mercy of others. Before the advent of Islam, those insured by tribal affiliation benefitted from the mutuality of such insurance, but it might not reliably extend to the indigent who did not belong to a tribe or to those who were excommunicated. *Zakat* may even be interpreted as a flat-rate social security tax earmarked for redistribution of wealth. Schiller (2003) and McCleary and Barro (2006) note that *zakat* was a rudimentary but novel form of social insurance at the time the Messenger received the revelation. Kuran (2003) argues that *zakat* may have been a functional social safety net in an economic system based on personal exchange to the extent the system was in the Messenger's time. Kuran further argues that contemporary market economies are based on a system of impersonal exchange, and redistribution is carried out through large-scale and impersonal social safety nets established through legislation and financed by taxation. Thus, *zakat* is *not* an effective institution of income redistribution on a large scale in modern economies.

Interpretation of *zakat* as charity rather than an ordained instrument of wealth redistribution is one reason for the stagnation of its historical evolution as an effective social safety net in contemporary economies. However, if *zakat* were properly considered as a tax earmarked for redistribution of wealth based on the doctrinal principle of Islam, it could mobilize resources on a large scale similar to a social security tax (Kahf 1997). Islamic rules by no means prohibit large-scale organization of income redistribution and poverty relief by the hand of the state utilizing taxation, welfare payments, health care assistance, subsidies, and other transfers. At present, such institutional arrangements exist in most Muslim countries. However, impersonal welfare institutions, while by-and-large functional under legal sanctions, do not seem to inspire a personal spirit of sharing, perhaps precisely for the reason that they are impersonal. Taxpayers appear reluctant to pay personally for impersonal transfers. Donors to charity appear more motivated by causes for which they have a personal concern, notwithstanding the appeal of tax deductions that lower their marginal tax rates in many cases. But adherence to *zakat* motivated by faith can perform an important function at the personal level in contemporary Muslim countries. This function of *zakat* can be ignored, as much as charity can be ignored in modern economies, although *zakat* is not charity but is ordained.[33]

Market economies predicated on private property and free enterprise cannot thrive without protections for property rights and without rewards to individual effort and entrepreneurship. As wealth is redistributed, the collateral impact on incentives for innovation and investment may be so adverse that the society ends up with more equally distributed but less total wealth over time. We are reminded of the failure of command economies ostensibly aiming at income equality, while creating very little incentive for hard work and innovation. Islam does not prescribe that temporal wealth is to be divided equally between the rich and the poor. From the point of view of the donor, this view addresses the problem of adverse incentive effects that curb wealth accumulation. As noted, wealth is to be shared not only through prescribed and voluntary giving but also by enabling those who are not able to access resources or work or education. So, the rules also address disincentives to work effort by encouraging and enabling work and enterprise to overcome deprivation and poverty. In this sense, *zakat* has a "workfare" aspect. This view of economic justice appears to be incentives-based, aiming at harmonizing economic justice with incentives. That harmonization is one of the fundamental issues that preoccupy the contemporary public finance and labor economics literature, as well as the political discourse on taxation, welfare, health care, and other transfer schemes.

Research Agenda for Islamic Economics: A Proposal

The broad consensus in Islamic economics is that the Islamic economic principles are conducive to economic development and they can establish a moral market order, if applied. However, a cacophony of divergent views on operational specifics has directed the focus of critique of Islamic economics to the applicability of some Islamic market principles in modern markets.[34] The debate reflects literalist reading of the codex of market rules instituted during the Messenger's time based on guidance from the Qur'an, as well as of the catechisms attributed to the Messenger by tradition (*fiqh*). But undue focus on literalist views makes for literalist critique. There may be some merit to literalist critique because it may serve to disabuse some students of Islamic economics of the notion that literalist views must be strictly applicable in modern markets. On the other hand, literalist critique narrows the scope of comparative analysis of alternative market rules and institutional arrangements by utilizing the tools of modern economics. An analogy is the role of quantum physics in enabling a better understanding of the origins of the universe—but one wonders to what extent quantum physics can concern itself with the literalist views of creation. Literalist critique of literalist views of creation by flagging the so immodestly named "God particle" (Higgs boson) cannot be fruitful. At the literalist level, there can be no meaningful debate that enhances either the philosophy of science or the philosophy of religion. Similarly, literalist debate cannot contribute to robust research in Islamic economics by the standards of the modern discipline.

The burden of critical research utilizing the tools of modern economics falls on the discipline of Islamic economics, if it is to make contributions to economic literature with universal appeal. There is an acute need for critical focus on specific questions that challenge the Islamic economic principles in modern markets at the analytical level. A critical approach will also be instrumental in developing institutions that are operational in modern markets and in harmony with the Islamic principles. It is likely that innovations suggested by critical analysis will meet with resistance from the literalists. But it is also likely that such innovations will find wide acceptance among those who subscribe to the Islamic market principles and wish them applied in modern markets. It is even possible that some lessons emerge to serve as innovations that can improve conventional market arrangements.

At various junctures in this study, we have proposed some areas of research, including experimental examination of economic behavior in reference to religion, the significance of faith-based references in decision making in uncertainty, and efficacy and stability of Islamic contracts based on direct property claims with ex post and ex ante risk sharing. We think those areas, and myriad others that have not occurred to us, make for important testable hypotheses for research that can enhance the corpus of Islamic economics and teach lessons to improve Islamic market arrangements.

Concluding Remarks

A general case can be made for the economic relevance of faith-based rules. In particular, the foundational Islamic market principles provide a rule-based institutional framework that is conducive to economic development. They protect private property rights and freedom of exchange. They address uncertainty by ordaining adherence to contractual obligations and other rules for preferred market behavior. The rules for ex ante and ex post risk sharing address the vulnerability of incomplete contracts to unpredictable events and they may guard against financial instability. The rules aim at harmonizing incentives with economic justice by ordaining wealth sharing and enabling market access by the poor.

The fundamentals of economic decline in Muslim countries are richly variegated in their vast complexity and uniqueness in different historical contexts. Our line of analysis suggests moral and institutional decay as a significant reason for the decline. There are supporting hypotheses. Chapra (2010) suggests that a significant cause of the economic decline is path-dependency originating from violations of the Islamic rules in the first century following the Messenger's death. Kuran (2011) also emphasizes path-dependency as shaped by various historical circumstances that hindered the adaptation of the foundational Islamic market principles. Scheherazade Rehman and Hossein Askari (2010) have developed an index of adherence to the foundational principles. They find a low level of adherence in Islamic countries. Moreover, they note that their index indicates a higher level of adherence to those principles in the predominantly Christian developed countries (see chapter 11 in this volume).

The nature and causes of decline of wealth of Islamic nations have long preoccupied historians. That inquiry is likely to be on the research agenda for a long time to come. We hope for the welfare of the world that answers will inspire solutions.

Notes

1. Iannaccone (1998) provides a comprehensive review. More recent work includes qualitative studies by Kuran (2004a, 2004b, 2011) and McCleary (2007); and quantitative explorations by Barro and Mitchell (2003), Barro (2006), and McCleary and Barro (2006). Works on Islamic economics by other authors will be cited in the discussion that follows.
2. The Qur'an explicitly exhorts modesty in clothing. But the extent to which Muslim women are covered in different Islamic societies greatly varies from a modest headscarf to complete covering of hair and body; such variations from society to society indicate that orthopraxy may have a greater influence on covering than faith. This may also reflect variations in the interpretations of Islamic exhortations reflecting cultural differences between societies. Moreover, such orthopraxy is observed in both religious and secular behavior, such as the signature clothing of the Hassidic Jews, the business suit and tie, and fashionable clothing and hairstyles of *mode de jour*.
3. See http://www.worldvaluessurvey.org/.
4. Our expectation was formed along the lines of Guiso, Sapienza, and Zingales (2005), who found that trust in institutions and law had a favorable impact on some economic and financial outcomes in industrial countries.
5. Apparently in some support of the secularization hypothesis, for industrial countries (all non-Muslim), the index values including and excluding religion did not differ at all. Our finding for Muslim countries is not necessarily attributable to preference falsification by avowing false fealty to religion for purposes of social and political

correctness, motivated by, for example, potential gains from networking (Kuran 1995). The Islamic attitude to be content with whatever Allah has granted to individuals in His ineffable wisdom may be playing a significant role in the survey results concerning trust. An examination of this widely held Islamic attitude in relation to entrepreneurial behavior and risk taking might produce interesting results. In a recent study, Benjamin, Choi, and Fisher (2010) report experimental results on the impact of religious identity on risk behavior; among other things, they find that Catholicism decreases risk aversion. The set of religious identities they use does not include Islam.

6. For brevity, only the widely known seminal works and compilations in this area are cited here: on institutions, North (1991, 1993, 1994); on incomplete contracts, Williamson (1979, 1985, 2002); on behavior in uncertainty, Kahneman and Tversky (2000); Kahneman, Slovic, and Tversky (1999); on behavioral finance, Thaler (1993, 2005).

7. In the normative sense, we interpret *preferred* economic behavior as moral behavior. In the objective sense, we interpret preferred economic behavior as such behavior that reduces uncertainty and increases individual and social welfare, in the same way the concept is understood in welfare economics. In the latter sense, Heiner (1983) argues that the source of predictable behavior is uncertainty; behavioral rules arise because of uncertainty of distinguishing more preferred from less preferred behavior in market exchange. Such rules therefore have economic value.

8. In contrast, Iannaccone (1998, 1474–75) notes that some authors have argued that early Protestant theologians did not seem to understand markets; however, most were averse to credit and interest.

9. Arrow (1990) notes that rational expectations models are a stochastic variant of the neoclassical perfect foresight models. For a recent comprehensive critique of rational expectations hypothesis, see Frydman and Goldberg (2007); those authors underline that rational expectations hypothesis further assumes implicitly that the expectations technology of rational agents is not subject to innovation over time. We should add that rational expectations hypothesis seems to defer knowledge of only the final outcomes of human behavior in different ages and social contexts to the highest authority but, with a considerable measure of audacity, it assumes that the distributions of random error terms are known.

10. We will refer to Knightian uncertainty as *uncertainty* or *ambiguity*, and to simple measurable risk as *risk*. The term ambiguity, used by Ellsberg (1961), has a hold in the literature and will be familiar to most readers. The term *vagueness* is also used in philosophy, usually in reference to the impossibility of cognitive completeness. Uncertainty should be distinguished from ignorance, which implies complete lack of knowledge about possible future events; see Hogarth and Kunreuther (1997). Uncertainty falls between precisely known probabilities and ignorance.

11. The following excerpts are from Knight (2002, chapter 2), "Meaning of Risk and Uncertainty."

12. The statistician Bartholomew, in his book *God, Chance, and Purpose*, (2008, 200–30) notes: "The development of human freedom requires that there be sufficient space for that freedom to be exercised. Chance seems to provide just the flexibility required and therefore to be a precondition of free will. ... It could be plausibly argued that risk is a necessary ingredient for full human development. It provides the richness and diversity of experience necessary to develop our skills and personalities."

13. This observation is supported by recent research in neuroeconomics (Camerer, Loewenstein, and Prelec 2005; Zweig 2007); psychology (Gigerenzer 2007); and brain science (Linden 2007).
14. Evolutionary economics literature supports those observations (the seminal reference is Nelson and Winter 1982). The core argument is that broadly competitive market systems can emerge (but not necessarily) as a result of social and institutional evolution within the context of historical conditions, while procedurally rational economic agents can devise innovative means of exchange to improve efficiency without claim to the neoclassical axiom of universal rationality and Pareto optimality. Economic institutions evolve, but *not* necessarily in a progressive manner. Their evolution also reflects the evolution of human beliefs, preferences, norms, and practices.
15. For a review of the evidence from behavioral economics, see Camerer, Loewenstein, and Rabin (2004).
16. On various views on the impact of cultures on economic behavior and performance, see Harrison and Huntington (2000) and Harrison (2006). La Porta and others (1998) examine a fundamental institutional factor for the protection of equity holders: legal rules and their historical origins and enforcement. They provide evidence of a negative correlation between the concentration of equity ownership and investor protection, based on a sample of mature and emerging markets. Guiso, Sapienza, and Zingales (2005) define trust as the subjective probability of being cheated by equity issuers (corporate boards and managers) and by institutions that facilitate and regulate stock market participation (brokerage houses, hedge funds, regulatory and supervisory bodies). Subjective probability is partly determined by the characteristics of the financial system, including the quality of investor protection and its enforcement. Evidence indicates that low trust significantly accounts for low equity market participation and a low share of wealth invested in equity. In a more recent study, Algan and Cahuc (2010) find that inherited trust is a very significant determinant of per capita income, and evolution of trust also has an "economically tremendous" impact on income differences between industrial countries.
17. An example is the "ultimatum game." It involves one party sharing a monetary reward with another party. Broadly, fair sharing (in the range of 40–50 percent) is the most common result from experiments that prevails across cultures and between parties who do not know or are not likely to ever see each other again. Evidently, there is a human tendency for fairness. Faith-based rules elaborate on that tendency. On behavioral game theory, see Camerer (2003).
18. This is similar to motorists' observance of traffic rules facilitating efficient traffic flow, albeit incompletely, while sometimes violating them opportunistically, as much as they might not always be able to reason with many of those rules (the authors readily admit they do not understand the rationale behind many traffic rules).
19. Rees (2007) reports that 63 percent of International Chamber of Commerce (ICC) arbitration cases were settled in five countries (France, Singapore, Switzerland, the United Kingdom, and the United States) in 2004. In a remarkable historical parallel, Kuran (2004a) notes that before the eighteenth century (that is, before the evolution of contractual forms in adaptation to industrial and financial development in the West), non-Muslims living in the countries where Islamic law applied preferred contracts under Islamic law, even though they had the option of resorting to the ecclesiastic law of their denominations. This reflected, among other things, the more reliable contract enforcement and flexibility under Islamic law, which allowed for business partners to decide on profit shares and renegotiate terms of business contracts any

time during the partnership as events unfolded. The economic significance of decision flexibility in uncertainty is discussed below.

20. Here, only the broad Islamic rules for contracts and contractual behavior are outlined in relation to the basics of contemporary contract theory. Review of specific Islamic contractual forms is outside the scope of this study. The general outline above borrows from Hart and Holmstrom (1987), Kenney and Klein (1983), and Goldberg (1985). Madsen (1999) provides a comprehensive review of the main issues in modern contract theory.

21. *The New York Times*, "Biggest Defaulters on the Mortgages Are the Rich," July 8, 2010, http://www.nytimes.com/2010/07/09/business/economy/09rich.html?pagewanted=all.

22. Schiller (2008) points out that insurance against decline in housing values is scant. There is a missing market; if it existed, it might prevent decline of neighborhoods. A significant reason why such insurance markets are missing might be market failure because the price of the financial instrument cannot be determined ex ante in ambiguity. See Kunreuther and others (1995) on underwriter behavior in ambiguity. Erbaş and Sayers (2006) provide evidence that non-life insurance coverage in a cross-section of countries is very significantly correlated with institutional quality as a proxy for uncertainty.

23. A report by the Joint Economic Committee of the U.S. Congress (2009) documents various predatory lending practices, including large late payment penalties (reported at an estimated $20.5 billion in 2009 by CreditCards.com), the high cost of switching from high interest to low interest credit cards, and arbitrary rate increases of as much as 8–20 points higher than the current rate the card holder is paying. The recent financial sector reform delegates supervision of such practices to the Consumer Financial Protection Bureau. According to *The Survey of Consumer Finances, 2004–2007* (U.S. Federal Reserve Board 2009) in 2007, credit card debt made up 3.5 of total consumer debt. With increasing bankruptcies due to the recession, default risk has risen, passed on to debt holders in good standing by charging them higher rates, on average. The national Annual Percentage Rate (APR) currently stands at about 15 percent, rising to nearly 25 percent for borrowers with bad credit histories. A survey by Garcia and Wheary (2011) shows that, in 2008, low-income to middle-income family median credit card debt was $5,000 and mean debt was $9,800; more than 50 percent of such families had been late or missed a payment and had experienced an increase in their credit card debt relative to three years earlier.

24. For example, there are futures contracts that enable ex post risk sharing by specifying a range of exchange rate deviation from the strike rate.

25. This is surprising to us and calls for more in-depth research than we can provide here. Some financial development indicators are significantly correlated with Worldwide Governance Indicators (Erbaş and Mirakhor 2010; Erbaş and Sayers 2006). As table 3.1 shows, the level of economic development, as measured by per capita income, is also significantly correlated with those indicators.

26. The columnist David Brooks tells of (and we hope he does not foretell) a doomsday scenario in which economic malaise persists despite recapitalization and fiscal spending by the U.S. government at unprecedented levels. The scenario has it that the psychology of uncertainty results in a shift from a high-trust to a low-trust society. In this dystopian world, economists and policy makers are helpless because they can think only in terms of "economic models with primitive views of human behavior" (*The New York Times*, Op-Ed, February 13, 2009).

27. The U.S. *Financial Crisis Inquiry Report* (National Commission 2011) relates many cautionary tales from the recent crisis about managerial behavior; in particular, see chapter 10, entitled "Madness."
28. Arrow (1972) argues: "It [is] possible that the process of exchange requires or at least is greatly facilitated by the presence of several...virtues (not only truth, but also trust, loyalty, and justice in future dealings)." Arrow goes on to discuss the impact of those virtues on economic efficiency through creation of positive externalities. "The virtue of truthfulness in fact contributes in a very significant way to the efficiency of the economic system...Ethical behavior can be regarded as a socially desirable institution which facilitates the achievement of economic efficiency in a broad sense." He continues: "The price system is not, and perhaps in some basic sense cannot be universal. To the extent that it is incomplete, it must be supplemented by an implicit or explicit social contract" (345–57). Arrow's observations become more substantiated in Knightian uncertainty, in which even efficient price discovery might not be possible without moral market behavior and social trust—hence the missing markets. Against conventional wisdom, it seems ironic that social capital in the form of trust that is so difficult to price is so critical in price determination.
29. Quoted in Dryzek and Goodwin (1986).
30. There is a vast body of literature on Rawls's theory of economic justice. For an early exposition, see Phelps (1974). A well-known comprehensive critique is by Rawls's contemporary, the philosopher Nozick (1974), who first articulated these main lines of critique.
31. Ambiguity aversion is documented in various behavioral and neurological experiments; some related studies have already been cited. Erbaş and Mirakhor (2010) argue that ambiguity aversion can explain the equity premium puzzle without resorting to extreme degrees of risk aversion.
32. For similar Judaic teachings on just economic order, see chapter 4, "Justice: Commitment to a Culture of Justice and a Just Economic Order," in Küng and Homolka (2009).
33. In 2011, total federal expenditures in the United States on education, health care (Medicare), income security (welfare), and veterans benefits was budgeted at $1,178 billion and realized outcome was estimated at $1,267 billion (White House 2011). Total revenue and disbursements of the top 200 charities were respectively estimated at $84 billion and $77 billion (Forbes.com). The ratio of those charities' total revenue to total budgeted federal expenditure is 7.1 percent; the ratio of charities' total disbursements to total estimated actual federal expenditure is 6.1 percent. The share of federal expenditure in gross domestic product (GDP) is 8 percent and share of charity in GDP is 0.5 percent; charity's share is modest but significant. Those charities include Jewish and Christian charities that have about a 17 percent share in the total, so religion plays a significant motivational role in giving. The political and ideological polemic surrounding *zakat* notwithstanding, it can also play a significant role in income redistribution and poverty relief. It should be noted, however, that Kuran (2003) observes that *zakat* plays a negligible role in poverty alleviation in Muslim countries. Whether this reflects low compliance, an unaccounted share of private giving, or less effective public and private solicitation is unknown to us. We do not anticipate *zakat* telethons soon. However, there are Islamic-oriented networks that privately raise substantial sums on the basis of *zakat*.

34. For example, Kuran (2003) pertinently observes that divergent interpretations of Islamic economic rules create ambiguity to the detriment of market development, in the same sense as we have used the concept of ambiguity in this study. Our professional experience suggests that there is indeed some concern in financial markets about the ambiguity created by divergent judgments on the Shari'ah compliance of financial instruments being developed. The market for Islamic financial instruments is relatively new, but it is in the process of maturing in response to large demand. We observe an increasing convergence of injunctions on the fundamentals, such as injunctions on the operational design of exchange-based financial instruments and on the types of real assets against which those instruments may be collateralized.

References

Akerlof, George, and Rachel Kranton. 2010. *Identity Economics*. Princeton, NJ: Princeton University Press.

Algan, Yann, and Pierre Cahuc. 2010. "Inherited Trust and Growth." *American Economic Review* 100 (5): 2069–92.

Arrow, Kenneth. 1971. *Essays on the Theory of Risk-Bearing*. Chicago: Markham Publishing Company.

———. 1972. "Gifts and Exchanges." *Philosophy and Public Affairs* 1 (4): 343–62.

———. 1990. "Economic Theory and the Hypothesis of Rationality." In *Utility and Probability*, edited by John Eatwell, Murray Milgate, and Peter Newman, 25–37. New York: W. W. Norton and Company.

Barro, Robert. 2006. "Spirit of Capitalism: Religion and Economic Development." *Harvard International Review* 25 (4).

Barro, Robert, and Joshua Mitchell. 2003. "Religious Faith and Economic Growth: What Matters Most—Belief or Belonging?" *Heritage Lectures* 841 (June): 1–12.

Bartholomew, David. 2008. *God, Chance and Purpose*. Cambridge, U.K.: Cambridge University Press.

Benjamin, Daniel, James Choi, and Geoffrey Fisher. 2010. "Religious Identity and Economic Behavior." National Bureau of Economic Research Working Paper 15925, National Bureau of Economic Research, Cambridge, MA.

Bottéro, Jean. (1987) 2000. *Birth of God (Naissance de Dieu)*. University Park, PA: Pennsylvania State University Press. Citations refer to the 2000 edition.

Camerer, Colin. 2003. *Behavioral Game Theory, Experiments in Strategic Interaction*. New York: Russel Sage Foundation; Princeton, NJ: Princeton University Press.

Camerer, Colin, George Loewenstein, and Drazen Prelec. 2005. "Neuroeconomics: How Neuroscience Can Inform Economics." *Journal of Economic Literature* 43 (1): 9–64.

Camerer, Colin, George Loewenstein, and Matthew Rabin, eds. 2004. *Advances in Behavioral Economics*. New York: Russel Sage Foundation; Princeton, NJ: Princeton University Press.

Chapra, M. Umer. 2010. *Muslim Civilization: The Causes of Decline and the Need for Reform*. Leicestershire, U.K.: Islamic Foundation, Kube Publishing Ltd.

Cizakça, Murat. 2011. *Islamic Capitalism and Finance: Origins, Evolution and the Future*. Cheltenham, U.K.: Edward Elgar.

Dixit, Avinash, and Robert Pyndick. 1994. *Investment under Uncertainty*. Princeton, NJ: Princeton University Press.

Dryzek, John, and Robert Goodwin. 1986. "Risk Sharing and Social Justice: The Motivational Foundations of the Post-War Welfare State." *British Journal of Political Science* 16 (1): 1–34.

Ellsberg, Daniel. 1961. "Risk, Ambiguity, and the Savage Axioms." *Quarterly Journal of Economics* 75 (4): 643–69.

Erbaş, S. Nuri, and Abbas Mirakhor. 2010. "The Equity Premium Puzzle, Ambiguity Aversion, and Institutional Quality: Implications for Islamic Finance." *Journal of Islamic Economics, Banking and Finance* 6 (1): 37–86.

Erbaş, Nuri S., and Chera L. Sayers. 2006. "Institutional Quality, Knightian Uncertainty, and Insurability: A Cross-Country Analysis." *Infrastructure and Financial Markets Review* (previously *IFM Bulletin*), Inter-American Development Bank 12 (2): 1, 7–9.

Frydman, Roman, and Michael Goldberg. 2007. *Imperfect Knowledge Economics*. Princeton, NJ: Princeton University Press.

Garcia, Jose, and Jennifer Wheary. 2011. "Understanding the Debt Difference." http://www.Demos.org.

Gigerenzer, Gerd. 2007. *Gut Feelings: The Intelligence of the Unconscious*. New York: Viking Penguin Books.

Gilboa, Itzhak, Andrew Postlewaite, and David Schmeidler. 2009. "Is It Always Rational to Satisfy Savage's Axioms?" *Economics and Philosophy* 25: 285–96.

Goldberg, Victor. 1985. "Price Adjustment in Long-Term Contracts." *Wisconsin Law Review* 483 (1985): 527–43.

Guiso, Luigi, Paola Sapienza, and Luigi Zingales. 2005. "Trusting the Stock Market." National Bureau of Economic Research Working Paper 11648, National Bureau of Economic Research, Cambridge, MA.

Harrison, Lawrence E. 2006. *The Central Liberal Truth*. New York: Oxford University Press.

Harrison, Lawrence E., and Samuel P. Huntington. 2000. *Culture Matters: How Values Shape Human Progress*. New York: Basic Books.

Hart, Oliver, and Bengt Holmstrom. 1987. "The Theory of Contracts." In *Advances in Economic Theory*, edited by Truman R. Bewley, 369–98. Fifth World Congress. Cambridge, U.K.: Cambridge University Press.

Heiner, Ronald. 1983. "The Origin of Predictable Behavior." *American Economic Review* 73 (4): 560–95.

Hogarth, Robin, and Howard Kunreuther. 1997. "Decision Making Under Ignorance: Arguing with Yourself." In *Research on Judgment and Decision Making, Currents, Connections, and Controversies*, edited by William Goldstein and Robin Hogarth, 482–508. Cambridge, U.K.: Cambridge University Press.

Iannaccone, Laurence. 1998. "Introduction to the Economics of Religion." *Journal of Economic Literature* 36 (September): 1465–96.

Kahf, Monzer. 1997. "Instruments of Meeting Budget Deficits in Islamic Economy." Research Paper 42, Islamic Development Bank, Islamic Research and Training Institute, Jeddah, Saudi Arabia.

Kahneman, Daniel, Paul Slovic, and Amos Tversky, eds. 1999. *Judgment Under Uncertainty: Heuristics and Biases*. Cambridge, U.K.: Cambridge University Press.

Kahneman, Daniel, and Amos Tversky. 2000. *Choices, Values and Frames*. Cambridge, U.K.: Russel Sage Foundation and Cambridge University Press.

Kenney, Roy, and Benjamin Klein. 1983. "The Economics of Block Booking." *Journal of Law and Economics* 26 (3): 497–540.

Knight, Frank. (1921) 2002. *Risk, Uncertainty and Profit*. Washington, DC: Beard Books. Citations are to the 2002 edition.

Koopmans, Tjalling. 1964. "On Flexibility of Future Preference." In *Human Judgments and Optimality*, edited by Maynard W. Shelly II and Glenn L. Bryan, chapter 13. New York: John Wiley and Sons.

Kreps, David. 1992. "Static Choice in the Presence of Unforeseen Contingencies." In *Economic Analysis of Markets and Games: Essays in Honor of Frank Hahn*, edited by Partha Dasgupta, Douglas Gale, Oliver Hart, and Eric Maskin, 258–81. Cambridge, MA: MIT Press.

———. 1999. "Markets and Hierarchies and (Mathematical) Economic Theory." In *Firms, Markets and Hierarchies, A Transactions Cost Economics Perspective*, edited by Glenn Carrol and David Teece, 121–63. New York: Oxford University Press.

Küng, Hans, and Rabbi W. Homolka. 2009. *How to Do Good and Avoid Evil*. Woodstock, VT: Skylight Paths Publishing.

Kunreuther, Howard, Jacqueline Meszaros, Robin Hogarth, and Marc Spranca. 1995. "Ambiguity and Underwriter Decision Process." *Journal of Economic Behavior and Organization* 26: 337–52.

Kuran, Timur. 1995. *Private Truths, Public Lies: The Social Consequences of Preference Falsification*. Cambridge, MA: Harvard University Press.

———. 2003. "Islamic Redistribution through Zakat: Historical Record and Modern Realities." In *Poverty and Charity in Middle Eastern Contexts*, edited by Michael Bonner, Mine Ener, and Amy Singer, chapter 14. New York: State University of New York Press.

———. 2004a. "Why the Middle East Is Economically Underdeveloped: Historical Mechanisms of Institutional Stagnation." *Journal of Economic Perspectives* 18 (3): 71–90.

———. 2004b. *Islam and Mammon: The Economic Predicaments of Islamism*. Princeton, NJ: Princeton University Press.

———. 2011. *The Long Divergence: How Islamic Law Held Back the Middle East*. Princeton, NJ: Princeton University Press; New York: Oxford University Press.

La Porta, Rafael, Florencio Lopez-de-Silanes, Andrei Shleifer, and Robert W. Vishny. 1998. "Law and Finance." *Journal of Political Economy* 106 (6): 1113–55.

Linden, David. 2007. *The Accidental Mind*. Cambridge, MA: Belknap Press of Harvard University Press.

Madsen, Scott. 1999. "Contractual Choice." In *Encyclopedia of Law and Economics*, 25–45. Cheltenham, U.K.: Edward Elgar.

Marschak, Thomas, and Richard Nelson. 1962. "Flexibility, Uncertainty, and Economic Theory." *Metroeconomica* 14: 42–58.

McCleary, Rachel. 2007. "Salvation, Damnation, and Economic Incentives." *Journal of Contemporary Religion* 22 (1): 49–74.

McCleary, Rachel, and Robert Barro. 2006. "Religion and Economy." *Journal of Economic Perspectives* 20 (2): 49–72.

Mirakhor, Abbas. 2009. "Islamic Economics and Finance: An Institutional Perspective." *International Islamic University of Malaysia Journal of Economics and Management* 17 (1): 31–72.

———. 2010. "Whither Islamic Finance?" Paper presented at the Inaugural Malaysia Securities Commission and Oxford Center for Islamic Studies Conference, March 15.

Mirakhor, Abbas, and Idris Hamid. 2009. *Islam and Development: An Institutional Framework*. New York: Global Scholarly Publications.

Nelson, Richard, and Sydney Winter. 1982. *An Evolutionary Theory of Economic Change*. Cambridge, MA: Belknap Press of Harvard University Press.

North, Douglass. 1991. "Institutions." *Journal of Economic Perspectives* 5 (1): 97–112.

———. 1993. "Institutions and Economic Performance." In *Rationality, Institutions and Economic Methodology*, edited by Uskali Mäki, Bo Gustafson, and Christian Knudsen, 242–61. London: Rutledge.

———. 1994. "Economic Performance through Time." *American Economic Review* 84 (3): 359–68.

Nozick, Robert. 1974. *Anarchy, State and Utopia*. New York: Basic Books.

OIC (Organisation of Islamic Cooperation). http://www.infoplease.com/spot/oicstates1.html.

Phelps, Edmund, ed. 1974. *Economic Justice*. Penguin Modern Economics Readings. New York: Penguin Books.

Rawls, John. 1972. *A Theory of Justice*. Oxford, U.K.: Clarendon Press.

Rees, Peter. 2007. "The Conduct of International Arbitration in England: The Challenge Has Still To Be Met." *The Journal of the London Court of International Arbitration* 23 (3): 505–10.

Reilly, Robert R. 2010. *The Closing of the Muslim Mind*. Wilmington, DE: Intercollegiate Studies Institute (ISI) Books.

Rehman, Scheherazade, and Hossein Askari. 2010. "How Islamic Are Islamic Countries?" *Global Economy Journal* 10 (2): 1–30.

Reinhart, Carmen, and Kenneth Rogoff. 2009. *This Time Is Different, Eight Centuries of Financial Folly*. Princeton, NJ: Princeton University Press.

Rodrik, Dani, Arvind Subramanian, and Francesco Trebbi. 2002. "Institutions Rule: The Primacy of Institutions over Integration and Geography in Economic Development." Working Paper 02/189, International Monetary Fund, Washington, DC.

Sadr, Kazem. 1996. *The Economy of the Earliest Islamic Period*. Tehran: Shaheed Beheshti University.

Sargent, Thomas. 1993. *Bounded Rationality in Macroeconomics*. New York: Oxford University Press.

Schiller, Robert. 2003. *New Financial Order: Risk in the 21st Century*. Princeton, NJ: Princeton University Press.

———. 2008. *The Subprime Solution*. Princeton, NJ: Princeton University Press.

Shubik, Martin. 1978. "On the Concept of Efficiency." *Policy Science* 9 (2): 121–26.

Simon, Herbert. 1976. "From Substantive to Procedural Rationality." In *Method and Appraisal in Economics*, edited by Spiro J. Latsis, 129–48. Cambridge, U.K.: Cambridge University Press.

Sugden, Robert. 1989. "Spontaneous Order." *Journal of Economic Perspectives* 3 (4): 85–97.

Sumner, William. 1883. *What Social Classes Owe Each Other*. New York: Harper.

Tanzi, Vito. 2007. "Complexity and Systemic Failure." In *Transition and Beyond: Essays in Honor of Mario Nuti*, edited by Saul Estrin, Grzegorz Kolodko, and Milicia Uralic. New York: Palgrave.

Thaler, Richard, ed. 1993. *Advances in Behavioral Finance, Volume I*. New York: The Russel Sage Foundation.

———. 2005. *Advances in Behavioral Finance, Volume II*. New York: The Russel Sage Foundation; Princeton, NJ: Princeton University Press.

Thaler, Richard, and Cass Sunstein. 2008. *Nudge: Improving Decisions about Health, Wealth and Happiness*. New Haven, CT: Yale University Press.

Tversky, Amos, and Daniel Kahneman. 1999. "Casual Schemas in Judgments under Uncertainty." In *Judgment Under Uncertainty: Heuristics and Biases*, edited by Daniel Kahneman, Paul Slovic, and Amos Tversky, 117–28. Cambridge, U.K.: Cambridge University Press.

United States, Federal Reserve Board. 2009. *The Survey of Consumer Finances, 2004–2007*. http://www.federalreserve.gov/econresdata/scf/scfindex.htm.

United States, Joint Economic Committee, U.S. Congress. 2009. *Vicious Cycle: How Unfair Credit Card Practices are Squeezing Consumers and Undermining the Recovery*. Washington, DC (May 12).

United States, National Commission on the Causes of the Financial and Economic Crisis in the United States. 2011. *The Financial Crisis Inquiry Report, Final Report*. Washington, DC: U.S. Government Printing Office.

United States, White House. 2011. *Economic Report of the President*. http://www.WhiteHouse.gov.

Williamson, Oliver. 1979. "Transaction-Cost Economics: The Governance of Contractual Relations." *Journal of Law and Economics* 22: 233–62.

———. 1985. "Assessing Contracts." *Journal of Law, Economics and Organization* 1: 177–208.

———. 2002. "The New Institutional Economics: Taking Stock, Looking Ahead." *Journal of Economic Literature* 38: 595–613.

World Bank. 2008. "Worldwide Governance Indicators." http://info.worldbank.org/governance/wgi/index.asp.

———. Various years. "World Development Indicators." http://data.worldbank.org/data-catalog/world-development-indicators.

Zweig, Jason. 2007. *Your Money and Your Brain*. New York: Simon and Schuster Publishers.

PART 2

Developmental Aspects

CHAPTER 4

Finance and Development in Islam: A Historical Perspective and a Brief Look Forward

Murat Çizakça

Introduction

Islamic finance is generally considered to be a new discipline, which by implication also makes its impact on economic development a new phenomenon not yet fully understood. This way of thinking begs a huge unanswered question: if Islamic finance is, indeed, a relatively new discipline, how have Muslims managed their financial affairs from the time of the Prophet until the present? Alternatively, do those who argue that Islamic finance is a new discipline seriously imply that Muslims of the earlier centuries did not have any idea about finance?

Nothing could be further from the truth. Indeed, Islamic finance is as old as Islam itself and constituted an inseparable part of an entire economic system. This was basically an ethical, commercial, preindustrial capitalist system, which antedated Western capitalism by a millennium. Between the tenth and the fourteenth centuries, the West borrowed many of the principles and institutions of Islamic capitalism (Çizakça 1996, 2006). Medieval Europe even practiced a stringent prohibition of the rate of interest. But then between the sixteenth and the eighteenth centuries, first with the "Reformation" and then the "Enlightenment," the prohibition was relaxed, and equally importantly, the ethical constraints were compromised. In the process, the original ethical capitalist was replaced by the rational *homo economicus* who was an invention of the positivist mind, devoid of all ethical and religious concerns enshrined in holy texts. Thus, a new set of laws governing the behavior of *homo economicus* had to be invented. As Abbas Mirakhor has argued, ever since Adam Smith's *The Wealth of Nations*, Western economic theory has been busy trying to do just this (Mirakhor and Hamid 2009, 21–25).

Murat Çizakça is a professor of Islamic finance and comparative economic history at the International Centre for Education in Islamic Finance, the Global University of Islamic Finance, Kuala Lumpur, Malaysia.

By contrast, Muslims, who were not burdened by a highly centralized church and its ruthless Inquisition, never felt the need to discard the basic teachings of their religion (Baigent and Leigh 2000). Consequently, their economic reasoning has always been shaped by the classical sources of Islam. The discussion now turns to the basic characteristics of Islamic economics and finance, the outcome of this reasoning.

Basic Characteristics of an Islamic Economy and Finance

Islamic finance and economic development obey certain rules and principles, which originate in the basic teachings of Islam. The best known of these principles is the prohibition of interest. The immediate consequence of the prohibition is the problem of combining the factors of production. Put differently, if

$$Q = f(K, L, N, E, \ldots) \text{ is a simple production function,} \qquad (4.1)$$

where Q is production, K is capital, L is labor, N is natural resources, and E is entrepreneurship, then combining these factors becomes a *conditio sine qua non* for production. Indeed, unless a way is found to combine these factors, each owned by different persons, no production can take place.

In conventional economies, the capitalist is compensated for the use of his or her capital with interest, and the entrepreneur with profit. In an Islamic economy, however, since interest is prohibited, the system of rewards becomes more complicated. The capitalist cannot be rewarded with the rate of interest anymore, and the capitalist's capital cannot be transferred to the entrepreneur in conventional ways. The problem is solved by also rewarding the capitalist with profit. Put differently, the capitalist and the entrepreneur begin sharing the profits. But there is a further complication: since profits are generated by taking risks, this means that risks are also shared. Since some risks inevitably lead to losses, this means that losses too must be shared.

Thus, when the capitalist is rewarded not by interest but by profits, the capitalist and the entrepreneur end up sharing not only the profits, but risks and losses, as well. As a result, the economy changes its character, and what can be called a "share economy" emerges. In this way, the sharing of risks, profits, and losses is the most essential trait of an Islamic economy.

Another very important principle of the Islamic economy concerns profits. Unlike the conventional economy, where profit maximization, pure and simple, prevails, in an Islamic economy, constrained maximization is the rule. Muslim business people try to maximize their profits subject to ethical considerations imposed by their religion. Thus, providing profits are generated through *helal*, legitimate means, there is no upper limit imposed on them. It has been argued that Islam first equips a Muslim with ethical principles and then leaves him/her free to compete (Zaim [1976] 1994, 103).

Only a few taxes are mentioned in the Qur'an, leading some Islamic economists to wonder how additional taxes can be imposed. But this is missing the point. The message of the Qur'an should be obvious: in an Islamic economy, taxes should be few and the tax burden should be light. With government revenue thus limited, assuming a balanced budget, expenditures must be limited, as well. Since national defense constitutes the most important and inelastic government expenditure, which cannot be compromised, this means that the bulk of tax revenue must be earmarked for defense, leaving other important social services such as health and education inadequately funded. Ottoman budgets from the sixteenth century demonstrate that this was indeed the case (Barkan 1953–54).

The resulting gap in the provision of services was filled by the *waqf* system. Known as charitable or philanthropic foundations in the West, *waqfs* were voluntary endowments provided by high net-worth individuals in order to finance, organize, and maintain in perpetuity the most important services needed by the society. That this was not just a theory but found widespread application in the Islamic world is attested to by the magnificent architectural monuments all over the Islamic world, from the shores of the Atlantic to the ends of the Indian Ocean. But architecture represents just the tip of the iceberg. The predominant role *waqfs* played in Muslims' lives has been explained by the historian Bahaeddin Yediyildiz, who argued that "a person could be born in a house belonging to a *waqf*, sleep in a cradle provided by that *waqf*, be educated in the school of the *waqf* and read the books provided by it, become a teacher in the *waqf's* school, earn a *waqf*-financed salary and at his death be placed in a *waqf*-provided coffin for burial in a *waqf* cemetery."[1]

Implementation

The reader may wonder at this point *whether and how* the theoretical model of an Islamic economy very briefly presented above has ever been actually implemented. Considering the question "whether" is not a new question at all. Western historians of Islamic economic/social history have long debated whether the principles mentioned above were purely theoretical and were confined to law books. It was another Western historian, Abraham Udovitch, who brought the debate to a conclusion. Referring particularly to the interest prohibition, Udovitch was able to demonstrate that by and large the prohibition was observed in real life (1970, chapter 1; see also Goitein 1971).

This brings us to the question, "How?" How, indeed, was the prohibition observed and, by implication, how were the different factors of production combined? The simple answer is, through institutions. It was through various institutions that the classical principles of an Islamic economy were applied in real life. To give just a few examples: sharing profits, risks, and losses between the capitalist and the entrepreneur was made possible by the institution of business partnerships. It was through these partnerships that the capital owned by the capitalist could be transferred to the entrepreneur. Thus sharing risks, profits, and losses replaced the rate of interest. Moreover, despite modest government revenue, *waqfs* made provision of important services to the society possible.

There were serious efforts to maximize government revenue throughout the centuries by continuous reforms of public finance institutions, but these primarily aimed at financing ever-rising military expenditures, leaving services financed primarily through *waqfs* more or less untouched (Çizakça 1996, chapter 5).

All of this brings us to the next vital question, which constitutes the essence of the present volume, *Islamic Finance and Economic Development*. Namely, have the classical principles of Islamic finance and economy, together with the institutions that applied these principles, ever led to economic development? Is there any historical evidence of sustained and significant economic development in the Islamic world? The discussion now turns to these questions.

Historical Evidence

For obvious reasons, we cannot resort to the types of data used by modern economists, such as gross national product (GNP) or income per capita. Instead, we must rely on indirect evidence. Notwithstanding this, there is powerful historical evidence that from the early eighth century onward, Muslims acquired a core position from where they were able to link the two most important economic zones of the world at the time, the Mediterranean and the Indian Ocean. Andre Wink (1991, 10) has argued that by establishing an Islamic superstructure on "the rich urbanite substratum of late antiquity and by fusing the formerly rival Byzantine and Sasanid commercial circuits and forcing links between the two zones, the Islamic Caliphate from the eighth to the eleventh century achieved an unquestioned economic supremacy in the world." Muslim impact and economic might did not remain limited to the two seas. Vast swathes of not only northern India but even Europe were incorporated into the Islamic world-economy. Historians now even speak of the "economic Islamization of early medieval Europe" (Wink 1991, 36).

Substantial evidence has been found in Arab navigation manuals that circumnavigation of Africa, from east to west, was first achieved by Muslims. Thus the European "discovery" of the Cape of Good Hope was simply the discovery of the already discovered" (Abu-Lughod 1989, 19, 209)![2]

Post-Roman Europe, utterly destroyed by the *Völkerwanderung*, was drastically demonetized and desperately needed Islamic coinage.[3] Trade was the only way coins could be obtained. Not being able to produce the goods that Muslims needed, Europeans began to sell primarily furs and lumber. Muslims paid for these products with their coins. Fifty-four finds of Islamic coins have been discovered all over the Carolingian empire and even in distant Scandinavia—the land of the Vikings. McCormick (2001, 344–54) provides solid and irrefutable evidence about the monetary might of the Muslims. It is thanks to these coins that post-Roman Europe was able to remonetize its economy.

These successes were achieved by applying the principles of Islamic capitalism enshrined in the Qur'an and the prophetic traditions, *Sunnah*, with the help of specially designed, Shari'ah-based institutions. Consider, for instance, money itself, the most fundamental building block of any economy. Why, indeed, were

Muslim coins found all over medieval Europe and from where did this monetary power come? For this, we need to look into the way Muslims monetized their commerce. Put differently, we need to understand how Muslims were catapulted from the age of barter to the age of money.

Indeed, in the absence of money, barter is the only other known method of commerce. Yet barter necessitates a double coincidence of wants. That is to say, what merchant A wants to exchange should be needed by merchant B, and what B wants to exchange should be needed by A. Moreover, it is also necessary that both these individuals personally come together in a market. By contrast, in monetized trade, A can sell his merchandise to third persons and with the money he receives he can travel to another market and there purchase B's goods in exactly the amount he wishes. Furthermore, since it is possible to send money over long distances, he does not even have to travel himself and can have the transaction completed by correspondence. The commercial advantage of trading with money over barter is obvious. Finally, since it is nearly impossible to measure the exact value of the goods exchanged in barter, any such transaction may involve an element of unjustified enrichment. It is probably based upon such concerns that Prophet Muhammad discouraged barter while encouraging monetized trade.

This policy is revealed in two Prophetic statements, *ahadith*, one clear and the other subtle. The former is narrated in Malik's *Muwatta* (the famous treatise by Imam Malik ibn Anas):

> Someone brought some excellent dates to the Messenger of God as a gift. The Prophet asked "Are all dates of Khaybar like this?" The man said, "No, Messenger of God! We take a *sa'* of this kind for two *sa's*, or two *sa's* for three." Upon this, the Messenger of God said: "Do not do that. Sell the assorted ones for dirhams (coins) and then buy the good ones with the dirhams."

In this *hadith*, the Prophet clearly disapproves of barter and orders Muslims to resort to trade instead (Ibn Ashur 2006, 288–90). In the next *hadith*, narrated by al-Bukhari and Muslim on the authority of Ubadah ibn al Samit, the Prophet takes a dramatic step further and declares barter a form of *riba*—that is, interest—and condemns it.[4]

> Gold for gold, equivalent for equivalent; silver for silver, equivalent for equivalent; dates for dates, equivalent for equivalent; salt for salt, equivalent for equivalent; barley for barley, equivalent for equivalent, and whoever exceeds or asks for excess, he practiced *al-riba*. Sell gold for silver as you wish if it is hand to hand (prompt delivery), and sell barley for dates as you wish if it is hand to hand.

The wisdom behind this *hadith* is not easy to understand. Even today, more than 1,400 years after it had been actually stated, some important scholars admit they do not really understand it.[5] The reason they do not understand it is because they consider the *hadith* from a legal perspective and ignore the historical circumstances in which it had been stated. With this *hadith*, the Prophet clearly makes barter almost impossible and encourages monetized trade. This is because if the merchants wish to barter like objects—say, dates for dates—they are ordered to do so exactly equivalent for equivalent, with total disregard to quality differences—in actuality, a near impossibility. Indeed, they are told that when doing this particular case of bartering, if one of them does not obey the rule "equivalent for equivalent" and asks for his higher quality dates a higher amount of the lower quality dates from the other party, he would be committing *riba*. In short, merchants who wish to barter like-objects are not allowed to take quality differences into consideration and are restricted severely to barter only exactly "equivalent for equivalent." While with this particular *hadith*, the Prophet does not prohibit the barter of like objects outright but makes it entirely unpractical and almost meaningless, with the previous one, he teaches the merchants how to trade like-objects by utilizing a medium of exchange: that is, dirhams, or coins.

Bartering objects of the same genre—say, silver for gold—is less strict: it is permitted subject to prompt delivery. It has been argued that the wisdom behind this insistence on prompt delivery is the possible change in the relative values of the goods in question if deferred payment is allowed. Since this would lead to an unjustified enrichment for one of the parties, the condition of prompt delivery is imposed (Al-Qusi 1981–82, 149). While this is certainly possible, I would argue that the real wisdom must be sought in the entirety of the *hadith*. What the Prophet has done here is to apply a hierarchy of restrictions, with the purpose of gradually but surely leading merchants from barter to monetized trade. Indeed, while the barter of like-objects (gold for gold) is most severely restricted, the barter of objects of the same genre (silver for gold, or barley for wheat) is permitted subject to prompt delivery. Finally, the exchange (sale) of precious metals for commodities—say, gold for wheat—is not even mentioned in the *hadith*, implying that it is entirely unrestricted. To sum up, by progressively relaxing the restrictions, the Prophet has catapulted Islamic community from the age of barter to the age of monetized exchange.[6]

This progress from barter to monetized trade must have been the *conditio sine qua non* for the establishment of an intercontinental trade system from the Atlantic to the Pacific, which Muslims came to dominate soon after the birth of Islam. If the gradual elimination of barter and its replacement by monetized trade was the *conditio sine qua non* for the establishment of an intercontinental trade network, the *conditio sine qua non* for the monetization of trade must have been the very existence of money. Indeed, the transition from barter to monetized trade could not possibly have materialized without a massive increase in the supply of money.

In a bimetallic (gold and silver) system, which dominated world trade in this era, an increase in the supply of money was possible only with a corresponding increase in the supply of silver and gold. Under normal circumstances, a drastic increase in the supply of these precious metals is not possible. But in the seventh to eighth centuries, circumstances were by no means normal. For this was the period when Islam expanded at the expense of the two great empires of the period: the Byzantine and the Sasanid. What dramatically changed world economic history with the conquest of the Byzantine and Sasanid territories was the capture of massive amounts of hoarded gold and silver in the Byzantine churches and Sasanid temples.[7] The gold and silver treasures hoarded by these institutions were melted down and then minted. Aggregate money supply increased in this way, and a new economic system, based upon monetized trade and dominated by the Muslims, could thus become a reality (Wink 1991, 34).

A closer look at the radical increase in the money supply reveals that this was achieved in two steps. First, the coins of the conquered Byzantine and Sasanid territories continued to be the legal tender in the Islamic empire. Since Byzantine coins were gold and Sasanid coins were silver-based, this meant a de facto bimetallic system. The tolerance toward these earlier coins meant that the now much-enlarged economy of the Islamic community experienced minimum disruption. Second, when it was decided to mint new Islamic coins, the precious metal content of these new coins was kept deliberately lower than the earlier coins. Apparently, it was understood that the bad money would drive away the good money, and in this way Islamic coins came to replace the earlier Byzantine and Sasanid coins. That bad money replaces good money and the latter comes to be hoarded and taken out of circulation is, of course, known as the Gresham's Law. Muslims apparently understood the principle behind it almost a millennium before Gresham (Orman 2001, 28).

To sum up, Muslim coinage not only replaced the earlier imperial coins but also spread rapidly and dominated the economies of Europe and the Middle East, as well as India.[8] Herman Van Der Wee, an eminent Belgian economic historian, also confirms that remonetization of Europe after the *Völkerwanderung*, and the rebirth of the European banking system owe much to the flow of Muslim coinage to Europe (van der Wee 1994, 74).

International trade would not have been possible, however, without a sophisticated maritime law. A well-known French historian, Daniel Panzac (2002), has shown that this institution was also provided by Muslims. This originally Islamic law of maritime trade was transferred to Europe through various compilations.

The three most important compilations were made during the eleventh to twelfth centuries. These were the Maritime Laws of Rhodes, Oleron, and the *Consolato del Mare*. It is now definitively established that the first one, previously considered to be a derivative of the Roman-Byzantine digests, was in fact based on *Al-Mudawwana al-Kubra* by Sahnun Ibn Sa'id al Tanukhi (d. 854). It was commented upon by Ibn Rushd (known in the West as Averroes, d. 1198) and drafted in Sicily or southern Italy, both Muslim territories during the ninth to eleventh centuries. The second was authored by the Court of the Crusader Kingdom of Jerusalem in order to harmonize trade relations between occidental and oriental Christians as well as Muslims. This compilation was brought to Europe partly by Eleanor of Aquitaine and partly by her son Richard the Lionheart. The contents of the Oleron compilation are identical to the Muslim laws of the ninth to tenth centuries. Finally, the *Consolato del Mare* was written in Spain. The document originates in the Muslim Middle Eastern texts of the eighth to ninth centuries and was later brought to Andalusia. It was translated during the reign of King Alphonse in thirteenth century Castile as part of the great works of translation from Arabic (Panzac 2002, 351–58).

One of the most important components of the maritime laws transferred to Europe was the law of partnerships, or more specifically, the Islamic *mudarabah*. Italian merchants doing business in the Middle East encountered this particular form of partnership, so essential for financing entrepreneurship. It then became a custom among them, and as such was incorporated into the various compilations just mentioned, which facilitated the diffusion of *mudarabah* to Europe, where it came to be known as *commenda*. It is generally agreed that *commenda* was the most important business partnership of medieval Europe and that it played a crucial role in triggering the "commercial revolution."[9]

An equally important institution that was borrowed by the medieval Europeans from the Muslims was the *waqf*. As is well known, *waqf* establishes, finances, and maintains the most essential services any civilized society needs, often for centuries. Foremost among these services are the institutions of learning and health: in short, institutions that enhance human capital. There is now definitive evidence that once borrowed, *waqf* played an enormously important role in the borrowing civilization. To give a highly dramatic example, one of the earliest colleges of Oxford (Merton College) was established in the form of an Islamic college (*madrasa*) and its endowment deed was practically identical to an Islamic *waqf* deed (Çizakça 2000, chapter 1).

International trade soon necessitated a whole spectrum of new financial instruments. Indeed, the invention of other business instruments facilitating monetary transactions did not have to wait very long. Bills of exchange, letters of credit (*suftaja*), promissory notes, ordinary checks, and double-entry bookkeeping were all known to the Muslims. Historians in general agree that medieval Europe simply borrowed these instruments from the Muslims and could not improve upon them! (Braudel 1993, 472; Sayous 1929, 132–33; Wink 1991, 12). Without these financial instruments, long-distance trade simply would not have been possible.

Economic/financial principles enshrined in the classical sources undoubtedly point to a capitalist system. This was Islamic, ethical capitalism, which preceded that of the West by a millennium.[10] It is now well established that all the legal and institutional prerequisites for financing and administering capitalist production and exchange were in place in the Islamic world long before the Europeans started using them (Abu-Lughod 1989, 224; Çizakça 1996; Udovitch 1970, 261).

It appears that these institutions were highly efficient. The fact that they were borrowed by the West shows that they must have operated at lower transaction costs.[11] This is because the direction of institutional borrowing between two civilizations is from the low cost one to the higher cost one. Put differently, the civilization with the high cost institutions ends up borrowing the lower cost institutions of the other (Çizakça 2006). All of this was confirmed by the French historian Sayous (1929, 132–33) long ago: "The Muslims had, during tenth to eleventh centuries incontestably more perfect commercial methods than those of the Europeans…The Christians of Europe could not improve upon them."

Application of the economic/financial principles enshrined in the Qur'an and the *Sunnah* by efficient institutions, accompanied by the conquest of vast areas of the formerly Byzantine and Sasanid empires, created massive wealth.[12] The economic integration of new territories was achieved by merchants, particularly the so-called Karimi merchants, who connected the Indian Ocean to the Mediterranean via the Republic of Yemen. Karimis were operating as early as Fatimid times (909–1171), and their fabulous wealth is well known (Ashtor 1956; see also Labib 1965; Abu-Lughod 1989, 227–29).

Wealth made possible massive investments in education and research through the *waqf* system. The *magnum opus* of Fuat Sezgin (2003) provides a detailed and most impressive account of the scientific advances achieved by Muslims in this period.

Finally, the relentless attacks by Crusaders from the West and Mongols from the East attest strongly to the relative wealth of the Islamic world. After all, these attacks basically aimed at plunder, and it is the wealthy who attract plunderers.

Stagnation and Decline

A cursory look at the Islamic world today would suffice to indicate how far this region has declined from its original glory, described above. There is an ongoing debate about the causes of decline of the Islamic world. Most recently, Timur Kuran's arguments (2011) have become very popular. Although he has made quite convincing arguments, the initial enthusiasm with which the scholarly community welcomed his views is now waning (Boogert 2009). This is because, while he has boldly accused Islamic jurisprudence with weak evidence, more refined arguments have been made (Çizakça 2012a; Çizakça and Kenanoğlu 2008), which were supported by solid archival research (Boogert 2009). Moreover, his theoretical arguments have also been criticized (Çizakça 2011b, 2011c; Zaman 2010).

In a nutshell, new research has suggested that rather than the alleged rigidity of Islamic jurisprudence, the culprit for the decline of the Islamic world should be sought in a variety of factors. Of these, the increasing centralization and militarization of the region that occurred in response to the massive pincer attacks by the Crusaders and the Mongols appears to have been the most important. The degree to which this militarization occurred and led to the rise of a garrison state has been indirectly quantified by Maya Shatzmiller (1994, 258), who showed that from the eighth–eleventh centuries to the twelfth–fifteenth, the military/bureaucratic occupations in the Islamic world increased by 200 percent.[13]

Moreover, since the pincer actions did not cease (Mongols, though temporarily defeated in 1258, were still attacking in 1394, as were the Crusaders in 1403 and even later), the centralization/militarization must have intensified in the long run. Indeed, the decline of the famous Karimi merchants in the fifteenth century is attributed to the ever-increasing demands for funds of the central Mamluk government (Ashtor 1956, 53). The Mamluk government played an important role in transforming the very structure of the spice trade from the traditional competitive one to increasing government monopolization. Thus, competitive markets and entrepreneurship were steadily choked by the ever-increasing taxes, price-fixing, and monopolies that transformed classical Islamic capitalism into something new (Abu Lughod 1989, 228–29). Monopolization of the spice trade reached a zenith in 1429–34 and brought the Karimi era to a decisive end. After establishing a government monopoly over the pepper trade in 1429, Sultan Barsbay prohibited the Venetian merchants from disembarking in the harbor of Alexandria. Finally, in 1434, Barsbay forbade all contacts between the Venetians and the Karimis and then completely cornered the pepper market, later expanding his monopoly to other items (Abu-Lughod 1989, 246, fn. 22).

Although this transformation of the Arab Republic of Egypt and the Syrian Arab Republic into a garrison state allowed these states to regain and then preserve their territorial independence, it did so at the cost of gradually weakening the classical Islamic capitalism and replacing it with the ever-increasing state control of the economy.

Evidence pertaining to the evolution of the Egyptian sugar industry supports this argument. During the thirteenth and the early fourteenth centuries, this industry was able to satisfy both prodigious local demand and export large quantities to Europe, and was described as "capitalistic," in the sense that big trusts were systematically pushing aside the smaller enterprises. However, the capitalists themselves appear to have been eventually pushed aside by Mamluk officials.[14] Penetration of the Mamluks into this industry proved to be disastrous for the Egyptian economy in the long run: not only did these officials pay lower taxes than the capitalist plantation owners, but they could also mobilize peasants through *corvée* (forced labor). Eventually, during the fourteenth and particularly the fifteenth century, they even began to force merchants to buy their own and the sultan's sugar at inflated prices, and took full advantage of their oligopsony powers to purchase the products of civilian producers at depressed prices. Such market distortions and property rights violations undoubtedly caused the technological stagnation observed in the Egyptian sugar industry during the fifteenth century, precisely when the European sugar refining techniques began to improve substantially (Abu Lughod 1989, 232–33, 236).

These developments were by no means specific to Mamluk Egypt. They were observed in varying degrees in other Islamic empires as well, and culminated in the emergence of the so-called Ottoman proto-quasi socialism.[15] Thus, it can be argued that the constant warfare and the instinct for survival transformed the once capitalistic Islamic economies into proto-quasi socialism.[16] This argument has been supported by research conducted in the Ottoman archives, which has revealed widespread, consistent, and long-lasting price and profit controls, limitations on property rights, and even confiscations—all socialist traits.[17] The latest ongoing research by Mehmet Genç (forthcoming) in the Ottoman archives has also revealed powerful government monopolies, lending further support to this argument.

The centuries-long shift from the classical Islamic capitalism toward quasi-socialism had disastrous consequences—all the more so because Europe vigorously continued along its own capitalist path. Supported by the discovery of vast new continents, exploitation of huge deposits of precious metals, the financial revolution that enabled governments to borrow vast sums at very lost cost from the public, and finally the industrial revolution, Western capitalism financed European imperialism. Colonization and impoverishment of the bulk of the Islamic world by this Western juggernaut was inevitable. The latest research by Hossein Askari and Scheherazade Rehman (chapter 11 in this volume) provides quantitative evidence. They have shown that even in the late twentieth century, between 1980 and 2011, the gross national income of the members of the Organization of Islamic Countries (OIC), measured in terms of purchasing power parity (PPP), was a mere fraction of that of the member-countries of the Organisation for Economic Co-operation and Development (OECD) (see figure 11.5). Moreover, they have concluded that poverty levels as measured by the percentage of the population that lives on $1.25 (PPP) or less per day over the last 30 years has not only been persistent but appears to have increased (figure 11.7).

The impact of divergence from classical Islamic capitalism was also reflected in another platform: the *waqf* system. The centuries-old tradition of wealthy Muslims voluntarily providing essential services to society was gradually replaced by state provision. Two developments played a crucial role in this: Western pressure and the indigenous modernists. The story of how these two cooperated and how they undermined the *waqf* system during the nineteenth to twentieth centuries is well-known (Çizakça 2000). With the *waqf* system weakened, and in some countries even destroyed, and the state incapable of substituting for it adequately, education and health services suffered. Askari and Rehman's chapter provides quantitative evidence. They have followed the 30-year educational progress of the OIC as measured by the UN Education Index and have found that OIC performance has been consistently well below the world average. In matters of health, their finding is similar. To conclude, the diversion from classical Islamic capitalism and the undermining and destruction of the *waqf* system have together hit human capital: the most important component of economic development.

Relevance for Today: What Needs to Be Done?

If the above conclusion about the proto-quasi socialism and its long-lasting impact on the Islamic world is correct, then it should be possible to come up with a policy recommendation. Muslims inhibited for centuries by proto-quasi socialism should rediscover their own ethical capitalism, with all its principles and institutions enshrined in the classical sources of Islam. The new Islamic economics should focus primarily on the rediscovery of the classical economic principles and their implementation through institutions. Put differently, rather than mimicking the West, where very special circumstances prevailed and the need was felt to discover new laws of economics, Islamic economists should focus instead on the rediscovery of the major financial/economic principles and institutions of their own past and their adaptation to current needs.

Actually, this process has already started! The first building block, *Tabung Haji*, was laid down in 1959 by Ungku Aziz, a member of the royal family of

Johor and at the time an economist at the University of Malaya, when he submitted a memorandum to the Malaysian Parliament, which aimed at financing and organizing the modern pilgrimage. Ungku Aziz was able to transform the process of preparation for the pilgrimage into a powerful financial institution. Initially, the total number of depositors was recorded at 1,281, which increased to more than 5 million as of 2009. The original depositors had paid in RM 46,610, which increased to RM 897.1 million as of 2008.[18] In recognition of the enormous services he has rendered to Malaysia, the Royal Professor Ungku Aziz was offered the highest honorific title "Tun" by three different Prime Ministers, as well as the prestigious Royal Award for Islamic Finance, but declined to accept all as a matter of principle. It is to be expected that the *Tabung Haji* will be emulated by the rest of the Islamic world.

Still another success story occurred in the field of banking. This pertains to the classical *mudarabah* partnership and its successful modernization. As is well-known, the *mudarabah* partnership is a true profit-and-loss-sharing partnership originally practiced by the Prophet. The problem with this partnership, however, was that it was practiced in history usually by two partners: a *rab al-mal* and a *mudarib*. This meant that the capital entrusted to the agent remained quite limited. A mechanism by which the savings of thousands of people could be entrusted to a powerful agent did not exist in the early history of Islam.

The crucial step for this purpose was taken by Dr. Ahmad al-Naggar in 1963. This was the establishment of the first ever Islamic bank in Mit Ghamr in Egypt. This bank was envisaged as a multiple *mudarabah* with hundreds of depositors/investors entrusting their hard-earned savings to it acting as the *mudarib*, agent. Today, Islamic banks are flourishing all over the Islamic world, even in non-Muslim countries, collecting the savings of hundreds of thousands of Muslims and non-Muslims and channeling them for profitable projects. Islamic banks have transformed Muslim countries from being non-bank societies to banking societies. This modernization of a classical Islamic partnership is not an achievement to be underestimated.

But in this context it is important to remember that one of the most important goals of Dr. al-Naggar—enhancement of entrepreneurship through these banks—has not materialized. Had Dr. al-Naggar's original plan of applying the *mudarabah* not only at the liability side but also at the asset side been followed, the goal would have been fulfilled and Islamic banks would have been able to create thousands of entrepreneurs.[19] But as is well known, the asset side of Islamic banks is dominated by *murabaha* sales—not the most useful instrument to enhance entrepreneurship. Islamic banks preferred to utilize the *murabaha* primarily because they were worried about their commitments to pay back their depositors. Because *mudarabah* is a long-term and risky instrument, there were serious concerns about the mismatch of funds. *Murabaha*, by contrast, provided fixed returns that could be paid back to the depositors easily.

All of this indicates that, as far as encouraging entrepreneurship is concerned, the task is not yet completed. Scholars are now actively searching for other historical instruments that can be modernized so as to provide both fixed returns to the depositors, while at the same time also enhance entrepreneurship through equity finance. In short, there is an urgent need for the development of hybrid instruments.

One of these is *esham*, originally utilized by the Ottoman Caliphate back in 1775 to borrow large Shari'ah-based funds from the public in order to pay a huge war indemnity to the Russians.[20] A research team at International Centre for Education in Islamic Finance (INCEIF), the Global University of Islamic Finance in Kuala Lumpur, has identified *esham* as a true profit-loss sharing instrument, which also yielded fixed returns (Çizakça forthcoming). Thus, the battle to develop Shari'ah-based profit-and-loss-sharing funds that not only enhances entrepreneurship but also yields fixed returns to the investors has now reached a new level. The INCEIF team is convinced that *esham* can be used for government borrowing. Some team members also believe that it can be used by the central banks of Islamic countries for open market operations, as well as for small and medium enterprise financing.

A close look at *sukuk* (Islamic bonds), on the other hand, has revealed that this instrument also represents the modernization of not one but two historical instruments: cash *waqfs*, and once again, *esham*. To what extent the financial engineers who designed the *sukuk* were aware of these historical instruments is not yet clear; at least one engineer has claimed that he was. Be that as it may, the sale-lease back-repurchase method so often used in most *sukuk* was originally utilized in the Ottoman cash *waqfs*. The special purpose vehicle, the crucial part of any *sukuk*, is but a simple cash *waqf*. As for securitization—that is, the idea of dividing a revenue stream into equal parts to be sold to the public—this was first used in 1775, as explained above. In short, *sukuk*, which is currently the most popular instrument of borrowing in the Islamic world, whether sovereign or private, is also a highly successful example of financial engineering using historical instruments.

Still another successful modernization occurred in the field of insurance leading to *Takaful*. This involved the modernization of the age-old *al-Aqilah*, a tribal custom among the Arabs going back even to the pre-Islamic era.[21]

In short, the revival of historical financial instruments to enhance contemporary Islamic finance is well on its way. This is taking place either by an economist redesigning an ancient tradition (*Tabung Haji* and the Mit Ghamr Bank); or financial engineers, not aware of historical instruments, rediscovering them without realizing their origins (*sukuk*); or more deliberately and systematically, by economic/financial historians informing financial engineers and Shari'ah scholars about certain historical instruments and reviving them together in a joint effort (*esham*). The latter is the method used by INCEIF.

Conclusion

Islamic economics is unique in the sense that while one subbranch of it—finance—has developed by leaps and bounds, the discipline itself has by and large stagnated. This lopsided development of the field has generated expectations that Islamic finance almost singlehandedly will lead to economic development. But no financial system, no matter how perfect, can generate economic growth without the rest of the economy following—and the rest of the economy cannot follow the financial sector unless certain preconditions are satisfied.

These preconditions are, in a nutshell, the rule of law, the democratic package, the basic freedoms, and the avoidance of sectarian violence. A detailed analysis of these concepts and their compatibility with the Shari'ah, however, would be well beyond the confines of this chapter.[22]

Notes

1. Yediyildiz, quoted in Babacan (forthcoming).
2. If Muslims did not use this route despite their knowledge about circumnavigation of Africa, this was because they had better and shorter routes through the Red Sea and the Gulf at their disposal.
3. *Völkerwanderung* refers to the "barbarian" attacks on the late Roman and post-Roman settlements and cities. It was one of these attacks in the year 476 AD that led to the conquest of Rome and brought the Western empire to an end. The attacks and the resulting mass migrations lasted for at least two centuries.
4. Malik, Book 31 (Business Transactions), *hadith* 31.12.21, www.imaanstar.com. A *sa'* was an ancient measure of weight. See also Muslim, Book 10 (Book of Transactions), *hadith* 3861, and discussion in Al-Qusi (1981–82, 144).
5. Consider the following interview conducted with Sheikh Esam M. Ishaq, a board member of the Discover Islam Centre in Bahrain and Shari'ah advisor to several Islamic financial institutions. "If I am going to exchange with you one bushel of a certain quality of rice with a bushel of lesser quality of rice, and if this is consensual and based on spot, people ask 'Why is this forbidden?' I can try to extrapolate a reason, but this will be purely deductive. Outwardly, I can't give you a single reason or explanation, but I know that it is there explicitly in the theological text" (Parker 2009, 160–61).
6. That the Prophet has condemned unequal barter exchange, encouraging instead monetized trade, has been acknowledged by Iqbal and Lewis (2009, 83), as well.
7. Substantial amounts of treasury became available very early on. When Hayber was captured only seven years after the *Hejrah*, massive booty became available. When Bahreyn began to send regular revenue the next year, some 80,000 dirhams became available per year (Kallek 1992, 82–83). So, the advance into the Byzantine and Sasanid territories must have compounded an already favorable conjuncture.
8. On Islamic coins dominating European economies during the ninth century, see McCormick (2001, 332, 334–35, 340, 344). On their spread to India, see Wink (1991, 30–34).
9. On the debate about the origins of the *commenda* and its vast importance, see Çizakça (1996).
10. For more on this, see Çizakça (2011a, chapter 2).
11. For evidence and detailed discussion of Western borrowing of Islamic economic/financial institutions in the eighth to thirteenth centuries, see Udovitch (1969); Çizakça (1996, chapter 2); Çizakça (2000, 8–13); Çizakça (2006, 671–98).

12. On the question of how an Islamic economy redistributes aggregate income, and the institutions used for this purpose, as well as their evolution, see Çizakça (2011a, chapters 6–8, and 10). The relatively equitable distribution of wealth in this period is confirmed by the relatively small numbers of beggars in Ottoman Istanbul in comparison to Paris. See Genç (2008).
13. Shatzmiller has actually confirmed the earlier observation of Abu-Lughod (1989, 147).
14. Mamluks were Turkic boys bought as slaves and raised to form the backbone of the Egyptian military.
15. "Proto," because the socialism practiced first by the medieval Islamic states and then the Ottoman empire antedated Marxist socialism by centuries; "quasi," because it was not based upon Marxist principles and class conflict, but—on the contrary—aimed at creating harmony between all citizens, thus following the Qur'anic notion of "*ummatan wasatan*," a society of the middle. However, in doing so, it went to the other extreme and choked private enterprise.
16. For a full treatment of the concept of "proto-quasi socialism," see Çizakça (2012b).
17. Genç (2002). Pamuk (2009) is more cautious, and argues that Ottoman interventionism was selective rather than comprehensive.
18. For a detailed account of *Tabung Haji*, see Çizakça (2011a, chapter 12).
19. *Mudarabah* protects the entrepreneur by shifting all the pecuniary loss to the capitalist. It is therefore truly a profit/loss-sharing contract. The agent loses only his time and effort. Its closest Western equivalent is venture capital, which triggered the revolution in information technology in the United States.
20. For details on *esham*, based on the historical research of Mehmet Genç, see Çizakça (2011a, 71–74, 165, 178, 180).
21. See Çizakça (2011a, 195–96). *Al-Aqilah* was a tribal custom designed to avoid vendettas by compensating the victim's family (belonging to another tribe) with cash collected from all the members of the tribe of the murderer.
22. For further discussion, see Çizakça (2011a, part 5).

References

Abu-Lughod, Janet. 1989. *Before European Hegemony, the World System A.D. 1250–1350*. Oxford, U.K.: Oxford University Press.

Al-Qusi, Abd al Mun`im Mahmud. 1981–82. "Riba, Islamic Law and Interest." PhD thesis, Temple University, Philadelphia, PA.

Ashtor, Eliyahu. 1956. "The Karimi Merchants." *Journal of the Royal Asiatic Society* (new series) 88: 45–56.

Babacan, Mehmet. Forthcoming. "Islamic Philanthropic Institutions and Governance: Evidence from Turkish Experience."

Baigent, Michael, and Richard Leigh. 2000. *The Inquisition*. New York: Penguin Adult.

Barkan, Ömer Lütfi. 1953–54. "H. 933–934 Tarihli Bütçe Defteri ve Ekleri." *İstanbul Üniversitesi İktisat Fakültesi Mecmuası* c. 15 (1–4).

Boogert, Maurits H. Van den. 2009. "Legal Reflections on the 'Jurisprudential Shift' Hypothesis." *Turcica* 41: 373–82.

Braudel, Fernand. 1993. *Maddi Ekonomi ve Kapitalizm* 3.cu cilt. Istanbul: Gece.

Çizakça, Murat. 1996. *Comparative Evolution of Business Partnerships: The Islamic World and Europe, with Specific Reference to the Ottoman Archives.* Leiden, The Netherlands: Brill.

———. 2000. *A History of Philanthropic Foundations: Islamic World from the Seventh Century to the Present.* Istanbul: Bogazici University Press.

———. 2006. "Cross-cultural Borrowing and Comparative Evolution of Institutions between Islamic World and the West." In *Relazioni economiche tra Europa e mondo Islamicho, Secc. XIII–XVIII*, edited by S. Cavaciocchi, 671–98. Prato: Istituto di Storia Economica, F. Datini, Serie II, 38, vol. II.

———. 2011a. *Islamic Capitalism and Finance: Origins, Evolution and the Future.* Cheltenham, U.K.: Edward Elgar.

———. 2011b. "Timur Kuran, *The Long Divergence: How Islamic Law Held Back the Middle East*. Princeton: Princeton University Press." http://eh.net/bookreviews/library, posted June 30, 2011.

———. 2011c. "Timur Kuran, *The Long Divergence: How Islamic Law Held Back the Middle East*. Princeton: Princeton University Press." *Review of Middle East Studies* 45 (1).

———. 2012a. "Long-Term Causes of Decline of the Ottoman/Islamic Economies." In *Religion and Religious Institutions in the European Economy, 1000–1800*, edited by Francesco Ammanati, 361–77. Florence, Italy: Firenze University Press.

———. 2012b. "The Ottoman Government and Economic Life: Taxation, Public Finance and Trade Controls." In *Cambridge History of Turkey*, vol. 2, edited by Suraiya Faroqhi and Kate Fleet. Cambridge, U.K.: Cambridge University Press.

———. Forthcoming. "Esham: A Fixed Return, Yet *Shari'ah*-Based Instrument of Investment." *Global Islamic Finance Review.*

Çizakça, Murat, and Macit Kenanoğlu. 2008. "Ottoman Merchants and the Jurisprudential Shift." In *Merchants in the Ottoman Empire*, edited by Suraiya Faroqhi and Giles Veinstein, 195–213. Louvain, Belgium: Collection Turcica XVI.

Genç, Mehmet. 2002. *Devlet ve Ekonomi.* İstanbul: Ötüken.

———. 2008. "Osmanlı Dünyası'nda Dilencilik." In *Bir Kent Sorunu, Dilencilik Sempozyumu Tebligler Kitabı*, edited by Suvat Parin. Istanbul: B. B. Zabıta Daire Bşk.

———. Forthcoming. "Yed-i Vahid." In *Türk Diyanet Vakfı İslam Ansiklopedisi.* İstanbul: Diyanet Vakfı.

Goitein, Shelomo Dov. 1971. *A Mediterranean Society.* Vols. 1 and 2. Berkeley: University of California Press.

Ibn Ashur. 2006. *Treatise on Maqasid al-Shari~ah.* London: International Institute of Islamic Thought.

Iqbal, Zapir, and Mervyn K. Lewis. 2009. *Islamic Perspective on Governance.* Cheltenham, U.K.: Edward Elgar.

Kallek, Cengiz. 1992. *Hz. Peygamber Doneminde Devlet ve Piyasa.* Istanbul: Bilim ve Sanat Vakfi.

Kuran, Timur. 2011. *The Long Divergence, How Islamic Law Held Back the Middle East.* Princeton, NJ: Princeton University Press.

Labib, Subhi. 1965. *Handelsgeschichte Aegyptens im Spaetmittelalter.* Wiesbaden, Germany: F. Steiner Verlag.

McCormick, Michael. 2001. *Origins of the European Economy: Communications and Commerce AD300–900.* Cambridge, U.K.: Cambridge University Press.

Mirakhor, Abbas, and Idris Samawi Hamid. 2009. *Islam and Development: The Institutional Framework*. New York: Global Scholarly Publications.

Orman, Sabri. 2001. *Iktisat, Tarih ve Toplum*. Istanbul: Kure Yayinlari.

Pamuk, Sevket. 2009. "Ottoman Interventionism in Economic and Monetary Affairs." In *The Ottoman Economy and Its Institutions*, edited by Sevket Pamuk, chapter 2. Farnham: Ashgate Variorum Collected Studies.

Panzac, Daniel. 2002. "Le Contrat d'Affrètement maritime en Mediterranee." *Journal of the Economic and Social History of the Orient* 45 (3): 351–58.

Parker, Mushtak. 2009. "Shari'ah Advisories Must Be Regulated." *Islamic Banker*, May/June: 8.

Sayous, André-E. 1929. *Le Commerce des Europeens a Tunis depuis le XII Siecle jusqu'a la fin de XVIe*. Paris: L'Academie des Sciences Coloniales.

Sezgin, Fuat. 2003. *Wissenschaft und Technik im Islam*, Band I, *Einführung in die Geschichte der Arabisch-Islamische Wissenschaften*. Frankfurt am Main: Institut für Geschichte der Arabisch-Islamische Wissenschaften an der Johann Wolfgang Goethe Universitaet.

Shatzmiller, Maya. 1994. *Labour in the Medieval Islamic World*. Leiden, The Netherlands: Brill.

Udovitch, Abraham. 1969. "At the Origins of the Western Commenda: Islam, Israel, Byzantium?" *Princeton Near East Papers* 9–10.

———. 1970. *Partnership and Profit in Medieval Islam*. Princeton, NJ: Princeton University Press.

van der Wee, Herman. 1994. *A History of European Banking*. Antwerp, Belgium: Mercator.

Wink, Andre. 1991. *Al-Hind, The Making of the Indo-Islamic World*. Leiden, The Netherlands: Brill.

Zaim, Sabahaddin. (1976) 1994. "Ekonomik Hayatta Müslüman İnsanın Tutum ve Davranışları." Paper submitted at the First World Congress of Islamic Economics, Mecca, April 5–11. Reprinted in *İş Hayatında İslam İnsanı, Homo Islamicus*, edited by Hüner Şencan. İstanbul: MÜSİAD. Citations refer to the 1994 edition.

Zaman, Arshad. 2010. "Timur Kuran, *The Long Divergence: How Islamic Law Held Back the Middle East*. Princeton: Princeton University Press." *Islamic Studies* 49 (2): 277–89.

CHAPTER 5

Economic Development in Islam

Hossein Askari

Whenever I think about economic development, my thoughts invariably revert to my university days as a student in the 1960s. Economic development, or the study of countries that are underdeveloped, had become a distinct field in the years following World War II. Development was envisaged as an increase in gross domestic product (GDP) per capita to levels enjoyed by the industrialized countries and structural transformation from an agrarian to an industrial economy. A few economists did question whether development would necessarily increase human well-being, but it was not exactly a hot button issue. The major impediments to development were seen as insufficient domestic savings, foreign exchange, and technology; shortsighted policies; and the inability to benefit from economic externalities and economies of scale. New theories were popping up to alleviate these constraints. In essence, the outlook for the transformation of underdeveloped economies to developed status was relatively optimistic, if only resources and better policies were forthcoming; and financial assistance

---

Hossein Askari is the Islamic Republic of Iran Professor of International Business and International Affairs at the George Washington University. This chapter is taken from and is based on a number of coauthored studies that contain much more detail. Please refer to those studies, and to the reference list in the 2010 work I coauthored with Abbas Mirakhor, *Islam and the Path to Human and Economic Development*, for references to other works noted in this chapter. First and foremost, I am grateful to Abbas Mirakhor, to whom I owe a big debt of gratitude for being my teacher, and for his guidance and patience with my learning process; this collaboration has expanded my appreciation of the process of development. I have taken from our 2010 book but have had to limit the number of footnotes and references because of limitations of space. My collaborative work with Scheherazade Rehman on "Islamicity" indexes, although preliminary, has demonstrated that in many ways Western countries, such as Sweden and Norway, may be pursuing a more Islamic economic and social agenda and policy path than Muslim countries (see also, chapter 11, this volume). My work on Islamic finance and banking with Zamir Iqbal, Noureddine Krichene, and Abbas Mirakhor has for me demonstrated that Western thinkers have largely ignored the importance of morality so central to Adam Smith's prescription. I believe that the author of *The Theory of Moral Sentiments* would stress that his market-based system of *The Wealth of Nations*, built on effective institutions, is truly hollow if it does not incorporate a heavy dose of morality, humanity, compassion, generosity, and charity. While I am seriously indebted to my coauthors, I am responsible for the views expressed here and for any and all errors and shortcomings.

(foreign aid) and enlightened policy advice from the industrialized countries could provide the necessary inputs and ingredients for success.

This relatively doable transformation from underdeveloped to developed status seemed rather simplistic to me, a young man from the Middle East who had seen intrigue and the destructive effects of power and money first hand. My closest friend in graduate school, a budding brilliant macroeconomist from Latin America, did not share my suspicions. We used to debate about what was the binding constraint to development; he stressed inconsistent macroeconomic policies, while I argued in favor of political reform. Upon leaving graduate school, I saw a slow but steady transformation of the development field. Human development and well-being took on increasing importance; the foundational contributions of institutions were rediscovered (from Adam Smith); and the significant contribution of political reform to human and economic development became recognized. Most recently, the opportunity to work on economic development concepts of Islam has expanded my appreciation of the many dimensions of human and economic development.

While Western economic thinking on development has changed over the last 60 or so years—basically rediscovering one of Adam Smith's two books while at best paying only lip service to the other, and recognizing the central importance of human well-being to the development process—Islamic thinking on development has not changed with time because Muslims believe that the Qur'an is the divine and immutable word of God. The foundations of human and economic development in Islam were laid down centuries ago in the Qur'an and practiced by the Prophet Mohammad. Islam is a rules-based system with a prescribed method for humans and society to achieve material and nonmaterial progress and development grounded in rule-compliance and effective institutions. Unfortunately, today's Muslim countries have not embraced and adopted Islam's foundational elements (much less supervised rule-compliance) to support human and economic development (see chapter 11 in this volume).

This chapter is organized along the following lines. The next section summarizes the evolution of Western thinking on development to provide the background for comparing and demonstrating the convergence of modern thinking on development with Islamic teachings (its foundational framework, its dimensions, and its rules), which is explored in the subsequent section. The final section provides a summary and a few thoughts to explain why development has not flourished in Muslim countries: namely, not because they have, but because they have not, followed the teachings of Islam on development.

The Evolution of Western Thinking on Development

The concept of modern development owes its origin to the eighteenth-century writers of the Scottish Enlightenment, especially Adam Smith, who formulated the first systematic idea of economic development, starting in his seminal work, *The Theory of Moral Sentiments* (1759). Adam Smith believed that through effort and cooperation, motivated by self-love tempered by the moral value of "sympathy" for others, there would be continuous material improvement. Sympathy is the quality that each individual would take to the market as a mechanism that would translate the self-love, or self-interest, of each market participant into love for others. If individuals entering the market were devoid of sympathy and cooperation, progress would be undermined. The dimension of the self that is a reflective judge of a person's own actions and *sense of duty* would create an appropriate balance between the interests of the self and those of others. This guidance by an "invisible hand" would lead to positive economic and social change. The separate self-love of all individuals would be galvanized toward the benefit of all, leading to a stable social order.

Driven by self-love and regulated by sympathy, each individual would be directed to the most productive economic activity. Labor would be one of two major inputs for increasing the "wealth of nations." At the same time, the profit motive would increase capital accumulation, the other major input. Increasing labor productivity would finance investment in machinery and equipment, with increasing returns based on the division of labor providing the basis for Smith's optimism. Labor productivity could either be increased through the expansion of skills and dexterity, or through the adoption of new technology and the deployment of new machinery and equipment. Smith emphasized the limited but critical role of the state to guarantee the sanctity of property, to create the conditions enhancing free and voluntary exchange, and to ensure that commitments generated from contracts of exchange are honored. Under such circumstances, the only limit to continuous material progress would be the size of the market; this limit could be removed through trade among nations, which would in turn result in global peace and tranquility (Smith [1759] 2006, 128–50).

But it was not until World War II, and especially in the postwar era, that economists took special interest in the problems of underdeveloped countries, focusing on policies that might relax the constraints to sustained growth and development. In 1943, my teacher Paul Rosenstein-Rodan was one of the earliest economists to do so. He saw industry, with its strong backward and forward linkages to other industries, with a higher productivity than agriculture, and with its increasing returns, as the vehicle for rapid economic growth. To benefit from these linkages, a "big push" was needed and would have to be initiated by governments, because the scale of these strategic investments would be too large for the nascent private sectors. Following Rosenstein-Rodan in the 1950s, Ragnar Nurkse believed that the problem of developing countries was low productivity because of an insufficient level of capital, which, in turn, was the result of low capital accumulation, itself a consequence of low investment caused by low savings. To create a large enough impetus for the economy to break out of the vicious circle, governments would have to undertake large-scale investments in a sufficiently wide spectrum of industries. Arthur Lewis saw industrialization, with higher returns and savings, as the way for underdeveloped countries to break out of their low-level (income) equilibrium trap. As long as surplus labor existed in the agricultural sector, the real wages of labor (relative to food) in the industrial sector would not increase, affording industry expansion prospects without increasing labor costs. For Lewis and a number of other economists, developing countries that had a colonial past were presumed to have an enclave economy, where colonial policy promoted the growth of sectors that were owned and controlled by the colonial powers and left the remaining sectors neglected, resulting in a two-sector, or "dualistic," economy. Lewis considered the migration of rural or traditional workers to the industrial sector a positive factor, but Gunnar Myrdal believed that any stimulus to growth, which would mean higher wages and income in the nontraditional sector, would attract the more able and productive out of the traditional sector, leaving only the very young and the less productive workers behind. This would initiate a dynamic of ever-worsening income inequality in the country. An important contribution of Myrdal to the evolution of thinking on economic development was the role of institutions. He believed that the existence of a strong efficient state in most industrial countries was a major underpinning of their development.

While Albert Hirschman agreed with the essence of "big push" strategy, he believed that the resources required to successfully implement such strategies were beyond the reach of a typical developing country. Instead, Hirschman advocated a focus on a few key industries with critical strategic linkages to the rest of the economy. In the priority sector, where the key industries were located, excess capacity would be created, thus reducing the price of products while creating shortages in the rest of the sectors. Such a process would also create new industries, further expanding employment, income, and growth. Another of my teachers, Walt Rostow, saw the growth of developing countries from a traditional society to sustained high growth as consisting of five stages: (1) the traditional society; (2) the stage of precondition for take-off; (3) the take-off stage; (4) the drive to maturity; and (5) the age of mass consumption. During this process, each stage provides the preconditions for the next.

All these economists, who wrote during the 1950s, saw economic growth as synonymous with economic development. In 1957, Robert Solow, another teacher, decomposed the output-input relations to obtain the contribution of each element of the production process to the growth of output—the contributions of labor and capital—and what could not be attributed to these, the residual, was attributed to technology, or total factor productivity (TFP). Growth accounting performed over a large number of countries over a number of decades has provided convincing evidence that TFP is the major reason for differential growth rates across countries. In 1986, Paul Romer developed a growth model with an endogenous growth of technology or knowledge. While each individual firm would still face diminishing returns to investment in knowledge generation, society as a whole would experience increasing returns to knowledge. Romer argued that while the growth of output depends on factor inputs—namely, labor and capital—it also depends on the stock of knowledge, which has beneficial externalities and generates opportunities for innovation that, in turn, expand the range and availability of products, increasing growth. The mechanism for society to increase the stock of knowledge is research and development (R&D): the higher the level of current investment in R&D, the larger the stock of future knowledge. The externality, or the spillover effect, of past investments in R&D reduces its cost over time.

In the latter part of the twentieth century, in a throwback to Adam Smith, economists began to attribute some of the differential in economic performance to the quality of institutions. This explanation for economic performance had its more recent roots in the last decades of the nineteenth and the first few decades of the twentieth century in the writings of scholars who rejected many of the assumptions and the methodology of neoclassical economics. The new institutional economics (NIE) view of economic development is that in addition to factor endowment, human capital, and technological progress, institutional structure plays a significant role in development. Empirical analysis based on this model has produced results with significant policy implications. The starting point of why institutions matter in economic development is why countries with considerable resource endowments and access to finance are, nevertheless, economically (and politically) underdeveloped. While differences in capital per worker, investment in human capital, and technology may explain differences in the level of per capita income across countries, these cannot be considered a fundamental reason for the underdevelopment of many countries. This is particularly important in the age of globalization since capital is mobile and should move to countries where its rate of return is higher. Moreover, investment in human capital should have higher returns in countries with low investment in education. However, if the institutional structure of a country is weak, its ability to mobilize, organize, and finance growth is constrained.

Neoclassical growth theory implicitly assumed that economies have institutions that provide political stability, guarantee and enforce property rights, and protect and enforce private contracts and the rule of law. In addition to assuming that the countries had efficient markets, it was assumed they also had the financial, legal, accounting, and regulatory apparatus that ensure transparency, accountability, and good governance. Douglass North (1995, 2003) has over the years argued that while the growth of advanced economies is explained by productivity increases from division of labor, specialization, technical progress, and the competitive market, the key to their performance is low transaction costs, resulting from the institutional structure that developed over the last 250 years. Conversely, it is the existence of prohibitive transaction costs that was the main obstacle to development. A modern economy relies on impersonal relationships that, by their very nature, involve a great deal of uncertainty. Efficient institutions reduce uncertainties and related costs.

Much of the intellectual effort of major thinkers in the eighteenth and nineteenth centuries was focused on the search for appropriate ways of establishing social order in the face of rapid industrialization and resulting socioeconomic dislocations as disorder increases uncertainty, decreases confidence and increases transactions costs (North 2003). North argues that after a period of disorder resulting from radical changes and crises, whether social order will be established quickly depends on the stability of the institutional structure of society, with those having such stable institutions recovering more rapidly. The collectivity of institutions provides society with the social capability to establish a stable order by reducing uncertainties or ambiguities. The institutional structure of a society is composed of constitutions, laws, and rules of governance; its government, its finances, economy, and politics; written rules, codes, and agreements that govern contractual relations and exchange and trade relationships; and commonly shared beliefs, social norms, and codes governing human behavior. The clarity of rules, social norms, and enforcement characteristics are important to the degree of compliance exhibited by the members of a society. The higher the degree of rule-compliance, the more stable the social order and the lower the transaction costs in the society. For example, social norms that prescribe trust, trustworthiness, and cooperation have a significant impact on encouraging collective action and coordination (North 2003, 115–30).

North believes that poor performance is due to path-dependencies resulting from past institutional structure, reflecting a belief system that is difficult to change either because the needed changes that improve economic performance run counter to the belief system or these changes pose a threat to existing political or business leaders. While acknowledging that needed changes to improve economic performance may be slow to materialize because of cultural factors and path-dependency, North nevertheless envisions an ideal political-economic institutional structure that has potential for achieving good economic performance and societal well-being as a framework of (a) an institutional matrix that defines and establishes a set of rights and privileges; (b) a stable structure of exchange relationships in economic and political markets; (c) a government that is credibly committed to a set of political rules and enforcement to protect individuals, organizations, and exchange relationships; (d) rule-compliance as a result of internalization of norms as well as coercive enforcement; (e) a set of economic institutions that create incentives for the members of society and organizations to engage in productive activities; and (f) a set of property rights and an effective price system that lead to low transaction costs in production, exchange, and distribution. Contrasted with this ideal institutional structure, North argues that the institutional framework of poorly performing economies does not provide the right incentive structure for activities that can improve productivity because of vested interests that resist change and because factor and product markets are ineffective in getting relative prices right. A prerequisite to successful actions to improve economic performance is "a viable polity that will put in place the necessary economic institutions and provide effective enforcement" (North 2003, 157). In 2009, North, Wallis, and Weingast argued that countries do not develop when rulers and their cronies establish a rent-seeking coalition to limit the access of the majority to both the political and economic systems. Most recently, Acemoglu and Robinson (2012), following in the footstep of North, have essentially confirmed that institutions are important for growth and that the political environment in turn determines the form and quality of institutions; effective institutions require a supportive political system. Their contribution includes a number of historical episodes that they claim confirms that when the political system creates private gains for those in power (confiscating the rightful gains of others), society loses and the country becomes impoverished. In the case of the Middle East, they conclude that religion has nothing to do with the underdevelopment of the region.

On a parallel track, during the 1970s, the intellectual and practical field of development changed its focus to human beings, both as the means and the end of the development process. In the late 1970s and early 1980s, economists, inspired by the contributions of Mahbub ul Haq and Amartya Sen, began to question the popular definition of economic development and the path for its achievement. They argued that development was much more than an increasing level of per capita income and a simple structural transformation. For the first time, human development—including education, health care, poverty eradication, a more even income distribution, environmental quality, and freedom—was seen as an integral component of the economic development process. Thus, it has been through the passage of time that economists have come to see the process of economic development as much more than the quest for increasing average per capita income, as reflected in the United Nation's initiation of a Human Development Index in 1990. Although man needs bread to live, man does not live by bread alone! Following these footsteps, a number of academics have introduced additional components of human well-being: sharing with the less advantaged, belonging to a group, the avoidance of opulent living, and sustainability and natural resource management to benefit current as well as future generations.

In assessing human well-being in Sen's framework, capabilities represent the real opportunities individuals have to lead or achieve a certain type of life. Functionings, on the other hand, represent the actual life they lead. Defining development as a process that promotes human well-being would then mean expansion of capabilities of people to flourish. In this framework, freedom is "the real opportunity we have to accomplish what we value" (Sen 1994). Consequently, progress is assessed primarily in terms of whether freedoms are enhanced. Ananta Kumar Giri (2000) argues that Sen neglects the development of the "self," maintaining that self-development is a crucial aspect of societal development, without which Sen's approach would not succeed. John Cameron (2000) criticizes Sen for focusing only on the poor and lower levels of income, while ignoring or neglecting the upper levels of income and the impact of income inequality on the development of capabilities; he argues that in so doing, Sen deemphasizes the need for radical income distribution that would correct the patterns of functionings in society. Thomas Pogge (2001) argues that affluent functionings damage human well-being and that the behavior of the affluent is a direct cause of the underdevelopment of poor countries.

This discussion has traced the evolution of the concept of economic development—from a concern for social order, the role of civil society, culture, and state to development as material well-being, with ethics, freedom, development of the self, income equality, environmental preservation, and sustainability factored in. It should be stressed that Smith is the basis of Western thinking on development; however, the author of the *Wealth of Nations*, stressing the self-interest motive that is the basis of utility and profit maximization for the individual consumer and producer at any cost to society, including the impoverishment and exploitation of fellow human beings, is very different from the author of *The Theory of Moral Sentiments*. Smith makes clear in his less cited book that while compliance with the rules prescribed by the Creator is a must, compliance with the market, an instrument for achieving the greatest good, is also a necessity. Smith succinctly and clearly shares some of the foundational scaffolding of Islam: belief in the One and Only Creator; belief in the accountability of the Day of Judgment; belief in the necessity of compliance with the rules prescribed by the Creator; and belief that justice is achieved with full compliance with rules. To paraphrase Sen, no space need be made artificially for justice and fairness; it already exists in the rules prescribed by the Law Giver. Smith considers the internalization of rules—being consciously aware of the ever-presence of the Creator and acting accordingly—as crucial to all human conduct, including economics. Rules reduce uncertainty and transaction costs and promote coordination, making collective action possible and promoting social solidarity. All of these elements have been directly emphasized or strongly implied by the Qur'an and in the traditions of the Prophet.

Economic Development in Islam

Today, the Western concept of development is focused on efficient institutions; a political system that nurtures institutions and prohibits rent-seeking activities and the confiscation of legitimate wealth; and a social outlook that embraces human development, including education, health care, poverty eradication, a more even income distribution, sustainability, and freedom. This is akin to the Islamic view—with one big difference and one small one. Islamic teachings (not the practice of Islam today) embrace heavier doses of social and economic justice, morality, humanity, compassion, generosity, and charity; and Islam places more emphasis on rules and rule-compliance.

Foundational Framework of Development in Islam

The essential framework for individual and collective human progress is presented in the Qur'an, and is, in turn, made operational by the traditions of the Prophet Mohammad. The Prophet, who implemented in Medina the institutional structure specified in the Qur'an, provides the ultimate frame of reference for the implementation of the Qur'anic prescription. An important aspect of Prophet Mohammad's interpretation is that it operationalized and, to an extent, localized the conditions necessary for development specified in the Qur'an. The Qur'an provides the framework and specifies rules (institutions) that are, to a degree, abstract, while the traditions of the Prophet articulate the operational form of these rules.

The Qur'anic concept of development has three dimensions: individual self-development; the physical development of the earth; and the development of the human collectivity, which includes both. The first specifies a dynamic process of the growth of the human toward perfection. The second specifies the utilization of natural resources to develop the earth to provide for the material needs of the individual and all of humanity. The third concept encompasses the progress of the human collectivity toward full integration and unity. Together they constitute the rules-based compliance system, which is intended to assure progress on the three interrelated dimensions of development. Fundamental to all three is the belief that the Supreme Creator has provided the ways and means to facilitate the achievement of all three dimensions of development.

The three dimensions of development are closely interrelated to the point where balanced progress in all three is needed to achieve development. The four basic elements of the Western concept of development—namely, scarcity, rationality, and the roles of the state and of the market—are perceived somewhat differently in Islam. All three dimensions of Islamic development assign heavy responsibility to individuals and society—with both held responsible for any lack of development. Balanced development is defined as balanced progress in all three dimensions. Progress is balanced if it is accompanied with justice, both in its general (*ádl*) and in its interpersonal (*qist*) dimension. The objective of such balanced development is to achieve progress on the path to perfection by humans, through rule-compliance. Enforcement of the prescribed rules is accomplished by an internal and an external mechanism. The love of humans for one another is a part of their adoration of the Creator, and each human is responsible for ensuring that others are rule-compliant. The governance structure envisaged in Islam requires full transparency and accountability by the state and the full participation of all members.

There are four fundamental concepts supporting the foundational justification for the rule-based system that is Islam. The first is *walayah*, the unconditional, dynamic, active, ever-present Love of the Supreme Creator for His Creation, manifested through the act of creation and the provision of sustenance.[1] For humans, this means sufficient resources to sustain life and divine rules enabling humans to sustain and flourish on this plane of existence. Each human reciprocates His Love by extending His love to other humans and to the rest of creation. Second is the concept of *karamah*, human dignity. The Qur'an considers humans to be the crowning achievement of His Creation for whose personal and collective development everything else has been created. Humans are endowed with intelligence to know their Creator, to recognize and appreciate the universe and everything in it, and to understand that the reasons for their own existence are contingent upon the Will of their Creator. The third concept is the *meethaq*, the primordial covenant in which all humans were called before their Supreme Creator and asked to testify that they recognize in Him the One and Only Creator and Sustainer of the entire Creation and all other implications flowing from this testimony. The concept of *meethaq*, in turn, unfolds into three basic principles: (1) *Tawhid*, the One-and-Onlyness of the Creator, which unfolds into the one-and-onlyness of the created and its unity, including above all the unity of humankind; (2) *Nubuwwa*, the continuous chain of humans appointed by the

Creator to remind, warn, cleanse, teach, and induce humans to bring about and uphold justice within the created order through their position of agency-trustee assigned and empowered by the Supreme Creator; and (3) *Ma'ad*, the return of creation to its origin and the accountability of humanity (individually and collectively)—success and failure in achieving, establishing, and upholding justice toward their selves, toward others of their kind, and toward the rest of creation. The fourth concept is that of *khilafah*: agent-trustee relationship. Jointly, *walayah* and *karamah* provide the basis for *khilafah*. The Love of the Creator endows humans with dignity and intelligence so as to manifest *walayah* through the instrumentality of *khilafah*. *Khilafah* is the empowerment of humans by their Creator as agent-trustee to extend *walayah* to one another, materially through the resources provided to them by the Creator and nonmaterially through the manifestation of unconditional love for their own kind, as well as for the rest of creation.

The Qur'an uses two words for justice: *qist* and *ádl*. The first is the chief characteristic of appropriate human relations and of human relations toward the rest of creation. It is a human phenomenon; it is not a divine trait. *Ádl*, on the other hand, is a feature of Allah's Actions that manifests itself in the perfect balance of the cosmos; it characterizes the Action of Allah to place everything in its rightful place. Any injustice perpetrated by the individual against other humans and against the rest of creation is ultimately an injustice to the self; Allah loves justice; it is a central part of His Universal *Walayah*. The response of creation to Universal *Walayah* must mirror the Justice of Allah. *Qist* and *ádl* manifested by humans is a fundamental manifestation of positive *walayah* oriented toward Allah. The core activity of *walayah* is love manifested through knowledge and the upholding of justice. Therefore, *walayah* is (a) a powerful unifying force by means of which every aspect of Islam can be either defined and placed in context, and (b) a criterion for determining the degree to which any given phenomenon is Islamic—that is, to what degree it is in harmony with the essence of Islam. In recognition and acknowledgment of their dignity, the Supreme Creator has endowed humans with freedom of choice. The autonomy provided by the freedom of choice is exercised through compliance with rules (institutions). The agent-trustee office requires the activation of the nonmaterial gifts from the Creator that empower humans to perform their responsibility. To this end, however, a self-cleansing and purification process is required.

The importance of knowledge is also emphasized in Islam. The knowledge of rules describes the path from Islam to *iman* (belief) in its various stages and characteristics such as gratitude, patience, righteousness, honesty, justice, struggle, and forbearance. Much of becoming intimately and experientially familiar with the knowledge of just duty relates to the progress of the self. It empowers and strengthens the working of the spirit gifted to humans. For individuals, Islam is a process governed by "just duty," the second type of knowledge named by the Prophet. The knowledge of just duty—an intimate knowledge of the rules of behavior—and the implementation of that knowledge result in inner harmony.

Dimensions of Development in Islam

One of the important tests for humans comes about when some individuals and groups experience conditions of plenty while others are faced with scarcity. The rules prescribed by Allah specify the appropriate response to these tests, which are considered by the Qur'an to be signs for the true believer. The wealthy are the ones who reject the messages of sharing and giving that have been brought to them by the messengers of Allah. Those who share and spend their wealth in the way prescribed are the adorers of Allah and He recompenses them for their spending aimed at pleasing Him. These humans recognize that the source of their blessings of bounty is the Creator and not their own doing. There are those, however, who, when faced with an adverse trial, turn to their Creator for help, but once they achieve success they attribute it to themselves.

In stark contrast to conventional economics, *scarcity in Islam is not a binding constraint at the level of humanity*. It is only a constraint at a micro-individual level; at this level it is a test both for the person who is constrained and for the person who is not constrained. For the constrained, it is a test of the strength of belief that has been experientially revealed to the person and is a light shining on the strength and weakness of the self. For those economically better off, it is a test of their recognition of the real source of their wealth and the strength of their rule-compliance in helping remove economic constraints: namely, barriers from the path to perfection of those in need of help. There is recognition and an important role for legitimate authorities, those who have *Walayah/walayah*, *Rububiyyah/úbudiyyah* relationships and are fully familiar with and adhere to the prescribed rules. Such persons are referred to in the Qur'an as *ululamr*. The important point is that it is the strength of the rule-compliance of these people, not their cunningness, physical or military prowess, or other worldly advantages, such as riches, that legitimizes their authority to oversee the implementation of the prescribed rules. It is clear that the strength of belief for those who will be vested with legitimate authority must surpass that of a representative believer.

The traditions of the Prophet invest the legitimacy of leadership of the community with another dimension, that of *bay'ah*, a contract between the person who is deemed worthy of accession to the office due to demonstrated full compliance with prescribed rules and acceptability by the members of the community. The manner in which the Prophet organized the first community as specified in the Qur'an constitutes legitimate political authority, and he sought acceptability among the multireligious population of Medina. The central term of the contract between the ruler and the ruled is understood clearly: full compliance with the prescribed rules by the legitimate authority. The community and its members commit to following and obeying the legitimate ruler *so long as* he is rule-compliant. The legitimate ruler commits not only to complying with all the prescribed rules, among which is the imperative of consultation, but also to ensuring the preservation, cohesion, and well-being of the community in accordance with the duties of the trusteeship-agency office. The strength of its legitimacy is derived from the enforcement of the rules. No authority has any legitimate basis for creating new rules that contradict those specified in the

Qur'an and practiced by the Prophet. *No political authority selected on the basis of this framework could retain legitimacy in the face of noncompliance with or violation of the rules.* As history shows, governments that violated rules retained power only by force. But such an event is simultaneously and concurrently a failure of rule-compliance by the community being ruled by force. Commanding others to rule-compliance is part of the cognizance of the love-bond between the Creator and the created since rule-compliance is the necessary and sufficient condition for staying on the path to perfection. No political authority can violate the prescribed rules and retain legitimacy, and no community can claim that it has remained a believing community while being ruled over by an authority that is noncompliant with and in violation of the prescribed rules. In short, it is the noncompliance with rules that leads to the emergence of unjust, dictatorial, and totalitarian authority.

Commanding what is good and forbidding what is evil is a duty incumbent on individuals as well as on the whole community. It is a promoter of solidarity and achievement, and a preserver of social order in the community. *The very existence of oppression, corruption, massive inequality, and poverty in a community is* prima facie *evidence of noncompliance with or outright shirking of this duty on the part of the group's members.* Given the strength of the emphasis on rule-compliance by the individual, even the existence of a legitimate political authority does not absolve a human being from the necessity of performing the duty of commanding rule-compliance and forbidding rule-violation. Coupled with the prescribed rule of consultation, this duty gives every member of society the right, and imposes on him or her the duty of participating in community affairs. And since the primary responsibility of the legitimate political authority is to enforce rule-compliance, the more active the individuals' role in assuring that their own behaviors and those of others in the community are rule-compliant, the more limited the need for interference of the authority in the socioeconomic life of the community.

Turning to rule-compliance in economic transactions, the Qur'an acknowledges the existence of markets and places great emphasis on contracts of exchange (*bay'*) and trade (*tijarah*). *Bay'* refers to any contract of exchange, including the exchange of commitments of fidelity to prescribed rules by a leader and by followers. A contract of exchange is needed for the trade of goods and services and for other economic transactions, and is therefore more general than trade. In other words, *bay'* is a contract between two participants to exchange, while *tijarah* is an action involving, specifically, buying and selling. In *bay'*, the two sides of the contract share the risk contained in the agreement to exchange. On the other hand, *tijarah* refers to trade: buying in order to sell with the intention of making a profit. The Qur'an makes a distinction between a debt contract (*dayn*), a contract of exchange (*bay'*), and trade (*tijarah*). Debts must be repaid on the date specified in the contract, and contracts must be written and witnessed. The Qur'an commands that trade must be based on mutual consent. A contract of pledge of political allegiance is called *mubaya'ah*, and is also based on a contract of exchange.

Replacing interest rate–based debt contracts with exchange has significant economic implications. First, before parties can enter into a contract of exchange, they must have the property rights in what they are going to exchange. Second, the parties need a place or a forum to consummate the exchange: a market. Third, the market needs rules for its efficient operation. Fourth, market rules need enforcement. Exchange facilitates specialization and allows the parties to share production, transportation, marketing, sales, and price risk. Therefore, exchange is above all a means of risk sharing. From an economic standpoint, therefore, by prohibiting interest rate-based contracts and ordaining exchange contracts the Qur'an encourages risk sharing and prohibits risk transfer, risk shedding, and risk shifting. Islamic finance is basically a financial system structured on risk sharing and the prohibition of debt financing (leveraging).[2] The central proposition of Islamic finance is the prohibition of transactions that embody rent for a specific period of time as a percentage of the loaned principle without the transfer of the property rights claims, thus shifting the entire risk of the transaction to the borrower. The alternative to debt-based contracts, namely mutual exchange, where one bundle of property rights is exchanged for another, allows both parties to share production, transportation, and marketing risks. In order to fit into this framework, financial intermediation and banking in the Islamic financial system (and more generally in a risk-sharing system) has been proposed as having two tiers. The first is a banking system that accepts deposits for safekeeping without accruing any return and requiring 100 percent reserves, thus protecting the payment system of the economy while concurrently limiting the credit-creating ability of the banking system and thus obviating the need for a deposit guarantee, as in the conventional fractional reserve system. The second tier is an investment component that functions as a classical financial intermediary, channeling savings to investment projects, and where deposits in investment banks are considered as equity investments with no guarantees for their face value at maturity and subject to the sharing of profits and losses. Depositors are investors in the pool of assets maintained by the bank on the assets side of its balance sheet.

It is important to recognize—though it may be difficult, given our mindsets—that there is nothing magical about the recent historical prominence of debt financing. Before the rise of debt financing, equity financing was preeminent. But a host of factors and developments catapulted debt financing to the forefront. Risk-sharing finance is trust-intensive, and trade financing during the Middle Ages was based on risk sharing, which, in turn, was based on mutual trust. Upheavals of the late Middle Ages in the fourteenth and fifteen centuries, including the Black Death, strife within the Church and between the Church and hereditary rulers, and general economic decline, contributed to the breakdown of trust in communities and among their members. While risk-sharing techniques continued to prevail in Europe until the mid-seventeenth century, beginning in the mid-sixteenth century, the institution of interest-based debt financing also began to be used more widely and extensively. The catalyst for debt financing was primarily the breakdown of trust, in Europe and elsewhere, and the adoption of securitization in finance. Over time, government deposit insurance schemes, tax treatments, rules, and regulations have all heavily favored debt-based contracts over risk-sharing contracts. Thus, risk sharing is still at an early stage of development in all countries, to say nothing of its even more modest international practice. These developments have helped perpetuate a system that a number of renowned economists, such as Keynes, have deemed detrimental to growth, development, and equitable income and wealth distribution. More recently, a growing literature and proposed reforms have argued that the stability of a financial system can be assured only by limiting credit expansion and leveraging; this, in turn, requires the elimination of implicit and explicit subsidies that fuel moral hazard, such as subsidized deposit insurance schemes and guarantees that support institutions that are deemed "too large to fail."

The Qur'an makes it clear that prescribed rules require that economic transactions be based on freedom of choice and freedom of contract, which in turn require property rights over possessions to be exchanged. While the historical evidence strongly suggests that markets already existed in Arabia, it was the Prophet who created the first market that was structured with operations in accordance with the prescribed rules of conduct for justice to prevail in exchange and trade. He appointed a market supervisor to promote full compliance with the prescribed rules of market behavior. While the legitimate authority has the obligation of supervising and enforcing rule-compliance, market participants are rule-compliant as long as they are free from further interference. The history of the market created by the Prophet in Medina underlines the importance and centrality of the market and rules.

As stated earlier, the Qur'an and the traditions of the Prophet envision development as composed of three interrelated and interdependent dimensions, and the most important of all these is individual human development, without which the other two would not progress as envisioned. The process of human self-development is referred to in the Qur'an as *rushd*, which is the opposite of *qhay*, meaning deep ignorance. When the process of *rushd* strengthens, the person is said to becoming *rasheed*: that is, someone who is making progress on the path to perfection. This stands in stark contrast to Western economic thought, as it was only in the last three decades of the twentieth century that professionals looked at a broader concept of development beyond the growth of physical capacity to produce goods and services: namely, that economic growth is only an element of the overall progress of human beings and that humans should be the ends, rather than the means, of development. Even in the most sophisticated of concepts—Sen's development as freedom—the imperative of self-development as the prerequisite for a comprehension of the substantive meaning of freedom has received little attention. If development means freedom and functioning, then what guarantee is there that without self-development, doing what one values will not lead to fully self-centered, selfish outcomes? These selfish outcomes include massive poverty and misery for a large segment of humanity side by side with incredible opulence and wealth accumulation for a few. Some minimum level of income is doubtless necessary to avoid destitution and absolute poverty before one is able to reflect upon one's action-decision choices. But beyond that, self-development becomes an imperative for humans to recognize the responsibilities of their *Khalifal* state and to develop the earth so as to remove economic barriers and minimize the pain of material paucity for all humans.

Much of the concern with the early formulations of development focused on achieving and maintaining social order. The Islamic concept places great emphasis on the need to focus human energy on the achievement of social solidarity and unity. In turn, that unity is firmly grounded in the purpose of creation, the *Walayah* of the Creator for and over humanity, which invested high dignity in the human state and the responsibilities implied by that state. The *Khalifal* functions of each human can be meaningful only in collectivity with other humans. Islam's emphasis on the social dimension is so great that there is not one act of adoration and worship that is devoid of societal implications. The success of each human is dependent on patient and tolerant interaction and cooperation with other humans. The idea is that mutual support and social solidarity bring about a more tolerant and patient response to individual and collective difficulties, heighten cognizance and consciousness of the Creator and of the commonalities of humanity, intensify adoration of Allah through mutual service to others and the rest of the creation, and ease the path to perfection. Complete success is possible only through appropriate social interaction. Even if it were possible for a human to achieve a degree of felicity individually and in total isolation from the human collectivity, this verse (chapter 3, verse 200) would suggest that such success is far from complete. The Qur'an repeatedly urges humans toward social solidarity and a just social order; they must follow the prescribed rules that serve to purify the self and to create social cohesion: namely, the rules that position both individuals and society on a straight path. The fundamental objective is to create a society in which individuals become cognizant of all their capabilities, including the spiritual. When humans realize these capabilities, a life the Qur'an refers to as *Hayat Tayyibah*, the good life—a life free of anxiety, fear, and regrets—becomes possible; a life of full awareness of the beauty of the creation and Creator; a life of solidarity with other humans and the rest of creation; and a life lived in the full Grace of Allah.

The Rules and the Practice of an Islamic Economy

The Prophet Mohammad has provided the foundational structure of a *Tawhid*-centered society. Rules of governance, accountability, and transparency; rules regarding property ownership and protection; rules regarding the formation and the structure of the market; rules concerning the role of the state vis-à-vis the market; rules of behavior by market participants; rules regarding distribution and redistribution; rules related to education, technological progress, and society's infrastructure; and, finally, rules regarding sources of government income and its expenditures, were all promulgated during the 13 years the Prophet spent in Medina.

The central framework and operation of these rules is *justice*. The Prophet understood the essential objective of his selection, appointment, and message to be to encourage and insert justice in human societies, as emphasized in the Qur'an. The Prophet taught the responsibility of the individual, the collectivity, and the state. He particularly emphasized the equality of individuals before the law, and that all rules that are incumbent on individuals and their collectivity must be more strictly observed by those in positions of authority. Thence the famous saying attributed to him: *"Authority may survive disbelief but not injustice."* Insistence on justice became the hallmark of the institutional scaffolding of governance, a structure with full transparency and accountability. It was in Medina where the Prophet was able to put into operation and implement important rules. The first and the most important of the Prophet's efforts was the formation of a society based on Islamic teaching; this he achieved with the assistance of the critical mass of his followers who had migrated with him to Medina. It was first necessary to create peace, social stability, and the means of defending the nascent society from external threats. The social contract with the inhabitants of Medina constituted agreed-upon procedures for administering society. Given that Muslims who had migrated with him were either poor or had lost their wealth fleeing persecution in Mecca, he initiated a contract of mutual support. Next, the Prophet clarified rules of property rights over natural resources. Those who had property at the time they entered Islam were given full rights over their properties.

Humans, in their collectivity, are entrusted with the responsibility of agent-trustee of the resources Allah has gifted them to remove economic obstacles created on the path to perfection of individual humans, who otherwise face the scarcity of these resources. Before enumerating the rules regarding property rights, it is useful to understand what property means. It is a bundle of rights, duties, powers, and liabilities embodied in an asset. In the Western concept, private property is considered the right of an individual to use and dispose of, along with the right to exclude others from access to and use of that asset. Even in the evolution of Western economies, this is a new concept of property that is thought to have accompanied the emergence of the current form of free market economies. Before that, however, property rights did not include the right to dispose of an asset or to exclude others from its use. It was thought that the free market economy required a revision. In Islam, however, limitations on the disposal of an asset are retained without diminishing the role of the market.

The first of eight principles of property rights in Islam acknowledged the permanent, constant, and invariant ownership of all property by Allah. The second principle acknowledged transfer by Allah of the right of possession to all of mankind. The third principle mandated equal opportunity of access by all to the natural resources provided by the Creator, to be combined with their labor to produce goods and services. The fourth rule recognizes only two ways in which individuals gain legitimate property rights: (1) through their creative labor, and/or (2) through transfers—exchange, contracts, grants, or inheritance—from others who have gained the property rights title to an asset through their own labor. Thus work is the basis of the acquisition of right to property. Work, however, is not only performed for the purpose of satisfying one's desires, but also considered a duty and an obligation of all.

The fifth rule forbids gaining instantaneous property rights without working to earn them. The exception is lawful transfer. This rule also prohibits property rights gained through gambling, theft, earning interest on money lent, bribery, or generally from sources considered unlawful. Just as work is a right and obligation of all humans, access to and use of natural-physical resources provided by the Creator for producing goods and services are also every human's right and obligation. All humans are ordained to apply their creative labor to these resources to produce what society needs. If an individual, for whatever reason, lacks the ability to work, it does not deprive him or her of his or her original right to resources granted to every human by their Creator.

The rule of the "immutability of property rights" constitutes the sixth rule of property relations. This rule sanctifies the duty of sharing by transferring it into the principles of property rights and obligations. Before any work is performed on natural-physical resources, all humans have an equal right and opportunity to access these resources. When individuals apply their creative labor to resources, they gain a right to priority in the possession, use, and exchange of the resulting product without nullifying the original property rights of the Creator or the rights He granted to all humans in the final product or the proceeds from its sale.

The duty of sharing the product or the income and wealth proceeding from its sale constitutes the seventh rule of property relations, which relates to property ownership rights as a trust. This rule is made operational through the ordained duties imposed on income and wealth, which must be paid to cleanse income and wealth from the rights of others. This is perhaps the reason why the Qur'an refers to these duties as *zakat*, from the root word meaning cleansing and purification. These duties are likened to tree pruning, which simultaneously rids the tree of its undesirable parts and allows its further growth. Although the Qur'an acknowledges that in His Wisdom the Lord has created humans with differences, it also emphasizes that these differences are only apparent and that all humans are the same. The real difference between them, the one that ultimately counts, is the degree of awareness of Allah-conscious. No other difference matters.

In a society in which there is poverty amidst plenty, the roots of inequality must be traced to distortions in the pattern of resource endowments, in the workings of the exchange and/or distribution mechanisms, and/or in the redistributive framework. The most fundamental among these is the pattern of resource endowment. When one is granted the mental-physical capacity by the Creator to access more of these resources, it means others less able or unable to use these resources are in fact one's partners, whose rights in the final post-production, post-market proceeds must be redeemed. The Qur'an affirms that because these are rights to be redeemed rather than charity, extreme care must be taken of the recipient's human dignity.

The eighth rule of property relations imposes limitations on the right of disposing of property—a right that is absolute in the Western concept of property rights. In Islam, individuals have an obligation not to waste, squander, or destroy property, or to use property for opulence or unlawful purposes. Once the specified property obligations are appropriately discharged, including that of sharing in the prescribed amount and manner, property rights on the remaining part of income, wealth, and assets are held sacred and inviolate and no one can force their appropriation or expropriation. While the above rules strongly affirm mankind's natural tendency to possess—particularly products resulting from individual labor—the concomitant property obligations promote interdependence and cohesion among the members of society. Private initiative, choice, and reward are recognized as legitimate and protected but are not allowed to subvert the obligation of sharing.

To ensure the property rights of all members of society, property rights over natural resources (such as mines) were placed in trust of either the state, to be used for the benefit of all, or in the hands of society at large as commons (for example, surface and underground water).[3] A clear distinction was made between the right of ownership and the right of possession, particularly in the case of land. Any individual could combine labor, capital, and available land to produce a commodity over which the person would have full property rights. The land would remain in the person's possession as long as the land was in production. However, if the land was not used for continuous production (for a designated period, such as three consecutive years), the person would lose the right of possession, and another producer would have the right to take possession of the land to use labor and capital to produce a commodity.

To protect the interests of society and maintain social order and stability, the Prophet enunciated rules, based on those already prescribed by the Qur'an, to give priority to the rights of society over those of the individual. These include the rule of no harm or injury, the prohibition of the waste and destruction of resources and products, of extravagance and opulence in production and consumption, of individual behavior that could create instability in the system, and of illegal, immoral, and unethical sources of income and wealth. These rules, while general, tangentially relate to property rights in that while these rights for the individual are recognized and protected, they are not allowed to harm the interests of society. The Prophet focused attention of producers and consumers on the social costs and benefits of their action-decisions rather than on their private costs. This would induce greater efficiency in the use of resources to benefit society. The rule of *no harm, no injury* was promulgated by the Prophet based on the Qur'an to ensure that there is no adverse impact of private economic behavior on third parties or on society. The purpose of this rule appears to be to promote the convergence of the private and social costs of economic activity. The Prophet, in accordance with prescribed rules, prohibited theft, bribery, interest on money, the usurpation of the property rights of others by force, and other ethically and morally forbidden activities as sources of income and wealth. These activities create instantaneous property rights without commensurate exertion of labor in production and are socially unproductive and harmful.

Before the advent of Islam, trade had been the most important economic activity of the Arabian Peninsula. A number of thriving markets had developed throughout the area. Upon his arrival in Medina, the Prophet organized a market that was structured and governed by rules based on the Qur'an. He implemented a number of policies to encourage the expansion of trade and the market. The Prophet prohibited the imposition of taxes on individual merchants, as well as on transactions. He also implemented policies to encourage trade among Muslims and non-Muslims by creating incentives for non-Muslim merchants in and outside of Medina. After the conquest of Mecca and the rest of Arabia, these and other market rules were institutionalized and generalized to all markets. These rules included, in addition to those mentioned above, no restrictions on international or interregional trade (including no taxation of imports and exports); the free spatial movement of resources, goods, and services from one market to another; no barriers to market entry and exit; free and transparent information regarding the price, quality, and quantity of goods, particularly in the case of spot trade; the specification of the exact date for the completion of trade in instances when trade was to take place over time; the specification of the property and other rights of all participants in every contract; guaranteed contract enforcement by the state and its legal apparatus; the prohibition of the hoarding of commodities and of productive resources for the purpose of pushing up their price; the prohibition of price controls; a ban on sellers or buyers harming the interests of other market participants, for example, by allowing a third party to interrupt negotiations between two parties in order to influence the negotiations to the benefit of one of the parties; and a ban on the shortchanging of buyers, for example, by not giving full weight and measure. Moreover, sellers and buyers were given the right of annulment of a business agreement: (a) before leaving the location in which it was taking place; (b) in the case of a buyer who had not seen the commodity and after seeing it found it unacceptable; (c) if either the seller or the buyer discovered that the product had either been sold for less than, or bought for higher than, it was worth; (d) if the buyer discovered that the quality of the product was not as expected; (e) if side conditions were specified during the negotiations which were left unfulfilled; (f) if a delivery period was specified but the product was not delivered on time; and (g) when the subject of the negotiations were pack animals, the buyer had the right to return the animal up to three days after the deal was finalized. The moral-ethical foundation of market behavior prescribed by the Qur'an and implemented by the Prophet ensured the minimization of risk and of uncertainty for market participants and increased the efficiency of exchange, and intended to reduce transaction costs. Moreover, rules specified in the Qur'an regarding faith to the terms of contracts and the knowledge of their enforcement increased certainty and reduced transaction costs. Another important rule promulgated by the Prophet was the prohibition of interference with supply before entrance into the market. From the earliest period of operation of the Medina market, the Prophet appointed market supervisors, whose job was to ensure rule-compliance, which in turn would result in markets that are just. The Prophet advised the participants to go beyond mere rule-compliance and to treat their fellow humans with beneficence. The Prophet strongly encouraged market participants to accept the duty of "commanding the good and forbidding evil" by engaging in self-regulation.

The Prophet lived modestly, *commensurate with the standard of living of the poorest* among his followers. Litigations before him were settled quickly and fairly, with influence from the rich or powerful playing no role in his decisions. He consulted with experts in every affair in accordance with the rule of consultation. His insistence on the participation of all members of society in its affairs, his strong encouragement of education, and inducements for the adoption of technologies from neighboring states and people are evidenced in biographies about him, as are his efforts to promote the expansion of social infrastructure. His emphasis on health and hygiene was so strong that he considered it a religious duty. He emphasized productive work and, while he would use the public treasury to alleviate destitution and poverty, he strongly discouraged laziness and reliance by the able-bodied on handouts. To encourage work, one of his policies was to enforce risk-reward sharing in production and/or trade projects. He encouraged those among his followers who were better off to provide interest-free loans to the needy and to invest in public projects to benefit society instead of hoarding their wealth.

In Islam, property is considered a gift from the Creator, a source of wealth creation and a means of communal support. Property rights are assigned to humans by their Lord as a trust for the betterment of all members of society and to establish justice. The wealthy, pampered, and opulent are those who did not redeem the rights of others in their wealth. Their behavior led to their destruction. There are historic accounts of how the economic behavior of the rich and powerful becomes a major source of injustice, which, in turn is the major source of political and social injustice. In practical terms, the Qur'an is clear that justice means creating a balanced society that avoids extremes of wealth and poverty, a society in which its members recognize that property is a blessing afforded by the Creator for the sole purpose of providing support for the life of all members of society. It is not possible for a society to have numerous rich people without that same society simultaneously creating a mass of economically deprived and destitute humans. On the one hand, the rich consume opulently and, on the other, the poor suffer from deprivation because their rights in the wealth of the rich and powerful are not redeemed. Islam prohibits the accumulation of wealth and imposes limits on consumption through its rules against overspending and waste, and ordains that what is left after one has reached a modest living standard must be returned to the less able members of society. Therefore, while Islam ordains hard work, the development of the earth and natural resources provided by the Creator, and the use of proceeds for the satisfaction of the needs of all humans, it prohibits the concentration in the hands of a few.

Douglass North believes that cognition plays a central role in belief formation, which, in turn, affects preference formation, rational decision making, and institutions. Institutions (rules) have a reciprocal effect on cognition. Beliefs constitute what North refers to as a "mental model" (North 1995, 15–26). However, whereas North believes that institutions "are clearly an extension to the mental constructs the human mind develops to interpret the environment of the individual," in Islam, rules (institutions) are provided by the Law Giver. For a believer, the "mental model" is formed by these rules (institutions), which reduce uncertainty for individuals and society, and in turn reduce transaction costs. Above all, the entrepreneurs engaged in production are subject to the rules of economic behavior that stress not cheating, not wasting (*itlaf*) or overusing (*israf*), and not causing harm to anyone in carrying out production. The Prophet said: "There are two characteristics above which there are no other in evil: associating partners with Allah and causing harm to the servants of Allah (other humans)"; "The person who defrauds a Muslim is not of us"; and "Whoever shortchanges the wages of a laborer, his place will be in fire" (Al-Hakimi, Al-Hakimi, and Al-Hakimi 1989, vol. 5, 367). The exploitation of hired labor, particularly short-changing their wages or refusing to pay labor wages commensurate with their productivity, was the subject of admonishments by the Prophet: "Whosoever mistreats a laborer in repaying for the work done, Allah will render his own work fruitless and Allah will forbid him the perfume of the Garden" (Al-Hakimi, Al-Hakimi, and Al-Hakimi 1989, vol. 5, 366–70).

The next set of rules to be understood and internalized by individuals are those governing contract and trust. Islam forcefully places all social-political-economic relations on a contractual footing. More generally, the whole fabric of Divine Law is contractual in its conceptualization, content, and application. Its very foundation is the primordial covenant between Allah and humans—the *meethaq*. That covenant imposes on humans the duty of remaining faithful to the affirmation of humanity: humans recognize the Supreme Creator as their Cherisher Lord and their *Wali* (Protector/Guardian). That recognition, in turn, is an affirmation of the duty of rule-compliance, which serves the best interests of humans and is a contractual obligation, linking humans to their Creator and to one another. Justice demands rule-compliance as a demonstration of faithfulness to the terms of the primordial covenant. The contractual foundation of the Law in human behavior is not only with respect to the Creator but is also toward other humans. Not only will performance be judged in the carrying out of contractual obligations but also the essential attributes of intending with which a party enters into a contract. These attributes are sincerity, truthfulness, and the strength and rigor of the loyalty of the fulfillment of obligations a person is intending to take on by entering into the contractual relationship.

As Habachy suggests, Islam's strong emphasis on the strictly binding nature of contracts covers private and public law contracts as well as international treaties. Moreover, "every public office in Islam, even the *Imamate* (temporal and spiritual leadership), is regarded as a contract, an agreement (*áqd*) that defines the rights and obligations of the parties. Every contract entered into by the faithful must include a forthright intention to remain loyal to performing the obligations specified by the terms of contract" (Habachy 1962). The highest office of the leadership of the society, *Imamate* or *Khilafat*, is inaugurated by *Mubaya'ah* (from the word *bay'*), which is a contract between the ruler and the community stating that the leader will be rule-compliant in discharging the duties of the office. This provides a strong accountable basis for governance (Al-Hakimi, Al-Hakimi, and Al-Hakimi 1989, vol. 2, 448–59). Throughout the legal history of Islam, a body of rules, based on the Qur'an and on the traditions of the Prophet, has constituted a general theory of contracts. These rules covering all contracts has established the principle that any agreement not specifically prohibited by law was valid and binding on parties and must be enforced by the courts in a fair manner to all parties.

It should be noted that there is a strong interdependence between contract and trust; without trust, contracts become difficult to negotiate and conclude, and costly to monitor and enforce. When and where trust is weak, complex and expensive administrative devices are needed to enforce contracts. Moreover, it is generally recognized that unambiguous contracts—ones that foresee all contingencies—do not exist, as not all contingencies can be foreseen. As McMillan suggests, trust is an important element of a well-designed market. "For a market to function well, you must be able to trust most of the people most of the time ¼ your trust in your trading partner rests on both the formal devices of the law and the informal device of reputation" (McMillan 2002, 10–11). When and where property rights are poorly defined and protected, the cost of gathering and analyzing information is high, and trust is weak, it is difficult to clearly specify the terms of contracts and enforce them. In these cases transaction costs—that is, search and information costs, bargaining and decision costs, contract negotiation and enforcement costs—are high. Where and when transaction costs are high, there is less trade, fewer market participants, less long-term investment, lower productivity, and slower economic growth. As North has pointed out, when and where there is rule-compliance and enforcement, there is an increase in the likelihood that property rights will be protected and contracts honored. Under such conditions, individuals are more willing to specialize, invest in long-term projects, undertake complex transactions, and accumulate and share technical knowledge.

Throughout the ages, one of the most important questions confronting mankind has been: what criterion should determine the distribution of economic resources? The answer depends on the underlying concept of justice and fairness, which, in turn, depends on the belief system. Islam considers justice an important attribute of the Creator manifested in His Creation. The concept of justice for humans is simple and unambiguous: justice is obtained when all things are placed where intended by the Creator! How are humans to know where the right (just) place is for everything? The answer is: follow the rules prescribed by the Creator (Al-Hakimi, Al-Hakimi, and Al-Hakimi 1989, vol. 2, 2–25; vol. 6, 324–451; Qutb 1953). By the instrumentality of His *Walayah*, the Loving Creator has provided all that is necessary for humans to develop and achieve perfection of the human state. He has also designated the path to perfection and has marked it with rules of behavior in all facets of human life. Rule-compliance assures justice. In turn, justice assures balance for individuals and for their collectivity. Compliance with rules, however, does more than create balance; it guarantees that humans draw near to their ultimate objective, namely, their Creator. Morality is a result of just behavior. In contrast, nontheocentric thought considers justice "an important subclass of morality in general, a subclass which generally involves appeals to the overlapping notions of right, fairness, equality ..." (Arthur and Shaw 1991, 4). These systems must find ways in which a consensual agreement is reached on the concept of justice and fairness according to which goods and services produced can be distributed. To do so, they must first devise moral theories that provide reason to justify a particular distributional system. One such theory is utilitarianism, which puts forth a distributional system that avoids justice but is instead based on morality. An action is considered justified if it increases utility, or happiness, of all. Accordingly, there is only one moral issue involved in a course of action or social policy: does it achieve the greatest aggregate happiness? This is a criterion by which not only individual and social actions are judged but one according to which various societies are compared. There is much criticism of utilitarianism. Two stand out. It permits the sacrifice of innocent individuals and their interests if it means increasing the happiness of the whole, thus serving totalitarian objectives; and it assigns equal weights to happiness of all individuals.

In principle, in economics, it is assumed that a free market that operates on the basis of the self-interest of its participants promotes the general interest of all. Based on a utilitarian concept, welfare economics developed the analytic position that in such a system, in which prices were determined by the free interplay of supply and demand, all factors of production would receive rewards commensurate with their marginal contribution to the production of goods and services. It is important to note that here, too, initial resource endowments as well as the preferences of individuals are taken as a given. Unhappy with utilitarianism, Rawls searched for an alternative principle of distribution by relying on the concept of the social contract. Equating justice with fairness, Rawls attempted to find principles of just distribution with which members of society, with different concepts of good and just, all agree.

To Rawls, distributive justice is a matter of public rather than private choice, although he assumes that citizens are just. Therefore, his principle of justice applies only to social institutions he refers to as the "basic structure." He uses the device of "a veil of ignorance" to ensure fair results. Assuming that people in society are ignorant of all of their particularities, including race, color, creed, or social status, they would come together to choose a rule of distribution that would then govern all members of society. Rawls concludes that people would choose a rule according to which all "social values—liberty and opportunity, income, wealth, and the basis of self-respect—are to be distributed equally unless an unequal distribution of any, or all, of these values is to everyone's advantage" (Rawls 1971). From this principle, referred to as "the difference principle," two other principles are deduced. First, that each individual in society has "equal right to political liberty; freedom of speech and assembly; liberty of conscience and freedom of thought; freedom of the person along with the right to hold (personal) property; and freedom from arbitrary arrest and seizure, as defined by the concept of the rule of law. These liberties are all required to be equal by the first principle, since citizens of a just society are to have the same basic rights" (Rawls 1971). The second principle requires that if there are to be inequalities, they are (a) to everyone's advantage, and (b) "attached to positions and offices open to all." These principles are to apply sequentially to the "basic structure" of society. Sequential order is necessary for Rawls to rule out the possibility that a departure from the first principle of equal liberty could or would be compensated by greater economic advantages. Under the "veil of ignorance," a fair allocation of primary goods would be the one that members would agree on before they know where they would land in the outcome.

These ideas on distributive justice afford a perspective on Islamic notions position of just distribution. An important central difference between Islam's position and those above is the role of the market. All the above ideas apply to "market economies." Markets also play a crucial role in Islam, but with one major difference. Epistemologically, the difference is one of the concept of the market as an ideology and the concept of the market as an instrument. This difference is profound. In societies known widely as "market economies," market norms are central to social relations. In turn, market norms are determined by self-interest, which dictate "rational" behavior as maximizing what interests the self, narrowly labeled as satisfaction (utility or profit). Market norms, in turn, determine the pattern of preferences of individuals. As Gomberg (2007) argues, market norms and preference patterns are individualist, not communal. They have self-seeking orientations.

In Islam, by contrast, the market is an instrument. It is not an organism that determines the rules and norms of behavior, not even those of its own operation. Rules that determine the pattern of preferences of participants are determined outside the market. Participants internalize them before entering the market. The behavior of consumers, producers, and traders, informed by their preferences, are subject to rules determined outside the market. In a market where there is full rule-compliance, the price that prevails for goods, services, and factors of production is considered just. The resulting incomes are considered justly earned. Therefore, the resulting distribution is just. However, participants will not be allowed to keep their full earnings simply because their income was justly earned. There are rights and entitlements of others in the resulting post market distribution of income and wealth that must be redeemed. This is the function of post market redistribution, which is governed by its own set of rules. Any remaining wealth that is accumulated is broken up at the end of the person's life and distributed among a large number of beneficiaries spanning at least four generations, according to rules specified in the Qur'an to avoid the concentration of income and wealth in the hands of a few.

As we have said numerous times, justice is at the heart of an Islamic society. Who is ultimately responsible for establishing a just society? The state's role is one of administrator, supervisor, and protector of society. It is the members of society who ensure that justice prevails. It can be argued that there is no topic more emphasized in Islam than poverty and the responsibility of individuals and society to eradicate it. The Prophet said that poverty is near disbelief and that poverty is worse than murder (Al-Hakimi, Al-Hakimi, and Al-Hakimi 1989, vol. 4, 278–468; Qutb 1953). Thus in any society in which there is poverty, this is sufficient evidence that Islamic rules are not being observed. It means that the rich and wealthy have not redeemed the rights of others in their income and wealth and that the state has failed to take corrective action.

Concluding Comments

In Islam, development has dimensions of self-development, of the physical development of the earth, and of the development of society. The first is the process of the growth of the human toward perfection; the second specifies how natural resources are to be used for developing the earth to provide for the material needs of humanity; and the third dimension encompasses the progress of the human collectivity toward full integration and unity. Together they constitute the rules-based compliance system to assure progress on the three interrelated dimensions of development.

While Islam attaches great importance to development and the means for its attainment, it should be evident from our discussion that the underdevelopment of many Muslim societies has nothing to do with Islam. Back in time, foreigners, under colonial rule, plundered many of these countries. After the emergence of these lands from the yoke of colonialism, autocratic rulers with the support of foreigners grabbed the reins of power and exploited ethnic and sectarian divides. In most Muslim societies, efficient institutions, rules, and rule-compliance to promote development were not embraced and practiced. As a result, in many countries that profess Islam and are labeled as Islamic today, we see injustice and underdevelopment. This state of affairs, as shown in chapter 11, is not representative of core Islamic teachings. If a country displays characteristics such as unelected, corrupt, oppressive and unjust rulers, inequality before the law, unequal opportunities for human development, absence of freedom of choice (including that of religion), opulence alongside poverty, and above all injustice of any kind, it is prima facie evidence that it is not Islamic. While all along, Islam is, and has been for centuries, the articulation of the universal love of Allah for His Creation, its Unity, and all that it implies for all-encompassing human and economic development. There is thus a disconnect between Islamic teachings and its practice in many communities that today profess Islam. Their underdevelopment is largely due to the absence of the institutional scaffolding recommended in Qur'anic teachings and practiced by the Prophet.

Notes

1. There are about 220 verses in the Qur'an referring to *Walayah* and related concepts. A 2010 book (by His Royal Highness Ghazi bin Muhammad bin Talal, based on his PhD thesis written and approved at Al-Azhar University) most forcefully establishes and acknowledges the concept of *Walayah*, or the "Love of Allah."

2. For further details, see Askari and others (2011).
3. Western economists have long addressed the issue of natural resource depletion and intergenerational equity. Solow (1974, 41) reached the conclusion that "the finite pool of resources (I have excluded full recycling) should be used up optimally according to the general rules that govern the optimal use of reproducible assets. In particular, earlier generations are entitled to draw down the pool (optimally, of course!) so long as they add (optimally, of course!) to the stock of reproducible capital." This is essentially the Islamic prescription.

References

Acemoglu, Daron, and James Robinson. 2012. *Why Nations Fail*. New York: Crown Publishers.

Al-Hakimi, M. R., M. Al-Hakimi, and Ali Al-Hakimi. 1989. *Al-Hayat*. Vols. 2, 5, 6. Tehran: Maktab Nashr Al-Thaqrafa Al-Islamiyyah.

Arthur, John. and William H. Shaw. 1991. *Justice and Economic Distribution*. Upper Saddle River, NJ: Prentice Hall.

Askari, Hossein, Zamir Iqbal, Noureddine Krichene, and Abbas Mirakhor. 2011. *Risk Sharing in Finance: The Islamic Finance Alternative*. Singapore: John Wiley and Sons.

Cameron, J. 2000. "Amartya Sen on Economic Inequality: The Need for an Explicit Critique of Opulence." *Journal of International Development* 12(7): 1031–45.

Ghazi bin Muhammad bin Talal, His Royal Highness. 2010. *Love in the Qur'an*. Lahore: Kazi Publications.

Giri, A. K. 2000. "Rethinking Human Well-Being: A Dialogue with Amartya Sen." *Journal of International Development* 12(7): 1003–18.

Gomberg, Paul. 2007. *How to Make Opportunity Equal*. Malden, MA: Blackwell.

Habachy, Saba. 1962. "Property, Right, and Contract in Muslim Law." *Columbia Law Review I* 62 (3): 450–73.

McMillan, John. 2002. *Reinventing the Bazar: A Natural History of Markets*. London: W.W. Norton.

Mirakhor, Abbas, and Hossein Askari. 2010. *Islam and the Path to Human and Economic Development*. New York: Palgrave Macmillan.

North, Douglass C. 1995. "Five Propositions about Institutional Change." In *Explaining Social Institutions*, edited by Jack Knight and Itai Sened, 15–26. Ann Arbor, MI: The University of Michigan Press.

———. 2003. *Understanding the Process of Economic Change*. Princeton, NJ: Princeton University.

North, Douglass C., John J. Wallis, and Barry R. Weingast. 2009. *Violence and Social Orders: A Conceptual Framework for Interpreting Recorded Human History*. New York: Cambridge University Press.

Pogge, T. W. 2001. "Eradicating Systemic Poverty: Brief for a Global Resource Dividend." *Journal of Human Development* 2(1): 59–77.

Qutb, Shaheed S. 1953. *Social Justice in Islam*, translated by J. B. Hardie. Rev. ed. Reprint, American Council of Learned Societies.

Rawls, John. 1971. "A Theory of Justice." In *Justice and Economic Distribution*, edited by John Arthur and William H. Shaw, 13–60. Upper Saddle River, NJ: Prentice Hall.

Romer, Paul. 1986. "Increasing Returns and Long-Run Growth." *The Journal of Political Economy* 94 (5): 1002–037.

Rosenstein-Rodan, Paul. 1943. "Problems of Industrialisation of Eastern and South-Eastern Europe." *Economic Journal* 53 (210/211): 202–11.

Sen, Amartya. 1994. *Development as Freedom*. New York: Anchor Books.

Smith, Adam. (1759) 2006. *The Theory of Moral Sentiments*. Reprint, Mineola, NY: Dover Publications. Citations refer to the 2006 Dover edition.

———. (1776) 2003. *An Inquiry into the Nature and Causes of the Wealth of Nations*. Reprint, Mineola, NY: Dover Publications.

Solow, Robert M. 1957. "Technical Change and the Aggregate Production Function." *The Review of Economics and Statistics* 39 (3): 312–20.

———. 1974. "Intergenerational Equity and Exhaustible Resources." *The Review of Economic Studies* 41: 29–45.

CHAPTER 6

Islam's Perspective on Financial Inclusion

Zamir Iqbal and Abbas Mirakhor

Financial development and improved access to finance (also referred to as financial inclusion) is likely not only to accelerate economic growth but also to reduce income inequality and poverty in a country, a growing body of evidence indicates. Despite the essential role played by financial services in the progress of efficiency and equality in a society, 2.7 billion people (70 percent of the adult population) in emerging markets still have no access to basic financial services, and a great many of the them come from countries with predominantly Muslim populations (Demirgüç-Kunt, Beck, and Honohan 2007).

In conventional finance, financial access is especially an issue for the poorer members of society, including potential entrepreneurs. They are commonly referred to as "nonbanked" or "unbankable," and in the case of potential entrepreneurs, they invariably lack adequate collateral to access conventional debt financing. While access to finance may be important for economic growth, the private sector may not be willing to provide financing to some areas or some segments of the economy because of the high cost associated with credit assessment and credit monitoring and because of the lack of acceptable collateral.

Although the linkage of financial development with economic development exists, a high degree of the financial development in a country is not necessarily any indication of alleviation of poverty in the country. There is growing realization that in addition to financial development, the emphasis should be to expand the accessibility to finance and the financial services that can play a more positive role in eradicating poverty. Development economists are convinced that the goal should be improving access and making basic financial services available to all members of the society in order to build an inclusive financial system. Enhancing the access to and the quality of basic financial services such as

---

Zamir Iqbal is the Lead Investment Officer at the World Bank. Abbas Mirakhor is the First Holder of the Islamic Finance Chair at the International Centre for Education in Islamic Finance, Malaysia. The views expressed in this chapter do not represent the views of the management and Executive Directors of the affiliated institutions.

availability of credit, mobilization of savings, insurance, and risk management can facilitate sustainable growth and productivity, especially for small and medium enterprises (SMEs).

Conventional finance has developed mechanisms such as microfinance, SME finance, and microinsurance to enhance financial inclusion. Conventional techniques have been partially successful in enhancing access, but are not without challenges. This chapter provides Islam's perspective on financial inclusion. Islamic finance, based on the concept of risk sharing, offers a set of financial instruments that promote risk sharing rather than risk shifting in the financial system. In addition, Islam advocates redistributive instruments such as *zakat* (a 2.5 percent tax for the welfare of the less fortunate segment of society); *sadaqat* (voluntary charitable contributions), and *Qard-al-hassan* (loans with no expectation of repayment), through which the economically more able segment of the society shares the risks facing the less able segment of the population. Such instruments of wealth redistribution are used to redeem the rights of the less able in the income and wealth of the more able. These are not instruments of charity, altruism, or beneficence but are instruments of redemption of rights and repayment of obligations. In addition, the inheritance rules specify how the wealth of a person is distributed among current and future generations of inheritors.

This study argues that the core principles of Islam place great emphasis on social justice, inclusion, and sharing of resources between the haves and the have-nots. Islamic finance addresses the issue of financial inclusion from two directions: one by promoting risk-sharing contracts that provide a viable alternative to conventional debt-based financing; and the other through specific instruments of redistribution of wealth in society. Both risk-sharing financing instruments and redistributive instruments complement each other to offer a comprehensive approach to enhance financial inclusion, eradicate poverty, and build a healthy and vibrant economy. With these instruments, the poor are not forced to rely on their low-level income, or cope with an absence of income, as they endeavor to maintain a decent level of subsistence living for themselves and their families. Increasing access to financial services holds the promise of helping to reduce poverty and improve development outcomes by enabling the poor to smooth consumption, start or expand a business, cope with risk, and increase or diversify household income.

Islamic finance provides a comprehensive framework to enhance financial inclusion by promoting microfinance, SME financing, and microinsurance structured on the principles of risk sharing, and through Islam's redistributive channels, which are grossly underutilized in Muslim countries. The chapter argues that redistributive instruments should be developed as proper institutions to optimize the function of such instruments. Institutionalizing these instruments would require a better enabling environment, a sound legal framework, and transparent collection and distribution. Applications of financial engineering can devise innovative ways to develop hybrids of risk-sharing and redistributive instruments to enhance access to finance to promote economic development.

Economic Development and Islamic Finance • http://dx.doi.org/10.1596/978-0-8213-9953-8

Instruments offered by Islam have strong historical roots and have been applied throughout history in various Muslim communities. Islam offers a rich set of instruments and unconventional approaches, if implemented in a true spirit, and can lead to reduced poverty and inequality in Muslim countries plagued by massive poverty. Therefore, policy makers in Muslim countries who are serious about enhancing access to finance or "financial inclusion" should exploit the potential of Islamic instruments to achieve this goal.

What Is Financial Inclusion and Why Is It Important?

Many poor families in the developing world have limited access to formal financial services, including credit, savings, and insurance. They rely instead on a variety of informal credit relationships with moneylenders, relatives, friends, or merchants. Traditionally, banks and other formal financial service providers, including insurance companies, have not considered the poor a viable market, and penetration rates for formal financial services in developing countries are extremely low.

The concept of financial inclusion initially referred to the delivery of financial services to low-income segments of society at affordable cost. However, during the past decade, the concept has evolved into four dimensions: (1) easy access to finance for all households and enterprises; (2) sound institutions guided by prudential regulation and supervision; (3) financial and institutional sustainability of financial institutions; and (4) competition between service providers to bring alternatives to customers (Demirgüç-Kunt, Beck, and Honohan 2007). Typical indicators of the financial inclusion of an economy are the proportion of population covered by commercial bank branches, number of Automatic Teller Machines (ATMs), and sizes of deposits and loans made by low-income households and SMEs. However, availability of financial services can not necessarily be equated with financial inclusion because people may voluntarily exclude themselves from financial services for religious or cultural reasons, even though they do have access and can afford the services (Demirgüç-Kunt, Beck, and Honohan 2007).

What distinguishes the use of financial services from access to financial services? To what extent is the lack of use a problem? The users of financial services can be distinguished from nonusers, who either cannot access the financial system or opt out from the financial system for some reason. Within the group of nonusers, first, there is a subgroup of households and enterprises that are considered unbankable by commercial financial institutions and markets because they do not have enough income or present too high a lending risk. Second, there might be discrimination against certain population groups based on social, religious, or ethnic grounds. Third, the contractual and informational infrastructure might prevent financial institutions from reaching out to certain population groups because the outreach is too costly to be commercially viable.[1] Finally, the price of financial services may be too high or the product features might not be appropriate for certain population groups. In addition, there could be a set of users who voluntarily exclude themselves from the system due to conflicts with their religious or ethical or moral value system.

Understanding the linkage of financial inclusion with the economic development is important. There is voluminous literature in economics and finance on the contributions of finance to economic growth and development. The main reason why "finance" or "financial inclusion" or "access to finance" matters is that financial development and intermediation has been shown empirically to be a key driver of economic growth and development. Development economists suggest that the lack of access to finance for the poor deters key decisions regarding the accumulation of human and physical capital. For example, in an imperfect financial market, poor people may find themselves in the "poverty trap," as they cannot save in harvest time or borrow to survive starvation. Similarly, without a predictable future cash flow, the poor in developing countries are also incapable of borrowing against future income to invest in education or health care for children.

Given the significance of financial inclusion, a developed financial sector in a country can play a critical role in promoting growth and in reducing poverty by enabling the poor to borrow to finance income-enhancing assets, including human assets such as health and education, and to become microentrepreneurs to generate income and ultimately move out of the poverty (DFID 2004). In addition, financial sector development could enable the poor to channel savings to the formal sector: that is, to maintain bank accounts and other saving schemes and insurance, which would allow the poor to establish a buffer against future shocks, thus reducing their vulnerability and exposure to adverse events that otherwise would put undue strain on future income prospects.

Modern development theories analyzing the evolution of growth, relative income inequalities, and economic development offer two tracks of thinking. One track attributes imbalances in redistribution of wealth and income in the economy as an impediment to growth, while the other track identifies financial market imperfections as the key obstacle (Demirgüç-Kunt, Beck, and Honohan 2007). Proponents of the redistribution of wealth claim that redistribution can foster growth, and a focus on redistributive public policies in areas such as land or education reform targeting schooling, saving, or fertility changes that can lead to reduction in income inequalities and poverty.

The other school of thought traces the obstacle to growth to market failures and imperfect information leading to financial market frictions (Stiglitz and Weiss 1981). Financial market frictions can be the critical mechanism for generating persistent income inequality or poverty traps. Financial market imperfections, such as information asymmetries and transactions costs, are likely to be especially binding on the talented poor and the microenterprises and small enterprises that lack collateral, credit histories, and connections, thus limiting their opportunities and leading to persistent inequality and slower growth.

The main problems in delivering credit are linked to risks arising out of information asymmetries and the high transaction costs of processing, monitoring, and enforcing small loans, leading to an increase in the break-even interest rates for these loans. These asymmetries can result from adverse selection (the inability of the lender to distinguish between high-risk and low-risk borrowers) or from moral hazard (the tendency for some borrowers to divert resources to projects that reduce their likelihood of being able to repay the loan, and the inability of the lender to detect and prevent such behavior). Depending on the specific information asymmetry and the ability of potential borrowers to pledge collateral, lenders may try to use the interest rate or a combination of the interest rate and collateral as a screening and sorting mechanism. If collateral is not available, lenders are forced to rely only on the interest rate, but in doing so, they risk excluding, or crowding out, safe borrowers.

There is growing evidence identifying the linkage between economic development and financial inclusion. Galor and Zeira (1993) and Banerjee and Newman (1993) imply that financial exclusion not only holds back investment, but results in persistent income inequality, as it adds to negative incentives to save and work and leads to vicious cycles of income inequality across generations in a society. Empirical studies by Demirgüç-Kunt and Levine (2008) show that countries with deeper financial systems experience faster reductions in the share of the population that lives on less than one dollar a day. Almost 30 percent of the cross-country variation in changing poverty rates can be explained by variation in financial development.

Issues with the Conventional Approach to Financial Inclusion

Although the tension continues between the two approaches of either redistribution policies or financial market frictions, there is realization that the evolution of financial development, growth, and intergenerational income dynamics are closely intertwined. Aghion and Bolton (1997) point out that an approach centered on redistribution policies may create disincentives to work and save. By contrast, Demirgüç-Kunt and Levine (2008) argue that focusing on financial sector reforms and reducing financial market imperfections to expand individual opportunities creates positive incentive effects—not negative ones. They further conclude that building a more inclusive financial system also appeals to a wider range of philosophical perspectives than redistributive policies can: redistribution aims to equalize outcomes, whereas better functioning financial systems serve to equalize opportunities.

The approach to remove financial market frictions to enhance financial inclusion consists of two tracks. First, the emphasis is on developing the overall financial sector infrastructure, targeting the banking, capital markets, and insurance sectors by promoting enhanced regulations, supervision, and transparency. This is in addition to building economic and legal institutions, which are deemed necessary for the efficient functioning of any economy. The second track focuses primarily on expanding credit to micro, small, and medium enterprises (MSMEs). For example, in the past three decades, access to microcredit has expanded dramatically and has brought formal financial services to the poor, reaching nearly 200 million microborrowers by some estimates (see Bauchet and others 2011).

The experience with microcredit or microfinance has been mixed, as there is growing consensus that the expectations were overestimated and there are serious challenges in achieving sustainable impact on poverty alleviation. The key challenges facing the microfinance industry are summarized below:

- *High interest rates.* Conventional microfinance institutions (MFIs) are often criticized for charging very high interest rates on loans to the poor. These high rates are justified because of high transaction costs and the high risk premium. However, this imposes undue stress on the recipient to engage in activities that produce returns higher than the cost of funding—which may not be possible in many cases.

- *Recognizing that not every poor borrower is a microentrepreneur.* Merely making capital accessible to the poor is not the solution, without realizing that not every poor person or recipient of microcredit has the skills set or the basic business sense to become an entrepreneur. There is need to provide proper training, skills building, and institutional support to promote entrepreneurship among the poor. Building such capacity requires funds that often are not readily available.

- *Diversion of funds.* The possibility exists that the funds will be diverted to nonproductive activities, such as personal consumption. In some cases, microcredit may lead the poor into a circular debt situation, where borrowing from one mircolender is used to pay off the borrowings from another lender. Poor households clearly have other needs, such as school fees, risk mitigation against adverse events such as illness, disability, or failed crops, and even personal consumption.

- *Large-scale fund mobilization.* While some of MFIs have had a significant impact on poverty, others have been less successful. MFIs generally cannot mobilize funds on a large scale and pool risks over very large areas in the way that more traditional, formal financial institutions can. In addition, most MFIs have only limited coverage and are reaching only a minority of the bankable population (DFID 2004).

- *Product design.* The financial services needs of poor households may require different product features with different payment and delivery structures than typical debt-based lending to microborrowers. A more suitable product targeted to match the needs of the poor may prove to be more welfare-enhancing.

- *Absence of private sector participation.* As mentioned, the effectiveness of MFIs is often compromised because of limitations on the supply of funding, coverage, mix of products, and funding by the informal, semi-formal, and noncommercial sectors. There is a need to move toward a market-based or private sector-based solution within the formal financial sector or capital markets. Without participation by the private sector, some of the core issues may not be overcome.

It is worth looking at the evidence on the effectiveness of mircolending. Recent experimental evidence from three randomized impact evaluations suggests that while increasing access to credit does not produce the kind of dramatic transformations expected by earlier literature, it does appear to have some important—though more modest—outcomes. There is some evidence of a shift away from nonproductive activities in favor of productive ones, but it is not drastic enough to result in significant improvement in the poverty levels. This suggests that microloans help some households reprioritize their expenditures and smooth consumption—a valuable function for poor households that suffer from irregular and unpredictable income streams (Bauchet and others 2011).

The Concept of Financial Inclusion in Islam

The central economic tenant of Islam is to develop a prosperous, just, and egalitarian economic and social structure in which all members of society can maximize their intellectual capacity, preserve and promote their health, and actively contribute to the economic and social development of society. Economic development and growth, along with social justice, are the foundational elements of an Islamic economic system. All members of an Islamic society must be given the same opportunities to advance themselves: in contemporary terms, there must be a level playing field, which in the Islamic view includes access to the natural resources provided by God. For those for whom there is no work and for those that cannot work (including the handicapped), society must afford the minimum requirements for a dignified life by providing shelter, food, health care, and education.

The concept of development in Islam has three dimensions: individual self-development, the physical development of the earth, and the development of the human collectivity, which includes both (Mirakhor and Askari 2010). In Islam, all three dimensions of development assign heavy responsibility to individuals and society—with both held responsible for any lack of development. Balanced development is defined as balanced progress in all three dimensions. Progress is balanced if it is accompanied by justice, both in its general (*ádl*) and in its interpersonal (*qist*) dimension.[2] The objective of such balanced development is to achieve progress on the path to perfection by all humans, through rule-compliance. The first dimension specifies a dynamic process of the growth of the human being toward perfection. The second dimension addresses the utilization of natural resources to develop the earth to provide for the material needs of the individual and all of humanity. The third dimension refers to the progress of the human collectivity toward full integration and unity. Happiness and fulfillment in a person's life is not achieved by a mere increase in income but by full development of a person along all three dimensions. At the same time, economic progress and prosperity are encouraged in Islam, since they provide the means by which humans can satisfy their material needs and thus remove the economic barriers on the path to their spiritual progress.

Islam emphasizes financial inclusion more explicitly. However, two distinct features of Islamic finance differentiate its path of development significantly from conventional financial models the notions of risk sharing and redistribution of wealth.

Individuals face two types of risks. The first is the result of the exposure of the economy to uncertainty and risk due to external and internal economic circumstances of society and its vulnerabilities to shocks. How well the economy will absorb shocks depends on its resilience, which will in turn depend on the institutional and policy infrastructure of the society. How flexibly these will respond to shocks will determine how much these risks impact individual lives when they materialize. The second type of risk that individuals face relates to the circumstances of their personal lives. These include risks of injuries, illness, accidents, or bankruptcies.

This kind of risk is referred to as idiosyncratic, and when idiosyncratic risks materialize, they play havoc with people's livelihood. This is because often the level of consumption that sustains them is directly dependent on their income. If their income becomes volatile, so will their livelihood and consumption. Engaging in risk sharing can mitigate idiosyncratic risk and allow consumption smoothing by weakening the correlation between income and consumption so that should these risks materialize, and the shock reduce income, the consumption and livelihood of the individual do not suffer correspondingly.

In a society, risks can be shared among its members, between its members and the state, or even internationally. In both industrial and developing economies, people find ways and means of sharing risks to their livelihood. In particular, they use coping mechanisms to decrease the variability of their income relative to their consumption. In more developed financial systems, the coping mechanism is investing in financial assets or in acquiring insurance to mitigate against personal risks. In developing countries with weak financial markets, people rely on informal insurance, borrowing, or saving to cope with idiosyncratic risks. In such societies, theory suggests that perfect informal insurance is possible if communities fully pool their incomes to share risks.

According to Islamic perspective, risks are mitigated in various ways. First, the economic system is a rule-based system, which has provided rules of behavior and a taxonomy of decisions: actions and their commensurate payoffs based on injunctions in the Qur'an. Complying with these rules reduces uncertainty. Clearly, individuals exercise their freedom in choosing to comply with these rules—or not. That rules of behavior and compliance with them reduce uncertainty is an important insight of the new institutional economics. Rules reduce the burden on human cognitive capacity, particularly in the process of decision making under uncertainty. Rules also promote cooperation and coordination (Mirakhor 2009). Second, Islam has provided ways and means by which those who are able to, mitigate uncertainty by sharing the risks they face by engaging in economic activities with fellow human beings through exchange. Sharing allows risk to be spread and thus lowered for individual participants. However, if a person is unable to use any of the market means of risk sharing because of poverty, Allah (swt) has ordered a solution here as well: the rich are commanded to share the risks of the life of the poor by redeeming their rights derived from the Islamic principles of property rights (Iqbal and Mirakhor 2011; Mirakhor 1989). Islam ordains risk sharing through three main venues:

- Contracts of exchange and risk-sharing instruments in the financial sector;
- Redistributive risk-sharing instruments through which the economically more able segment of the society shares the risks facing the less able segment of the population; and
- Inheritance rules specified in the Qur'an, through which the wealth of a person at the time of death is distributed among current and future generations of inheritors.

Islamic finance is based on the belief that such a system facilitates real sector activities through risk sharing. It has its epistemological roots firmly in the Qur'an—specifically chapter 2, verse 275 (Mirakhor 2011a; Mirakhor and Smolo 2011). This verse, in part, ordains that all economic and financial transactions are conducted via contracts of exchange (*al-Bay'*) and not through interest-based debt contracts (*al-Riba*). Since in the verse, the contract of exchange appears first and the stipulation against *riba* follows, it is reasonable to argue that requiring that contracts be based on exchange constitutes a necessary condition of a permissible contract. Based on the same logic, the requirement of "no *riba*" (no interest) constitutes the sufficient condition of contracts. The necessary condition (*al-Bay'*) and sufficient condition (no *riba*) must be met for a contract to be considered Islamic. Classical Arabic lexicons of the Qur'an define contracts of exchange (*al-Bay'*) as contracts involving exchange of property in which there are expectations of gains and probability of losses (Mirakhor 2010), implying that there are risks in the transaction.

One reason for the ban on interest-based contracts (*al-Riba*) is surely due to the fact that this type of contract transfers all risk, or at least a major portion of it, to the borrower. It is possible to imagine instruments that on their face are compatible with the no-*riba* requirement, but are instruments of risk transfer, and ultimately shift risk to taxpayers.

By entering into contracts of exchange, parties improve their welfare by exchanging the risks of economic activities, thus allowing division of labor and specialization. Conceptually, there is a difference between risk taking and risk sharing. The former is antecedent to the latter. An entrepreneur must first decide to undertake the risk associated with a real sector project before seeking financing. In nonbarter exchange, it is at the point of financing where risk sharing materializes or fails to do so. The risk of the project does not change as it enters the financial sector seeking financing. Not clarifying this distinction has led to a confusion that the two concepts are one and the same. In the contemporary economy, at the point of financing, risk can be shared, but it can also be transferred or shifted. The essence of financial intermediation is the ability of financial institutions to transfer risk. All institutional arrangements within the financial sector of contemporary economies are mostly geared to facilitate this function. One of the chief characteristics of the 2007–09 global crisis was the fact that many financial institutions shifted the risk of losses, but internalized the gains of their operation. Hence, the concept of "privatized gains and socialized losses" (see Sheng 2009).

Arrow (1971) demonstrated that in a competitive market economy, in which markets are complete and Arrow Securities—whose payoffs are state-contingent—are available, it would be Pareto optimal for the economy if its members were to share risk according to each participant's ability to bear risk (Mirakhor 2010). In the absence of complete markets, which include all possible future contingencies, the efficiency of risk-sharing mechanisms will depend on the institutional structure, the degree and intensity of informational problems, and the effectiveness of policies designed to render the economy resilient to shocks.[3]

To summarize, the Islamic system advocates risk sharing in financial transactions, and a financial system based on risk sharing offers various advantages over the conventional system based on risk shifting. Use of risk-sharing instruments could encourage investors to invest in sectors such as MSMEs, which are perceived as high-risk sectors. Given an enabling environment, investors with an appetite for taking on such higher risks will be attracted to providing capital for these sectors. This argument can be supported by growing the market for private equity. If funds for these sectors become more available, financial inclusion in the system could be expected to increase.

Redistributive Instruments of Islam

The second set of instruments meant for redistribution are used to redeem the rights of the less able in the income and wealth of the more able. Contrary to common belief, these are not instruments of charity, altruism, or beneficence but instruments of redemption of rights and repayment of obligations.

The Qur'an makes clear that wealth is a blessing provided by the Creator for the sole purpose of providing support for the lives of all mankind. Thus, in practical terms, creating a balanced society that avoids extremes of wealth and poverty is desirable. The Islamic view holds that it is not possible to have many rich and wealthy people who continue to focus all their efforts on accumulating wealth without simultaneously creating economically deprived and destitute masses. The rich consume opulently while the poor suffer from deprivation because their rights in the wealth of the rich and powerful are not redeemed. To avoid this, Islam prohibits wealth concentration, and imposes limits on consumption through its rules prohibiting overspending (*israf*), waste (*itlaf*), and ostentatious and opulent spending (*itraf*). It then ordains that the net surplus, after moderate spending necessary to maintain a modest living standard, must be returned to the members of the society who, for a variety of reasons, are unable to work; hence the resources they could have used to produce income and wealth were utilized by the more able.

The Qur'an considers the more able as trustee-agents in using these resources on behalf of the less able. In this view, property is not a means of exclusion but inclusion, in which the rights of those less able in the income and wealth of the more able are redeemed. The result would be a balanced economy without extremes of wealth and poverty. The operational mechanism for redeeming the rights of the less able in the income and wealth of the more able are the network of mandatory and voluntary payments such as *zakat* (a 2.5 percent levy on asset-based wealth), *khums* (a 20 percent levy on income), and payments referred to as *sadaqah* (voluntary charitable contributions).

The most important economic institution that makes the objective of achieving social justice in Islam operational is the distribution-redistribution rule of the Islamic economic paradigm. Distribution takes place after production and sale, when all factors of production are given what is due to them, commensurate with their contribution to production, exchange, and sale of goods and services. Redistribution refers to the phase after distribution, when the charges due to the less able are levied. These expenditures are essentially repatriation and redemption of the rights of others in one's income and wealth. Redeeming these rights is a manifestation of belief in the Oneness of the Creator and its corollary, the unity of creation in general and of mankind in particular. It is the recognition and affirmation that Allah (swt) has created the resources for all of mankind, who must have unhindered access to them. Even the abilities that make access to resources possible are due to the Creator. This would mean that those who are less able or unable to use these resources are partners of the more able.

The expenditures intended for redeeming these rights are referred to in the Qur'an as *sadaqat*, which is the plural of the term *sadaqah*, a derivative of the root meaning truthfulness and sincerity. Their payments indicate the strength of the sincerity of a person's belief (Qur'an, 2:26; 2:272). The Qur'an insists that these are rights of the poor in the income and wealth of the rich; they are not charity (2:177; 17:26; 19:51; 38:30; 70:25). Therefore, the Qur'an asks that extreme care be taken of the recipients' human dignity—of which the recipients themselves are fully aware and conscious, to the point that they are reluctant to reveal their poverty. The Qur'an consequently recommends that payment to the poor be done in secret (2:271–273). Moreover, the Qur'an strictly forbids that these payments be made either with reproach or accompanied by ill treatment of the recipient, or with any annoyance displayed by the person making the payment (2:262–265).

Sadaqat are a very important redistributive institution in Islam for two reasons: first, they operationalize the truthfulness of one's belief in Allah (swt) in voluntarily giving of one's income and wealth. Second, the importance of this institution derives from the fact that the receiver is not the person to whom *sadaqat* is given, but Allah (swt). In two verses of the Chapter of Repentance, it is noted that:

> Of their goods (wealth) take *sadaqat*, so that you might purify and sanctify them; and pray on their behalf. Indeed, your prayers are a source of security for them: and Allah (swt) is One Who Hears and Knows. (9:103)

Do they not know that Allah (swt) accepts repentance from His servants and Receives their *sadaqat*, and that Allah (swt) is indeed He, the Oft-Returning, Most Merciful. (9:104)

Zakah is considered a component of *sadaqat*, but it has been given a special status in the Qur'an because it is ordained with obligatory prayer in at least 20 verses (see, for example, chapter 2, verse 110). Moreover, its collection was enforced by the governments in early Muslim history following the passing of the Messenger.

Qard-al-hassan is a loan mentioned in the Qur'an as "beautiful" (*hassan*), probably because in all the verses in which this loan is mentioned, it is stipulated that it is made directly to Allah (swt) and not to the recipient (see, for example, Chapter 64, verse 17). It is a voluntary loan, without any expectation by the creditor of any return on the principal. In addition, while the debtor is obligated to return the principal, the creditor, of his own free will, does not press the debtor for an exact timing of its return. Allah (swt) promises multiple returns to the "beautiful loan." Unfortunately, the full potential of this institution to mobilize substantial resources for the empowerment of the economically weak or dispossessed has not been realized. Much has been written about microfinance and its potential to reduce poverty. However, it is an irony that institutions of microfinance are growing rapidly in Muslim countries, but it is seldom realized that Islam's own institution of *Qard-al-hassan* is a more effective means of providing credit to those who cannot access formal credit channels.

Very early in the history of Muslim societies, the institution of *waqf* appeared, through which individuals could contribute the third of their wealth over which they are allowed by Shari'ah to exercise control at the time of their death. A *waqf* is a trust established when the contributor endows the stream of income accruing to a property for a charitable purpose in perpetuity. This institution has already been partially instrumentalized—although not in the sense intended in this discussion—since the legality of cash *waqf* (endowing the future income stream of a cash trust instead of a physical property) has been recognized in most Muslim countries. This instrument also offers substantial potential to mobilize large amounts of financial resources through instrumentalization of this institution by a globally credible Islamic financial institution.

The third dimension of distributive justice in the institutional scaffolding of an Islamic society is the institution of inheritance, which is crucial in the intergenerational justice framework envisioned by the Law Giver. Rules governing production, consumption, and distribution assure conservation of resources for future generations. Rules of redistribution ensure that those unable to benefit by participating directly in production and consumption in the market, through a combination of their labor and their right of access to resources provided by the Supreme Creator for all humans, are redeemed their rights through *zakah*, *khums*, *sadaqat*, *waqf*, and other redistributive mechanisms. Once these rights have been redeemed out of the income and wealth of the more economically able, the latter's property rights on the remaining income and wealth are held inviolable. These rights, however, expire at the point of passing of a person. At death, the person loses the right to allocate his/her wealth as he/she pleases except on one-third of income, which believers can use to make *waqf*, *sadaqat*, or other transfer contributions as the person wishes. The remainder is broken up and must be distributed among a large number of persons and categories according to strict rules of allocation specified in the Qur'an (see 4:1–13).

Public Policy Implications

Analysts suggest that public policy and strengthened institutional framework in developing countries can go a long way to enhancing financial inclusion. Examples of policy improvements include better corporate governance, including supervision, monitoring, and management, which can reduce damage to households due to economic and financial mismanagement; achieving and sustaining economic and political stability; and developing the financial sector. In terms of the institutional framework, clear and secure property rights; contract enforcement; and the securing of trust among people and between government, citizens, and other institutions can reduce risk, uncertainty, and ambiguity; strengthen social solidarity; bring private and public interests into closer harmony; and ensure coordination to improve risk sharing (Mirakhor 2009, 2010). Public policy could also help in mobilizing savings of poor households and thus reduce their vulnerability to income shocks.

With regard to microfinance, as discussed, there is empirical evidence suggesting that while these contracts help reduce poverty in low-income countries by providing small, uncollaterized loans to poor borrowers, there is no evidence to suggest that those contracts allow businesses to grow beyond subsistence. High interest rates can reduce available resources. Moreover, the structure of typical microfinance contracts has features that can create tension between risk taking and risk pooling, such as peer monitoring and joint liability designed to reduce the risk of moral hazard risk. Risk pooling allows greater opportunity for informal risk sharing due to repeated interaction among the borrowers. Joint liability and peer monitoring are common to most microfinance programs; small groups of borrowers become responsible for one another's loan, and all members are held responsible for the consequences of one member's failure to repay the loan but do not reward other members in case of success. This arrangement can have the unintended effect of discouraging risk taking and dampening the development of entrepreneurial impulses among borrowers (Armendariz De Aghion and Morduch 2005; Chowdhury 2005; Fischer 2010).

In addition to mobilizing savings and encouraging microfinance, better access to the financial sector by developing microcredit and insurance markets in rural and poverty-stricken regions are promising ways by which public policy can assist the development of risk sharing to allow households to cope with risk.

There are powers available to a government that the private sector does not have. For one thing, in its capacity as the risk manager of the society and as its agent, government can promote risk sharing broadly. It can reduce information problems, such as moral hazard and adverse selection, through its potentially vast investigative, monitoring, and enforcement capabilities. Through its power of implementing civil and criminal penalties for noncompliance, a government can demand truthful disclosure of information from participants in the economy. It can force financial concerns that would attempt to appropriate gains and externalize losses by shifting risks to others to internalize them by imposing stiff liabilities or taxes. Using its power to tax and to control money supply, a government has the significant ability to make credible commitments on current and future financing issues. It can use its power to tax to create an incentive structure for intergenerational risk sharing whereby the proceeds from taxation of the current income-earning generation is redistributed to reduce risks to human capital of the youth of current and future generations. Without government intervention, individuals are unable to diversify the risk to their most valuable asset: their human capital. The young have significant human capital but insufficient financial capital. For the old, the opposite is the case.[4]

Government as the Risk Manager Promoting Risk Sharing[5]

It could well be argued that in contemporary societies, risk management is the central role of government, and therefore, government is the ultimate risk manager in a society. In most economies, governments play a major role in bearing risk on behalf of their citizens. For example, governments provided social safety net measures and insurance for a variety of financial transactions. The history of economic explanation for government's role in the economy spans more than a century, as economists have attempted to justify the role as being necessitated by the divergence between public and private interests. Some six decades ago, Arrow and Debreu (1954) focused on finding precise conditions under which public and private interests would converge, as envisioned in Adam Smith's conjecture of the invisible hand. The result was an elegant proof that competitive markets would indeed have a stable equilibrium, provided some stringent conditions were met. It was clear, however, that even under the best of actual conditions, markets did not perform as envisioned either by Smith or Arrow-Debreu. Consideration of violations of the underlying conditions spawned a voluminous body of literature on the theory and empirics of market failure. This concept became the starting point of analytic reasoning that justifies government's intervention in the economy to protect the public interest (Stiglitz 1993).

The reason that contemporary societies implement social safety nets, such as social security, health care, and public unemployment insurance programs, is that individual households face substantial risk over their life span, such as mortality risk, wage and other income-wide risks, and health risks. Because private insurance markets do not provide perfect insurance against all risks, there is said to be a market failure, and government intervention is called for to correct it. What has become clear in the wake of the global financial crisis is that even in the most advanced industrial economies, existing social safety nets have become incapable of coping with the adverse consequences of the crisis. Not only has the crisis shaken previous levels of confidence in markets, but nearly all analyses of its causes attribute it to market failure in one dimension or another. This has intensified calls for government interventions to counter the adverse effects of the crisis on income and employment, to strengthen the social safety nets, and to reform the financial sectors. The most important lesson of the crisis has been that people at large carry too large a risk of exposure to massive shocks originating in events that are beyond their influence and control. Hence, attention has been focused on ways and means of expanding collective risk sharing.

Before the recent subprime crisis, it was assumed that government intervention, in the form of activities such as providing social safety nets, public goods, and deposit insurance, was solely for the purpose of addressing various kinds of market failure. While this is a crucial justification for intervention, there is an important dimension of government's role that has not attracted much attention. Many of the steps to provide a social safety net, from a minimal amount in some countries to substantial amounts in welfare states, are also about collective risk sharing. This dimension has been particularly neglected in the analysis of government provision of social insurance and services, in which the sole focus has been on the issue of trade-off between equity and efficiency: the issue at the heart of debates about the roles of the state versus the market.

Need for Developing a Supportive Institutional Framework

As discussed, access to finance is hampered by informational asymmetries and market imperfections, which need to be removed before one can think of enhancing finance. When it comes to developing countries, where the financial sector is not very developed and the formal financial sector is underdeveloped, it is important that attention be paid to improving institutions critical for financial sector development. Improved access to finance in many developing countries is constrained by an underdeveloped institutional framework, inadequate regulations, and lack of a specialized supervisory capacity. Policy makers need to take steps to enhance key institutions such as the legal, informational, and regulatory institutions in the country.

Regulators should make financial inclusion a priority. Despite the significance of financial inclusion, it is still not a priority for financial regulators in most of the 57 member-countries of the Organization of Islamic Cooperation (OIC). OIC countries need to develop a regulatory and supervisory framework that supports wide financial inclusion based on sound risk management and with sufficient consumer protections. Financial inclusion should be considered as a goal alongside prudential regulation and financial system stability. The survey of financial regulators worldwide concerning financial access (CGAP 2010) found that regions that include financial access in their strategies and mandate their financial regulators to pursue such agendas are also the countries that reform the most. Regulators with a financial inclusion strategy are more likely to have more financial inclusion topics under their purview and more resources and staff dedicated to working on these matters (Pearce 2010).

Priority should be given to improving financial infrastructure, especially the current credit information system. Core components of the financial infrastructure such as credit information, investors' rights, and insolvency regimes are essential, irrespective of the type of financing: whether conventional or Islamic. Deficiencies in financial infrastructure are one of the major obstacles blocking further SME lending in the Middle East and North Africa (MENA) region.[6] Sharing borrower information is essential to lowering the costs of finance and overcoming information constraints. Lack of access to credit information and the fact that only a small portion of the population has established a credit history (low coverage ratio) are two main features that contribute to financial exclusion in OIC countries, especially for SME financing. Muslim countries interested in enhancing financial inclusion need to improve their financial infrastructure, which will entail expanding the range of collateral, improving registries for moveable assets, and improving enforcement and sales procedures for both fixed assets and movables. Public credit registries should be upgraded. More importantly, private credit bureaus should be introduced; they are capable of significantly expanding coverage and the depth of credit information (Rocha and others 2011). Improvements in financial infrastructure will reduce the information asymmetry that constrains access to credit and raises the costs and risk of financial intermediation.

Infrastructure conducive to products compliant with Shari'ah should be developed. The growth of Islamic microfinance will depend to a large degree on whether financial institutions can develop sufficiently attractive financial products and services that are competitive with conventional products in terms of pricing, transparency, processing time, and burden on the client. Shari'ah-compliant microfinance and SME financing is limited in its scope and scale because of lack of knowledge concerning Shari'ah products, absence of accounting and regulatory standards for Shari'ah-compliant microfinance, and adequate monitoring and supervisory setups.

Integrating Shari'ah-compliant products and customer information into the formal financial sector will not only enhance access, but will also help integrate Islamic finance with conventional finance. For example, by bringing borrowers' information to credit bureaus, financial institutions of all types could extend access to new customers, while managing risks and costs more effectively. This will also help Shari'ah-compliant financial institutions expand their funding source and enhance their risk-sharing mechanisms, as institutions with their clients' credit information available to the public can establish their reputation much more easily than institutions with a system based on informal credit histories.

Microinsurance should be developed and promoted. There is evidence of a positive causal relationship at the country level between insurance penetration and economic growth. At the individual level, the policyholder benefits from increased access to a wider range of products with increased coverage and greater sustainability, and the partnering insurance company has access into a new market without taking on extensive marketing, distribution, or administration costs. More importantly, the partner-agent model facilitates the pooling of risks between the formal and informal sectors.

Despite the success and rapid growth of Islamic insurance (*Takaful*) and the contribution of microinsurance to poverty reduction, micro*Takaful* institutions are still significantly underdeveloped in OIC countries. Like low-income individuals, SMEs are also less covered by insurance services in poorer OIC countries. In the MENA region, 34 percent of SMEs in Gulf Cooperation Council (GCC) countries have the access to insurance services, compared to only 19 percent of the SMEs in non-GCC countries (Rocha and others 2011). One major reason for the slow expansion of micro*Takaful* may be linked to the fact that MFIs in populous Muslim countries are less likely to offer insurance services that are Shari'ah-compliant (Kwon 2010).

If the policy makers in Muslim countries wish to promote Islamic microfinance and SMEs, these measures need to be complemented by promotion of micro*Takaful* by designing adequate regulatory frameworks and by providing incentives to insurance carriers to enter into this market. A study by the Islamic Development Bank rightly suggests that *Qard-al-hassan* funds could be used to develop micro*Takaful* capacity in a country in addition to credit guarantee systems (Obaidullah 2008). Similarly, *zakat* funds can be utilized to cover the default risk of microenterprises run by poor microentrepreneurs, to build capacity and skills, and to reduce operating costs of microfinance and microinsurance. Implementation of such ideas and innovations require development of institutions that support transparent governance to ensure the effectiveness of such mechanisms.

Engagement by the formal sector should be encouraged. Based on the experience of microfinance, the development community is shifting the emphasis away from microcredit institutions to an array of other financial institutions, such as postal savings banks, consumer credit institutions, and—most importantly—the banking system, with the view that this broader approach can lead to overall financial system efficiency and outreach to the entire population. Widening of financial services to the poor and small enterprises by private sector institutions (particularly commercial banks) in the formal financial sector requires proper incentives and removal of regulatory barriers, without sacrificing promotion of stability or security of the financial system (DFID 2004).

Institutionalization of Islamic Redistributive Instruments

As discussed, Islam provides a set of redistributive instruments that could play a critical role in enhancing financial access and reducing poverty. Given Islam's emphasis on social and economic justice and the eradication of poverty, Islamic instruments that address inequity, such as *zakat*, *khairat* (charitable donations), *waqf*, and *Qard-al-hassan*, could be expected to play an important role if the required institutional structures are developed.[7] Therefore, there is a need to formalize or institutionalize Islamic redistributive mechanisms designed to empower the economically weak segments of society.[8]

By institutionalization, we mean building nation-wide institutions and the related legal infrastructure to maximize the effectiveness of these redistributive mechanisms. This institution-building exercise can take place in three steps. The first step is the development of institutions. An institution is nothing more than the legalization of the rules of behavior, and therefore, would require crafting rules pertaining to these instruments as envisioned by Shari'ah. The second step would be to establish these institutions and to integrate them with the rest of the economic and financial system. In this process, either existing channels of distribution, such as banks and post offices, can be utilized to interact with the customers, or new means can be introduced, leveraging new technologies. Finally, there should be mechanisms to ensure enforceability of rules through transparent means.

The objective of institutionalization of redistributive instruments is to formalize and standardize the operations to facilitate each instrument. For example, for *zakat*, *khairat*, and *Qard-al-hassan*, a formal network of institutions needs to be developed to collect, distribute, and recycle the funds in the most efficient and the most transparent fashion.[9] In some countries, point of sale mechanisms such as ATMs or cash-dispensing machines are used to give the customers the choice and to make it easier for them to make donations or contributions on the spot. The financial institution can collect and aggregate funds and then disburse them to needy through selected channels.

The use of *Qard-al-hassan* for the microfinance sector should be exploited further. Many of the characteristics of the *Qard-al-hassan*–based funds could be shared by MFIs. Therefore, the infrastructure of the latter can be utilized to effectively achieve the objectives of the former. While it is difficult to explain why this very important Islamic redistributive institution is so underutilized in the Islamic world—and requires some research effort by sociologists and economists to investigate the behavioral causes—one can speculate that lack of knowledge, in the first instance, and concerns about safety and security of the contributed principal, in the second, may be important factors. The latter could be addressed by a credible Islamic financial institution by issuing financial instruments that would provide safety and security to the contributors. The Islamic financial institution could also instrumentalize the asset side of its balance sheet. Furthermore, it could provide *Qard-al-hassan* resources to existing MFIs to reduce the burden of their interest rate charges on their borrowers. How would such an Islamic financial institution cover its administrative costs? There are two possible sources. The first is by investing a fraction of the mobilized resources. The second is through profit-sharing via *Qard-al-hassan* resources. The Islamic financial institution could invest in productive investment projects of young entrepreneurs that have no access to formal credit markets.

Policy makers need to pay attention to this set of tools to enhance access. They should encourage development of such institutions through development of the legal framework to protect the institutions, donors, and stakeholders, and to ensure transparent governance. With well-developed redistributive institutions, supplemented by formal and semi-formal sector financial institutions, a more effective approach to poverty reduction could be undertaken.

Financial Engineering

Financial innovation and financial engineering have changed the face of the global financial landscape in the last three decades. Although some of the innovations have been criticized and have been the source of volatility in the markets, their positive contribution cannot be denied. There is no reason why financial engineering cannot be used in the area of financial inclusion and to enhance financial access. One way would be to securitize assets generated by microfinance and SMEs. *Sukuk* (Islamic bonds) are a successful application of securitization. Along the same lines, a marketable instrument could be introduced to provide funding for much-needed microfinance and SME financing. With the introduction of securitization of microfinance and SME financing, financial institutions would be able to pool their assets and issue marketable securities. In this way, they could share risks with the market, as well as free up the capital for further mobilization of microfinance and SME financing.

Several researchers have suggested ways to formalize and institutionalize Islamic modes of redistribution through an integrated approach by applying financial engineering and by combining different modes (see Mohieldin and others 2011 for details). These approaches include establishing a nonprofit financial intermediary based on the *Qard-al-hassan* model or establishing MFIs based on a hybrid of *zakat*, *awqaf*, and *sadaqat*. The institution of *awqaf* (trust or endowment) was once a very well-established institution in Muslim societies, but with gradual decline, the institution has lost its effectiveness. Policy makers need to encourage revival of these institutions and should encourage financial engineering to create hybrid solutions whereby Islam's redistributive instruments are mixed with market-based instruments to address the issue of sustainable development.

Consider an example of financial engineering where a market-based solution is combined with a redistributive instrument to strengthen its viability in the market. As argued, securitization could be used to securitize assets in the MSME sector and to mobilize funding from the market. However, given the perception of high risk for such undertakings, and the lack of credit enhancement tools—which are a standard feature in conventional securitization—both the originators and structurers shy away from securitization of such portfolios. In addition to conventional credit enhancement techniques through tranching, sufficient funds could be raised based on *Qard-al-hassan* to provide an additional buffer of security to the investors against the credit risk. If the securitized portfolio consisted of microlending, a default by the microborrower could be covered by the *Qard-al-hassan*, which could be forgiven if a business loss occurs despite the earnest efforts of the borrower.

Similarly, issuing an equity instrument on the portfolio of domestic development projects has an added advantage of improving domestic income distribution. Provided that these instruments are issued in low denominations sold in the retail market, these instruments could serve households and firms in their attempts to hedge their idiosyncratic risks. In essence, they would be macro-market instruments similar to those proposed by Shiller (1993, 1999, 2004).

These instruments could anchor the development of the high-end of the risk spectrum.

Innovative techniques like these should be explored further by the Islamic financial institutions. Policy makers should aim to develop a financial system where financial innovation is encouraged, but where there are checks and balances as well as incentive mechanisms to avoid misuse of financial engineering. An enabling environment and the supporting institutions are prerequisites, and should be developed before such innovations could take place.

Conclusion

Risk sharing serves one of the most important goals of Islam: the unity of mankind. Islam is a rules-based system in which a network of prescribed rules governs the socio-economic-political life of society. Compliance with these rules renders the society a union of mutual support by requiring humans to share the risks of life. Risk sharing intensifies human interaction. The dazing pace of financial innovations of the several decades preceding the recent financial crisis created opportunities and instruments of risk shifting—whereby risks were shifted to investors, borrowers, depositors and, ultimately, to taxpayers—rather than risk sharing. The financial sector became increasingly decoupled from the real sector, with the growth of the former outpacing that of the latter by double-digit multiples (Epstein 2006; Menkoff and Tolksdorf 2001; Mirakhor 2010).

Instruments of Islamic finance allow risk sharing and risk diversification with which individuals can mitigate their idiosyncratic risks. On the other hand, mandated levies, such as *zakah*, are means through which the idiosyncratic risks of the poor are shared by the rich as an act of redemption of the former's property rights in the income and wealth of the latter. Other recommended levies, beyond those mandated, such as *sadaqat* and *Qard-al-hassan*, also play the same role. They help reduce the poor's income-consumption correlation. In other words, the poor are not forced to rely on their low-level income, or cope with an absence of income, to maintain a decent level of subsistence living for themselves and their families. It is possible that at some future time, even these levies could be instrumentalized to be included in the full-spectrum Islamic finance menu of instruments for risk sharing. In such a way, Islamic finance could help governments become better risk managers for society.

Islamic instruments of risk sharing could help blunt the impact of economic shocks, disappointments, and suffering for individuals by dispersing their effects among a large number of people. Instruments of finance could be available for all classes of people to allow them to reduce their idiosyncratic risks and smooth their consumption. They could help ensure that innovators, entrepreneurs, and micro, small, and medium firms have access to financial resources without the need to bear all risks themselves or, alternatively, to abandon productive projects altogether. Instruments of insurance could not only provide protection against health and accident risks but also insure against risks to livelihoods and home values to protect people's long-term income and livelihood. Such a full-spectrum Islamic finance could then truly be said to have "democratized finance" without transferring risks of any venture to a particular class or to the whole society. This would be in sharp contrast to the results of the "democratization of finance," which led to the recent global financial crisis of the conventional system, in which the risks of financial innovations were shifted away from financiers. The consequence was that while the gains were privatized, the pain was socialized (Sheng 2009).

Given the rules governing property rights, work, production, exchange, markets, distribution, and redistribution, it is reasonable to conclude that in an Islamic society—that is, a rule-complying and Allah-conscious society—absolute poverty could not exist. It can be argued that there is no economic topic more emphasized in Islam than poverty and the responsibility of individuals and society to eradicate it. The Prophet said that poverty verges on disbelief, and that poverty is worse than murder. It is almost axiomatic that in any society in which there is poverty, Islamic rules are not being observed. It means that the rich and wealthy have not redeemed the rights of others in their income and wealth, and that the state has failed to take corrective action.

Notes

1. For example, in Bangladesh, Pakistan, and the Philippines, it takes more than one month to get a small business loan processed. In Denmark, the wait is only one day (Demirgüç-Kunt, Beck, and Honohan 2007).
2. The Qu'ran uses two words for justice: *qist* and *ádl*. *Qist* is the chief characteristic of appropriate human relations and of human relations toward the rest of creation. It is entirely a human phenomenon; it is not a divine trait. *Ádl*, on the other hand, is a feature of Allah's Actions that manifests itself in the perfect balance of the cosmos; it characterizes the Action of Allah to place everything in its rightful place (Mirakhor and Askari 2010).
3. Mirakhor (2010). The economy-finance nexus defined by Arrow-Debreu-Hahn general equilibrium models were risk-sharing conceptualizations in which securities represented contingent financial claims on the real sector. Equity share claims represent first-best instruments of risk sharing and satisfy characteristics required of Arrow Securities. It would appear that had the financial markets in industrial countries developed their financial sector along the lines suggested by the Arrow-Debreu-Hahn model, they could have had much more efficient risk sharing and, perhaps, avoided the crises that have plagued conventional financial system. See Arrow and Debreu (1954) and Arrow and Hahn (1971).
4. As Merton (1983) suggested, a trade is possible between these generations, but laws prohibit trade in human capital (except through wage employment). The young cannot make credible commitment of their human capital through private contracts. There is no possibility for private contracts to commit future generations to current risk-sharing arrangements. This, in effect, represents another case of commitment failure. Using its powers of taxing and spending, unparalleled monitoring and enforcing capabilities, and its control of money supply, government can resolve these issues. No private entity can credibly commit not to default on an obligation, as can government.

5. This section is based on Mirakhor (2011b).
6. The Doing Business Report, as the most comprehensive measurement of business environment faced by SMEs across countries, shows that OIC countries as of 2011on average rank 118, much lower than the average developing countries (100) in terms of ease of doing business (World Bank 2011). In addition, OIC countries lag far behind in all four aspects of ease of getting credit: depth of credit information, public credit registry coverage, strength of legal rights, and private credit bureau (Mohieldin and others 2011).
7. For example, Mohieldin and others (2011) estimate the resources needed to fill the poverty gap using *zakat* collection. They find supporting evidence that 20 of 39 OIC countries could lift the poorest (those living on less than $1.25 per day) above the poverty line simply with collection of *zakat* from domestic payments and remittances. They argue that they do not consider *zakat* a totally new poverty reduction mechanism, as it is already collected and distributed to the poor in several Islamic countries. However, they argue that proper collection, streamlining, accountability, prioritization, and allocation to productive activities can have significant impact on enhancing access and opportunity for the poor segment of the society, which will ultimately lead to a reduction in poverty.
8. See Mirakhor (2004) for further details. Mirakhor argues that given the number of poor in Islamic countries, critics argue that, a priori, Islamic institutions, which were meant to redistribute income and wealth from the more well-to-do to the weaker segment of the society, have not shown the necessary potency in performing their function, and they could be right (see also chapter 11). It is a serious problem that very little effort has been expended by Islamic and other researchers and scholars to empirically investigate the behavior of Muslims vis-à-vis these institutions: that is, why the latter have failed to achieve the objectives for which they were designed and how the situation could be remedied. Admitting that these institutions have, by and large, failed to alleviate poverty in Muslim countries does not obviate the need to consider their potential.
9. An example of a Muslim country where the institution of *Qard-al-hassan* has been utilized effectively to provide microfinance is the Islamic Republic of Iran, where these institutions are widespread throughout the country. They provide small consumer and producer loans and, in some cases, engage in profit-making activities that supplement the principal amounts deposited with the fund. These *Qard-al-hassan* funds are usually associated in each locality with mosques or other religious organizations and, at times, with guilds or professional group associations. The capital is contributed by the more well-to-do, who are at liberty to withdraw their funds at any time. These funds operate with very low administrative costs, since most are managed through volunteer services contributed by the people within the group. See Sadr (2007).

References

Aghion, Philippe, and Patrick Bolton. 1997. "A Theory of Trickle-Down Growth and Development." *Review of Economic Studies* 64 (2): 151–72.

Armendariz De Aghion, Beatriz, and Jonathan Morduch. 2005. *The Economics of Microfinance*. Cambridge, MA: MIT Press.

Arrow, Kenneth J. 1971. *Essays in the Theory of Risk-Bearing*. Chicago, IL: Markham Publishing Company.

Arrow, Kenneth J., and Gerard Debreu. 1954. "The Existence of an Equilibrium for a Competitive Economy." *Econometrica* 22 (3): 265–90.

Arrow, Kenneth J., and Frank Hahn. 1971. *General Competitive Analysis*. San Francisco, CA: Holder Day.

Banerjee, Abhijit V., and Andrew F. Newman. 1993. "Occupational Choice and the Process of Development." *Journal of Political Economy* 101 (2): 274–98.

Bauchet, Jonathan, Cristobal Marshall, Laura Starita, Jeanette Thomas, and Anna Yalouris. 2011. "Latest Findings from Randomized Evaluations of Microfinance." Access to Finance Forum, No. 2 (December), Consultative Group to Assist the Poor (CGAP), Washington, DC.

CGAP (Consultative Group to Assist the Poor). 2010. *Financial Access 2010: The State of Financial Inclusion through the Crisis*. Washington, DC: CGAP and World Bank.

Chowdhury, Prabal R. 2005. "Group-Lending: Sequential Financing Lender Monitoring and Joint Liability." *Journal of Development Economics* 77 (2): 415–39.

Demirgüç-Kunt, Asli, Thorsten Beck, and Patrick Honohan. 2007. *Finance for All? Policies and Pitfalls in Expanding Access*. A World Bank Policy Research Report. Washington, DC: World Bank.

Demirgüç-Kunt, Asli, and Ross Levine. 2008. "Finance and Economic Opportunity." Policy Working Paper 4468, World Bank, Washington, DC.

DFID (Department for International Development, United Kingdom). 2004. "The Importance of Financial Sector Development for Growth and Poverty Reduction." Policy Division Working Paper, DFID, London.

Epstein, Gerald A. 2006. *Financialization and the World Economy*. New York: Edward Elgar.

Fischer, Greg. 2010. "Contract Structure, Risk Sharing, and Investment Choice." The Suntory Centre, London School of Economics, London.

Galor, Oded, and Joseph Zeira. 1993. "Income Distribution and Macroeconomics." *Review of Economic Studies* 60 (1): 35–52.

Iqbal, Zamir, and Abbas Mirakhor. 2011. *An Introduction to Islamic Finance: Theory and Practice*. 2nd ed. Singapore: John Wiley & Sons.

Kwon, Jean W. 2010. "An Analysis of Organisational, Market and Socio-Cultural Factors Affecting the Supply of Insurance and Other Financial Services by Microfinance Institutions in Developing Economics." Geneva Papers on Risk and Insurance 35 (1): 130–60.

Menkoff, Lucas, and Norbert Tolksdorf. 2001. *Financial Market Drift: Decoupling of the Financial Sector from the Real Economy?* Heidelberg-Berlin: Springer-Verlag.

Merton, Robert. 1983. "On the Role of Social Security as a Means for Efficient Risk Sharing in an Economy Where Human Capital Is Not Tradeable." In *Financial Aspects of the United States Pension System*, edited by Zvi Bodie and John Shoven. Chicago, IL: University of Chicago Press.

Mirakhor, Abbas. 1989. "General Characteristics of an Islamic Economic System." In *Essays on Iqtisad: The Islamic Approach to Economic Problems*, edited by Baqir Al-Hasani and Abbas Mirakhor, 45–80. Maryland: Nur.

———. 2004. "Islamic Finance and Instrumentalization of Islamic Redistributive Institutions." Paper presented at Ibn Rushd Memorial Lecture, London, April.

———. 2009. "Islamic Economics and Finance: An Institutional Perspective." *IIUM Journal of Economics and Management* 17 (1): 31–72.

———. 2010. "Whither Islamic Finance?" Presented at the Securities Commission of Malaysia, March.

———. 2011a. "Epistemological Foundation of Finance: Islamic and Conventional." Keynote address presented at the Foundations of Islamic Finance Conference Series, Kuala Lumpur, March 8–10.

———. 2011b. "Islamic Finance and Risk Sharing: Role of Public Policy." Paper presented at 5th International Islamic Capital Market Forum Securities Commission of Malaysia, Kuala Lumpur, November 10.

Mirakhor, Abbas, and Hossein Askari. 2010. *Islam and the Path to Human and Economic Development.* New York: Palgrave Macmillan.

Mirakhor, Abbas, and Edib Smolo. 2011. "Do Conventional and Islamic Finance Share Common Epistemology?" *Global Islamic Finance*, August: 49–53.

Mohieldin, Mahmoud, Zamir Iqbal, Ahmed Rostom, and Xiaochen Fu. 2011. "The Role of Islamic Finance in Enhancing Financial Inclusion in Organization of Islamic Cooperation (OIC) Countries." Policy Research Working Paper WPS5920, World Bank, Washington, DC.

Obaidullah, Mohammed. 2008. *Role of Microfinance in Poverty Alleviation: Lessons from Experiences in Selected IDB Member-Countries.* Jeddah, Saudi Arabia: Islamic Research and Training Institute (IRTI) and Islamic Development Bank (IDB).

Pearce, Douglas. 2010. "Financial Inclusion in the Middle East and North Africa: Analysis and Roadmap Recommendations." World Bank, Washington, DC.

Rocha, Roberto, Subika Farazi, Rania Khouri, and Douglas Pearce. 2011. "The Middle East and North Africa Region: The Results of a Joint Survey of the Union of Arab Banks and the World Bank." World Bank, Washington, DC.

Sadr, Kazem. 2007. "Gharzul-Hasaneh Financing and Institutions." First International Conference on Inclusive Islamic Financial Sector Development, Jointly Organized by Islamic Research and Training Institute of the Islamic Development Bank and the Centre for Islamic Banking Finance and Management, Universiti Brunei Darussalam.

Sheng, Andrew. 2009. *From Asian to Global Financial Crisis.* New York: Cambridge University Press.

Shiller, Robert J. 1993. *Macro Markets: Creating Institutions for Managing Society's Largest Economic Risks.* New York: Oxford University Press.

———. 1999. "Social Security and Institutions for Intergenerational, Intragenerational, and International Risk Sharing." *Carnegie-Rochester Conference Series on Public Policy* 50: 165–204.

———. 2004. "Radical Financial Innovation." Discussion Paper 1461, Cowles Foundation, New Haven, CT.

Stiglitz, Joseph. 1993. "Perspectives on the Role of Government Risk-Bearing within the Financial Sector." In *Government Risk-Bearing*, 109–130. Federal Reserve Bank of Cleveland.

Stiglitz, Joseph, and Andrew Weiss. 1981. "Credit Rationing in Markets with Imperfect Information." *American Economic Review* 71 (3): 393–410.

World Bank. 2011. *Doing Business Report 2011.* Washington, DC. http://www.doingbusiness.org/

CHAPTER 7

Financial Inclusion and Islamic Finance: Organizational Formats, Products, Outreach, and Sustainability

Habib Ahmed

Introduction

Provision of financial services to the poor is an important tool for achieving the first Millennium Development Goal of cutting absolute poverty by half, the United Nations has stated (2006, 4). Similarly, the Asian Development Bank (2000, 1) asserts that providing different financial services to the poor is "a critical element of an effective poverty reduction strategy." It is widely agreed that provision of credit used in productive activities for successive years can increase the income of the poor to levels where the households will eventually graduate beyond poverty. Until recently, however, the majority of the poor did not have access to financial services in most countries, either involuntarily because of economic and social factors or voluntarily because of cultural and religious reasons (World Bank 2008, 29).

The poor face many risks that make them vulnerable to falling back to poverty. As a result, they need mechanisms not only to increase their income levels but also to help them cope with shocks and reduce their vulnerability. In general, the vulnerability of a household, community, or country depends on the characteristics of risk events they face and their ability to manage them. Given the multifaceted nature of poverty and the risks facing the poor, there has been discussion of a paradigm shift from microfinance to "inclusive finance," which entails providing a variety of financial services to the poor, including savings, credit, and insurance facilities (Matin, Hulme, and Rutherford 2002; UN 2006). These financial services enable the poor to

Habib Ahmed holds the Sharjah Chair in Islamic Law and Finance at the Institute of Middle Eastern and Islamic Studies, School of Government and International Affairs, Durham University, the United Kingdom.

acquire capital to engage in productive ventures, manage risks, increase their income and savings, and move out of poverty. The impact of finance on poverty can be enhanced if the depth of outreach of financial services can be expanded.[1]

A large segment of the poor population is excluded from the formal financial services involuntarily due to low income, high risk, price, and the information framework, among other reasons (World Bank 2008). The key constraints to providing financial services to the poor arise due to asymmetric information problems and the costs involved with the size of financial service and scale of production. Private information about poor households is scant, which leads to moral hazard and adverse selection problems, among other difficulties. In the face of extreme information problems and costly state verification, markets tend either to break down or function poorly (Holzmann and Jorgensen 2000). Furthermore, as the size of the current financial services market for the poor is small, the costs of per unit of financial services are relatively high. Given the high risks and costs, sustainability becomes an important issue for organizations providing financial services to the poor. Sustainability in the long run relates to providing services without subsidies.

An important demand-side factor that can hinder access to finance to the poor in Muslim countries are cultural norms; people may choose to exclude themselves voluntarily from financial services for religious reasons. Many poor people in Muslim countries would not deal with conventional interest-based financial institutions (FIs) because of the prohibition of *riba* (interest) by Islamic law. This is confirmed in a study by Karim, Tarazi, and Reille (2008), who found that an estimated 72 percent of the people living in Muslim countries do not use formal financial services, and a large percentage of the population (ranging from 20 to more than 40 percent) would not use conventional microfinance to avoid interest. Thus, access of finance to the poor in many Muslim countries would require provision of *Shari'ah*-compliant services.

To keep the scope of this discussion manageable, this chapter will focus mainly at micro-level organizational features of FIs and identify some regulatory issues affecting their operations. After reviewing the background literature on financial inclusion to identify the factors affecting provision of financial services to the poor, the discussion on Islamic financial inclusion focuses on four key elements. First, it identifies different organizational models used to deliver services to the poor. Second, it examines the provision of the range of services by these organizations. Third, it assesses the sustainability and outreach of the service providers. Finally, it evaluates the role of *zakat* (obligatory alms) and *waqf* (religious endowment) in operations of organizations providing financial services to the poor. Because the information and data used are drawn from secondary sources, the assessments of outreach and sustainability of different organizations are anecdotal in nature.

Inclusive Finance: Scope and Constraints

As mentioned, inclusive finance for the poor would include financing facilities to promote productive income-generation, savings opportunities to build up the assets, and insurance facilities to protect them against risks. This section reviews the key issues in the provision of these services at the organizational level. Organizations face a trade-off between outreach and sustainability in providing these services to the poor. Sustainability and outreach has been debated rigorously in the literature on inclusive finance. While various research papers present contradictory evidence on the issue, a comprehensive study by Hermes, Lensink, and Meesters (2011) using data from 435 microfinance institutions (MFIs) covering 11 years clearly identifies the trade-off between the two. The issues related to provision of different services to the poor and the implications for outreach and sustainability are discussed next.

Microfinance

Although microfinance has existed in different forms for a long time,[2] the initiation of the microcredit programs as tool for poverty alleviation through formal institutions was initiated in the 1970s. Microfinance schemes provide credit to the poor and operate quite differently from conventional commercial banks.[3] To obtain finance from these institutions, the client or beneficiary must be poor.[4] Small amounts of credit are extended at reasonable rates of interest and paid back in weekly or monthly installments. Sometimes, MFIs also extend credit to individuals to build houses and for collective enterprises.

Although different approaches to microfinance have evolved, the group-based Grameen Bank model serves as the dominant model for most MFIs (Morduch 1994). Under the group-based programs, a person must form a group of like-minded people with similar socioeconomic status to get credit. A number of groups are federated into a center, and members elect a center chief and deputy center chief. Weekly meetings of the center are held at a convenient place in the locality. All members (that is, clients) of the center are required to attend these meetings. An official from the MFI attends the weekly meetings to conduct the banking transactions and other businesses with the members of the center.

Most of the initial MFIs provided credit facilities only. Some MFIs have various (forced) savings schemes and risk mitigation funds. However, these pools of savings usually are "not designed to meet the poor's need for savings mechanisms" but rather are "a means of collateralizing loans and providing low-cost capital," Hulme (2000, 26) notes. While group-based microfinance is one of the dominant models, MFIs have evolved to various other types whereby both nonprofit and for-profit organizations provide various financial services to the poor. Many commercial banks, including large international banks such as Citigroup, Deutsche Bank, and HSBC, have also started to provide microfinance (Hermes, Lensink, and Meesters 2011). Most of the financing provided by commercial organizations is individual-based lending, rather than group-based lending.

Many studies indicate that microfinance has a positive impact on income levels and reduction of vulnerability.[5] Although a large literature shows the success of MFIs, some studies point out the failure of these institutions in targeting the core poor. For example, Dichter (1996), Hulme and Mosley (1996a), and Montgomery (1996) report that MFIs do not serve the poorest, as they are either not given loans or drop out of the credit schemes.[6] A key problem for the MFIs, however, is the trade-off between sustainability and depth of outreach. Due to lack of fund mobilization and the high administrative costs, the costs of providing finance for MFIs become exorbitantly high. For example, Bennett (1998, 116) reports that the administrative costs of five MFIs in South Asia range from 24 percent to more than 400 percent per dollar lent.[7]

Microinsurance

The insurance sector is complementary to the banking and securities markets in promoting growth (Brainard 2008).[8] The insurance industry can play an important role in alleviating poverty if services can be provided to the poor to reduce their risks and vulnerability. However, compared to microfinance, microinsurance is relatively new and its provision is miniscule, with only 0.5 percent of the poor covered in Africa and less than 3 percent in Asia in 2007 (Bhatty 2010).

While the core principles of microinsurance are similar to that of traditional insurance, many things are different, McCord, Zenklusen, and Steinmann (2011) assert. The International Association of Insurance Supervisors (IAIS 2007, 10) defines microinsurance as "insurance that is accessed by low-income population, provided by a variety of different entities, but run in accordance with generally accepted insurance practices." This definition thus excludes certain government social welfare and emergency support programs, as these are not funded from a pool of funds that depends on risk-related premiums.

The key features of microinsurance compared to traditional insurance are identified by McCord, Zenklusen, and Steinmann (2011). The clients of the former are poor, face more risks—resulting in volatility in their incomes—and can afford to pay only a very small premium. To understand the problems of providing insurance services to the poor, it is important to know the risks they face and the ways in which they can be managed. There are various ways to classify risks that the poor face. Holzmann and Jorgensen (2000, 11) maintain that risks can be natural or a result of human activity. The World Bank (2001) identifies sources of risks arising from shocks at the micro, meso, and macro levels. While micro risks are idiosyncratic, arising at the individual or household level, the meso and macro risks are covariant risks that affect communities and national economies, respectively.

Risks also differ in terms of their frequency of occurrence and intensity, which relates to the expected welfare losses. SwissRe (2010) identifies four key risk types that low-income families face. The first are health risks, which result in either direct costs due to unexpected medical treatment or indirect losses of income due to health related reasons. The second risk is related to lifecycle events such as old age and death of the breadwinner in the household. Third, financial risks result in lower income due to different reasons, such as loss of property, decrease in price of products, or crop failure. Finally, households face disaster risks arising from natural events that can cause loss of lives and property. In a survey of insurance providers in 11 countries, Roth, McCord, and Liber (2007) find demand for protection against health risks to be ranked highest, followed by property and death risks.

Insurance is sold to clients through different delivery channels, which include agents and intermediaries of insurance companies. There are several limitations that make providing insurance to the poor difficult. These include lack of actuarial data on poor households and limited distribution options, which make the provision of insurance riskier and costly. Thus, commercial insurance companies and their agents and intermediaries shy away from providing insurance to the poor. As a result, there may be a need for nonprofit organizations to provide microinsurance (Roth, McCord, and Liber 2007).

Although relatively new, microinsurance faces the same problems of sustainability and outreach as microfinance. Mosley (2003) identifies key issues related to sustainability and outreach related to microinsurance. As with microfinance, the information problems of adverse selection and moral hazard exist in provision of insurance to the poor. While the former implies that the riskiest households would end up using insurance services, the latter would induce more risky behavior after the insurance has been provided. The asymmetric information problems of moral hazard and adverse selection exist in microinsurance in extremes. Higher risks due to these informational problems mean that the premium charged is high, which makes insurance costly to the poor. This leads to a demand-side factor, whereby poor choose not to avail the insurance, partly due to higher costs.

Other than asymmetric information problems, the cost of providing insurance is also high due to small size of insurance coverage. Costs are also pushed up because transactions cost increases due to lack of economies of scale and contract enforcement mechanisms are lacking (Morduch 2006). Along with high risks, high transactions costs associated with low scale of operation and low demand can lead to a situation where the costs of provision of microinsurance becomes exorbitantly high and its sustainability becomes difficult. The implication is that until a certain scale of operation in terms of client numbers is reached, provision of microinsurance may require subsidies (Mosley 2003, 147).

Organizational Features, Sustainability, and Outreach

The trade-off between outreach and sustainability is closely related to the organizational features used to deliver the financial services to the poor. Roth, McCord, and Liber (2007) identify four main categories of organizations that provide financial services to the poor. The first are commercial firms that provide financial services with an objective of profit-making. The second are nongovernmental organizations (NGOs) that provide financial services as nonprofits to fulfill social objectives. The third category consists of mutuals or cooperatives that are owned by members and professionally managed. Finally, community-based organizations (CBOs) are member-owned and managed. One difference between the mutuals and CBOs are that the former are regulated and professionally managed organizations. Given their social mission, nonprofit organizations are better suited to provide services to the poorer sections of the population.

Depending on the missions of organizations, two broad approaches can be identified in delivering financial services. The first is the poverty approach, in which the FIs operate as nonprofits, with the goals of providing finance to the poor and core-poor (Schreiner 2002). Under this approach, financial services are provided by NGOs, government agencies, cooperatives, and development finance institutions (Bennett 1998). As it is costly to finance the poor, long-term sustainability of the operations of these organizations without subsidies becomes an issue. Hermes, Lensink, and Meesters (2011) call the proponents of the poverty approach "welfarists," who emphasize outreach as a key goal for microfinancial services.

The second approach focuses on self-sufficiency; institutions operate like other for-profit institutions (Schreiner 2002). The operations of FIs are sustained by providing larger loans to the less poor at higher interest rates. One way this is done is the linking approach, whereby formal FIs provide services to the poor through intermediaries or special programs (Bennett 1998). While a commercial approach to providing financial services can help the growth of microenterprises, it may fail as a tool to eliminate core poverty (Weiss and Montgomery 2005). In contrast to the welfarists, the institutionalists support this approach, focusing on efficiency and sustainability (Hermes, Lensink, and Meesters 2011).

Beyond the mission of organizations, the appropriate type of organizational format used will also depend on the nature of services provided. For example, McCord, Zenklusen, and Steinmann (2011) point out that one difference between microcredit and microinsurance is that in microcredit, the lenders' funds are at risk, while in microinsurance, the clients' funds are at risk. This requires more trust of the clients on the part of providers of microinsurance compared to microfinance. One way to resolve the trust problem in microinsurance—which faces the underwriting challenge of riskier clients and weak infrastructure—is to use the format of cooperatives and mutual organizations (Weidmaier-Pfister and Klien 2010).

Given the factors discussed, the following organizational features can be identified as relevant and key to delivery of inclusive finance:

Organizational format. The organizational format is ascertained by examining the legal status of the organization. This will partly depend on the menu of organizational formats that different countries have. The organizational format will fall broadly among the four categories identified by Roth, McCord, and Liber (2007): commercial firms, NGOs, mutuals or cooperatives, and CBOs.

Regulatory environment. The regulatory regime, among other factors, defines the scope of Islamic financial products that different organizations can offer and also determines the conditions under which certain financial products are permitted. Regulations on the one hand provide opportunities for certain products such as demand deposits, and on the other hand can introduce constraints for offering financial products.

Sources of funds. Depending on the organizational format and type of business, the sources of funds will vary. Beyond initial capital, funds for MFIs come from two broad categories of sources: liabilities, such as deposits and loans, and donations, which provide funds at subsidized rates. For microinsurance, the premium contributed by participants is the main source of funds.

Products and services offered. As discussed, the products of interest for financial inclusion are savings opportunities, financing, and insurance for the poor. Savings can be distinguished as having either restricted investment, where opportunities to save are limited to certain forced or illiquid forms of deposits, or unrestricted opportunities, which offer wider savings opportunities, including demand deposits. Most unregulated organizations are not allowed to offer unrestricted savings services. Similarly, insurance can also be restricted or unrestricted. Restricted insurance is tied to the credit line of microfinance; clients contribute to a risk fund to cover defaults. Unrestricted insurance includes schemes in which participants voluntarily participate by paying contributions to protect themselves against certain specific risks.

Outreach. As mentioned, two types of outreach are considered. The *width* of the outreach is measured in terms of the number of clients served. The *depth* of outreach is measured by the proportion of poor served. While the width of outreach can be examined in relative terms and depends on the scale of operations of the organization, the *depth* of outreach can be measured by proxies such as size of the savings, financing, and contributions to insurance.

Sustainability. Sustainability indicates the ability of an FI to sustain its activities without subsidies. While the variables used to measure sustainability include operational self-sufficiency and returns on assets, other indicators can also be used. The variables used to measure sustainability include operational self-sufficiency and return of assets (Cull, Demirgüç, and Morduch 2007; Hartarska and Nadolnyak 2007). Other variables can also be used, such as borrowers per branch and access to funds, to ascertain efficiency and sustainability.

Islamic Finance and Inclusive Finance

The social role of the Islamic financial sector can be best exemplified by providing financial services to the poor so as to increase their income and wealth.[9] Specialized poverty-focused Islamic FIs provide services to the poor using Shari'ah-compliant modes and instruments. Thus the assets and liabilities of the Islamic FIs will differ from their conventional counterparts. Important aspects of Islamic modes of finance are that financial capital cannot claim a return on itself and that the transaction must involve a real good or object.

Islamic Microfinance Institutions

Given that interest (one form of *riba*) is prohibited in Islam, the composition of assets and liabilities of Islamic MFIs will comprise different types of non–interest-bearing financial instruments. The innovative group-based format used by MFIs introduces social collateral, thereby minimizing credit risks and ensuring higher recovery rates. As most microfinance schemes have an integrated social development program, adopting the approach of microfinancing can imply a much broader program of wealth creation for the poor and bring about more extensive development.

Modes of Islamic financing are many and varied. The type of financing instrument will depend on the type of activity for which funds are granted. Other than interest free loans (*Qard-al-hassan*), the principles of Islamic financing can be broadly classified as partnerships (*sharikat*) and exchange contracts (*mu'awadat*).[10] Partnership can be on the basis of profit sharing or output sharing. Profit sharing again can take two forms—*musharakah* and *mudarabah*. Whereas in *musharakah*, more than one party can supply finance and participate in a project and distribute the profit at an agreed ratio, in *mudarabah*, one party supplies the funds and the other party manages the project and shares the profit at an agreed upon ratio.

Although there are different kinds of exchange contracts, the most important among these is the deferred-trading principle. A deferred-trading contract can either be a price-deferred sale or an object-deferred sale. What is relevant for microfinancing is the price-deferred sale (*bay-mua'jjal*), in which the object of sale is delivered at the time of the contract, but the price is paid later. The price can also be paid in the future in installments. One type of financial transaction under this format is mark-up sale (*murabahah*), in which the Islamic MFI buys a good or asset and sells it to the client at a mark-up. The client pays for the good or asset at a future date or in installments. *Ijarah* is a leasing contract in which the client uses an asset by paying rent. One form of this arrangement can be the hire-purchase scheme or lease-purchase scheme (*ijarah wa iqitina*), in which the installment includes rent and part of the capital. When the installments are fully paid, the ownership of the asset is transferred to the client.

Various kinds of financing arrangements can be used to finance different kinds of activities. *Musharakah* principle can be adopted in production (agricultural and nonagricultural). The Islamic MFI can provide part of the financial capital to produce an output and in return receive a share of the profit. In trading, the Islamic MFI and the client can jointly finance the purchase and selling of a certain good and distribute the profit. Production undertaken under the *mudarabah* principle would imply that the Islamic MFI finances and the client manages the project. In agricultural production, output sharing can take the form of *muzara'a*. The Islamic MFI may fund the purchase of irrigation equipment, fertilizer, and the like, which the landowner uses on his land to cultivate a certain crop. The harvested crop is then shared by the landowner and the Islamic MFI at an agreed ratio. Other than the profit-sharing principle discussed above, *murabahah* and *ijarah* forms of financing can also be used in production. For example, if a client is in need of initial physical capital (such as equipment or gadgets), the Islamic MFI can buy the items and sell these to the client at a mark-up. In agriculture, the item may be a cow or poultry that the Islamic MFI sells at a mark-up.

The client pays back the price in agreed upon installments in the future. Similar transactions can take place under a leasing (*ijarah*) contract.

In trading, profit sharing schemes and deferred trading contracts can be used. Under a profit-sharing scheme, the Islamic MFI becomes a partner in the trading business and gets a share of the profit. The *murabahah* principle can also be applied where the items to be traded are first bought by Islamic MFI and then sold at a mark-up to the clients. The clients pay back the Islamic MFI once they sell the goods. In transport services, both mark-up principle and the leasing principle can be applied. For example, if a client wants to buy a rickshaw, the Islamic MFI can purchase it and sell it to the client at a mark-up. The client then pays the price on an agreed installment plan. Alternatively, hire-purchase arrangements can be made in which the client pays rent plus a part of the capital in his installments. Once the installments are fully paid, the client becomes the owner of the rickshaw.

*Micro*Takaful

The conventional insurance contract, whereby periodic premium payments are made for a future indemnity, has been deemed as non-Shari'ah-compliant by most Shari'ah scholars because of the existence of excessive uncertainty (*gharar*). While declaring conventional insurance to be prohibited—in Resolution No. 9 (9/2)—the Islamic Fiqh Academy proposes using cooperative insurance based on charitable donations (*tabarru'*) and cooperation or mutual help (*ta'awun*) (IRTI and IFA 2000, 13). As a result, various models of *Takaful* (mutual guarantee) were developed to come with Shari'ah-compliant insurance schemes. The key organizational feature of the *Takaful* is that of mutual insurance, whereby the function of a policy holder takes up the role of ownership and risk bearing and the managerial function is performed by a *Takaful* operator (TO).[11]

The basic structure of a *Takaful* model is shown in figure 7.1. Depending on the relationship between the *Takaful* participants and the TO and the nature of the participants' *Takaful* fund, three key models of *Takaful* can be identified.[12] The first is a *mudarabah* model, in which the TO and the participants have a partnership relationship. The participants contribute (*tabarru'*) in the participants' *Takaful* funds, which is managed by the TO. The TO invests the funds in income-generating activities and gets a share of the profit. After meeting the claims of the participants, the surplus is distributed among the participants. A *wikala* model is very similar to a *mudarabah* model, except that the TO acts as an agent, instead of a partner. As such, the TO gets management fees as compensation instead of profit. Note that *Takaful* can include features of both *mudarabah* and *wikala* contracts. Finally, in the *waqf* model, the participants' *Takaful* fund takes the form of a *waqf* fund. The *waqf* is initially created by the TO, and the contributions of the participants add to this fund. The relationship between the participants and the TO in a *waqf*-based model can be either *mudarabah* or *wikala*.

Hussain (2009) points out that the operational model of *Takafuls* raises a fundamental legal question: Is a *Takaful* a mutual or a proprietorship corporation?

Figure 7.1 The Basic Structure of *Takaful* Models

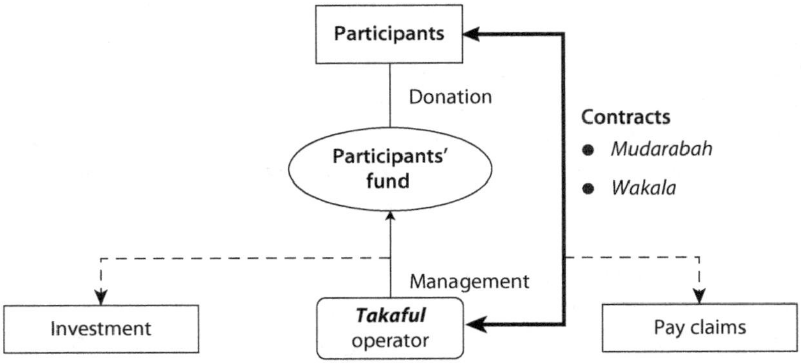

```
                    Participants ◄─────────┐
                         │                  │
                      Donation              │
                         │              Contracts
                    Participants'         • Mudarabah
                       fund              • Wakala
                         ▲
                         │
                     Management
    ┌────────────┐       │         ┌────────────┐
    │ Investment │◄──  Takaful  ──►│ Pay claims │
    └────────────┘     operator    └────────────┘
```

Source: Adapted from Ali and Odierno 2008, 33.

A mutual is owned by the participants in case of *Takaful*, and they as shareholders have the right to appoint managers or TOs. This, however, is not the case. On the one hand, the participants own the *Takaful* fund along with the assets and liabilities attached to it. On the other hand, the corporation or the TO manages the fund with absolute discretion (Hussain 2009). While this legal dilemma is difficult to resolve, for purposes of this chapter, *Takaful* will be identified as for-profit or nonprofit in terms of their legal status. Thus, if a TO is issued a license as a corporation in which shareholders provide it with capital, it will be considered a for-profit organization. If the *Takaful* is registered as mutual such as cooperative or a society, it will be considered a nonprofit entity.

Use of Zakat and Waqf in Inclusive Finance

Whereas *waqf* can be integrated in the *Takaful* model, literature on Islamic microfinance identifies additional religious instruments of *zakat* (obligatory alms) to complement financing to the poor. *Zakat* is one of the fundamental pillars of Islam that has direct economic bearing upon others. It requires Muslims to distribute a part of their wealth among the specified heads in order to achieve economic emancipation of the poor. Similarly, *waqf* is a voluntary charitable act that has wide economic implications. These institutions were able to solve the problems of poverty and extend social services in the classical times.[13] *Sadaqat* (charities) and *Qard-al-hassan* (interest-free loan) are tools for supporting the poor and redistribution of income in their favor.

Zakat and income from *waqf* can be integrated into microfinancing, which can prevent fund diversions and benefit the poorest beneficiaries (Ahmed 2002). *Zakat* given to the poor can be used for consumption, asset building, and production purposes to complement funds of Islamic MFIs. These complementary funds can either be given as grants or interest-free loans (*Qard-al-hassan*) according to the needs of the beneficiary. As these complementary funds will reduce the need for diverting money for consumption and/or purchase of assets, it is expected that the funds taken for productive activities will be invested accordingly. As a result, the overall return on invested funds is expected to be higher and the probability of default relatively lower. Thus, integrating Islamic institutions of *zakat*, charities, and *waqf* with microfinancing will increase the probability of repayment of the funds to the Islamic MFI. In addition, *zakat* can be given out to the poor for consumption purposes to avoid diversion of funds from productive heads.

Çizakça (2004) suggests a model in which the concept of cash *waqf* can be used to serve the social objectives in the society. One use of cash *waqf* would be to provide microfinance to the poor. Similarly, El-Gari (2004) proposes establishing a nonprofit financial intermediary, the *Qard-al-hassan* bank, which gives interest-free loans (*Qard-al-hassan*) to finance the poor. The capital of the bank would come from monetary (cash) *waqf* donated by wealthy Muslims. Kahf (2004) and Ahmed (2004) propose establishing a MFIs based on *zakat* and *waqf*. They suggest that the returns from *waqf* can be used to finance productive microenterprises at subsidized rates. Ahmed (2011) suggests a model of *waqf*-based Islamic MFI that can provide microfinancing and facilitate wealth creation of the poor. Cash *waqf* would form the capital of the MFI. The capital along with deposits would be used to finance the poor.

Given the charitable nature of *zakat* and *awqaf*, these instruments can be used to resolve the problem of the trade-off between outreach and sustainability to some extent. For nonprofit organizations focusing on poverty, charitable funds from these sources can provide support to sustain their activities. For commercial for-profit organizations, *zakat* and *awqaf* can provide subsidized sources to funds that can be use to expand their outreach to the poor.

Islamic Inclusive Finance: An Overview and Comparison

This section presents different models of organizations providing various Islamic financial services to the poor. As the information gathered on different features is from secondary sources, some information of certain variables was not available, and in certain cases the conclusions related to a few variables are anecdotal. The variables used to assess the organizational features of different organizations providing financial services to the poor were identified in the third section, as organizational format, regulatory environment, sources of funds, products and services offered, outreach, and sustainability. The features of these variables, for a sample of organizations that provide Islamic microfinancial services to the poor using both the poverty and commercial approaches, are presented below.

Rescue, Bangladesh (NGO)
While NGOs in Bangladesh can be registered under different formats, most of the MFIs opt to register as voluntary social welfare organizations under the Voluntary Social Welfare Agencies (Registration and Control) Ordinance 1961.

Organizations operating on public donations or government aid are regarded as voluntary social welfare agencies and are registered with the Ministry of Social Welfare. The registered organizations get legal status and become eligible for grants from the government and other sources, including foreign ones. As a NGO, the registered organizations are not regulated by any regulatory body.

Rescue, a registered NGO providing Islamic microfinance in the Rangpur district of the country, adopted the group-based lending format of the conventional MFIs and adapted Islamic principles and values. It started operations in 1991. Key donors of Rescue who initiated the MFI became members of the board of directors, which is the policy-making body of the institution. The executive director runs the institution and is responsible for implementing the decisions taken by the board of directors.

Other than the initial start-up capital provided by a few donors, most of the funds for MFIs come from external sources and forced savings of clients. In 2001, Rescue had assets of Tk 3.91 million[14] (US$70,045), which was financed on the liability side as follows: 2.2 percent by a total capital fund; 4.4 percent through savings of clients; 92.4 percent from borrowing from government agencies; and the remaining 0.9 percent from other liabilities. In the same year, Rescue had 2,515 clients and an average disbursement of Tk 2,148 per member, at a 16 percent rate of return. Nearly all beneficiaries (97.5 percent) are female, and the dropout rate was 3.8 percent. The average savings per client was Tk 352.7 and the risk fund per client was only Tk 62.3. The rate of return on assets (ROA) for Rescue was 3.6 percent, which is lower than that of Grameen Bank. Similarly, efficiency, measured in terms of a beneficiaries-to-employee ratio, was 132.4, which was much less than the corresponding figure of 174.2 for Grameen Bank.

Islamic MFIs, including Rescue, face certain problems in obtaining funds from external sources, according to Ahmed (2002). Although some funds are available from government agencies, they impose certain terms and conditions. Some of these terms are contrary to Islamic principles and limit the flexibility of the operations of Islamic MFIs. For example, the funds are given with interest and the MFIs are required to recover a certain fixed rate of return on their investments. As a result, funds from these sources cannot be employed in microfinancing using certain Islamic modes of financing like *mudarabah* and *musharakah*. Islamic MFIs in Bangladesh identify lack of funds as one of the major constraints to growth and efficient operations.

Other than limiting the expansion of operations of MFIs, lack of funds has other detrimental implications. MFIs cannot hire sufficient workers at competitive wages. Lack of funds also means employing fewer field-level workers, lowering the employee-beneficiary ratio, and adversely affecting supervision and monitoring. Paying lower wages implies that they employ relatively low-productivity workers. In the same survey, the officials of Islamic MFIs indicate that the benefits package given to employees is not as good as the established MFIs operating in the neighborhood. This sometimes induces employees with experience to move on to other MFIs that have better pay and benefits. These factors increase the probability of default and lowering the expected income of MFIs.

Takaful T&T Friendly Society, Trinidad and Tobago (Friendly Society/Cooperative)

Takaful T&T Friendly Society (TTTFS) is a multipurpose cooperative established in 1999 under the Friendly Societies' Act (18 of 1950) of Trinidad and Tobago for the Muslims of the country. Of the alternatives available, the friendly society option was selected under the Act because it did not restrict using Shari'ah-compliant alternatives. Furthermore, there was no requirement for large paid-in capital and the option allowed for a small start-up with potential for gradual growth. One disadvantage of the organizational format was that not all types of insurance products could be offered. Other than offering a microinsurance scheme under the Funeral Benefit Scheme (FBS), TTTFS has several investment funds, which include an Investment Fund, a *Hajj* (a mandatory pilgrimage for Muslims who can afford it) Fund, and a *Waqf* Fund for charitable purposes. By paying a membership fee of TT$20 annually, members can avail themselves of various services offered by the Society. Since its inception, there have been a total of 474 members in the FBS scheme, of which 411 were active members in 2012. During this period, 24 participants died and another 39 dropped out of the scheme.

The FBS is structured as *wikala*-based *Takaful*-model. Members of the scheme contribute TT$120 annually to cover three family members and pay an additional TT$30 for each household member in excess of three. As a representative (*wakil*), TTTFS charges a fee of 15 percent of the contributions to manage the funds and pay the claims; the fee goes to the General Fund. The proceeds of the *Takaful* fund are invested with the other investment funds of the Society on a *mudarabah* basis on a 70:30 profit-sharing ratio. A funeral grant of TT$2,500 is paid by TTTFS upon the death of the member or any dependent. A part of the surplus generated after payment of claims due to death is put aside as reserves and the remainder is distributed among the members. To complement the *Takaful* operations, an additional TT$2,000 was added as payments to the claimants of the bereaved family in 2008. This additional amount is paid as grant of TT$1,000 from the *Waqf* Fund surplus and another TT$1,000 from the General Fund. The FBS scheme has sustained itself over the years, resulting in surpluses, which led to the distribution of rebates every year and accumulated reserves of TT$16,523 as of the end of 2011.

Peramu Foundation, Indonesia (Nonprofit Organization)

Based in Bogor, Indonesia, Peramu Foundation (Yayasan Pengembangan Masyarakat Mustadh'afiin, Empowering the Oppressed) was established in 1993 as a multipurpose social development organization.[15] It is registered as a nonprofit foundation that provides various services to the poor. Peramu Foundation is governed by three boards/committees. The founders, who pledged the initial capital of Rp 250 million[16] of the foundation, are also members of the board of trustees.

Peramu operates three different microfinance programs, structured as Baitul Maal Tamwil (BMT), Bank Perkerditan Rakyat Syari'ah (BPRS), and Koperasi Baytul Ikhtiar (BAIK). These MFIs provide financing to different types of clients. Peramu uses *zakat* funds in its microfinance programs. Takaful Mikro Indonesia (Takmin), a working group of Peramu, intermediates *Takaful* services to poor clients through a network of Islamic MFIs in the country. Established in 2006 as a pilot project, it is the newest in the group. The Islamic micro*Takaful* working group adopts partner-agent model aims to provide access to *Takaful* services for the clients and members of MFIs within Peramu and others. As microfinance has been covered in other cases, the features of micro*Takaful* scheme are presented here.

The initial funding for initiating Takmin came from an international NGO, Oxfam-Novib of the Netherlands, in 2006. Partnering with an established TO, Takaful Indonesia, Takmin provides various *Takaful* services as an agent to the clients of MFIs located in West Java, Central Java, and Lampung provinces. It uses an efficient online data storage and transfer system for enrollment and claims information and data, which is shared by Takaful Indonesia in real time. Whereas Takaful Indonesia is regulated by the Ministry of Finance as a *Takaful* company, Takmin being an agent does not fall under their regulatory purview.

Takmin's first product was credit life *Takaful* for MFI clients called Takaful Mikro Sakinah. While Takmin's credit life scheme covers payments of debt of clients in case of death, it excludes coverage due to suicide, participation in a crime, political risks, war, riot, invasion, terrorism, sabotage, and events that are drug- and alcohol-related. Rates and premium collections are remitted monthly to the insurer, and amount to 0.05 percent per month on the outstanding portion of the loan. Coverage remains in effect until the loan is repaid. Takmin receives 25 percent of the monthly remitted amount. Aside from being Shari'ah-compliant, an interesting and unique feature is the combination of premium collection and remittance modes by the MFI.

Recently Takmin introduced a micro*Takaful* scheme for both clients of MFIs and non-clients called Takaful Ukhuwah Mikro. Under the scheme, a client of an MFI can be insured for Rp 1 million (US$109.1) for death for any cause, and for Rp 5 million (US$545.50) for accidental death by contributing Rp 20,000 (or US$2.18) annually per person. Of this contribution, the MFI keeps 25 percent (Rp 5,000) as an administration fee, Takmin keeps 25 percent of Rp 15,000 (or Rp 3,750) as its commission, and the remaining Rp 11,250 goes to Takaful Indonesia. Takmin served around 15,000 clients from 47 MFIs in 2011.[17] There were 11 cases of death in 2008 and 20 cases in 2009. Overall, the scheme is operating at a surplus. A key issue to the expansion of the scheme lies in convincing the MFIs to enroll their clients in the micro*Takaful*.

Rural Development Scheme of IBBL, Bangladesh (Commercial Bank)

Islamic Bank Bangladesh Limited (IBBL) is an Islamic commercial bank regulated by the central bank, Bangladesh Bank. Though most of the bank's products constitute traditional banking services, it also provides microfinance through its Rural Development Scheme (RDS). RDS was initiated in 1995 and started operations in 1996 to cater to the investment needs of poor microentrepreneurs, particularly in rural areas. While the RDS program is within the ambit of operations of the bank and overseen by the board of directors and senior management, it is headed by a manager who had extensive experience in microfinance prior to joining IBBL.

RDS is funded from IBBL's general investment fund. Like other banks, IBBL's main source of funds is deposits. The opportunity cost of using these funds is investment in alternative projects/investments. Most Islamic banks, however, have excess liquidity, given the lack of Islamic-compatible money market instruments to park funds for shorter periods of time. Given this excess liquidity, the opportunity cost of using these funds is close to nil.

The objective of RDS is to eliminate rural poverty through the community development approach. The target group of RDS is the rural poor, defined as the landless or those households having less than 0.5 acres of cultivable land. The RDS program uses group-based financing, as this format suits the poor. No physical collateral is required for obtaining funds. Instead, social collateral is introduced by forming groups and centers. The dominant mode of financing used by RDS is *murabahah* or deferred-price sale. Small amounts (ranging from Tk 3,000 to Tk 25,000) are given to individuals and repaid in small weekly installments. The clients save Tk 5 per week as personal savings and have to give Tk 1 per week for the center fund.

As of June 2010, RDS has provided microfinance services in 12,857 villages in 177 branches of IBBL. A total of Tk 42.28 billion had been disbursed to 382,319 clients (organized in 132,268 groups and 22,206 centers). The average financing size was Tk 15,369, provided at 12.5 percent rate of return, with a 2.5 percent rebate given for timely repayment. This rate is much lower than what is charged by a typical MFI. The recovery rate of outstanding finance was 98.8 percent. IBBL also manages the Islamic Bank Foundation (IBF), a fund created from *zakat*, charitable donations, and income of the bank that cannot be included in profit of the bank. The activities of IBF include provision of various social services.

Using RDS as an example, Ahmed (2004) asserts that Islamic banks can provide microfinance to the poor more efficiently and effectively. The operating costs of providing microfinance in case of Islamic banks will be much smaller than MFIs. As Islamic banks will provide microfinance from existing branches, they will not incur any extra fixed costs (such as for rent or utilities). Furthermore, they will not require a whole range of professionals/employees, particularly at the top management level at the head office and regional offices. This will reduce the cost of operations at the head-office level. The wages paid to the field workers and supervisors in the case of Islamic banks are expected to be higher than their MFI counterparts. This will have two offsetting effects. On the one hand, higher wages will attract more productive field-level workers. On the other hand, it will increase the wage bill. As the field-level workers are paid relatively low salaries compared to professionals at the management level, the total wage bill for microfinance operations in Islamic banks is expected to be much lower than that of MFIs. Thus, the total operating costs of providing a certain amount of microfinance to a given number of beneficiaries will be lower in the case of Islamic banks than that of MFIs.

Bank Perkreditan Rakyat Syari'ah (BPRS), Indonesia (Rural Bank)

Indonesia has one of the most diverse financial sectors in the world, catering to different segments of the population. Among the institutions providing microfinance are rural banks, both conventional and Islamic. Although the country has a long history of rural banks, these were formalized in 1988 with a presidential decree called Paket Kebijakan (Policy Package) through the President's Decision No. 38, National Act No.7/1992 and National Act No. 10/1998. The law allowed privately owned rural banks to be established; these are regulated by Bank Indonesia, the central bank of the country. The first rural bank, Badan Perkreditan Rakyat (BPR), was established in 1989; the Islamic counterpart, BPRS, was established in 1991. Since then, the number of BPRS branches have grown and are playing an important role in providing Islamic microfinance in Indonesia. The central bank of the country, Bank Indonesia, actively regulates and supervises BPRS (Seibel 2005).

While conventional BPR has a commercial orientation, the owners of BPRS tend to have a social mission Seibel (2005, 24) notes. The mission of BPRS includes assisting the enterprising poor, while covering the bank's costs of operations. In a sample of four BPRS, Seibel finds that 6 percent of the clients had income levels below the official poverty line. Though BPRS provide Islamic financial services, their services are open to people of all religions.

BPRS are privately owned, and have a variety of owners, who can be individuals, foundations, or companies. In a sample of five BPRS, Seibel and Agung (2006) find from 3 to 118 owners. In many cases, the major shareholder also manages the BPRS. Along with a management board and a supervisory board, there is a Shari'ah board to oversee Shari'ah-related issues (Seibel 2005). Bank Indonesia, the regulator, requires that the management include one or two directors who have banking experience.

Being a regulated bank, BPRS can accept deposits (demand, savings, and time) and borrow funds. Using Bank Indonesia's consolidated balance sheet in 2003, Seibel (2005) estimates that the average total assets of BPRS is Rp 2.28bn (US$270,000), which is about 38 percent of their conventional counterparts. He further reports that the main source of funds of BPRS come from deposits by clients, amounting to Rp 110.0bn (or 57.4 percent of total assets). Other sources of funds are equity (22.9 percent) (which includes reserves and profits of the current year), bank deposits (11.5 percent), and borrowing (3.8 percent).

BPRS can use different modes of financing depending on the type of client (Seibel 2005). The first type of client has existing businesses and can demonstrate a track record of success in their operations for at least two years. The second type consists of new entrepreneurs who do not have any previous business experience. The vast majority of clients fall into the first category and are financed by different modes, which include *murabahah*, *musharakah*, and *mudarabah*. The second group of clients, who constitute a small minority, are financed through *Qard-al-hassan*. In general, BPRS does not provide consumer loans or loans for speculative investments.

In terms of outreach, Seibel (2005) estimates that in 2003, the average number of depositors of 84 BPRS was around 1,000, which is much lower than BPR, which has 2,594. Similarly, the average borrower outreach for BPRS was 355, compared to 934 for BPR. The disparity in numbers is also reflected in average total financing, which was Rp 1.65bn (US$195,200) per BPRS, compared to an average of Rp 4.41bn (US$522,000) for a conventional BPR. Seibel (2005, 29) compares the performance of five BPRS and find their average NPL ratios to be 4.6 percent, which is higher than that for Bank Rakyat Indonesia (BRI) units (2.5 percent)—and which is considered the benchmark of microfinance in the country. Similarly, the average ROA for the five BPRS was 3.2 percent, which is lower than the average of 5.7 percent for the BRI units.

Bank Rakyat ArRahnu Programme, Malaysia (Cooperative Bank)[18]

Established in 1954, Bank Kerjasama Rakyat Malaysia (Bank Rakyat, or BR) is the largest cooperative bank in Malaysia. While the bank is owned by the members (depositors), the members of the board of directors are appointed by the government. As it is a cooperative, it is registered with the Ministry of Cooperatives. Since it accepts different types of deposits, BR is regulated by the central bank, Bank Negara Malaysia (BNM). In addition to providing deposit facilities, BR also provides financing through other mechanisms, such as personal loans and lease-purchase. Though BR started as a conventional FI, it converted to Islamic finance in 1993. By the end of 2010, BR had 134 branches in the country and assets worth RM 1.91 billion.[19] Whereas the BR is a cooperative bank, it operates like a commercial firm.[20]

BR offers a variety of services, including savings; investments; consumer financing; commercial financing; financing small, medium, and cooperative entrepreneurs; financial planning; and electronic banking services. The bank offers microfinance in the form of Islamic pawning services under the *ArRahnu* programme through all of its branches and 23 ArRahnu centers. The operational details and contracts of the programme are cleared by the Shari'ah board of the bank, and the compliance department ensures that all operations are undertaken according the approved rules and guidelines.

To obtain financing from the *ArRahnu* programmes, clients must use jewelry made of yellow gold. When a client brings the jewelry to a branch, it is checked for authenticity and its value is ascertained. For a first-time customer, 65 percent of the value is given as an interest-free loan (*Qard-al-hassan*);

existing customers receive 70 percent of the value. The loan is made for six months, but can be extended for another six months. The gold is kept in safes in the bank, and safe-keeping charges or storage fees are changed. The storage fee is calculated based on the value of the gold and equals 65 cents per month for every RM 100. This rate converts to about 13.8 percent per year, which is lower than the charges of conventional pawnbrokers (which can go as high as 2 percent per month).

The loans are taken mostly for consumption purposes and can include paying fees for universities. About 80 percent of the loans are small amounts and are in the range of RM 10,000–15,000. Loans greater than RM 30,000 account for around 15 percent of the loans, and are mainly taken for businesses. Two weeks before the due date, a reminder is sent to the debtor about the repayment date of the outstanding dues. Another reminder is sent on the due date. A final reminder is given two weeks after the due date. If the loan is not paid back, then the gold is auctioned off, after waiting seven months and seven days from the beginning of the transaction date. The starting bid price is 90 percent of the day's gold price. After deducting the loan amount and the storage charges, the remaining amount is returned to the client. The default rate is relatively low and ranges from 2 to 5 percent.

BR also offers micro*Takaful* products as an agent of other TOs. It operates a personal protection *Takaful* scheme called Takaful Hayati in collaboration with Etiqa Takaful Berhad. By paying RM 50 annually, the scheme provides coverage of RM 13,000 for accidental death. Another *Takaful* program, called Amani Takaful, is a personal accident protection scheme, which is provided in collaboration with Takaful Ikhlas Snd Bhd. For annual contributions of RM 50, it covers up to RM 40,000 for accidental death or permanent disability and RM 1,000 for funeral expenses.

Organizational Formats, Services, Outreach, and Sustainability

Provision of different Islamic financial services by various organizations presents interesting perspectives on the various issues. Table 7.1 compares the various features of the organizations discussed above. The legal formats include both for-profit and nonprofit types. Two organizations (IBBL and BPRS) are for-profit banks, two (BR and TTTFS) have cooperative formats, and two others (Rescue and Takmin) are nonprofit organizations. As both banks and BR can offer different types of deposits, these are regulated by central banks in their respective countries.

The sources of funds fall into five categories: equity, membership contributions, deposits, subsidized funds, and donations. Whereas nonprofit organizations depend on donations and subsidized funds, the sources for for-profit banks are equity and deposits. The cooperatives and TOs get their funds from membership contributions.

Table 7.1 shows the three key services (savings, financing, and insurance) provided by different organizations. As mentioned, savings and insurance can be distinguished as restricted and unrestricted. Unlike unrestricted savings, which include demand deposits, restricted savings are illiquid and forced on the clients as an integral part of provision of financing. Similarly, insurance is restricted when it is part of the provision of financing to protect against credit risk. In order to assess the services provided by different organizations, the provision of unrestricted services is given a value of 2, restricted services are valued 1, and nonprovision of service is designated 0. The highest score for provision of services is scored by BR and Peramu. Interestingly, both are nonprofit organizations: one is a cooperative and the other is a foundation. However, Peramu provides savings and microfinance services through its microfinance subsidiaries. Table 7.1 shows that regulated organizations (with the exception of BR) have limits to providing all range of services provided.

Outreach and Sustainability

As noted, two features of outreach are considered for different organizations. Whereas the breadth of outreach indicates the number of clients served by an organization, the depth of outreach shows the extent to which the clientele is poor. An indicator of depth of outreach is the financing size; the smaller the size of the financing, the more accessible the financing is to the poor. For *Takaful*, the amount paid out after the occurrence of the risk event is used to assess the depth of outreach. As the sample of organizations are from different countries and from different years for a country, one way to ascertain the depth is to examine the size of financing divided by gross domestic product (GDP) per capita. Both outreach concepts are ranked according to a scale of good, moderate, and poor, as shown in table 7.2.

The criteria to rank different organizations as poor, moderate, and good are shown in table 7.2. Besides using rate of ROA and operating surplus variables when available, access to funds is also used to assess sustainability. Tables 7.3 and 7.4 use the criteria in table 7.2 to assess the outreach and sustainability of the organizations described above.

Table 7.3 shows that organizations that have poverty approaches are able to fulfill the outreach much better than the organizations with commercial approaches. Specifically, all three nonprofit organizations in the sample (Rescue, TTTFS, and Peramu) have a ranking of good, and commercial organizations (BPRS and BR) get a score of poor in terms of depth of outreach. Table 7.4 shows the ranking of sustainability of different organizations by looking at returns and access to funds. As expected, the commercial organizations perform better than organizations with poverty approaches. One key feature related to access to funds is that commercial organizations depend on their own funds (particularly deposits), and organizations with a poverty approach depend on donations or subsidized funds. Thus, lack of funds availability can be a constraint to the expansion of the scale of operations in poverty-focused organizations.

Table 7.5 summarizes the results of different organizations in terms of provision of services, outreach, and sustainability and use of *zakat/awqaf*. Nonprofit organizations appear to serve the poor better than for-profit

Table 7.1 Organizational Types and Services Provided

Organization	Legal format	Approach	Regulated	Sources of funds	Savings	Financing	Insurance	Services score[a]
Rescue	Nongovernmental organization (NGO)	Poverty	No	Donations Subsidized funds	Restricted	Yes	Restricted (credit line)	1+2+1 = 4
TTTFS	Society (Co-op)	Poverty	No	Membership contributions	Restricted	No	Unrestricted (funeral)	1+0+2 = 3
Peramu	Foundation	Poverty	No[b]	Donation, membership contributions	Yes	Yes	Unrestricted (credit line)	2+2+2 = 6
IBBL (RDS)	Commercial bank	Commercial	Yes	Equity Deposits	Unrestricted	Yes	Restricted (credit line)	2+2+1 = 5
BPRS	Rural bank	Commercial	Yes	Equity Deposits	Unrestricted	Yes	No	2+2+0 = 4
BR (ArRahnu)	Cooperative	Commercial	Yes	Membership contributions, deposits	Unrestricted	Yes	Unrestricted (life)	2+2+2 = 6

Note: TTTFS = Takaful T&T Friendly Society; IBBL = Islamic Bank Bangladesh Limited; BPRS = Bank Perkerditan Rakyat Syari'ah; BR = Bank Rakyat.
a. Yes and unrestricted = 2; Restricted = 1; No = 0.
b. While Peramu's microTakaful operations are not regulated, its microfinance program with BPRS is regulated.

Table 7.2 Criteria Used to Rank Outreach and Sustainability

Rank	Depth of outreach (size of financing/GDP per capita)	Return on assets (ROA)/ operating surplus	Access to funds
Poor	Over 0.50	Negative ROA/deficit	Dependent on donations
Moderate	0.11–0.50	Low ROA/surplus	Dependent on subsidized funds
Good	0.0–0.10	High ROA/surplus	Dependent on own funds

Table 7.3 Outreach of Different Organizations

Organization	Approach	Outreach (depth)	Rank[a]
Rescue	Poverty	0.10	Good
TTTFS	Poverty	0.04	Good
Peramu (Takmin)	Poverty	0.10	Good
IBBL (RDS)	Commercial	0.42	Moderate
BPRS	Commercial	0.65	Poor
BR (ArRahnu)	Commercial	0.73	Poor

Note: TTTFS = Takaful T&T Friendly Society; IBBL = Islamic Bank Bangladesh Limited; BPRS = Bank Perkerditan Rakyat Syari'ah; BR = Bank Rakyat.
a. 0.0–0.1 = good; 0.1–0.5 = moderate; more than 0.5 = poor.

Table 7.4 Sustainability of Different Organizations

Organization	Approach	Return on assets (ROA)/ operating surplus	Access to funds	Overall sustainability rank
Rescue	Poverty	ROA = −3.57 (less than Grameen Bank)	Dependent on subsidized funds	Poor
TTTFS	Poverty	Moderately in surplus	Limited to members' contributions	Moderate
Peramu	Poverty	Moderately in surplus	Dependent on donations	Moderate
IBBL (RDS)	Commercial	Surplus	Own funds	Good
BPRS	Commercial	ROA = 3.2 (less than BPR)	Own funds	Moderate
BR	Commercial	20% dividend	Own funds	Good

Note: TTTFS = Takaful T&T Friendly Society; IBBL = Islamic Bank Bangladesh Limited; BPRS = Bank Perkerditan Rakyat Syari'ah; BR = Bank Rakyat.

Table 7.5 Inclusive Finance, Outreach, and Sustainability

Organization	Approach	Provision of services	Outreach	Sustainability	Zakat/Waqf
Rescue	Poverty	4	Good	Poor	No
TTTFS	Poverty	3	Good	Moderate	Yes
Peramu	Poverty	6	Good	Moderate	Yes
IBBL (RDS)	Commercial	5	Moderate	Good	No
BPRS	Commercial	4	Poor	Moderate	No
BR	Commercial	6	Poor	Good	No

Note: TTTFS = Takaful T&T Friendly Society; IBBL = Islamic Bank Bangladesh Limited; BPRS = Bank Perkerditan Rakyat Syari'ah; BR = Bank Rakyat.

organizations. However, nonprofits face problems of sustainability partly because they serve the poor and partly because they do not have access to funds. One way to resolve the sustainability problem is to integrate *zakat* and *waqf* with inclusive finance. Of the six organizations considered, only two have used these instruments with financial services. TTTFS has integrated *waqf* into operations whereby the poor claimants are given an additional TT$1000 from the *waqf* fund to cover funeral expenses. Peramu has integrated *zakat* into their financing program. While IBBL collects *zakat* and uses the collections for various socioeconomic activities, it has not integrated it with its microfinance program.

Conclusion

Provision of financial services to the poor is considered an important tool for alleviating poverty. Given the complex nature of poverty, there have been calls for a paradigm shift from microfinance to inclusive finance. Inclusive financial services would include savings, financing, and insurance facilities for the poor. These services enable the poor to move out of poverty, as they can invest funds in productive ventures, manage various risks, and increase their income and savings. Because providing services to the poor is costly and risky, a key issue in providing inclusive finance is the trade-off between outreach and vulnerability. There are two broad approaches to provision of services to the poor. One is the poverty approach, which focuses on outreach, but which needs subsidies to sustain the activities. The other is the commercial approach, in which the organizations providing financial services are profitable, partly because they exclude poor clientele. Nonprofit organizations usually adopt the former approach, and for-profit firms usually adopt the latter.

As eradication of poverty is considered an important objective of an Islamic economic system, institutions providing financial services can play an important role in achieving this goal. The chapter presented different organizational approaches to Shari'ah-compliant microfinance and micro*Takaful* (insurance). The products that can mitigate poverty and vulnerability were examined, and the implications related to sustainability and outreach in relation to different organizational approaches were discussed. Examination of six organizations that provide inclusive Islamic financial services substantiates the trade-off between outreach and sustainability. The results show that nonprofit organizations adopt the poverty approach and rank well for outreach, but have problems with sustainability. For-profit organizations are sustainable, but rank low in terms of outreach.

As noted, *zakat* and *awqaf* can be integrated into Islamic inclusive finance to resolve the outreach and sustainability problems. While the nonprofit organizational model appears to serve the poor better than the for-profit model, the weakness of the nonprofits is sustainability. This can partly be resolved by using *zakat* and *waqf* as additional complementary funds to support their activities. The outreach of for-profit organizations can be expanded by using funds from these sources to cover provision of financial services to the poor. However, only two organizations in a sample of six considered are using *zakat* and *awqaf* in their operations. The potential of using these instruments in inclusive Islamic finance to resolve the trade-off between outreach and sustainability needs to be further explored, both in research and practice.

Notes

1. Navajas and others (2000) and Schreiner (2002) identify six dimensions of outreach. Of these, only two are relevant here. Whereas *breadth* of outreach is the number of clients served, *depth* relates to the number of poor covered by the program.
2. For as history of microfinance in Europe, see Seibel (2003).
3. Although different approaches to microfinance have evolved, the format discussed here is that of Grameen Bank.
4. Different MFIs define their target group in different ways. For example, to be eligible to receive credit from Grameen Bank, a household must own less than 0.4 acres of land and must not have assets exceeding the market value of one acre of cultivable land.
5. See Hossain (1983, 1987); Fuglesang and Chandler (1993); Bornstein (1996); Goetz and Gupta (1996); Hashemi, Schuler, and Riley (1996). For a survey of studies showing the impact of microfinance on poverty see Morduch and Haley (2002).
6. Karim and Osada (1998) observe that there is a steady increase in the dropout rate from Grameen Bank (15 percent in 1994) and that 88 percent of the total dropouts did not graduate to the status of nonpoor. Asaduzzaman (1997) finds that while microfinance does increase the income level of the poor, the current operations of MFIs are not very effective in improving the lives of the extreme poor.
7. Reed and Befus (1994, 190) study five MFIs and find average ROA for three of these below 2 percent, one at 3.5 percent, and the other at 14.6 percent. Hashemi (1997) and Khandker, Khalily, and Khan (1995) point out that Grameen Bank would operate at a loss without grants. A Subsidy Dependence Index (SDI) developed by Yaron (1992) indicates that in 1996, Grameen Bank would have to increase its lending interest rate by an additional 21 percent in order to breakeven without subsidies (Hashemi 1997). Similarly, Hulme and Mosley (1996a, 52) find that 12 out of 13 MFIs from six countries have a positive SDI, ranging from 32 to 1,884 percent.
8. In a study of 55 industrialized and developing countries, Arena (2008) finds a robust relationship between the size of the insurance market and economic growth. He finds that while life insurance positively impacts growth in industrialized countries, other forms of insurance besides life insurance significantly affect economic growth in both.
9. Khan (1997) suggests a variety of activities like *Qard-al-hassan*, financing housing, meeting basic needs, and promoting and financing small entrepreneurs. All these aspects, however, can be covered in a comprehensive integrated program with a focus on microfinance.
10. Detailed expositions of the different principles of Islamic financing are found in Kahf and Khan (1992) and Ayub (2007).
11. For a discussion on the different organizational models of insurance, see Mayers and Smith (1988).
12. For a detailed study on *Takaful* models, see Ali and Odierno (2008).

13. For detailed discussions on *zakat*, see El-Ashker and Haq (1995); on *waqf*, see Basar (1987); Çizakça (1996, 1998).
14. Tk stands for taka, the currency of Bangladesh. The average exchange for 2009 was US$1 = Tk 69.
15. I am grateful to Murniati Muklisin, International Relations Manager of Takmin, for providing me with the information and data on Takmin.
16. Rp stands for rupiah, the currency of Indonesia. The exchange rate was US$1 = Rp 9,165 as of April 5, 2012.
17. Takmin had 15,459 clients in August 2011 and 14,470 clients in September 2011.
18. The information on the ArRahnu Programme of Raykat Bank was gathered from an interview with officials of the bank in 2009 and public information available at http://www.bankrakyat.com.my/web/guest/home.
19. RM stands for ringgit, the currency of Malaysia.
20. The mission of BR is "to help improve the economic well-being of members by providing financial facilities at an affordable rate for agriculture, production, marketing, fishing, transportation, housing and business activities deemed beneficial to members and to also promote thrift and savings."

References

ADB (Asian Development Bank). 2000. *Finance for the Poor: Microfinance Development Strategy*. Manila: Asian Development Bank.

Ahmed, Habib. 2002. "Financing Microenterprises: An Analytical Study of Islamic Microfinance Institutions." *Islamic Economic Studies* 9 (2): 27–64.

———. 2004. "Role of *Zakah* and *Awqaf* in Poverty Alleviation." Occasional Paper 8, Islamic Research and Training Institute, Islamic Development Bank, Jeddah, Saudi Arabia.

———. 2011. "Waqf-based Microfinance: Realizing the Social Role of Islamic Finance." In *Essential Readings in Contemporary Waqf Issues*, edited by Monzer Kahf and Siti Mashitoh Mahamood. Kuala Lumpur: Cert Publications Sdn. Bhd.

Ali, Engku R. A., and Hassan Scott P. Odierno. 2008. *Essential Guide to Takaful (Islamic Insurance)*. Kuala Lumpur: CERT Publications Sdn. Bhd.

Arena, Marco. 2008. "Does Insurance Market Activity Promote Economic Growth? A Cross-Country Study for Industrialized and Developing Countries." *Journal of Risk and Insurance* 75 (4): 921–46.

Asaduzzaman, Mohammed. 1997. "Role of Microcredit in Poverty Alleviation." In *Poverty and Development: Bangladesh Perspective*, edited by Rushidan I. Rahman. Dhaka: Bangladesh Institute of Development Studies (in Bengali).

Ayub, Muhammad. 2007. *Understanding Islamic Finance*. West Sussex: John Wiley & Sons.

Basar, Hasmet. 1987. *Management and Development of Awqaf Properties*. Research Seminar-Workshop Proceedings 1. Jeddah, Saudi Arabia: Islamic Research and Training Institute, Islamic Development Bank.

Bennett, Lynn. 1998. "Combining Social and Financial Intermediation to Reach the Poor: The Necessity and the Dangers." In *Strategic Issues in Microfinance*, edited by Mwangi S. Kimenyi, Robert C. Wieland, and J. D. von Pischke. Hants, U.K.: Ahsgate Publishing Ltd.

Bhatty, Ajmal. 2010. "Protecting the Forgotten through Microtakaful." Microinsurance Centre. http://www.microinsurancecentre.org/resources/documents/doc_details/767-protecting-the-forgotten-through-microtakaful.html.

Bornstein, David. 1996. *The Price of a Dream: The Story of Grameen Bank and the Idea That Is Helping the Poor to Change Their Lives*. Dhaka: University Press.

Brainard, Lael. 2008. "What is the Role of Insurance in Economic Development." Zurich Government and Industry Affairs, Zurich, Switzerland.

Çizakça, Murat. 1996. "The Relevance of the Ottoman Cash Waqfs (Awqaf al Nuqud) for Modern Islamic Economics." In *Financing Development is Islam*, Seminar Proceedings Series 30, edited by M. A. Mannan. Jeddah, Saudi Arabia: Islamic Research and Training Institute, Islamic Development Bank.

———. 1998. "Awqaf in History and Implications for Modern Islamic Economics." Paper presented at International Seminar on Awqaf and Economic Development, Kuala Lumpur.

———. 2004. "Cash *Waqf* as Alternative to NBFIs Bank." Paper presented at the International Seminar on Nonbank Financial Institutions: Islamic Alternatives, jointly organized by Islamic Research and Training Institute, Islamic Development Bank, and Islamic Banking and Finance Institute, Malaysia, Kuala Lumpur, March 1–3.

Cull, Robert, Asli Demirgüç, and Jonathan Morduch. 2007. "Financial Performance and Outreach: A Global Analysis of Leading Microbanks." *Economic Journal* 117: F107–33.

Dichter, Thomas W. 1996. "Questioning the Future of NGOs in Microfinance." *Journal of International Development* 8: 256–69.

El-Ashker, Abdel-Fattah A., and Muhammad S. Haq, eds. 1995. *Institutional Framework of Zakah: Dimensions and Implications*. Seminar Proceedings 23, Jeddah, Saudi Arabia: Islamic Research and Training Institute, Islamic Development Bank.

El-Gari, Mohamed A. 2004. "The *Qard Hassan* Bank." Paper presented at the International Seminar on Nonbank Financial Institutions: Islamic Alternatives, jointly organized by Islamic Research and Training Institute, Islamic Development Bank, and Islamic Banking and Finance Institute, Malaysia, Kuala Lumpur, March 1–3.

Fuglesang, Andreas, and Dale Chandler. 1993. *Participation as Process–Process as Growth: What We Can Learn from Grameen Bank*. Dhaka: Grameen Trust.

Goetz, Marie A., and Rina S. Gupta. 1996. "Who Takes the Credit? Gender, Power, and Control over Loan Use in Rural Credit Programmes in Bangladesh." *World Development* 24: 45–63.

Hartarska, Valentina, and Denis Nadolnyak. 2007. "Do Regulated Microfinance Institutions Achieve Better Sustainability and Outreach? Cross-country Evidence." *Applied Economics* 39: 1207–22.

Hashemi, Syed M. 1997. "Building up Capacity for Banking with the Poor: The Grameen Bank in Bangladesh." In *Microfinance for the Poor*, edited by Hartmut Schneider. Paris: Development Centre of the Organisation for Economic Co-operation and Development, OECD.

Hashemi, Syed M., Sidney R. Schuler, and Ann P. Riley. 1996. "Rural Credit Programs and Women's Empowerment in Bangladesh." *World Development* 24: 635–53.

Hermes, Niels, Robert Lensink, and Aljar Meesters. 2011. "Outreach and Efficiency of Microfinance Institutions." *World Development* 39 (6): 938–48.

Holzmann, Robert, and Teen Jorgensen. 2000. "Social Risk Management: A New Conceptual Framework for Social Protection and Beyond." Social Protection Discussion Paper Series 006, World Bank, Washington, DC.

Hossain, Mahabub. 1983. *Credit Programme for the Landless: The Experience of Grameen Bank Project*. Dhaka: Bangladesh Institute of Development Studies.

———. 1987. "Employment Generation through Cottage Industries-Potentials and Constraints: The Case of Bangladesh." In *Rural Industrialisation and Employment in Asia*, edited by Rizwanul Islam. New Delhi: International Labour Organisation, Asian Employment Programme.

Hulme, David. 2000. "Is Microdebt Good for Poor People? A Note on the Dark Side of Microfinance." *Small Enterprise Development* 11 (1): 26–28.

Hulme, David, and Paul Mosley. 1996a. *Finance against Poverty*. Vol. 1. London: Routledge.

———. 1996b. *Finance against Poverty*. Vol. 2. London: Routledge.

Hussain, Mohammad M. 2009. "Legal Issues in Takaful." In *Takaful Islamic Insurance: Concepts and Regulatory Issues*, edited by Simon Archer, Rifaat Ahmed Abdel Karim, and Volker Nienhaus. Singapore: John Wiley & Sons (Asia) Pte. Ltd.

IAIS (International Association of Insurance Supervisors). 2007. *Issues in Regulation and Supervision of Microinsurance*. International Association of Insurance Supervisors.

IRTI and IFA (Islamic Research and Training Institute and Islamic Fiqh Academy). 2000. *Resolutions and Recommendations of the Council of the Islamic Fiqh Academy*. Jeddah, Saudi Arabia: Islamic Research and Training Institute, Islamic Development Bank.

Kahf, Monzer. 2004. "*Shari'ah* and Historical Aspects of *Zakah* and *Awqaf*." Background paper prepared for Islamic Research and Training Institute, Islamic Development Bank.

Kahf, Monzer, and Tariqullah Khan. 1992. "Principles of Islamic Financing, A Survey." Research Paper 16, Islamic Research and Training Institute, Islamic Development Bank, Jeddah, Saudi Arabia.

Karim, Rezaul Md., and Mitsue Osada. 1998. "Dropping Out: An Emerging Factor in the Success of Microcredit-based Poverty Alleviation Programs." *The Developing Economies* 36 (3): 257–88.

Karim, Nimrah, Michael Tarazi, and Xavier Reille. 2008. "Islamic Microfinance: An Emerging Market Niche." CGAP Focus Note 49, Consultative Group Against Poverty, Washington, DC.

Khan, Fahim M. 1997. "Social Dimensions of Islamic Banks in Theory and Practice." Islamic Research and Training Institute, Islamic Development Bank, Jeddah, Saudi Arabia.

Khandker, Shahidur R., Baqui Khalily, and Zahed Khan. 1995. "Grameen Bank: Performance and Sustainability." World Bank Discussion Paper 306, World Bank, Washington, DC.

Matin, Imran, David Hulme, and Stuart Rutherford. 2002. "Finance for the Poor: From Microcredit to Microfinancial Services." *Journal of International Development* 14: 273–94.

Mayers, David, and Clifford W. Smith Jr. 1988. "Ownership Structure across Lines of Property-Causalty Insurance." *Journal of Law and Economics* 31: 351–78.

McCord, Michael J., Oliver Zenklusen, and Roland Steinmann. 2011. "Not So Fast! Towards Realistic Growth Expectations in Microinsurance." Key Issues Discussion Papers, Series 1: 2011, Micro Insurance Centre.

Montgomery, Richard. 1996. "Disciplining or Protecting the Poor? Avoiding the Social Costs of Peer Pressure in Micro-credit Schemes." *Journal of International Development* 8: 289–305.

Morduch, Jonathan. 1994. "Poverty and Vulnerability." *American Economics Association Papers and Proceedings* 84 (2): 221–25.

———. 2006. "Micro-insurance: The Next Revolution?" In *Understanding Poverty*, edited by Abhijit Banerjee, Roland Benabou, and Dilip Mookherjee, 337–56. New York: Oxford University Press.

Morduch, Jonathan, and Barbara Haley. 2002. "Analysis of the Effects of Microfinance on Poverty Reduction." NYU Wagner Working Paper 1014, New York University.

Mosley, Paul. 2003. "Micro-insurance: Scope, Design and Assessment of Wider Impacts." *IDS Bulletin* 34 (4): 143–55.

Navajas, Sergio, Mark Schreiner, Richard Meyer, Claudio Gonzalez-Vega, and Jorge Rodriguez-Meza. 2000. "Microcredit and the Poorest of the Poor: Theory and Evidence from Bolivia." *World Development* 28 (2): 333–46.

Reed, Larry R., and David R. Befus. 1994. "Transformation Lending: Helping Microenterprises Become Small Businesses." In *The New World of Microenterprise Finance*, edited by Maria Otero and Elisabeth Rhyne, 185–204. West Hartford, CT: Kumarian Press.

Roth, Jim, Michael J. McCord, and Dominic Liber. 2007. *The Landscape of Microinsurance in the World's 100 Poorest Countries*. Appleton, WI: The Microinsurance Centre.

Schreiner, Mark. 2002. "Aspects of Outreach: A Framework for Discussion of the Social Benefits of Microfinance." *Journal of International Development* 14: 591–603.

Seibel, Dieter H. 2003. "Taking Stock." *Small Enterprise Development* 14 (2): 10–12.

———. 2005. *Islamic Microfinance in Indonesia*. Eschborn, Germany: Division of Economic Development and Employment, Federal Ministry for Economic Cooperation and Development.

Seibel, Dieter H., and Wahyu D. Agung. 2006. "Islamic Microfinance in Indonesia." Working Paper 2006, 2, University of Cologne, Development Research Center.

SwissRe. 2010. *Microinsurance—Risk Protection for 4 Billion People*. Zurich: Swiss Reinsurance Company Ltd.

UN (United Nations). 2006. *Building Inclusive Financial Sectors for Development*. New York: United Nations.

Weidmaier-Pfister, Martina, and Brigitte Klien. 2010. "Microinsurance Innovations in Rural Finance." Innovations in Rural and Agricultural Finance, Focus 18, Brief 12, International Food Policy Research Institute and the World Bank, Washington DC.

Weiss, John, and Heather Montgomery. 2005. "Great Expectations: Microfinance and Poverty Reduction in Asia and Latin America." *Oxford Development Studies* 33 (3–4): 412.

World Bank. 2001. *World Development Report 2000/2001: Attacking Poverty*. New York: Oxford University Press.

———. 2008. "Finance for All? Policies and Pitfalls in Expanding Access." World Bank Policy Research Report, World Bank, Washington, DC.

Yaron, Jacob. 1992. "Assessing Development Finance Institutions: A Public Interest Analysis." Discussion Paper 174, World Bank, Washington, DC.

CHAPTER 8

Theory and Instruments of Social Safety Nets and Social Insurance in Islamic Finance: *Takaful* and *Ta'min*

Kamaruddin Sharif and Wang Yong Bao

> *Verily! Allah will not change the condition of a community if they do not change their state themselves.*
>
> Surah Ar-Rad 13:11

Poverty is one of the oldest enemies of mankind (Iqbal 2002). It has topped the agenda in world economic conferences and gatherings held by the various United Nations (UN) agencies and other related parties like the World Bank and the International Monetary Fund (IMF). The United Nations had even designated the years 1997–2015 as the period for the eradication of poverty. The United Nations Millennium Summit in 2000 set a target of eradicating the number of people categorized as extremely poor and hungry by half between 1990 and 2015.

For believers in Islam, this task takes on special urgency. Islam views poverty not only as a social disgrace but also as an avenue to apostasy, against which the poor need protection (Sahl 2009). In Islam, despite the fact that all Muslims are to believe in *Qadha-o-Qadr* (the Divine Decree and the Will of God), they must look for ways and means to mitigate risk and to avoid misfortunes and sufferings wherever possible, and to minimize their financial losses should such disasters occur. This is in line with the verse (*Surah Ar-Rad* 13:11) that states, "Allah will not change the condition of a community if they do not change their state themselves."

There is much work to be done. World population stood at 7.009 billion as of 2011, of which 5.135 billion (75.3 percent) live in Asia and Africa (U.S. Census Bureau). More than half the world's population lives on less than $2.50 a day. An estimated 925 million people are hungry and undernourished, and this figure has

---

Professor Kamaruddin Sharif is a Professor of Takaful and Wealth Planning at the International Centre for Education in Islamic Finance, Malaysia. Associate Professor Wang Yong Bao was a visiting Professor at INCEIF.

increased since 1995, the UN Food and Agriculture Organization (FAO) reported in 2010. Three factors have been cited for this increase: first, the neglect of agriculture, which is relevant to the very poor; second, the current worldwide economic crisis; and third, the significant increase of food prices. According to United Nations Children's Fund (UNICEF), 22,000 children die each day due to poverty, and around 28 percent of all children in the developing countries are estimated to be underweight or stunted. The two regions that account for the bulk of this calamity are South Asia and Sub-Saharan Africa, where the population is predominantly Muslim in many areas.

About 72 million children of primary school age in the developing world were not in school in 2005, and 57 percent of them are girls. Nearly 1 billion people who entered the twenty-first century are unable to read a book or sign their name. The world needs less than 1 percent of what it spends every day on weapons to put every child into school by the year 2000—and yet it has not happened. The poorest (40 percent of the world's population) account for 5 percent of global income, while the richest (20 percent of the world population) account for 75 percent of world income (Anup 2009). Why such a disparity?

How can reform-related economic efficiency and distributive justice be blended into a coherent strategy? As Ghosh (1997) argues, three main points need to be clear:

- In a nonegalitarian society, economic reforms cannot be left exclusively to market forces and ruthless competition, but need to be managed and guided by laws and socially accepted codes of behavior.
- The social cost of economic reform must be shared fairly by different income groups.
- Poverty alleviation should be built into the reform process. Safety nets should be extended to the needy as a way of empowering them to participate in the economy and contribute to it.

With respect to safety nets to protect the incomes and human capital investments of the poor and the vulnerable in times of crisis, public social safety can be sourced as an important countercyclical tool. Without relying extensively on administration discretion, effective safety nets can be installed so as to respond to any form of distress in a timely and flexible manner. Evidence in various parts of the world has shown that it is better to put safety net mechanisms in place beforehand and adjust them accordingly later.

Islamic Social Safety Nets

Beyond all doubt, Islam has forever contained all necessities and needs (Al-Shatibi 2005, vol. 2, 13–19) as Allah's guarantee for all humans to coexist in this temporal world.[1] We surely can observe and perceive this from rules of the Qur'an: "And do not kill your children for fear of poverty. We provide for them and for you. Indeed, their killing is ever a great sin" (17:31). "Let them worship the Lord of this House Who has fed them, (saving them) from hunger and made them safe, (saving them) from fear" (106:3–4). It is worth noting here that the root of *iman* (belief) and *aman* (safety and security) applied by the Qur'an imply a significant meaning: once someone embraces Islam, he or she enters into the safety and security provided by Allah the Almighty.

With comprehension of the principles and fundamentals of Islamic belief, one may easily realize his or her dignity: "We have honored the sons of Adam; provided them with transport on land and sea; given them for sustenance things good and pure; and conferred on them special favors, above a great part of Our creation" (17:70). As a Muslim, one should recognize his/her duties and obligations as a *Khilafa* (Allah's vicegerent on earth) to exploit and utilize all given resources in pursuing the bounty of Allah and improving the livelihood of fellow humans (2:30).[2] This is done in order to satisfy not only the needs of man but also the requirements of Shari'ah in accordance with the rules of Allah and the practice of the Prophet (pbuh). Obviously, there is an intimate and inseparable relationship between social safety and justice—the ultimate economic objective of society. In this area, the leaders of the state have the inescapable responsibility to take care of their citizens. The Prophet (pbuh) said, "All of you are shepherds and each of you is responsible for his flock. A man is the shepherd of the people of his house and he is responsible. A woman is the shepherd of the house of her husband and she is responsible. Each of you is a shepherd and each is responsible for his flock" (Ibn Hajar 2004, vol. 9, no. 5188, 291).

To achieve economic adequacy, a fair and just distribution and redistribution system is an essential prerequisite. Thus, Islam always links social safety and security with Divinely inspired and ordained institutions. This constitutes the fundamental pillar of the social-political-economic system in Islam. This system is supported by two subsystems. The first is the distribution system, upon which the principle rights of humans are based on what can be achieved; hence Islam urges or obliges each member of society to struggle to ensure his or her adequacy independently. By doing so, the members will simultaneously enjoy their rights and fulfill their duties toward the distribution. However, there are members of society who are not independent, such as those who are disabled, orphaned, widowed, or unemployed, and they need to be looked after collectively by the *Ummah* (community) at local and international levels. The Qur'an has designated this as a "Right": "And those within whose wealth is a known right, for the petitioner and the deprived" (70:24–25).[3]

The second subsystem is the property ownership system in Islam, which encourages private possessions but prohibits extreme consumption and conditions that could lead to exploitation. Although property is considered private, it is bound by social rights, or as the Qur'an prescribes it, "A Known Right" to pay *zakat* for the poor, the needy, or those related to the poor or needy. In addition, Islam has ordained another dictum, which requires society at large to meet the public needs that the state should undertake—that is, social safety and security—which includes helping those who are unable to work or unemployed with a legitimate excuse and have no one to depend on.

It is the nature of humans to utilize their energy to earn a livelihood and accumulate resources to satisfy their needs and the needs of those who are dependent on them. Islam considers such responsibility as obligatory and compulsory for every Muslim who is able to work, and requires that he or she focus his or her positive attitude toward the life in this world, as well as promises that he or she will be rewarded. Since labor is attached to dignity and honor, and examples fill the Qur'an as well as the sayings of the Prophet (pbuh) that encourage Muslims to obtain this dignity.[4] Idleness is the greatest prodigality; Islam condemns a person who sits idle and enjoys the fruits of others' labor, such as usury, speculation, and gambling, all of which are prohibited in the Shari'ah.

The Institutional Framework of Social Safety Nets in Islam

In order for humans to bring about social safety and achieve its objectives, Islam has established a set of institutional frameworks to redistribute income to the poorest and most vulnerable, with an immediate impact on poverty and inequality. The most well-known are described next.

The Duty of Necessary Expenditures on the Family

While humans have gathered together in the form of a family, they, with their interdependent nature, are motivated to help, support, and take care of one another. The Shari'ah confirms not only this nature, but also the necessary expenditures for the family and its members. The Qur'an demonstrates how we should spend: "They ask you, [O Muhammad], what they should spend. Say, 'Whatever you spend of good is [to be] for parents and relatives and orphans and the needy and the traveler. And whatever you do is good—indeed, Allah is Knowing of it'" (2:215). An unquestionable, natural, and moral principle is our interdependence, which has been fostered by the Shari'ah and has been enforced through the juridical system (personal status codes) to protect every family member's rights of financial assurance. Even a newly born infant has rights. As the Qur'an explicates: "Mothers may breastfeed their children two complete years for whoever wishes to complete the nursing [period]. Upon the father is the mother's provision and their clothing according to what is acceptable. No person is charged with more than his capacity. No mother should be harmed through her child, and no father through his child. And upon the [father's] heir is [a duty] like that [of the father]" (2:233). It is a unanimous consensus of Muslim scholars that it is for the husband to expend on his wife, children, and his poor relatives (Al-Jaziri 2004, vol. 4, 423–32, 446–52). All Islamic legislatures, judicial bodies, and educational institutions emphasize this principle of social security. If a person has not taken his responsibility toward his family, then he has committed a sin and he should be rebuked and enforced to fulfill his duty. On the contrary, Islam encourages believers to undertake this honorable duty and even this is considered as giving charity and struggling for the path of Allah the Almighty (Ibn Hajar 2004; see also Al-Jaziri 2004, vol. 4, 423–32 and 446–52).

The Rules of Inheritance

Social security has been fortified and consolidated through the implementation of Islamic rules of inheritance, which underscore the interdependent dimensions and measurements among members of a society by obligating them to apportion the inheritances and patrimonies of the deceased among the inheritors in accordance with the degrees or levels of kinship or relationship to the deceased. The Qur'an says: "For men is a share of what the parents and close relatives leave, and for women is a share of what the parents and close relatives leave, be it a little or much—an obligatory share" (4:7–12,176).[5] Islam takes mutual care into consideration by starting with family members, who are the cornerstone of the social security system. Inheritance is an essential element of this system. On the basis of the rules of Islamic social security, the property of the deceased should be justly treated and distributed among the members of his or her family. If the inheritance is not enough to cover the needs of heirs, the community will look after them. However, if there is no heir or relative left behind, then the entire estate of the deceased would return to *Bait al-Mal* (the public treasury) and the property would be distributed for those in need (Abu Yusuf 1999, 185).

Care of Orphans

Islam has obligated those who share the same origin with orphans(their relatives initiating from the nearest one to the farthest) to ensure that the orphans' basic livelihood, education, and other related needs are met. In addition, Islam encourages the entire Muslim community to undertake this social responsibility to obtain Allah's pleasure. Therefore, Muslims in general have deemed that the best family is one that includes an orphan because of their response to this divine call from Allah the Almighty, their commitment to undertake this moral and social responsibility, and their compliance with the sacred instructions. Accordingly, the Prophet (pbuh) said, "I and the person who looks after an orphan and provides for him, will be in the Paradise like this (putting his index and middle fingers together)" (see Ibn Hajar 2004, vol. 10, no. 6005, 491–92). This means that the person will be honored to accompany the Prophet in Paradise. This saying indicates the magnitude of the matter. Remarkably, the physical needs of orphans are a major concern in Islam; at the same time, their spiritual needs are also treated with utmost importance. To avoid hurting their feelings (dignity), the Qur'an says, "So as for the orphan, do not excoriate [him]" (93:9).

The Neighborhood

The neighborhood is a firmly interdependent relationship that has been highlighted by Islam. The Qur'an says, "Worship Allah and associate nothing with Him, and to parents do good, and to relatives, orphans, the needy, the near neighbor, the neighbor farther away, the companion at your side, the traveler, and those whom your right hand possesses. Indeed, Allah does not like those who are self-deluding and boastful" (4:36). In this verse, the neighborhood has been divided into three categories: a neighbor who is a relative; a neighbor who is a stranger;

and a casual or temporary neighbor with whom one happens to live or travel for a certain time. All of them deserve our respect and kind treatment, regardless of their religion, race, or color. Islam requires us to show consideration toward our neighbors. This was continually emphasized by the angel Gabriel to the Prophet (pbuh), which almost made him think that neighbors might even share one's inheritance (see Ibn Hajar 2004, vol. 10, no. 6015 and 6016, 499; Ibn Iyadh 2005, vol. 8, no. 2624 and 2025, 105).

The Prophet (pbuh) reminds us to be friendly and helpful toward our neighbors; we cannot achieve such a good relationship unless we share with them their happiness as well their sorrows. Thus, the Prophet (pbuh) said, "He who has not affirmed faith in me (i.e., he is not a true follower) is he who eats to his satisfaction and sleeps comfortably at night while his neighbor goes hungry—and he is aware of it" (see Ibn Hajar 2004, vol. 10, no. 6015 and 6016, 499; Ibn Iyadh 2005, vol. 8, no. 2624 and 2025, 105). *Iman*, which links with our generosity toward our neighbors (Ibn Hajar 2004, vol. 10, no. 6019, 502–03), enjoins us to establish social relations in which one can depend upon the other with regard to his or her life, honor, and property. Only when our neighbors' social conditions (physical and mental health) are developed and improved can we achieve a strong and cohesive neighborhood, which may possibly enhance social order, reduce or prevent poverty, and serve as a buffer against various forms of adversity.

Charitable Activities
By addressing the suffering of people who are not the relatives of a contributor or those who are not covered by a social safety net, charitable activities can be a major factor that contributes to solving the problems of the poor. Charity can provide essential assistances and services that are geared toward redressing social inequality. Charity is encouraged by the Prophet (pbuh). He said, "The one who looks after and works for a widow and for a poor person is like a warrior fighting for Allah's cause, or like a person who fasts during the day and prays throughout the night" (Ibn Hajar 2004, vol. 10, no. 6006 and 6007, 492–93). Islam praises and encourages its believers to do good deeds, including voluntary and benevolent behavior and charitable activities. They always connect with *iman*, meaning that they are the reflection of belief in Allah the Exalted and are the means of obtaining Allah's pleasure. "And they give food out of love for it to the needy, the orphan, and the captive, [Saying], "We feed you only for the countenance of Allah. We wish not from you any reward or gratitude" (76:8–9).

Al-Waqf
In order to achieve the real functions of social security, it is not good enough for governments to mobilize charitable and voluntary activities in general and *waqf* institutions in particular. Special attention should be given to the *waqf* institutions in the Muslim world, since the *waqf* [6] (or endowment) system plays an important role of financing many entities that have contributed substantially to

society by providing services to the poor and the needy, such as schools, libraries, clinics, hospitals, sanatoriums, nursing homes, orphanages, old-age homes, boarding houses for foreign workers, hostelries for guests and travelers, water cooling machines, water dispensers, water installations, wells, roads, bridges, parks and gardens for entertainment. Even the contemporary practices of *waqf* have gone beyond these ranges and has entered in fields related to finance and productivity, such as the *Waqf* Banks of Seeds for equipping needy farmers (which stores seeds as a source for planting in case seed reserves are destroyed) and Awqaf al-Nuqud (cash endowments) (Qahf 2000; Al-Avna'ut 2001).

Al-Zakat

Zakat is one of five pillars of the Islamic faith. It is compulsory for every Muslim whose wealth reaches a certain level. With its far-reaching effect, *zakat* is considered the most important framework of social security in the Islamic society. There is great wisdom in establishing *zakat* as a duty for the rich and a right of the poor. The Qur'an emphasizes the responsibility of individuals in society: "And establish prayer and give *zakat* and bow with those who bow [in worship and obedience]" (2:43). Allah the Almighty highlights the responsibility of the state (official institutions) for collecting *zakat*: "Take, [O, Muhammad], from their wealth a *sadaqah* (*zakat*) by which you purify them and cause them increase, and invoke [Allah's blessings] upon them. Indeed, your invocations are reassurance for them. And Allah is Hearing and Knowing" (9:103). Paying *zakat* purifies the affluent from the base qualities of stinginess and avarice. It also purifies them from sin. It is indeed a means by which the person's wealth becomes blessed and by which it will find increase. Then Allah the Exalted ordains the state to distribute whatever it has collected from *zakat* to those in need: "*Zakat* expenditures are only for the poor and for the needy and for those employed to collect [*zakat*] and for bringing hearts together [for Islam] and for freeing captives [or slaves] and for those in debt and for the cause of Allah and for the [stranded] traveler—an obligation [imposed] by Allah. And Allah is Knowing and Wise" (9:60).

Zakat is a constant and persistent mechanism for redistributing resources and income among the members of the society, which is based on the principle, "to be taken from the rich among them and then distributed to their poor" (see Ibn Hajar 2004, vol. 3, no. 1395, 297). Thus, the poor have a right to share amounts of up to 2.5 percent of one year's savings, or one-tenth tax (*ushr*) on agricultural produce, or one-fifth charged on the product of mines or mineral wealth (*khums*). Zakat benefits both the affluent and the needy, elevating their status and preserving their dignity. One of the greatest aspects of its wisdom with respect to the poor is that it preserves their dignity by sparing them from having to beg. Begging is a humiliation. By contrast, when a poor person receives *zakat*, he is taking that which is his right as set forth in Allah's Law. The same can be said for any of the other categories of people who are eligible to receive *zakat*. The dignity of the recipient is even more safeguarded where the *zakat* is collected by the Muslim government and distributed to those who deserve it.

Accordingly, unlike charity, Muslims are encouraged to disclose the payment of *zakat* because *zakat* is the rule of the Law Giver; its disclosure will manifest that the giver is rule-compliant. Some people are afraid that their money will decrease or that they will become poor by giving money to the poor, but Islamic belief says the contrary: "The likeness of those who spend their wealth in the way of Allah, is as the likeness of a grain that sprouts seven spikes. In every spike there are 100 grains, and Allah multiplies for whom He will" (2:261).

If the resources of *zakat* are insufficient to satisfy the poor, then the liability is transferred to *Bait al-Mal* (public treasury). "The Imam (the leader of the Islamic state) must be Allah-conscious of distributing the wealth, he leave not any poor unless he gave him his right (or his portion) from *zakat* until deemed satisfactory for himself and his dependents; if there are some Muslims in need and there is nothing left in the department of *zakat* of Bait al-Mal, the Imam should gave him what is needed from its department of *Kharaj*" (Al-Sarakhsi 1993, vol. 3, 18). Another example of adequacy is family expenditure that is the obligation on the husband. A wife has the right to obtain sufficient livelihood for herself and her children. She is even allowed to take from her husband's property without his knowledge if he falls below this basic level of supporting her.

Bait al-Mal *(House of Wealth)*

Bait al-Mal is considered the last shelter for ensuring the adequacy or delivery of social benefits. When members of the society personally lack the resources to achieve, and when the safety frameworks have reached their limits in the Muslim society, the role of *Bait al-Mal* is initiated, for the security of citizens. This is social security in its narrow sense, and pertains to the liability of the state with respect to its citizens to ensure the social adequacy of benefits for the needy. This crucial responsibility is originated from the Prophet (pbuh)— the founder as well as the leader of the archetype model of the Islamic state in Medina—who said, "I am closer to the believers than their own selves, so whoever of them dies while being in debt and leaves nothing for its repayment, then it is on me to pay his debts on his behalf, and if he dies leaving some property then that property is for his heirs" (see Ibn Hajar 2004, vol. 12, no. 6731, 12).

This approach is embodied in the Islamic concept of social safety and security. It is a system that satisfies not only the physical material needs, but also the spiritual needs. It is the real concept of philanthropy in Islam because what is given to the poor or the needy must be from lawfully earned money. As the concept of ownership of wealth in Islam is that all wealth belongs to Allah, man has only been entrusted with that wealth; as prescribed in the Qur'an, all philanthropy should be made for the pleasure of Allah alone. In short, this philanthropic approach always targets human development projects in areas like education, health, water supply and sanitation, law, justice and public administration, industry, infrastructure, and agriculture and rural development. While establishing and improving the social security system, there is also a right path for managing investments and establishing, supervising, and managing funds in accordance with the fund management principles of matching the characteristics of the various projects. By working hard, these investments and funds will guarantee an increase in the value of the social security funds and resolve the operational risks of the security funds, in such a way as to safeguard social safety and stability.

The Concept of Social Security in Islam

The story is told that the Second Caliph, 'Umar bin al-Khattab, met a Dhimi (a non-Muslim citizen of the Islamic state) begging on the road. He quickly brought him to his house and gave him charity. Then he issued an order to the treasurer of *Bait al-Mal*, "Look at this (the Dhimi) and ascertain whom is as much as his condition, by Allah, we have not done justice to him if we had consumed his youth and then we abandoned him when he became aged" (Abu Yusuf 1999, 126). Accordingly, his *jizyah* (a per capita tax levied on a non-Muslim citizen who meets certain criteria) was exempted. Moreover, guarantees for his sufficient livelihood were met through *Bait al-Mal*. The Caliph 'Umar bin 'Abd al-'Aziz followed the same approach toward Dhimi, who lived under the security provided by the Islamic state (Abu Yusuf 1999, 126). As these examples show, the responsibility for social safety and security that the Islamic state has undertaken has not been restricted to its citizens, but has also included all residents (even those living temporarily in the Islamic state). Its best witness is the treaty that had been concluded between Khalid bin al-Walid with the people of al-Hirah (an ancient city located south of al-Kufah in south-central Iraq) that any aged person who was weak, had lost his or her ability to work, fallen ill, or who had been rich but became poor, would be exempt from *jizyah*, and his or livelihood and the livelihood of his or her dependents (who were not living permanently in the Islamic state) would be met by *Bait al-Mal* (Abu Yusuf 1999, 126).

Accordingly, it is the responsibility of an Islamic state to be fully concerned with the safety and security needs of its citizens. In contemporary society, the social safety system is not wholesome. It is based on a number of risks and is offered with many conditions, such as the period of effective service, period of insured, and period of least residency. Consequently, with the diminution or shrinkage of the state's liabilities or responsibilities toward its citizens, the spectrum of insured citizens has been critically narrowed. This has simultaneously opened the door for commercial insurance to play its role. Unfortunately, the presence of conventional insurance has not been well received by the Muslim community. Since the second half of the twentieth century, the Muslim world has witnessed the emergence of legislation that enacted what is now known as the social security system. The idea of the system is based on mandatory insurance, in which the burdens are shared by the beneficiaries, employers, and the state through the mechanism of proportional participation pooled in the special fund. Its spectrum is limited and related to state security projects where the participants would include state employees, military personnel, and workers attached to large state projects. The benefits of such a system include remuneration for retirement, pension, health insurance, compensation for work-related accidents, disability, occupational diseases, death, maternity leave, and family aid ('Abdullah 1989, 173–85; Isa 1989, 11). Such a system is considered a reflection of the principle of cooperation, which the state is obliged to abide by to actualize *al-Masalih al-Mursalah* (the public interest). The contemporary social security system is not aimed at generating profits, even though the security funds have been invested and wealth has been increased by the management of the state for the benefits of the related institutions (Al-Fanjari 1982, 30; Shabir 2001,103). The needs of individuals can either be satisfied by their own resources or through public programs transferred through the social security system. Even though these needs are private in nature, they are necessities that need to be provided to citizens because they are considered prerequisites for their revival and prosperity in society. The following are public programs that need to be provided.

Education

Islam has dignified the role and importance of knowledge, honored those who pursue knowledge, and even emphasized that the acquisition of knowledge is an obligation for every Muslim (Ibn Majah 1984). Thus providing the necessary facilities to pursue and acquire knowledge is also an obligation. Therefore, schools, colleges, universities, libraries, laboratories, and so on are all qualified to obtain support to meet the objectives of Shari'ah. *Al-Fuqha* (Muslim jurists) have affirmed that *zakat* can be distributed to students of knowledge to cover the costs of education (Al-Qardhawi 2000, vol. 2, 560). Such payments encourage families to enroll their children, as well as older students to pursue higher education.

Health Care

The protection of life is one of the objectives of Shari'ah. To achieve this objective, it is required that either individuals or organizations in society fight for their lives and ward off any disease. The Qur'an says, "And whoever saves one—it is as if he had saved mankind entirely" (5:32). Not surprisingly, many hospitals, medical centers, and clinics have been set up by Muslim as *waqf*, together with the state, to protect members of the society. From an Islamic point of view, it is obligatory for every Muslim to take care of him or herself. The Qur'an says, "And spend in the way of Allah and do not throw [yourselves] with your [own] hands into destruction [by refraining]. And do good; indeed, Allah loves the doers of good" (2:195).

Training

Training is another significant instrument provided for the members of the society to teach them vocational or practical skills. The Islamic society in the archetypal model of Medina emphasized the competencies and qualifications of its members and has encouraged them to be competent in their professions, careers, businesses, and so on. The Prophet (pbuh) teaches us that Allah the Almighty loves the professional who is also a believer; one who does his job skillfully and professionally, and is a strong believer in the sight of Allah is worthier than a weak believer (Ibn 'Ayyadh 1986, vol. 8, no. 2662, 157). Training will make us reach perfection in our job after we have mastered certain related skills; then, through the skills we have learned, we may produce more products and services that may improve our life and reduce poverty.

Security, Protection, and Jurisdiction

By applying Islamic principles to safeguard peace, the Islamic society is protected by its sovereignty against dangers, damages, losses, and crimes. According to the Shari'ah, all citizens—Muslims and non-Muslims—have the same responsibilities and rights; thus their life, religion, wealth, dignity, and lineage are sacred and inviolable in the Islamic state. The legislation of the *Hisbah* institution, under the authority of an Islamic state, appoints officials of the state to carry out the responsibility of enjoining what is right (whenever people start to neglect it) and forbidding what is wrong (whenever people start to engage in it) (Al-Mawardi 2006, 349). Allah says in the Qur'an, "And let there be [arising] from you a nation inviting to [all that is] good, enjoining what is right and forbidding what is wrong, and those will be the successful" (3:104). The purpose of the *Hisbah* institution, obviously, is to safeguard society from deviance, protect the faith, and ensure the welfare of the people. Apart from this, the authority must also be prepared to defend the Islamic state against any type of invasion and aggression (economical, cultural, political, and so on) with all its might. Allah ordains the believers in the Qur'an, "And prepare against them (enemies) whatever you are able within your power" (8:60).

Infrastructure

Infrastructure, such as roads, water supply, electrical grids, and telecommunications, includes the basic physical structures of interrelated systems that society needs to provide essential services to establish, sustain, or improve societal living conditions (Fulmer 2009; Sullivan and Sheffrin 2003, 474). A society that lacks infrastructure will handicap its development. Hence the state should consistently finance infrastructure development projects of society. Classical Islamic jurisprudence, which elaborates the allocation of revenues of *Bait al-Mal*, has emphasized that *Bait al-Mal* should also allot revenues to building bridges, repairing roads, digging wells, improving irrigation-drainage systems, broadening river canals, and the like) (Al-Sarakhsi 1993, vol. 3, 18; Ibn Qudamah 1980, vol. 3, 334).

Social Insurance: *Takaful* and *Ta'min*

To make the concept of helping one another based on cooperation a reality, contemporary Muslim scholars urge Muslims to participate in social security through their own capabilities and potential. Two Arabic terms, in particular, relate to social insurance and social security: *ta'min* and *Takaful*.

Ta'min

The term "*ta'min*" in Arabic is a derivation from the verb "*amman*" and its current form is "*yuammin*," which literally means "pray or supplication"(Al-Zamakhshri 1960, 20). It is crucial to point out that the basic letters of its root "A-M-N" have several meanings, but all are significantly interrelated. First, "*aman*" means security, peace, safety and the feeling of tranquility.[7] Second, "*amanah*" means loyalty, honesty, and fidelity. Third, "*iman*" means certification, authentication, and attestation (Ahmad bin Faris 1969; Ibn Faris 2008, vol. 1, 72; Ibn Manzur 2007). Thus, a believer who states his attestation "of *iman* (believes in Allah the Almighty) is one who is cognizant, believing and acting, knowing that not only one is safe and secure, but is actively and consciously aware of the source of that safety and security" (Mirakhor and Hamid 2009, 144); thus, he or she lives with the feeling of tranquility.

Technically, the word *ta'min* refers to someone who paid a sum of money for something in installments in order for himself or his heirs to acquire an agreed amount of money or compensation for something he has lost (Al-Mu'jam al-Wasit 1960, 27–28). This meaning of *ta'min* is not different from the conventional concept of insurance. If we look at insurance as a cooperative system, we find that Muslim scholars like Al-Sanahuri, Al-Zarga', 'Abduh, and others have similar definitions: that is, a contractual system based on *ta'awun* (cooperation) of a group of people who are committed to pay a sum of money as donation through a managed arrangement to indemnify for the damages or losses that may befall one member when contingent events occur (Al-Mu'jam al-Wasit 1960). In accordance with the understanding of those scholars, it seems that social cooperation or mutual assistance is the main purpose of *ta'min*. However, this is not the purpose of commercial insurance, which is profit-oriented[8] and which might be executed in the form of individuals or companies or organizations, or the state itself, with the intention of fulfilling the public benefits of the society or the interests of a group of people or even individuals. Further extending the concept of *ta'min*, so as to be more inclusive, is *al-Ta'min al-Ijtimai* (social insurance), a system of ensuring a necessary livelihood for certain people who meet the conditions stipulated by the state while their earnings cease for certain reasons. In practical terms, in its modern form, social insurance is a nonprofit system of either a state-sponsored compulsory program or a heavily subsidized program that most eligible individuals choose to participate in. The programs often and largely have been carried out by governmental organizations to protect the income of eligible people when confronted with work-related disability, or unemployment, retirement, disease, death, or the like ('Abdullah 1976, 500; Al-Jammal 1975, 41).

Takaful

Takaful is another frequently used Arabic word that refers to social security. It is also a derivation of the verb "*kaffal*," which literally means "to provide, support, sponsor, spend and guarantee." Through these meanings, it shares the notion of *kafalah* (social security). "*Takaful*" as a root of the verb indicates behaviors that always happen between two or more people, and each of them provides supports to the other; hence it entails the idea of interdependence, love for one another, and solidarity in society (Al-Zawi 1980, vol. 4, 68). The Qur'an ordains believers to implement such cooperation: "And cooperate in righteousness and piety, but do not cooperate in sin and aggression" (5:2). The Prophet (pbuh) said, "A Muslim is a brother of another Muslim, so he should not oppress him, nor should he hand him over to an oppressor. Whoever fulfilled the needs of his brother, Allah will fulfill his needs; whoever brought his (Muslim) brother out of a discomfort, Allah will bring him out of the discomforts on the Day of Resurrection, and whoever screened a Muslim, Allah will screen him on the Day of Resurrection"(Ibn Hajar 2004, vol. 12, no. 6851, 374). In another *Hadith* [report of statement or actions of Prophet Muhammad (pbuh)], the Prophet (pbuh) said, "The example of the believers in their mutual love, mercy, and compassion is like the example of a body. If one part feels pain, then the whole of it is affected by sickness and fever"(Ibn Ayyadh, 1986, vol. 8, no. 2586, 56). And "If *Al-Ash'ariyyin* (the tribe) lacked supplies during a raid or their families lacked food in the city, they gathered what they had in one garment and distributed it among themselves equally; then they are part of me and I am part of them"(Ibn Hajar 2004, vol. 5, no. 2486, 146).

In accordance with this ideology, *Takaful* is a system of joint liability among individuals, or a group of people, or organizations in a society, to meet the needs of the needy, support one another, and fund as well as protect their common benefits (Abu Zahrah 1994, 4; Al-Mahmud 1994, 82). The *Takaful* system is based on the healthy principles of the human consciousness of solidarity and legal enforcement to ensure equality, and is a reflection on all aspects of human life (Qutub 1967, 28–35, 62–76). It is a manifestation of *iman* (belief) that every individual has responsibility toward others in society, and accordingly, he or she must treat others the same as he or she treats himself or herself (Salim 1965). The system implies social, economic, political, judicial, cultural, and educational dimensions, among others (Shaltut 1962, 910–13; Al-Abrashi 1969, 280), along with corresponding virtues and enactment of them in society. The individuals' spirit of cooperation and solidarity would be enhanced in this way; hence the needs of the society would be satisfied (Al-Khayyat 1972, 74–75, 321–22). The best example is one mentioned in the section of *al-Aqilah* that the Prophet (pbuh) emphasized in the first Treaty concluded in Medina among believers and between the believers and the followers of other religions (Ibn Hisham 2009, vol. 1, 501–504).

If the *Takaful* system is compared to a social security system incorporating the social insurance system, there are certain similarities in terms of satisfying the needs of members of a society and by virtue of both being the factors of social-political-economic security. However, they differ from one another in several dimensions (Al-Mahmud 1994, 89–90).

- Social insurance is a legal system ruled and executed by specific law; *Takaful* is a faith-based and ethical system that originates from the consciousness of the individual.

- Social insurance is a compulsory system carried out for people who meet certain conditions; *Takaful* is an optional system based on the interrelationship and interdependence among the members of society.
- The scope of *Takaful* is more comprehensive than social insurance. *Takaful* covers all members of the society, whereas social insurance is restricted to certain people who meet the stipulated conditions, such as income class.
- The authority of social insurance is limited and often dominated by government organizations; *Takaful* is widespread in society.
- The returns of social insurance are available only to the participants in the system because it is a legal financial system; *Takaful* extends much more widely since it is based on donation and cooperation. Beneficiaries may not even know who provided the assistance—or that they would even receive assistance—and donors may remain anonymous.

The *Takaful* system in Islam has a wider significance and normally refers to social security in the Muslim world. Recently, however, the concept of *Takaful* has been applied in *ta'min* and is being made operational along the lines of a commercial insurance company. It is a collective insurance contract, whereby its subscribers are committed to pay a specific amount of money as a donation to indemnify the beneficiaries on the basis of *Takaful*—that is, cooperation and solidarity—when the risk actually occurs. Its insurance operations are borne by a specialized company as a *wakil* (representation) or *ajir* (employee) or *mudarib* (one who provides his time and skills) for a fixed fee. Such a company is ready to provide insurance services and manage the funds for the benefits of participants in a specific form of contract.

However, the functions of social insurance and commercial insurance are not too different from each other. For the insured, it is a way to achieve economic protection. For the insurer, it is a means of generating profits, since the surplus of the fund can be invested. For the state and the society, it is an enormous financial resource for economic development. Nevertheless, the scope of social insurance is much broader than the commercial one, since social insurance is generally a legal security system that often aims at eliminating poverty and protecting society, whereas commercial insurance always seeks profits (Al-Mahmud 1994, 318–20). Therefore, the main objective of social insurance is to achieve economic protection for the insured. This does not contradict the Islamic point of view toward social security. Islam deems that security is one of the blessings of Allah the Exalted, Who says in the Qur'an, "Allah has promised those who have believed among you and done righteous deeds that He will surely grant them succession [to authority] upon the earth just as He granted it to those before them and that He will surely establish for them [therein] their religion which He has preferred for them and that He will surely substitute for them, after their fear, security, [for] they worship Me, not associating anything with Me. But whoever disbelieves after that—then those are the defiantly disobedient" (24:55). To achieve security, we need to work hard and struggle against poverty. Even this is urged by the Prophet (pbuh), who says that Muslims should always make *doa'* or pray to Allah the Almighty to seek His protection from poverty.[9]

The means of achieving the objective of social insurance can be in the form of benefits to be distributed, since the majority of members of the society are lower-income and middle-income who need assistance to alleviate the poverty that threatens them. There is no objection from Shari'ah law for the state to intervene to actualize the objective of social insurance, since it is based on the public interest. Social insurance can be a compulsory system that the state has implemented, since the Shari'ah emphasizes obtaining the maximum benefits for the *Ummah* (Al-Mahmud 1994, 339–45). In terms of a contract, Muslim scholars have deemed that social insurance is a contract based on *tabarru'* (donation) (Al-'Attar 1974, 248; Hassan 1978, 45–46; Shalabi 1980, 85). Although this kind of *tabarru'* is compulsory, it is under the supervision of the state for purposes of the public interest and is not transferred to private property. The state can invest the funds collected from the participants to enhance the program's capability to meet the needs of the poor in case the adverse events occur (Al-Mahmud 1994, 346–56).

Takaful in Practice

Modern *Takaful* began in Sudan in 1979. By 2011, the *Takaful* industry was operating through more than 200 entities around the world and was worth an estimated US$12 billion (Ernst & Young 2011). Growth has been considerable, as seen in table 8.1.

Over a period of one year (2011–12), Indonesia recorded the largest *Takaful* market growth rate (67 percent), followed by Bangladesh (58 percent) and Saudi Arabia (34 percent).

The gross global family *Takaful* contribution in 2010 was US$1.7 billion, 29 percent higher than in 2009, according to the *Global Family Takaful Report 2010* (Milliman 2010). Between 2007 and 2010, the global family *Takaful* contribution increased at a compound growth rate of 36 percent. In 2010, Southeast Asia's share of the global family *Takaful* contribution was 73 percent, followed by the Middle East, with 25 percent, and South Asia, with 2 percent. While most of the general *Takaful* market is centered in the Middle East and the Gulf Cooperation Council (GCC) region, the family *Takaful* market is focused in Southeast Asia, especially in Malaysia. In 2010, family *Takaful* in Malaysia was estimated to contribute 77 percent of net *Takaful* contributions in the country (Ernst & Young 2011).

Table 8.1 Increase in Regional Growth Rates in *Takaful*, 2010–11

Region	Increase in growth rate (percent)
Indian subcontinent	85
Middle East	40
Gulf Cooperation Council (GCC)	31
Southeast Asia	29
Africa	26

Source: Ernst & Young 2011.

In the past three decades, the development and growth has been greater on the commercial side of *Takaful*—that is, *Takaful al-tijari*—where the focus is mainly on personal benefits or interests of *Takaful* participants, rather than the poor and the vulnerable in society at large. However, Muslims should not overlook the spirit that underlies these operational efforts. This spirit comes under the form of *Takaful al-ijtimai* (mutual social responsibility), which includes all material and moral aspects of life that are implicit in the *Maqasid al-Shari'ah* (the objectives of Shari'ah). According to Al-Morsy (2006), *Takaful al-ijtimai* can be defined as the solidarity of all members of society, caring for public as well as private interests, keeping others from evil and harm so that each individual realizes that he has duties to others, corresponding to the rights they have, especially to those who are not able to achieve their own needs. 'Ulwan (2001), on the other hand, states in his book *Al-Takaful al-ijtimai fi al-Islam* that *Takaful al-ijtimai* is the act of guarantee and supports each member in the society, whether individually or in a group. It is driven by a deep sense of empathy, stemming from Islamic faith, through which individuals can serve society. By acting on these principles, everyone can cooperate in order to develop a better society. While Islam acknowledges the business aspect of *Takaful* as developed through *Takaful al-tijari*, it also emphasizes inculcating the facet of *Takaful al-ijtimai*. Therefore, rebalancing both aspects of *Takaful* should complement the roles and functions played by the *Takaful* operators.

Takaful participants are part of society, hence ensuring the well-being of other people's lives should be considered as an *ibadah* [obedience, submission and devotion to Allah (swt)], and together we should uphold the responsibility. As stated by Imam Ahmad Ibni Hambal, "Nobody will enter Paradise if he does not protect his neighbor who is in distresses" (Shakir 1995). Operationalizing the concept of *Takaful al-ijtimai* takes two forms: namely, through the promulgation of cash *waqf*, and through introduction of micro*Takaful* programs. Al-Morsy (2006) believes that the activation of the *waqf* system is necessary to continue the progress of *Takaful al-ijtimai* in the global environment. Funds accumulated through the cash *waqf* programs, especially in developing countries, can be allocated to socially related development areas, including agriculture, education, and health, as well as urban poverty alleviation programs. Such a focus would eventually reduce poverty levels and uplift the spirit of helping one another among the *Ummah*.

There are some historical models, such as the cash *waqf* in operation in Bursa, Turkey, which between 1555 and 1823 offered funding to 10 percent of the total population of Bursa (60,000 inhabitants) (Çizakça 1995, 314). In Bangladesh since 1997, the Social Investment Bank Limited (SIBL) has issued cash *waqf* certificates to collect funds from the rich and distribute profits of the managed funds to the poor (Masyita and Telaga 2005). Currently, a number of Muslim countries, including the Arab Republic of Egypt, Indonesia, the Islamic Republic of Iran, Iraq, Malaysia, Pakistan, the Syrian Arab Republic, and Turkey, have accepted the practice of cash *waqf* (Mohammad Tahir Sabit 2006).

Islam, being egalitarian in nature, emphasizes the importance of fulfilling the basic needs of the poor and the vulnerable. This is the objective of the

Figure 8.1 Dynamics of Poverty Reduction

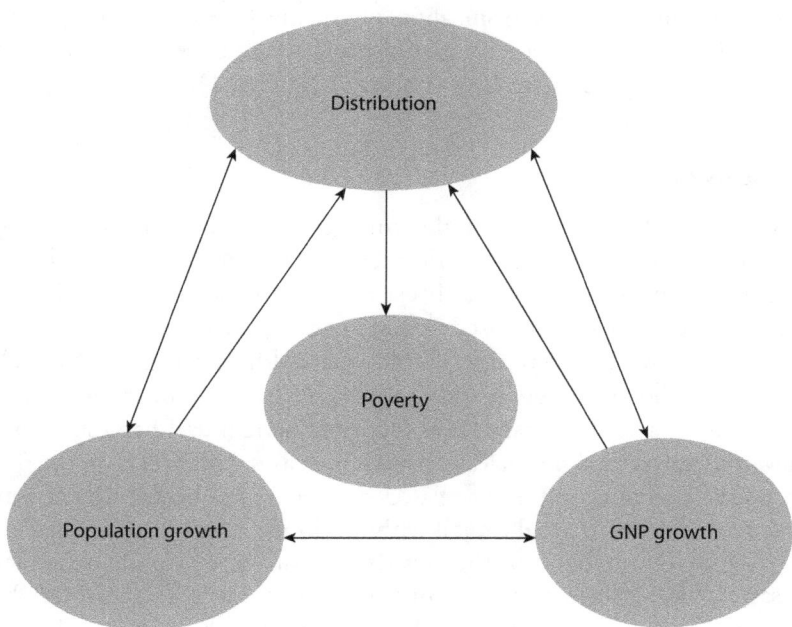

Source: Adapted from Iqbal 2002.

Islamic distributive system. Together with a good economic growth, a controlled population growth rate, and an efficient distribution scheme, they "could form the dynamics of poverty reduction," as Iqbal (2002, 9) puts it (see figure 8.1). Distribution ranks quite high in the hierarchy of values of Shari'ah and is an explicit Qur'anic criterion for evaluating a society, as evident in chapter 69, verse 34, "And would not encourage the feeding of the indigent!" and in chapter 89, verse 18, "Nor do you encourage one another to feed the poor!"

Refusal to share with the needy is considered a transgression. Combating poverty, or fulfilling needs, is the primary goal of redistribution in Islam and is one expression of the divine verdict to honor the children of Adam.

Another operational approach to activate *Takaful al-ijtimai* is through microfinance, or more specifically, through micro*Takaful* programs. According to Bhatty (2010), while *Takaful* deals with manageable risks for those who can afford them, micro*Takaful* targets the type of risks that are excluded on normal yardsticks. The risk in the micro*Takaful* proposition is a function of low income, poverty, and vulnerability, which relates to loss of property due to theft or fire, loss from natural and man-made disasters, agricultural losses, accidental death, disability, or illnesses. An example of micro*Takaful* can be found in Indonesia. Peramu, a nongovernmental organization (NGO), has been closely involved in the Indonesian government's charity trust fund for the poor. They have established the Takmin Working Group to run the micro*Takaful* program as a pilot project in Bogor, with technical assistance provided by the Microinsurance Association of Netherlands (MIAN) (Haryadi 2007, 62–63; see also chapter 7).

Micro*Takaful* needs to be part of national agendas to alleviate poverty. The member-states of the Organization of Islamic Countries (OIC) should make micro*Takaful* and microcredit part of the 2015 goals set by the United Nations Millennium Development Plan (Bhatty 2010, 60–61).

Conclusion

Over the past 30 or so years, the emergence of a number of economic crises, coupled with waves of natural disasters, have disproportionately hurt the poor and the vulnerable, and have thrust many into the quagmire of poverty. The economic crises have increased unemployment, increased the prices of essential items, and lowered the returns on physical and financial assets. Natural disasters such as earthquakes, floods, and droughts have caused physical destruction and loss of lives, and at the same time, depleted agricultural harvests, which in turn have generated food shortages and price increases. The effects on the poor of cuts in public spending and other related measures have become more intense, and this has eroded the social capital within communities.

The adverse impacts of the covariate nature of economic crises and natural disasters have attracted the attention of most countries of the world. Poverty has topped the agenda in many global gatherings assembled by the United Nations, the World Bank, and the IMF. These crises have also prompted many countries to reassess the adequacy of their safety nets to help the poor and the vulnerable. Various social safety net programs have been examined and implemented as a countercyclical tool in times of crises.

This study proposes the implementation of Islamic social safety nets through the application of the *Takaful* and *ta'min* concepts. Under a *Takaful* contract, participants agree to contribute to a *Takaful* fund, which can be used in an act of mutual help in the event of a misfortune.

Each member of society should help those in need so that they can at least lead a decent life and meet their basic needs, as Al-Gamal (Mahmoud 1992) puts it. This involves all members of society, regardless of their religion or nationality.

Notes

1. See the verses of the Qur'an regarding the needs provided by Allah the Almighty to humans: (2:35), (7:26), (8:66–69), (14:80–81), (16:5), (20:118–19), (35:12), (36:33–35), (43:12), (56:68–69), (67:15).
2. Also see the verses of the Qur'an: (2:36), (7:24), (11:61), (62:10), (73:20).
3. Also see the verse of the Qur'an: (6:141).
4. Also see the verses of the Qur'an: (7:10), (11:38), (18:77), (28:26–27), (34:10–11), (62:10), (67:15). For the sayings of the Prophet (pbuh), it is reported by Zubiar ibn 'Awam and Abu Hurairah that the Messenger of Allah said, "That one of you takes his rope and then comes with a load of wood upon his back and sells it, and that thereby Allah guards his face, is better for him than that he should beg of men whether they give him or refuse him." See Ibn Hajar (2004, vol. 3, no. 1470 and 1471, 380).

5. See the rules prescribed for the inheritance in the Qur'an: (4:7–12, 176).
6. The most appropriate definition of *waqf* is "Holding the origin (property) and giving away (donating) the usufruct (of property for the sake of Allah)," which is defined by Ibn Qudamah (1980, vol. 2, 308).
7. The word of *"aman"* recoded in the Qur'an refers to security, peace, safety, and the feeling of tranquility, such as: "And [as mentioned also in the Quran] when We made the House a place of return for the people and [a place of] security…" and the Prophet Ibrahim prayed Allah the Almighty, "O my Lord, make this a secure city and provide its people with fruits—whoever of them believes in Allah and the Last Day" (2:125–126). See also: (2:125), (3:97), (16:112).
8. See Al-Sanahuri (1952, vol. 2, 1087); 'Abduh (1977, 130); Al-Zarqa' (1980, 394–95). Commercial insurance is prohibited in the Islamic Shari'ah for three basic reasons. The first is excessive *gharar* (uncertainty). A subscriber pays premiums, but if the adverse event does not occur, he will not receive any compensation for what he paid. In an extreme case, he may pay a single premium at the beginning of the term, and then the adverse event may occur; in that case, he will receive a vast amount of money. The second reason is *riba* (usury or interest). There is a time difference between the payment of the premium and the receipt of compensation and it is *Riba al-Nasi'ah* (on credit). If the subscriber pays a little and received a larger amount, it is *Riba al-Fadl* (surplus). The third reason is *maysir* (gambling). See the verses of the Qur'an prohibiting *riba, gharar,* and *maysir*.
9. It is narrated by 'Ai'shah that the Prophet (pbuh) used to say, "O Allah! I seek refuge with you from laziness from geriatric old age, from being in debt, and from committing sins. O Allah! I seek refuge with you from the punishment of the Fire, the afflictions of the grave, the punishment in the grave, and the evil of the affliction of poverty and from the evil of the affliction caused by Al-Masih Al-Dajjal. O Allah! Wash away my sins with the water of snow and hail, and cleanse my heart from the sins as a white garment is cleansed of filth, and let there be a faraway distance between me and my sins as You have set far away the East and the West from each other." See Ibn Hajar (2004, vol. 11, no. 6375, 6376, 6377, 204).

References

'Abduh, 'Isa. 1977. *Al-'Uqud al-Shar'iyyah al-Hakimah lil-Mu'amalat al-Maliyyah al-Mu'asirah*. Cairo: Dar al-I'tisam.

'Abdullah, Salamah. 1976. *Al-Khatar wal-Ta'min: al-Usul al-'Ilmiyyah wal-'Amaliyyah*. Cairo: Dar al-Nahdhah al-'Arabiyyah.

'Abdullah, 'Uthman Husain. 1989. *Al-Zakat wal-Dhaman al-Ijtmai al-Islami*. Mansoura, Egypt: Dar al-Wafa'.

Abu Yusuf, Ya'qub. 1999. *Kitab Al-Kharaj*. Beirut: Dar al-Ma'arif.

Abu Zahrah, Muhammad. 1994. *Al-Mujtam 'al-Islami*. Cairo: Dar al-Fikr al-'Arabi.

Ahmad bin Faris bin Zakariyya. 1969. *Mu'jam Maqayis al-Lughh by 'Abud al-Salam Muhammad Harun*. 2nd ed., vol. 1. Cairo: Sharikah Maktabah wa Matba'ah al-Babi al-Halabi wa Awladih.

Al-Abrashi, Muhammad. 1969. *'Atiyyah, Ruh al-Islam*. 2nd ed. Cairo: Dar Ihya' al-Kutub al-'Arabiyyah.

Al-'Attar, 'Abd al-Nasir Tawfiq. 1974. *Ahkam al-Ta'min fi al-Qanun al-Madani wa al-Shariah al-Islamiyyah*. Cairo: Matba'ah al-Sa'adah.

Al-Avna'ut, Muhammad. 2001. *Dirasat fi Waqf al-Nuqud*. Tunis: Mu'assah al-Tamimi.

Al-Fanjari, Muhammad Shawqi. 1982. *Al-Islam wal-Dhaman al-Ijtma'i*. Riyadh: Dar Thaqif.

Al-Jammal, Gharib. 1975. *Al-Ta'min fi al-Shariah al-Islamiyyah wal-Qanun*. Cairo: Dar al-Fikr al-'Arabi.

Al-Jaziri, 'Abd al-Rahman. 2004. *Al-Fiqh 'ala al-Mazahib al-Araba'ah*. Vol. 4. Cairo: Dar al-Hadith.

Al-Khayyat, 'Abd al-'Aziz. 1972. *Al-Mujtama' al-Mutakafil fi al-Islam*. Beirut: Mu'assisah al-Risalah wa Maktabah al-Aqsa.

Al-Mahmud, 'Abd al-Latif Mahmud. 1994. *Al-Ta'min al-Ijtima'i fi Dhaw' al-Shariah al-Islamiyyah*. Beirut: Dar al-Nafa'is.

Al-Mawardi. 2006. *Al-Ahkam al-Sutaniyyah*. Cairo: Dar al-Hadith

Al-Morsy, Al-Sayyid Hegazy. 2006. "The Role of Waqf in Achieving *Takaful* Ijtimai within the Islamic Environment." Jeddah, *Journal of King Abdulaziz University* 19 (2): 55–94.

Al-Mu'jam al-Wasit. 1960. *Al-Mu'jam al-Wasit*. Cairo: Majma' al-Lughah al-Arabiyah.

Al-Qardhawi, Yusuf. 2000. *Fiqh al-Zakat*. Vol. 2, 563–69. Beirut: Mu'assisah al-Risalah wa Maktabah Al-Aqsa.

Al-Sanahuri, 'Abd al-Razzaq Aímad. 1952. *Al-Wasit fi Sharh al-Qanun al-Madani*. Vol. 2. Cairo: Dar al-Nashr lil-Jami'at wa Dar al-Nahdhah al-'Arabiyyah.

Al-Sarakhsi, Shamsuddin. 1993. *Kitab al-Mabsut*. Vol. 3. Beirut: Dar al-Marifah.

Al-Shatibi, Abu Ishaq Ibrahim bin Musa al-Lakhmi al-Gharnati. 2005. *Al-Muwafiqat fi Usul al-Shariah*. 7th ed., vol 2. Beirut: Dar al-Kutub al-Ilmiyah.

Al-Zamakhshri, Abu al-Qasim Mahmud bin 'Umar bin Muhammad. 1960. *Asas al-Balaghah*. Cairo: Dar wa Matabi' al-Sha'b.

Al-Zarqa', Mustafa Ahmad. 1980. *Nizam al-Ta'min: Mawqi'uh fi al-Maidan al-Iqtisadi bi Wajh 'Am wa Maqifu al-Shariah al-Islamiyyah minah*. Jeddah: Al-Markaz al-'Alami li Abhath al-Iqtisad al-Islami.

Al-Zawi, Al-Tahir Ahmad. 1980. *Tartib al-Qamus al-Muhit 'ala Tariqah al-Misbah al-Munir wa Asas al-Balaghah*. Vol. 4. Libya: Al-Dar al-'Arabiyyah lil-Kutab.

Anup, Shah. 2009. "Poverty Facts and Stats." GlobalIssues.org. March 22. http://helppoor.wordpress.com/statistics/.

Bhatty, Ajmal. 2010. "Protecting the Forgotten through Microtakaful." *Global Takaful*, July: 60–61.

Çizakça, Murat. 1995. "Cash Waqf of Bursa, 1555–1823." *Journal of the Economic and Social History of the Orient* 38 (3): 313–54.

Ernst & Young. 2011. *World Takaful Report 2011: Transforming Operating Performances*. London: Ernst & Young.

Fulmer, Jeffrey. 2009. "What in the World is Infrastructure?" *Infrastructure Investor*, July/August: 30–32.

Ghosh, Bimal. 1997. "Economic Reform and Safety Nets Go Together." *New York Times*, January 9.

Haryadi, A. 2007. "Reaching Out to the Poor with Microtakaful." *Middle East Insurance Review*, July: 62–63.

Hassan, Husain Hamid. 1978. *Hukum al-Shariah al-Islamiyyah fi 'Uqud al-Ta'min*. Cairo: Dar al-I'tisam.

Ibn, 'Ayyadh. 1986. *Ikmal al-Mu'allim bi Fawai'd Muslim*. Vol. 8, no. 2664, 2586. Al-Mansurah, Egypt: Wafa Dar al-Wafa.

Ibn Faris, Abu al-Husain Ahmad bin Faris bin Zakariyya al-Razi. 2008. *Mu'jam Maqayis al-Lughh*. 2nd ed., vol. 1. Beirut: Dar al-Kutub al-'Ilmiyyah.

Ibn Hajar, Ahmad bin Ali al-Asqalani. 2004. "Fath al-Bari bi Sharh Sahih al-Bukhari." Vols. 3, 5, 9, 10, 11, and 12. Cairo: Dar al-Hadith.

Ibn Hisham. 2009. Al-Sirah al-Nabawiyyah. Vol. 1. Cairo: Sharikah Maktabah wa Matba'ah al-Babi al-Halabi wa Awladih.

Ibn Iyadh, Abu al-Daghl 'Ayyadh bin Musa al-Yahasabi. 2005. *Ikmal al-Mu'lim bi Fawai'd Muslim*. 3rd ed., vol. 8, no. 2624, 2025. Al-Mansurah, Egypt: Dar al-Wafa'.

Ibn Majah. 1984. "Al-Sunan." *Al-Sunan Ibn Majah*. 228. Beirut: Dar al-Kutub al-'Ilmiyyah.

Ibn Manzur, Abu al-Fadhl Jamal al-Din Muhammad bin Mukrim bin 'Ali. 2007. *Lisan al-'Arab*. 4th ed. Beirut: Dar Sadir li al-Tiba'ah wa as-Nashr.

Ibn Qudamah. 1980. *Al-Muqni'*. Vols. 2 and 3. Riyadh: Maktabah al-Riyadh al-Hadithah.

Iqbal, M. 2002. *Islamic Economic Institutions and the Elimination of Poverty*. Leicester, U.K.: The Islamic Foundation.

Isa, 'Ali. 1989. *Al-Dhaman al-Ijtmai*. Oman: Dar al-Nafa'is.

Mahmoud, Gamal El Dine Mohamed. 1992. *'Usul al Mujtama' al Islami*. Cairo: Dar al Kitab al Masry.

Masyita, D. T. M., and A. S. Telaga. 2005. "A Dynamic Model for Cash Waqf Management as One of the Alternative Instrument for the Poverty Alleviation in Indonesia." Research paper presented at the 23rd International Conference of the System Dynamics Society, Massachusetts Institute of Technology (MIT), Cambridge, MA, July 17–21.

Milliman. 2010. *Global Family Takaful Report, 2010*. Milliman Research Report.

Mirakhor, Abbas, and Idris Samawi Hamid. 2009. *Islam and Development: The Institutional Framework*. New York: Global Scholarly Publications.

Mohammad Tahir Sabit, Mohammad. 2006. "Innovative Models of Financing the Development of Waqf Property." Paper presented at the Konvensyen Wakaf Kebangsaan, The Legend Hotel, Kuala Lumpur, September 12–14.

Mudhari, 'Abd al-Halim 'Abd al-Qawi. 2004. *Al-Targhib wal-Tarhib*. Vol. 3. 3780–3781. Cairo: Dar al-Hadith.

Qahf, Mudhir. 2000. *Al-Waqf al-Islami: Tatawwuruh, Idaratuh, Tanmiyatuh*. Beirut: Dar al-Fikr al-Muasir.

Qutub, Sayyid. 1967. *Al-'Adalah al-Ijtima'iyyah*. 7th ed. Beirut: Mu'assissah al-Risalah wa Maktabah Al-Aqsa.

Sahl, Ibrahim M. G. 2009. "Challenging the Concept of Poverty: Does Islam Provide a Solution?" Societal Studies 217–49.

Salim, Muhammad Farh. 1965. *Al-Takaful al-Ijtima'I*. Cairo: Shaikh al-Tiba'ah Al-Faniyyah al-Muttahidah.

Shabir, Muhammad. 2001. *'Uthman, Al-Mu'amalat al-Maliyyah al-Mu'assarah fi al-Fiqh al-Islami*. Oman: Dar–al-Nafa'is.

Shakir, Ahmad Muhammad. 1995. *The Musnad of Ibn Hanbal*. Cairo: Dar al-Ma'arif.

Shalabi, Ahmad. 1980. *Al-Islam wa al-Qadhaya al-Iqtisadiyyah al-Nahdlah*. Cairo: Maktabah al-Nahdhah al-Misiriyyah.

Shaltut, Mahmud. 1962. "Al-Islam wal-*Takaful* al-Ijtima'i." *Majallah al-Azhar* 8.

Sullivan, Authur, and Steven M. Sheffrin. 2003. *Economics: Principles in Action*. Upper Saddle River, NJ: Pearson Prentice Hall.

'Ulwan, 'Abd Allah Nasih. 2001. *Al-takaful al-ijtimai fi al-Islam*. Cairo: Dar al-Salam.

CHAPTER 9

Islamic Capital Markets and Development

Obiyathulla Ismath Bacha and Abbas Mirakhor

Introduction

The question of whether capital markets (and the financial sector) are necessary for economic growth and development appeared to have been settled. However, the recent spate of financial crises and the devastating effect they have had on growth and macroeconomic stability have re-stoked questions; not so much about whether the capital markets are necessary for growth as whether they are playing the role expected of them. Questions have also been raised about whether there are inherent imbalances within capital markets that could cause economies to veer off into crises. Some have even questioned the viability of free market systems and called for regulation so tight that it could harken back to the bad old days of financial repression and controls. Yet given the frequency and depth of financial crises, and the diverse nature of economies that have had to suffer through them, it seems appropriate to question the workings of the system. This study argues that conventional capital markets that are heavily biased toward debt and debt-based instruments are inherently unstable, and that mere reregulation would miss the point. We propose a risk-sharing framework that minimizes debt—if not avoids debt completely—and brings about renewed stability.

Are Capital Markets Necessary?

Whether capital markets are necessary for growth and development has been debated for quite a while: to be precise, for at least a hundred years, from Walter Bagehot (1873),[1] who argues that an efficient financial system is needed for economies to grow, to Robert Lucas (1988, 42), who argues that economists "badly over-stress" the role finance plays in growth. In between these polar arguments is Joseph Schumpeter ([1911] 1982), who argues that the services

---

Obiyathulla Ismath Bacha is a professor of Finance and Head of Graduate Studies Department at the International Centre for Education in Islamic Finance, Malaysia. Abbas Mirakhor is Professor and the first holder of the Islamic Finance Chair at INCEIF.

offered by financial sector players are essential for technological innovation and overall economic development. Raymond Goldsmith (1969) and Ronald McKinnon (1973)[2] empirically illustrate the close links between financial sector and economic growth. The one notable study that is in line with Lucas (1988) is Joan Robinson (1952), which finds that rather than being a determinant of growth, financial sector development follows economic growth. A number of later studies by Pagano (1993), King and Levine (1993), Bekaert and Harvey (1997), and Beck, Demirgüç-Kunt, and Levine (2007) all find financial and capital market development to be a key contributing factor to economic growth. In fact, Beck, Demirgüç-Kunt, and Levine (2007, 27) show that financial development not only contributes to aggregate economic growth, but also "disproportionately boosts incomes of the poorest quintile and reduces income inequality." This finding is in direct contrast to the commonly held perception that financial development has little impact on the poorer segments of society.

Using data from 80 countries over the 30-year period 1960–89, King and Levine (1993) show evidence consistent with Schumpeter's view that financial development promotes economic growth. They document strong correlation between financial sector growth and the real per capita gross domestic product (GDP) growth, the rate of physical capital accumulation, and the efficiency of physical capital use. They also find that financial development is a good predictor of long-run growth over the next 10–30 years. They conclude that "policies that alter the costliness and efficiency of financial intermediation exert a first-order influence on economic growth" (735).[3]

The fact that financial markets are relevant to economic growth is well established, but one might want to know why and how the two are correlated. To answer this question, the next section briefly examines the functions of financial/capital markets.

Functions of Capital Market

If capital markets are so critical to well-functioning economies and economic growth, what is it that they do? Traditionally, four functions have been attributed to capital markets: intermediating between surplus and deficit units; facilitating the payments system; enabling intertemporal transfers; and serving as a medium for transmitting monetary policy.

Modern capital markets have an expanded role. In addition to the four functions described, modern capital markets provide the means and avenue for risk management. The derivative markets and instruments are the enabler for this function. By providing debt, equity, and money markets, capital markets also allow for price discovery. Critical to all this is the ability of capital markets to assimilate the actions of participants and reflect them as market information. The ability of capital markets to disseminate information in a timely manner and in a cost-effective way is perhaps the most important function of markets these days.

The efficacy with which a capital market plays these roles ultimately determines the efficient allocation of resources within an economy. The market-determined prices provide the price signals for this allocation. The transformation of savings into investments in an efficient way is the ultimate function of capital markets. It is obvious that where the pricing mechanism is hindered, prices would be distorted, leading to misallocation of resources. Worse, as Bekaert and Harvey (1997, 2) show, "Inefficient financial institutions will have the effect of taxing productive investment and thus reducing scope for increasing the stock of equipment needed to grow and compete globally." Thus, retarded capital markets lead to retarded national competitiveness.

Issues Concerning Capital Markets

While capital market inefficiency is a reality in the Muslim world and other less developed countries, the developed world has of late experienced a different kind of problem emanating from capital markets. Banking and financial crises that used to be the bane of developing countries have started to plague developed ones. It is now apparent that these problems related to the financial sector and capital markets can seriously increase the vulnerability of the overall economy. There is little doubt about the potentially systemic nature of these problems or the devastating effect they have on the real sector. Decades of hard work and capital accumulation can be lost in matter of weeks. The resulting pain both in terms of human misery and economic costs can take years—or perhaps even decades—to ameliorate.[4] Japan is a classic case in point. Regardless of where these crises originate, whether from developed or developing countries, they all seem to have a single root cause: debt. Every economic or financial crisis in the last 50 years has its root cause associated with excessive leverage (Reinhart and Rogoff 2010). When rational players, driven by their own goals to maximize profits, come face to face with a bad policy environment that incentivizes debt while also providing implicit/explicit guarantees, a volatile mixture forms. Left unchecked, this combination always results in huge social costs. A large part of this bad policy environment has its origins in the pro-growth inclination of governments that has led to artificially low interest rates.

When an entrepreneur decides to undertake a project in the real sector, he or she considers all the risks to the project. These risks do not increase when the project is being considered for financing in the capital/financial markets. However, the method of financing can differ. The project can be financed via risk transfer, risk shifting, or risk sharing. Risk transfer is what financial intermediation has long been expected to do: to transfer risk from the depositor to the borrower. Risk shifting occurs in case of insurance: the risk of life or property is shifted to the insurer, for a fee. Risk sharing occurs in equity markets where, presumably, the Arrow Principle of risk bearing applies: all participants bear risk according to their ability to do so. It is worth noting that whereas in case of insurance, the insurer is presumably fully informed of factors that affect the risk of the venture being undertaken and, hence, charges an appropriate fee, at times risk is shifted without the knowledge or consent of the ultimate risk bearer.

Such was the case of the massive bailout of financial institutions, where risks of their operations were shifted ultimately to the taxpayers without prior knowledge or consent. Consent of taxpayers was given ex post via parliaments or legislative bodies. The 2007–09 crisis demonstrated how risk transfer can quickly convert to risk shifting and then to ex post forced risk sharing. The case of Greece and the recent "settlement" through haircuts is a prime illustrative example of ex post mandatory risk sharing. It also demonstrates the limit of ex ante risk shifting through moral hazard associated with deposit guarantees.

Unlike risk-sharing finance, where parties to the transaction share (ex ante) in the risk of the project or asset being financed, and therefore have symmetry of incentives, interest-based debt financing involves a host of asymmetries. For shareholders of firms, there are several incentives to leverage (borrow). Leverage increases their return on equity (ROE); is cheaper than equity financing, especially given the tax shelter on interest; and leads to no dilution in ownership. Moreover, leveraged equity represents a call option on the firm.[5]

For the lender, on the other hand, there are also incentives to provide debt financing. The lender does not have share in the risk of the underlying asset/project. Though the lender does not share in the risk, he or she has a claim on the asset. The lender is "assured" of a fixed return, regardless of the asset's performance.

Given the apparent advantages to both the borrower and lender, debt transactions would appear to be a "win-win" for both parties. However, in a world with limited resources, true win-win transactions are rare. The reality is that for most win-win situations, there is typically a third party for whom it would be "lose-lose." In the case of excesses with debt, society at large ultimately takes the losses. In an environment of implicit or explicit guarantees and artificially low interest rates, the incentives for debt from both the demand and supply side will lead to a buildup in debt and inevitably veer the economy toward excessive leverage. This tendency toward debt build-up is self-evident. According to a 2012 estimate by the International Monetary Fund, the gross government debt of G-20 economies was expected to grow from 118 percent of their GDP to 122 percent in 2014. Reinhart and Rogoff (2010) estimate the total global outstanding amount of financial paper to be about US$200 trillion. Of this, 75 percent ($150 trillion) constitutes interest-bearing debt paper. With global GDP in 2011 estimated at about $65 trillion, the ratio of global debt to GDP would be an astounding 230 percent! Judging by these numbers, there is no doubting the inherent tendency of debt-based systems to veer toward excess (see Mirakhor 2011).

In a risk-sharing situation, on the other hand, there are self-correcting mechanisms that would ensure the avoidance of such excesses. For example, lenders will be less inclined to fund any project that comes by, simply because they now must share in the risk of the business. Similarly, shareholders would think twice about resorting to external financing because risk-sharing finance requires the sharing of future benefits with the financier. In other words, there is dilution in shareholders' claims to the profits. Given the high stakes involved with risk-sharing finance, it will be in the interest of both parties to be more careful with the investments they undertake. The resulting advantage to society is that risk-sharing finance raises the threshold of scrutiny, thereby avoiding bad/wasteful projects, which translates directly into improved resource allocation and economic efficiency. More importantly, the nature of risk-sharing finance in avoiding excessive leverage minimizes the vulnerability of economies to financial crises and the resulting boom-bust cycles. Development has a better chance of taking root when stability is prevalent.

Concept of Islamic Capital Markets

What would an Islamic capital market (ICM) look like? It would simply be a capital market that met the requisites of Shari'ah law. Both the instruments and trading processes would be in line with Shari'ah requirements for transactions. Some Shari'ah requirements are common to all properly functioning capital markets, including the avoidance of corruption such as bribes (*rishwah*), the prohibition on gambling (*maysir*), proscriptions against the use of poorly defined contracts (*gharar*), and insistence on the enforceability of contracts. What truly separates an ICM from others would be the reliance on risk-sharing contracts/transactions. Since no business has fixed returns, the avoidance of fixed returns, as in interest-based debt, is automatically avoided. As is evident from the description of requirements for an ICM that follows, many capital markets—excluding debt-based ones—and especially those of developed countries, would come close to fulfilling most of the requirements. The two elusive features are the use of risk-sharing contracts in lieu of debt and the avoidance of *riba* (interest). In fact, one could argue that risk-sharing and avoidance of *riba* are two sides of the same coin. One cannot coexist with the other. Risk sharing by definition excludes interest-based lending. Risk sharing is such a differentiating feature that a true ICM will have features vastly different from that of conventional capital markets. These features are examined in the remainder of this chapter. A quick overview of some of the key requisites follows.

Requisites for an Islamic Capital Market
Risk Sharing

The underlying principle or starting point for this requirement is probably verse 275 of *Surah Al-Baqarah*, which declares that while Allah (swt) has permitted *Al-Bay'*, he has prohibited *Al-Riba*. Broadly, *Al-Bay'* "is a contract covering all types of exchange except those prohibited by the Shari'ah" (Mirakhor and Hamid 2009, 265).

The Qur'an establishes all human relations firmly on the basis of contract (*áqd*). These include the entire spectrum of relations from marriage to economic/financial transactions to legitimacy of political authority. The most fundamental contract underlying human transactions is the contract of *Al-Bay'*. In all etymodogical studies of the terms used in the Qur'an, *Al-Bay'* is defined as "the exchange of property with property." Contemporary economic language would render this definition as "exchange of one bundle of property rights for another." In part of verse 275, those economic/financial transactions that are based on contract of exchange are considered legitimate. This means that permissible contracts are those that allow full transfer of property rights over the subjects of transactions.

The same part of the verse declares contracts of *Al-Riba* as nonpermissible. In contrast to contracts of exchange, *Al-Riba* contracts are those where property rights over the subject of contracts are not exchanged fully. Such is the case with interest-based debt contracts. In these contracts, the property rights over the amount loaned are not transferred to the debtor. While the creditor maintains full property rights for the amount loaned, the contract creates an instantaneous property right for the creditor for the property of the debtor to the amount of an ex ante determined interest payment tied to the amount loaned. Such contracts are not considered legitimate bases for economic/financial transactions.

The five words "commanding the good and forbidding evil" that constitute this part of verse 275 of chapter 2 of the Qur'an are so crucial that they could arguably be considered the organizing principle of the Islamic economic and financial system (Mirakhor and Hamid 2009, 271). The reason is rather clear. To base economic transactions on exchange means freedom of contract, freedom of production, and freedom of selecting one's partner to exchange. In turn, exchange promotes specialization, a concept which from the time of the classical economist has meant risk sharing, coordination, cooperation, and trust, all leading to efficiency in resource allocation. Exchange needs markets, and markets need rules governing participants' behavior. For an ICM, these rules are prescribed in the Qur'an and in the Tradition of the Prophet.

The essence of verse 275 has been inferred to mean that "by mandating *Al-Bay'*, Allah (swt) has ordained risk sharing in all exchange activities" (Abbas 2009, 265). *Riba*-based transactions, on the other hand, constitute risk transfer rather than risk sharing. In interest-based financing, the financier takes no part in the risks of the business for which the money is being borrowed. All risks are transferred to the borrower.

Balance and Equity (Fairness)

Riba-based transactions also violate the requirements for balance and fairness in transactions. In interest-based debt financing where the lender has claims on both the underlying asset of the transaction (collateral) and on his or her money, as well as on the debtor in an amount equal to the interest payment, there is neither balance nor equity.

Property Rights

The Islamic philosophy of property rights is based on the premise that as Creator, Allah (swt) is the ultimate owner of all property. Humans can claim ownership rights over property if it is acquired either through work (physical, or intellectual, or both) or through transfer (such as inheritance). Winnings from gambling, theft, corruption, and interest-based lending, which may result in instantaneous property rights claims, are not recognized and are prohibited.

Markets and Market Prices

The repeated emphasis on *Al-Bay'* exchange in the Qur'an and the abhorrence of earning through interest has meant an emphasis on markets, their proper functioning, and a reliance on market-derived prices. As a merchant and businessman, the Prophet (saw), in several sayings (*hadiths*), emphasizes the need for price determination through market trading. As part of the all-important rule of encouraging compliance with prescribed rules and discouragement of their violation (*al 'amr i bi al Ma'ruf wa anNahi 'anil Munkar*), the Prophet (saw) required that prices be determined by competition among market participants and that their practices be subject to oversight by market regulators/supervisors (*muhtasibs*), to ensure their accountability. This arrangement entails a clear placement of faith in the function of markets, but with appropriate regulatory/supervisory oversight.

Contracts and Trust

Trust is the very essence of Islam. The faithful, in submitting to the will of Allah, place all trust in the Creator. Contracts "enforce" trust, and Islam forcefully places all social-political and economic relations on the firm footing of *contractus*. In very unambiguous terms, the Qur'an requires all believers to "fulfill all contracts." The requirements to be trustworthy and to comply with contracts come directly from the emphasis on exchange (risk sharing) and on markets and market prices. Markets cannot function well unless one is free to contract and can enforce the trust inherent in exchange. Risk sharing requires parties to the transaction to be rule-compliant and also requires means to enforce compliance in the face of incentives to do otherwise. Trust, rule-compliance, and contracts go together. If parties to a transaction know that violation will be met with swift reprisals, behavior is checked. Thus, the emphasis in Islam is not only for individuals to be trustworthy, for contracts to be clear and transparent, and for rule-compliance, but also for the enforceability of contracts. The end result of these requirements would be the lowering of transaction costs, potential for widespread participation, and the smooth functioning of markets.

No Fixity of Returns

Emanating from the requirements to have exchange based on risk sharing and market-traded price discovery, and the prohibition of interest, the implication is that Shari'ah-compliant transactions should have no fixity in returns. More specifically, returns to a transaction should not be fixed and determined before the outcome of the investment is known. In other words, there should be no a priori determination of returns from an investment. In fact, it would be an oxymoron to have a risk-sharing contract with fixed predetermined returns to one party.

In addition to these six requirements, there are three other Shari'ah requisites for all transactions, ICM-based or not. These are the avoidance of corrupt practices such as bribery (*rishwah*); gambling or the taking of unnecessary/excessive risks (*maysir*); and ignorance (*jahl*), which refers to the presence of asymmetric information, and taking advantage of those less knowledgeable or ignorant. To see the virtues of these simple prohibitions, one need only examine the causes of the recent U.S. subprime crisis. It was a crisis that had its roots in debt and excessive risk taking: first, by investment banks in the funding of their assets and their lending to hedge funds; second, by companies like AIG, in originating credit default swaps; and finally, through the extensive use of teaser loans, adjustable rate mortgages (ARMs), and the like to take advantage of ordinary families looking to house themselves. The use of highly complicated structured products that had embedded options to fund these activities could be considered yet another extension of *jahl*. Viewed in the context of recent financial crises and their causal factors, it appears that the requirements of the Shari'ah, despite its origins of more than a thousand years ago, are as relevant today as at any time.

One would be tempted to ask if indeed there is an ICM anywhere in the world. The short answer is no: not because an ICM would be detached from reality, for there are other risk-sharing markets and well-functioning ones. These are the equity markets. The problem is that, today, equity markets are but a mere component of capital markets, heavily linked to debt markets. Thus, stock market bubbles can be created when debt is cheap and easily available. In other words, when debt coexists with risk sharing, excesses can and do happen. An ICM would be a market where risk sharing is the predominant type of contract, if not the only one.

Equity and *Sukuk* Markets in an Islamic Capital Market

Equity and debt markets are typically the two pillars of capital markets. This section examines the key features of an ICM-based equity and *sukuk* market.

The Equities Market in a Risk-Sharing Framework

Equities are essentially risk-sharing instruments. As such, their use and propagation would move closer to risk-sharing finance, the essence of ICMs. Though equity instruments like stocks are congruent with Shari'ah requirements, not all listed stocks would be eligible for Shari'ah compliance. A range of filter techniques have been developed to evaluate the compatibility of listed stocks with Shari'ah. Rather than revisit this issue of Shari'ah filters for equities, the discussion turns instead to two critical issues for equities in general, in a move toward risk-sharing finance. These are the implication on the firm's cost of capital and the resulting dynamics, and the implication for portfolio diversification, including cross-border diversification.

The Implication for Cost of Capital

The cost of capital for a firm is typically the weighted average of the component sources of capital within its capital structure. The two most common sources of capital are equity and debt. From the company's view point, debt is initially cheaper than equity. Debt becomes even cheaper when the tax shelter on interest expense is taken into account. However, debt, though cheaper, has a number of problems. First, the use of debt (leveraging) makes the firm riskier. Leverage increases the volatility of profit and cash flows. Thus, a leveraged firm is riskier than an unleveraged one, all other things being equal. Second, the use of debt, given the fixed nature of its claim, increases the probability of financial distress. Third, the use of debt reduces a firm's financial flexibility. Finally, again due to its fixed nature, the use of debt raises the firm's breakeven point, as the fixed charges arising from debt add to the firm's total fixed cost. In view of these disadvantages, one would have to ask whether cheaper really is better.

For shareholders, the use of debt, especially to meet new funding requirements, is advantageous for two reasons. First, there will be no dilution in ownership. Second, leveraging increases the ROE by way of increasing the value of the firm. Much of this increase in the value of the firm really comes from the present value of the tax shelter received by the firm from taking on debt. Thus, the increased return to shareholders when their firms take on debt comes from a government subsidy for borrowing and not from some inherent feature of debt. The cost of the debt (borrowing) may be cheaper than equity, but this is precisely because the lender is not sharing the underlying business risk. All business risks are borne by shareholders. So, if one thinks about it, the benefit from debt to a borrowing company really comes from tax arbitrage. Companies often borrow precisely to take advantage of this tax shelter. To put it another way, the government subsidizes borrowing. Why should there be such a subsidy? There is logic to subsidizing basic food staples; the poorer segments of society get to consume something they may otherwise not be able to afford. But subsidizing debt enables financiers to gain an "unfair" advantage without giving up anything in return for this subsidy. That governments continue to give this subsidy is testimony to the influence and patronage of the banking sector—something that the "Occupy Wall Street" and other "Occupy" movements seek to dislodge.

Without this subsidy and the attendant tax arbitrage benefit for corporations, the sole benefit of debt—that it is cheaper—may not be sufficient to overcome its many disadvantages. Absent tax benefits, the Modigliani-Miller (MM) world of capital structure irrelevance would prevail: that is, debt financing has minimal impact on firm value. Under the assumptions of the MM model (Modigliani and Miller 1958), firm value remains unchanged regardless of the debt-to-equity ratio.

In a risk-sharing framework without debt, a firm's cost of capital will converge to its cost of equity, which in turn will be reflective purely of its business risk. This brings about a number of benefits:

- Stock and equity values will be priced based on their business risk, uncluttered by compensation needed for the higher risk due to leverage.
- The incentive for companies and shareholders to leverage in order to increase expected earnings/returns will be eliminated.
- Tax arbitrage, which increases government revenue without necessarily causing a reduction in growth, will be eliminated.
- Corporate earnings and stock returns should become less volatile.
- On a macro level, the absence of debt reduces economic vulnerability and the potential for sudden stops in capital flows.

Company Cost of Capital in a Risk-Sharing Framework

Would a company's cost of capital be cheaper in a risk-sharing framework? Yes, in some cases, but not necessarily in most cases. This has to do with the fact that there would be counterveiling forces at work. To take the easy case first, companies with capital structures near their optimal level would likely experience a marginal increase in their cost of capital. The replacement of equity with debt causes this. In the case of companies with excessive leverage, with debt levels beyond optimal, the logic of Modigliani and Miller would imply that the cost of capital would be lower.

The countervailing forces affecting the cost of capital are as follows. A moderately leveraged firm could have a lower overall cost of capital, even though its cost of equity would be higher than a similar firm that is totally unleveraged. The higher cost of equity reflects the firm's higher risk due to leverage; however, the lower cost of debt reduces its overall weighted average of cost of capital. It is easy to see what the likely impact on the firms' overall cost of capital would be, if the economy moved to a pure risk-sharing arrangement. Two things would happen simultaneously: as debt was replaced with equity-like, risk-sharing finance, the weighted average cost of capital (WACC) would creep up. However, the cost of equity, which was high due to leverage, would begin to fall. The final WACC would converge to the unleveraged cost of equity, which would be a pure reflection of the underlying business or asset risk. In such a situation, equity stock values would reflect the underlying asset/business risk.

The Equities Market and its Impact on the Overall Economy

The creation of a deeper and wider equities market would have several positive effects on the overall economy.

Better Resource Allocation

With asset (stock) values reflective of their actual business risk, resource allocation ought to be better. Sectors that have relatively higher risk but lower returns would be avoided; thus resources would flow into assets/sectors that provide the best risk-return trade-offs. This is unlike conventional debt financing, where a high risk, low-return activity can be made profitable purely by adding several layers of leverage. Equity holders can earn a decent return from such an investment, mainly because the extensive use of debt makes the venture profitable. Absent the debt, the venture would be unprofitable. Much of hedge fund activity that seeks to "arbitrage" very minute mispricing would fall in this category. It is precisely the extensive use of leverage that makes their effort worthwhile. In a world with limited resources, there is a social cost to such diversion of resources. Resources that could have been gainfully employed to build real assets get diverted into speculative activity that provides gains to a very small group.

Reduced Vulnerability

Flowing from the above, another advantage of risk-sharing finance would follow: the advantage of avoiding the provision of one-way options for speculative play, or in the words of Paul Krugman (1998), avoiding the creation of "Pangloss value." When the ability to leverage multiple times goes hand in hand with implicit or explicit guarantees, speculative play becomes not only highly profitable but has minimal downside risk—thus the one-way option. When financial institutions that had literally speculated have to be bailed out with public funds, society loses not only the bailout money but also the loss arising from diversion of funds from real productive uses. Pangloss value can also result from capital budgeting in which discount factors are used that are lower than they should be. One common situation would be one in which the cost of capital used is lower than it should be because of heavy reliance on debt in capital structure. As noted, the use of debt can reduce overall cost of capital. As a result, projects that are marginal and which in normal circumstances would be rejected are accepted, leading to what Krugman calls "overinvestment." In industries where market share can be acquired only through new investment, the use of leverage to make marginal investment profitable is often justified in the name of competitive advantage. While there indeed may be a temporary improvement in competitiveness, over the long term the company and industry become vulnerable because they are being set up for a fall. With risk-based financing, such losses are minimized, largely because the incentive is being tempered. Without being able to leverage, most speculative plays become unattractive. Thus, risk-sharing reduces the moral hazard that leads to destructive risk-taking behavior.

Avoidance of Financialization
The next key advantage of risk-sharing finance to the overall economy is the avoidance of "financialization (see Mirakhor 2010), and by extension, the creation of asset bubbles. Financialization refers to the growth of pure financial instruments, totally detached from the real sector and having a life of their own. Other than the private gains of the few who design and trade these instruments, society benefits little if at all. Worse, such instruments typically divert funds into sectors of the economy that are most malleable to speculative play: usually commodities, real estate, stock, and the like. The result is the creation of asset bubbles, leading to overall economic vulnerability. The fact that in many developing countries asset bubbles can coexist with productive sectors that are starved for funds is the irony of financialization.

In a risk-sharing economy with little or no debt, the banking sector would have to readjust. Much of its key roles, such as intermediation, facilitating the remittance and payments systems, and even making intertemporal transfers, would remain the same. The kind of products and services they offer, however, would differ. In fact, their expertise in areas such as business evaluation and project assessment would become even more valuable in a risk-sharing framework. By offering more equity-like products on the deposit (liability) side, and participating in the risk of the assets they finance, banks would have to be much more vigilant in their evaluation of customer financing. This has the added advantage of automatically reducing the moral hazard arising from the implicit guarantee of banking deposits. In a risk-sharing framework, risks are not transferred to the banks, but like equity mutual funds, banks share the risk with their depositors. And, like equity mutual funds, banks would be evaluated for their performance in a risk-return framework. In such a world, banks' lending at Pangloss values would be a thing of the past.

Impact on Portfolios and Diversification

One of the key functions of capital markets is value preservation through risk management. Aside from the use of derivative instruments for risk management, diversification is one of the most basic means of risk management. An ICM based on risk-sharing finance should enable the same level of diversification as a conventional capital market. Since diversification is dependent on diversity and the correlation between stocks, there is no reason why portfolio diversification should be any less efficient in a risk-sharing system. As will be argued below, it is foreseeable that equity risks could be lower in risk-shared capital markets. In the case of diversification within a domestic market, it can be argued that the residual risk that remains even with full diversification, also known as systematic risk, ought to be lower in a risk-sharing context. In today's equity markets, where debt is seen as an attractive financing choice by shareholders and where businesses see leveraging as a competitive edge, a domestic portfolio, even a fully diversified one, will have high betas.[6] Portfolio betas that are higher than they should be reflect the inherent leverage. Since interest rates are an economy-wide variable and therefore systematic, their risk does not get diversified away like other idiosyncratic risks of a stock would, thus the higher portfolio beta.

It is easy to see the beneficial impact of risk sharing on the residual risk of fully diversified asset portfolios. For the same portfolios, beta will be lower in the absence of leverage. Since riskiness is lower, risk premiums and therefore required returns for stocks would also be lower. The reduced riskiness of stocks should also make it better suited for lower rungs of society to participate in equity markets. Currently, equity investment is unsuited to most ordinary folk given the volatility of equity markets. Yet to keep things in perspective, there is no reason why equity markets should be much more volatile than the underlying real sectors that they represent. If real sector returns are fairly stable, the volatility in stock returns is not attributable to changes in the real sector, but to external factors like leverage, investor psychology, herding, and the like. The need to understand and make sense of these externalities has not only led to the spawning of an entire industry of equity analysts and investment advisors, but has further distanced ordinary folk from stocks. In many ways, this is sophistication that is not necessary.

In the absence of leveraging, including share margin financing and short-sales, there is no a priori reason why an Islamic equities market should in any way be suboptimal. In the context of the Markowitz model[7] and modern portfolio theory (MPT), a short sale has no role in the formulation of an optimal portfolio. Share margin financing, on the other hand, like all leverage, increases returns but also risk. In fact, the capital market line[8] has no difference in slope, even if the cost of leveraging is the risk-free rate, implying that there is no net benefit to leveraging in a risk-return context.

The absence of short-sale and margin financing could dampen liquidity at times, but once again there is no reason why there should be a systematic reduction in liquidity over time. The potential negative impact of reduced liquidity, however, must be balanced against the positive benefit of reduced volatility and "forced" overshooting of markets and asset prices. In the absence of such overshooting, price discovery should be more attuned to changes in the real sector, and therefore more reflective of real values—not artificially induced changes to value.

Seen from the viewpoint of international portfolio diversification, a risk-sharing economy ought to be an attractive market for international investors. For a country to be attractive for diversification purposes, its equity market should have low correlation with the rest of the world, especially those of developed markets. A debt-based open economy would by definition have equity and financial markets closely linked with developed markets. The movement of "hot money" and speculative capital across borders to arbitrage interest differentials would ensure the close correlation. Even emerging equity markets are pulled into the orbit of developed equity markets by way of speculative capital that seeks to arbitrage individual country differences in interest rates. In this regard, a policy of moving away from debt to a risk-sharing framework has two benefits. First, it reduces the economy's susceptibility to speculative flows, thereby improving overall stability. Second, with equity asset returns anchored to real sector returns, the correlation in returns is reduced, thereby making the domestic economy attractive to foreign equity capital in search of diversification.

Keep in mind that even in a risk-sharing framework, attracting foreign equity capital is positive since the cost of capital can be lowered. Since such capital is also based on risk sharing, it does not increase risk the way that inflows of debt-based speculative capital would.

Sukuk *in a Risk-Sharing Framework*

Sukuk, which is plural for *sakk*, refers to an investment certificate. It could also mean a trustee certificate. *Sukuk* was used extensively by Muslim merchants in the Middle Ages as paper denoting financial obligations arising from commercial activities. Some have argued that the contemporary term "check" has its origins in the word *sakk*. In his famous treatise, the *al-Muwatta*, Imam Malik ibn Anas describes the use of *sakk* by the Ummayad government. *Sakk* was used as partial payment to soldiers and government servants. The *sakk*, which came to be known as "grain permits," entitled holders to receive a predetermined amount of commodities from the state treasury on the maturity date. Since the *sakk* represented a state obligation, they were often traded/exchanged among *sukuk* holders (see Haneef 2009). *Sukuk* have therefore been a tradable instrument in Muslim societies in times past.

Today, *sukuk* are used as instruments for raising external financing. Being a fundraising product, *sukuk* have often been referred to as "Islamic bonds" and subjected to comparison with conventional bonds. While the objective of a *sukuk* issuance may be the same as that of a bond—that is, to raise financing—there are many differences between the two instruments. To begin with, one must keep in mind that there is no such a thing as "debt" financing in Islamic finance. The only debt there is in Islam is *Qard-al-hassan*, which is a benevolent loan: that is, a non-interest loan that does not have a compulsory term of repayment (see chapters 1 and 6). Given this, while *sukuk* are intended to raise external financing just like bonds, their operational, legal, and regulatory frameworks are vastly different. Seen in the light of conventional debt and equity, a *sukuk* would constitute a hybrid instrument. That is, it has a definite maturity and is therefore terminal as is debt. However, the returns to *sukuk* holders are not fixed and predetermined, but are typically dependent on the profits/cash flow generated by the asset or investment financed using *sukuk* proceeds. In this sense, *sukuk* is very much like equity, in that returns come from profits, and the magnitude of return is dependent on the size of profits.

Sukuk are perhaps the most visible Islamic finance product today. Given the range and international diversity of *sukuk* issuers, it is obvious that *sukuk* have become an internationally accepted Islamic finance product. Malaysia, which is currently the world's largest originator of *sukuk*, has been the product's main supporter/champion. Global *sukuk* issuance has been very impressive within the Islamic financial industry but its size relative to conventional securitized markets is still negligible. From virtual nonexistence in 2000 (US$0.3 billion), total global issuance had grown to US$84.4 billion by 2011, at a cumulative average annual growth rate nearing 60 percent.

Despite the double-digit growth in global *sukuk* issuance, the true capabilities of the instrument have yet to be harnessed. Like options—which followed the evolution of forwards and futures but built upon them to provide a degree of flexibility not found with either forwards or futures—*sukuk*, given their hybrid nature, can have tremendous advantage over conventional debt or equity. Recall that there is a tradeoff for existing shareholders of a firm in deciding between to finance with debt or equity. Choosing debt to finance new funding requirements, whether by way of bank borrowing or bond issuance, increases financial leverage, increases the volatility of returns and earnings, and reduces financial flexibility. Issuing new equity, on the other hand, has the huge cost of diluting ownership. Now suppose that existing shareholders of a firm choose to fund new needs by way of risk-sharing *Sukuk al Mudharabah* (a term partnership) instead of conventional debt or equity. They get access to new funds *without* the disadvantages of *either* debt or equity.

As a risk-sharing instrument, the *sukuk* will provide returns based on profits/losses. The fact that there is no fixed additional claim on the company's cash flow—as would be created by the fixed interest on debt—implies that there will be no increase in the firm's breakeven point, nor will there be an increase in the firm's financial leverage. Since *sukuk* holders' returns are tied to company earnings, the implication is that financing by way of such a *sukuk* acts as an built-in stabilizer. The firm is a more stable entity after the *sukuk* has been issued. Of course, shareholders could have reached this same result by issuing new shares (equity) by way of a rights issue, instead of *sukuk*; however, there is a huge difference. By issuing new equity, they would have diluted their ownership of all assets of the firm, including existing (old) assets. This would be the case because new shares are on equal footing with existing shares in all cases. Additionally, as Hellman, Murdock, and Stiglitz (2000) have pointed out, there is adverse signaling effect when a firm issues additional equity (Mirakhor 2010). In the case of *sukuk* issuance, however, there is a major if subtle difference. Since *sukuk* is issued to finance the acquisition of new asset(s), *sukuk* holders have a right of claim on only the profits generated by the new asset(s). This is unlike new shareholders, who will have a claim on *all* of the firms' assets, including assets that existed before they were shareholders.

Since the risk/profit sharing feature of *sukuk* resembles equity financing, financing with *sukuk* does not reduce the firm's financial flexibility, as debt would. Further, the fact that there are no fixed claims on the firm resulting from the issuance of *sukuk* implies reduced volatility of cash flow and reduced risk premiums for both the firm's currently outstanding stocks and bonds. All else being equal, for the firm with a mixture of both equity and debt in its capital structure, funding new requirements with *sukuk* should reduce risk, and thus the required returns of both its current equity and bondholders. Existing equity holders (shareholders) and bond holders of the firm should see the market values of the instruments increase in value, given the reduced required returns. This happens because of the equity-like features within the *sukuk*. The company's equity holders and debt holders experience a gain in wealth simply because the new *sukuk* holders come in to share the risk of the new asset being acquired by the firm. Unlike the use of debt, which gives a firm's shareholders advantages that come at the expense of the rest of society (as described earlier), the gains experienced here are real and do not come at the expense of others. Thus, society is simply better off with the use of risk sharing.

Recently, there have been proposals to have *sukuk* that are based not on the performance of a single underlying asset but on such things as GDP growth, a price index of a nation's export commodities, and the like. Linking *sukuk* returns to GDP performance is not unlike the Shiller proposal for "*trills*" that have been made in the conventional space (Shiller 2012).[9] Though most *sukuk* issuance has been sovereign issues by governments, none have used these novel concepts. Yet it is easy to see how governments of low-income and less developed countries can use *sukuk* to raise development financing. For example, a less developed country with limited resources could use *sukuk* to finance needed development expenditure such as roads, railways, ports and other infrastructure within a Build-Operate-Transfer (BOT) framework. A needed highway project could be undertaken by issuing *sukuk*, whose returns during the period of construction would be a percentage tied to export earnings of the country and on completion would yield returns that are a percent of toll collected over say, the subsequent 20 years. If the period of construction is five years, then the overall maturity of the *sukuk* would be 25 years. Such a risk-sharing instrument, aside from avoiding any economic vulnerability to the issuer, would have the added advantage of removing the bottleneck of limited funds. Furthermore, the government would suffer no loss of ownership of the asset financed. Currency risk could also be shared by denominating returns in the main currency of the issuing country's export earnings. After the construction period, the return could be in the home currency of the issuer. It is obvious that the percent of profit due to the *sukuk* holders should depend on the stability of the home currency and other risks related to the *sukuk*. In other words, the percentage of profit attributable to *sukuk* holders should also reflect country risk premiums. Islam requires fairness in transactions, and unless the returns expected are justified given the risk, there may be insufficient take up of the *sukuk*. That returns be commensurate to risks is a requirement for all financial instruments and is not unique to *sukuk*.

Several other variants of the *sukuk* structure above are also possible. For example, the financing of projects that are highly capital-intensive and require extensive upfront investments, like power generation plants, intra-city mass rapid transit systems and the like, have always been problematic for developing countries. Given infantile and shallow domestic equity markets, such projects have typically been financed largely with debt, which usually is foreign sourced. Such borrowing has two inherent problems. First, the borrowing entity commits Eichengreen's "Original Sin."[10] Second, as a result of the long gestation period for these projects and the compounding nature of debt, the projects come on stream carrying a massive debt overload. Without government subsidies, the cost to consumers would be prohibitive. The usual result in such cases has been either perpetual subsidization from the government or nationalization, which then shifts the debt burden to the government. It is precisely projects of this nature that would be well suited for *sukuk*-based financing. For example, a mass rapid transit system that typically requires several years of construction but would provide stable cash flow for a long period subsequently could be financed with *sukuk* that pays nothing in the initial years but converts into profit-sharing instruments, for say the next 30 years; this could be a very attractive investment. The advantage is that such financing would place no strain on government budgets but would get development going. At the end of the 30 years, the government would own a very lucrative asset that it never paid for but only facilitated.

The risk-sharing framework obviously has much promise, especially for the development financing of lower-income/less developed countries. What is needed is often a change in mindsets and an ability to resist the temptation for familiarity.

The Reality of Capital Markets in the Muslim World

The underdevelopment of most capital markets of the Muslim world is apparent to even the casual observer. With the exception of a few countries, the majority can be said to be in various stages of financial repression. These are markets replete with controls and regulations—in many cases, a carryover from earlier days of socialism or socialist inclinations. As a direct result of the neglect and the complacent attitude toward needed capital market development, the financial sector in these countries is highly bank-centric. Even banks, which are highly protected and subject to credit controls, are noncompetitive. The equity markets, on the other hand, are closed, disjointed, and small, with only a few listed firms. The lack of good governance and poor means of enforcement have meant low investor participation and therefore highly illiquid and volatile equity markets. To cap it all, there is probably no Muslim country with freely floating exchange rates. The vast majority have pegged exchange rates, implying a lack of flexibility in domestic monetary policy. For many countries in the Middle East and North Africa, exchange rates are clearly overvalued.

The state of neglect and the financially repressive policies have meant not only infantile capital markets but a stunted and highly uncompetitive real sector. With the exception of companies involved in the exploitation of naturally endowed resources, the Muslim *Ummah*, despite being close to a quarter of the world's population, has not produced a single globally competitive business entity. Going by the arguments of macroeconomic theory and capital market equilibrium, this should not be surprising. Well-developed capital markets can enhance the private rate of saving, increase the social marginal productivity of capital, and increase the proportion of savings funneled to investment (Pagano 1993). When the financial sector fails, the real sector is inevitably held back. As Brandl (2011) shows, it is possible for businesses within an economy to experience difficulty in borrowing, even when there are savings, if capital markets are unable to intermediate between surplus and deficit units. He further argues that just as a lack of attention to education can entrench one within the poverty trap, neglect of capital markets can mean the same for economies. A recent report that examined 130 countries in terms of property and legal rights found that in Tunisia, "92 percent of the population holds its real estate extralegally—without formal property rights—while 99 percent of entrepreneurs operate outside the law." In the case of the Arab Republic of Egypt, the study found that "it takes up to 10 years to get authorization to build on a vacant plot of desert and one and a half years to incorporate a bakery. The result is an astonishing amount of dead capital languishing in the region's informal economies" (see Luxembourg for Finance 2012). Conditions in other Muslim countries, by and large, are not much better. Muslim countries, on the whole, have clearly ignored the injunctions of the Shari'ah concerning the sanctity of property rights. There cannot be a better way to stultify development and entrap a society in poverty. In such environments, markets simply ossify and cease to function effectively.

The irony of disintermediation of capital markets at the domestic level is played out at the international level in three different ways. First, in the case of low-income Muslim countries, where savings that are unable to be funneled into investments typically leak out through capital flight. For the better-off Muslim countries, the savings, given the insufficient demand domestically, leave as capital outflow in search of investments—typically to financial centers in the West. The third irony is that the growing economies within the Muslim world are unable to tap the savings of the better-off countries directly, but only through capital markets of the West. The fact that intermediation of Muslim funds must happen through Western capital markets and the lack of a single truly global financial center anywhere in the Muslim world is testimony to how far behind the Muslim world is with regard to capital market development. The fault for this lies not in a lack of infrastructure or technology; the financial institutions in the likes of Dubai, Bahrain, or Kuala Lumpur can match the infrastructure of any in the West. The problem is the absence of other requisites, such as good governance, property rights, rule of law, sanctity of contracts and their enforcement, and the building of trust—all of which are requirements of the Shari'ah, too.

Concluding Remarks: Implementing the Risk-Sharing Framework

A key advantage of the risk-sharing framework is that it works through and within market forces and not against them. As described in the section on the requisites for an ICM, any efforts at improving the function of markets would be positive for risk sharing. Thus, implementing an ICM or a risk-sharing framework would require nothing extraordinary. Strengthening the rule of law, minimizing corruption, enhancing property rights, and the like, would improve existing markets while also enabling increased risk sharing. The easiest and least resistant means to increasing risk sharing within an economy would be by expanding equity markets by deliberately reducing reliance on debt markets. Creating a level playing field for debt and equity by eliminating the tax shelter on interest rates would be a good beginning. Educating the public on the need to share rather than transfer risks would be necessary. Pointing out that relying on real rates would be both more stable and lucrative compared to debt-based time deposits would also be necessary. Removing the blanket deposit insurance currently being offered to all deposits should be considered.

Banks and banking themselves would have to change. Banks would have to be more like mutual funds or funds of funds. Assets and liabilities are inherently mismatched in many ways in conventional banking, and a mismatch in risk has been a key contributor to banking crises. The funding a bank provides (its asset side) is uncertain, but the deposits (liability side) with which it funds these loans are required to be guaranteed. In a risk-sharing context, depositors would have to share in the risk. Their returns would be linked directly to net returns from the asset side, in the manner of mutual funds. In effect, matching savers with borrowers is true intermediation. Depositors with no risk appetite—the proverbial widows and orphans—would have to be provided safe (*wadi`ah*) deposit accounts that provide safekeeping and conveniences of banking, but provide no returns. Like Kotlikoff's (2010) limited purpose banks, banks in a risk-sharing ICM would be limited to intermediation.

Building a trusting society would perhaps be the most challenging and time-consuming. Yet headway could be made with rule of law, strict enforcement, policy consistency with well-announced policies, and a willingness to stay the course without falling for political expediency. For risk-sharing systems to work, it is critical that investors be made to bear only the risks of the underlying asset/business. They should not also bear other risks, like political and regulatory risks.

A failure to keep such risks in check would lead to an inevitable relapse to debt-based financing. One could make the case that fixed rate debt financing is popular not because investors want to avoid business risk but because of all the nonbusiness risks that come attached. Most if not all Muslim states are notorious for their ambiguities. Once again, rule of law and sanctity of property rights and contracts, as well as their enforcement, would have to be paramount for a risk-sharing system to work.

Risk sharing does have its downside. Being equity based, the agency problems of equity could be prevalent. Thus, the controls used by equity holders, especially venture capitalists, to manage these issues would have to be considered. In this regard some of the Shari'ah-based contracts at the heart of risk sharing—contracts like *mudarabah* and *musharakah*—may have to be modified to be applicable to contemporary settings. As some scholars have pointed out, there is nothing sacrosanct about these contracts that they cannot be modified. The kind of modifications needed for these contracts are of a control nature to check for moral hazards and agency-related problems. Controls are needed at least until a time when trust makes these controls redundant.

A number of countries, most notably Malaysia and Bahrain, have attempted to build ICMs. Malaysia has a functioning ICM with all the components of a capital market operating in a Shari'ah-compliant way. Thus, there is an Islamic Interbank Money Market for Islamic Bank and other institutions to manage their liquidity. There is an Islamic equities market with Shari'ah-screened stocks, a thriving mutual fund industry, and listed real estate investment trusts (REITs) and exchange-traded funds (ETFs). There is also the very active market in *sukuk*s. While providing for the Muslim populace with Shari'ah-compliant alternatives and despite impressive growth rates, the overall emphasis appears to be on short-term, low-risk, and highly liquid instruments. The longer tenured *sukuk*s are highly illiquid, with nearly absent secondary markets. The *sukuk*s also are not all necessarily risk-sharing, but mostly mimic conventional bonds. Unless there is deliberate attempt to change this, path-dependency would mean more of the same. A large part of this may have to do with the fact that although governments, such as those of Malaysia, are determined to develop their ICM, policy making at the macroeconomic level remains conventional—especially monetary policy. Thus, interest rate targeting and the use of debt-based instruments to execute monetary policy continue. For a nation aspiring to a full-blown ICM, this is a paradox that needs to be looked into. One cannot continue with monetary policy that is designed for a debt-based system to grow a risk-sharing ICM.

Traditional debt-based financing has proven repeatedly to be unstable. Regulation, no matter how fine-tuned, will be meaningless because debt is inherently destabilizing. One cannot expect different results from continued use of debt. Risk-sharing financing, which is the basis of ICMs, promises inherent stability. Since risk is being shared and spread, the logic of this stability is clear. What needs to be done is to give risk sharing a chance. Now may be a good time to begin.

Notes

1. See Brandl (2011).
2. See King and Levine (1993).
3. In the light of such strong evidence, perhaps the answer to the malaise plaguing economic growth of Muslim countries is self-evident.
4. It took Indonesia 25 years to reduce poverty by 50 percent before the 1997/98 Asian Crisis, and it lost almost that entire gain during and after the crisis.
5. The risk profile of levered equity resembles that of a long call position. Like the payoff of a long call, the downside is limited, but the upside potential is unlimited. It also means that for the borrower, it will make sense to repay the loan only if it is in-the-money (successful).
6. Beta is a measure of the degree to which the price of a stock or portfolio is correlated to a benchmark, such as the overall financial market (measured by an index like the S&P 500 for U.S. stocks.) The stronger the correlation, the larger the beta. The beta of the portfolio is simply the weighted average beta of assets within the portfolio.
7. In 1952, Harry M. Markowitz proposed a portfolio construction model based on mean-variance analysis.
8. The Capital Market Line (CML) is a line that plots the increase in return an investor can expect to get in return for taking an additional risk. The CML with the highest slope would reflect the Markowitz efficient portfolio. The slope of the CML determines the equilibrium market price of risk.
9. Shiller, along with economist Mark Kamstara, has proposed that countries replace much of their existing national debt with shares of the "earnings" of their economies. The shares, or "trills," would pay a quarterly dividend equal to exactly one-trillionth of a country's quarterly gross domestic product.
10. Eichengreen and Hausmann (1999). The original sin refers to the fact that most governments/companies are unable to borrow abroad in their domestic currency; as a result, foreign borrowing always results in currency mismatch. This mismatch brings in a new dimension of risk-currency risk.

References

Bagehot, W. 1873. *Lombard Street: A Description of the Money Market.* London: Henry S. King and Co.

Beck, T., A. Demirgüç-Kunt, and R. Levine. 2007. "Finance, Inequality and the Poor." *Journal of Economic Growth* 12: 27–49.

Bekaert, G., and C. R. Harvey. 1997. "Capital Markets: An Engine for Economic Growth." National Bureau of Economic Research, Cambridge, MA. Unpublished.

Brandl, M. W. 2011. "The Role of Financial Institutions in Long-Run Economic Growth." McCombs School of Business, The University of Texas at Austin. Unpublished.

Eichengreen, B., and R. Hausmann. 1999. "Exchange Rates and Financial Fragility." *Proceedings*, Federal Reserve Bank of Kansas City, 329–68.

Goldsmith, R. 1969. *Financial Structure and Development.* New Haven, CT: Yale University Press.

Haneef, R. 2009. "From Asset-Backed to Asset-Light Structures: The Intricate History of Sukuk." *ISRA International Journal of Islamic Finance* 1 (1): 103–26.

Hellman T. F., K. C. Murdock, and J. E. Stiglitz. 2000. "Liberalization, Moral Hazard in Banking and Prudential Regulation: Are Capital Requirements Enough?" *American Economic Review* 90: 147–65.

IMF (International Monetary Fund). 2012. *Fiscal Monitor. Taking Stock: A Progress Report on Fiscal Adjustment* (October). Washington, DC: International Monetary Fund.

King, R. G., and R. Levine 1993. "Finance and Growth: Schumpeter Might Be Right." *The Quarterly Journal of Economics* 108 (3): 717–37.

Kotlikoff, L. J. 2010. "Limited Purpose Banking." In *Jimmy Stewart Is Dead. Ending the World's Ongoing Financial Plague with Limited Purpose Banking*, 123–51. Hoboken, NJ: John Wiley & Sons.

Krugman, P. 1998. "What Happened to Asia?" http://web.mit.edu/krugman/www/DISINTER.html.

Lucas, R. 1988. "On the Mechanics of Economic Development." *Journal of Monetary Economics* 22 (February): 3–42.

Luxembourg for Finance. 2012. "Freedom and Property Rights Are Inseparable." http://www.luxembourgforfinance.lu/news/freedom-and-property-rights-are-inseparable.

McKinnon, R. 1973. *Money & Capital in Economic Development*. Washington, DC: Brookings Institution Press.

Mirakhor, A. 2010. "Whither Islamic Finance? Risk Sharing in an Age of Crises." Paper presented at the Inaugural Securities Commission Malaysia (SC)–Oxford Centre for Islamic Studies (OCIS) Roundtable, "Developing a Scientific Methodology on *Shariah* Governance for Positioning Islamic Finance Globally," March 15.

———. 2011"Risk Sharing and Public Policy." The 5th International Islamic Capital Market Forum, Securities Commission of Malaysia.

Mirakhor, A., and I. S. Hamid. 2009. *Islam and Development: The Institutional Framework*. New York: Global Scholarly Publications.

Modigliani, F., and M. Miller. 1958. "The Cost of Capital, Corporation Finance and the Theory of Investment." *American Economic Review* 48 (3): 261–97.

Pagano, M. 1993. "Financial Markets and Growth: An Overview." *European Economic Review* 37: 613–22.

Reinhart, C., and K. Rogoff. 2010. "Growth in a Time of Debt." NBER Working Paper 15639, National Bureau of Economic Research, Cambridge, MA.

Robinson, J. 1952. *The Rate of Interest, and Other Essays*. London: MacMillan.

Schumpeter, J. (1911) 1982. *The Theory of Economic Development: An Inquiry into Profits, Capital, Credit, Interest, and the Business Cycle*. Reprint, Transaction Publishers.

Shiller, R. 2012. "Tackling the World Economy: Give People Shares of GDP." *Harvard Business Review* January–February.

CHAPTER 10

Islamic Stock Markets in a Global Context

Andrew Sheng and Ajit Singh

Introduction

This study is a sequel to the 2012 Sheng and Singh article that identified and explained the significance of the two central tenets of Islamic finance: namely, its underpinning by a strong ethical system, and the absolute prohibition of the use of interest rates. That study also argued that the cooperation between the conventional Western system and the Islamic system is eminently sensible and will lead to a Pareto optimal increase in world welfare.[1]

Our earlier study noted that Islamic finance has been growing at a fast rate over the last two decades, and concluded that it is a complete system that has the potential to satisfy the financing and banking needs not only of Muslims worldwide but also of non-Muslims in various countries. It offers the world an additional financial system favoring profits derived from capital and labor working together, rather than interest, and with a rather different ethical basis than that of current Western capitalism.[2]

This study looks at a much narrower but current issue of establishing and operating Islamic stock markets within a global context. Islamic stock markets would compete against non-Islamic markets. If Islamic stock markets were successful, they would strengthen and enhance the international appeal and practice of Islamic finance. Leading Islamic scholars have long argued in favor of Islamic stock markets, even though they recognize that many practices in conventional stock markets may be incompatible with Islamic teaching. In 1984, Professor Mokhtar Metwally observed:

> In an Islamic economy where interest-bearing loans are prohibited and where direct participation in business enterprise, with its attendant risks and profit sharing, is encouraged, the existence of a well-functioning Stock Exchange is very important.

The authors are, respectively, President of the Fung Global Institute, and Emeritus Professor of Economics at the University of Cambridge. They are grateful to the Perdana Foundation for funding this research, but all opinions and errors and omissions are their own.

It would allow for the mobilization of savings for investment and provide means for liquidity to individual shareholders. However, existing Stock Exchanges in non-Islamic economies have many drawbacks. They generate practices such as speculation and fluctuations in share prices which are not related to the economic performance of enterprises. These practices are inconsistent with the teachings of Islam. (Metwally 1984, 19)

In 2011, one of the foremost scholars of Islamic economics and finance, Professor Abbas Mirakhor, argued in the Islamic Finance Forum for government intervention to develop truly vibrant and active Islamic stock markets. He noted that risk sharing is central to Islamic finance and observed that "arguably, the stock market is the first-best instrument of risk-sharing. Developing an active and efficient stock market can promote international as well as domestic risk sharing which render the economy and its financial system resilient to shocks" (Mirakhor 2011, 23).

Coincidentally, Islamic scholars' positive interest in Islamic stock markets arose at the same time as a vigorous debate in economics on the non-Islamic stock market's negative consequences. The role of the stock market in propagating if not generating important dimensions of the current international financial crisis, has been a subject of many serious commentaries. As this study intends to draw suggestions for an Islamic stock market from the experience and analysis of the stock market in non-Islamic countries, we intend to explore what are the weaknesses of the current stock market model.

Most analysts agree that one of the significant causes of the 2007–09 Great Recession was the U.S. housing bubble.[3] The ending of this bubble led to a fall in share prices not only in the United States but also around the world due to the close integration of world stock markets that had occurred in the previous two decades. Olivier Blanchard (2009) estimates bank losses due to the failure of the subprime mortgage market to be around $250 billion. However, the consequent financial crisis led to "contagion" and a sharp fall in aggregate world stock market capitalization of the order of $26 trillion—nearly 100 times larger than the losses associated with subprime mortgages. Similarly, Robert Solow (2009) notes that the combined result of the housing and stock market shocks was a decline in U.S. household wealth from $64.4 trillion in mid-2007 (before the crisis) to $51.5 trillion at the end of 2008. Thus $13 trillion of household wealth disappeared in the space of about one year. Solow (2009) notes: "Nothing concrete had changed. Buildings still stood, factories were still capable of functioning; people had not lost their ability to work or their skills or their technology. But a population that thought in 2007 that they had 64.4 trillion dollars with which to plan their lives discovered in 2008 that they have lost 20 percent of that."

Thus one important aspect of a stock market regime is that globalization may make an economy unstable through contagion, even though there is no intrinsic reason for the country to be subject to fluctuations. Such external shocks often end up with a procyclical feedback loop between two volatile financial markets: namely, the stock market and the market for foreign exchange.

These macroeconomic effects of the stock market are usually neglected in the economic literature and policy analysis. This is mainly because the corporate finance economists who specialize in this area tend to work with microeconomic models. This study attempts to address this lacunae.

In 2011, the British government invited a committee under London School of Economics professor John Kay to review the U.K. equity market and its impact on long-term decision making (Kay 2012). Its report, published in July 2012, identified two important principles that turn out to be relevant to the establishment of stock markets in Islamic countries:

1. All participants in the equity investment chain should act according to the principles of stewardship, based on respect for those whose funds are invested or managed, and trust in those by whom the funds are invested or managed.
2. Relationships based on trust and respect are everywhere more effective in promoting high performance of companies and securing good returns to savers taken as a whole than trading transactions between anonymous agents.

These notions of stewardship, trust, and respect are clearly more closely aligned with the Islamic precepts and beliefs of the participants. There is a strong pressure toward the promotion of these more ethical values in Islamic culture.

The discussion that follows examines the problems of primary and secondary aspects of the non-Islamic stock markets and other critiques of corporate governance, and explores how Islamic stock markets should avoid these defects. We do this because the stock market is not only an important symbol of capitalism, but also has a wider role in the economy to promote investment and create employment. The case for and against the stock market inevitably involves a discussion of important related subjects of corporate finance, corporate governance, and corporate law. The relationship between the legal system and the stock market, and the relationship between corporate finance and the stock market, are salient to any assessment of the role of the stock market in economic development. This study presents a nuanced and balanced view of the feasibility and desirability of Islamic stock markets. It suggests that Islamic stock markets can compete effectively against non-Islamic stock markets by improving on corporate controls and serving the real sector by helping small and medium enterprises (SMEs) raise capital. This requires the creation of a class of intermediaries that nurture the SMEs before they access capital markets.

Specifically, this study reflects on the following questions:

- Do stock market economies grow faster than economies where stock markets are relatively little used?
- Stock markets have an ability to finance technological developments and therefore have an important role in principle in supporting new technology. Are stock market economies more conducive to technical change and economic development than non-stock market economies?

- To be compatible with Shari'ah law, an Islamic stock market will need to eliminate short-termism, speculation, and strategic pricing by stock market participants among other practices. What kind of regulation, formal or informal, will be required to achieve this?
- How well does the stock market perform its essential task of pooling society's savings dispersed among individual savers, to channel these savings selectively to companies with the best investment prospects?
- How does the stock market ensure the efficient use of assets that embody past savings?
- What are the implications of the stock market development for corporate governance?
- What are the implications of the mode of financing of corporate growth for stock markets in emerging countries?

The discussion will review the evidence on some of the more important above issues from the data on non-Islamic stock markets and examine the implications of this analysis for the potential development in Islamic stock markets.

Do Stock Markets Help Economic Development?

The mainstream free market ideology that permeated financial market theory and development economics thinking recommended almost without reservation the establishment of stock markets in emerging markets as a positive factor for growth. In the 1990s, the International Finance Corporation (IFC) helped establish stock markets in many emerging markets and led the wave of portfolio investment in emerging stocks as an asset class.

Their argument for stock markets is two-fold. First, the World Bank concluded that the bank-dominated financial systems of developing countries in the 1980s were failing. The debt-based system, together with policy-based allocation of government funds, particularly to big domestic corporations to promote industrialization, was unsatisfactory because of excessive leverage, crony capitalism, and inefficient and inflationary finance.

The second argument was what may be called natural progression. The basic idea is that stock market development is a part of a natural progression of countries toward higher stages of development. As countries become richer, they also expand and modernize their capital markets, with the stock markets as the foundation of deep derivative markets. Stock market development became an emblem of economic development, just as airports were emblems in the 1960s.

These views were supported by advanced market fund managers and some emerging market intellectuals. The former wanted a wider range of assets to diversify their risks, with opportunities to improve their risk-return frontier. The latter group argued that long-term capital for developing countries should come from the huge accumulated savings of Western investment institutions, such as pension funds and insurance companies. This would reduce emerging market debt overhang. Stock markets would also enable government assets to be privatized and foreign exchange to be obtained. Emerging market companies would be able to raise capital to expand overseas.

The proponents of the conventional stock market model suggest that deep and liquid stock markets improve four key functions of capital markets: resource allocation, price discovery, risk management, and corporate governance. Enhancing deep and liquid capital markets in emerging markets not only enable long-term direct and portfolio investments to be channeled from developed markets, but long-term capital to be raised, which in turn can create jobs and growth. Furthermore, price discovery is improved as stock markets "signal" the attractiveness of "undiscovered" emerging market firms. With the arrival of advanced market investors and intermediaries, risk management and corporate governance are improved.

There is no question that primary and secondary stock markets enable emerging market entrepreneurs to raise capital and "double leverage" their assets, since they can not only raise capital in primary issues, but also use their (now) liquid holdings as collateral to raise more capital in the secondary market or through the banking system.

While there has been substantial financial deepening in many emerging markets, the volatility of such markets, with booms and busts and sharp fluctuations in capital flows, has resulted in a more nuanced reexamination of the cost and benefits of stock markets for economic development. The following sections examine these more systematically in order to see what lessons can be drawn for Islamic stock markets.

First, the series of stock market debacles since the Asian financial crisis, tech stock bubble, the Gulf stock market crash, and the Great Recession all suggest that short-termism, excessive market volatility, lack of corporate control, social inequities, and weak risk management are endemic in the existing structure.

Second, the case against speculative stock markets was powerfully argued in the depths of the Great Depression by John Maynard Keynes in his *General Theory*:

> Speculators may do no harm as bubbles on a steady stream of enterprises. But the position is serious when enterprise becomes the bubble on a whirlpool of speculation. When the capital development of a country becomes a by-product of the activities of a casino, the job is likely to be ill-done. The measure of success attained by Wall Street, regarded as an institution of which social purpose is to direct new investment into the most profitable channels in terms of future yield, cannot be claimed as one of the outstanding triumphs of laissez-faire capitalism. (Keynes 1936, 159)

Third, these critiques of the stock market were given fresh impetus by a report of a Blue Ribbon Committee of 25 leading U.S. finance specialists established in the 1990s. The Committee was chaired by Harvard professor Michael Porter, and its purpose was to investigate to what extent the American financial system and the stock market in particular were responsible for the poor overall American economic performance, particularly during the period 1980–95, when the U.S.

economy was stagnant; the trend rate of growth of U.S. productivity was virtually zero during this period. The Committee concluded:

> The change in nature of competition and the increasing pressure of globalization make investment the most critical determinant of competitive advantage. Yet the U.S. system of allocating investment capital both within and across companies is failing. This puts America at a serious disadvantage in global competition and ultimately threatens the long term growth of the U.S. economy. (Porter 1992, 4)

Fourth, the Kay Review (2012, 9) uncovered serious deficiencies in the current model: "Short-termism is a problem in the U.K. equity markets, and [the] principal causes are the decline of trust and the misalignment of incentives throughout the equity investment chain." Indeed, the Kay Review found that U.K. companies have not been investing as much as their foreign competitors and that smaller companies are finding difficulty in accessing capital. Furthermore, successful companies are beginning to privatize themselves because of the regulatory burdens, while investors are complaining that the long-term returns on investing in listed companies have been disappointing.

Lessons for Islamic Stock Markets

Given these contrasting perspectives, what are the appropriate lessons to be drawn for the construction of Islamic stock markets? A good place to begin is with regard to the question of financing of corporate growth and to ask what role the stock market plays in this task.

The textbook function of the stock market is to help increase savings by providing an additional investment instrument, (namely, share purchase). It enables individuals to buy a fraction of a steel plant or a shipyard, thus spreading the risks across the board. This also helps investment, as without such fractional buying and risk sharing, big projects may not have been undertaken at all.

However, the experience of non-Islamic countries in the real world does not quite square with this textbook account. In leading industrial countries such as the United Kingdom and Germany, most large firms listed on the stock markets in these countries do not raise new equity capital at all. Instead, they rely on their retained profits for financing almost all of their investment needs. The few, usually small, companies that do go to the stock markets do not use the new capital for investment purposes. Rather, they employ it as a means of acquiring liquidity in the early stages of their development. The Kay Review concludes that the main role of equity markets is not to monitor allocation of capital between companies, but instead to oversee its allocation within companies. The Review goes on to suggest that "promoting good governance and stewardship is....the central rather than an incidental function of the U.K. equity markets" (10). Similarly, there are relatively few initial public offerings (IPOs) in continental European countries such as Germany and Italy. This suggests that the role of public equity markets in these countries is also likely to be small (Pagano, Panetta, and Zingales 1998).

What has happened in advanced markets like the United Kingdom is that companies now raise more capital through private equity and debt, which leads to a closer relationship between providers and users of capital. Such a relationship is much more difficult for listed companies due to the fragmentation of share ownership, extensive restrictions on information that listed companies are allowed to share, and operational difficulty of "managing good earnings" without huge listed share price shocks.

The experience of the U.S. stock market is quite different from that of the United Kingdom or European countries. There are many more IPOs and more listed companies and a greater resort to the stock markets by small companies. More importantly, the U.S. stock markets act as an "exit mechanism" for the public flotation of companies in the hi-tech sectors, and for private equity and venture capital that play important roles as incubators of dynamic entrepreneurs and innovators.

In the case of fast-growing developing countries in Asia, the behavior of the stock market in mobilizing savings and financing corporate growth is also different from the U.S. or the European experience. First, these countries enjoyed an enormous expansion of savings over the last 30 years, with savings as a proportion of national gross domestic product (GDP) growing from about 5 percent of GDP at the beginning of the period to 30 percent or more now. In this huge increase in national savings, the stock market has played a relatively small role.

Second, as studies by Glen and Singh (2003, 2005) and Singh (1993) have suggested, large firms in developing countries raise a much larger proportion of their capital from the stock markets than large firms in advanced countries. This so-called Singh-paradox is counterintuitive and defies most explanations offered for it. The closest reasonable interpretation is that the growth rate of a developing country's firms is greater than that of an advanced country's corporations, leading to a greater demand for funds by the former. But this explanation does not answer the question of why this "greater demand" should be met by equity issues rather than other sources. Indeed, the question of fairness in access to capital markets arises: why should large state-owned enterprises (SOEs) and large multinational and local firms have greater access to financing than the SMEs?

According to both traditional economic theory and its further development in the seminal paper by Myers and Majluf (1984), the financing of corporate growth should follow the pecking order outlined below: firms should in the first instance rely as far as possible on retained earnings for their investment needs; if that is not adequate, they should resort to debt; and only as a last resort should they raise any funds from the stock market. Myers and Majluf show that this is mainly due to asymmetrical information between managers and outsiders. Glen and Singh (2005) confirm the earlier Singh (1995) and Singh and Hamid (1993) results for the 1980s. Their new results for the 1990s suggest that the pecking order theory is comprehensively rejected by the data for this decade. As shown in table 10.1, on the financing of corporate growth in 19 developing and 22 advanced countries from 1995 to 2000, developing countries during this period financed 39 percent of their growth from equity issues, 27 percent from retained

Table 10.1 Financing of Corporate Growth in 19 Developing Economies and 22 Advanced Economies, 1995–2000
Percent

Developed markets	Liabilities	External finance	Internal finance	Emerging markets	Liabilities	External finance	Internal finance
Australia	58	32	11	Argentina	46	16	38
Austria	52	3	45	Brazil	74	11	15
Belgium	56	6	38	Chile	44	33	23
Bermuda	41	23	36	Colombia	73	16	11
Canada	56	32	12	Czech Rep.	33	21	46
Cayman Islands	90	8	2	Hong Kong SAR, China	44	20	35
Denmark	72	6	23	Hungary	28	1	71
Finland	53	26	22	India	53	5	43
France	61	7	31	Indonesia	110	12	−23
Germany	62	5	33	Israel	54	6	40
Greece	52	34	14	Korea, Rep.	27	48	25
Ireland	76	5	18	Malaysia	40	18	42
Italy	68	5	27	Mexico	61	30	10
Japan	62	6	32	Philippines	34	17	49
Netherlands	65	9	26	South Africa	49	10	41
Norway	50	23	27	Taiwan, China	59	40	1
Singapore	66	15	19	Thailand	74	11	15
Spain	68	−9	40	Turkey	61	18	21
Sweden	57	4	39	Venezuela, RB	27	54	19
Switzerland	54	7	39				
United Kingdom	52	21	27				
United States	47	21	32				
Group average	53	17	30	Group average	35	39	27
Global average	49	22	29				

Source: Glen and Singh 2005.
Note: The basic accounting identity in this table is as follows: Total finance for corporate growth consists of the growth of liabilities, growth of equity capital, and the growth of internal finance.

earnings, and 35 percent from debt, on average. In contrast, for advanced countries, the corresponding figures were 17, 30, and 53 percent, on average. This clearly indicates a much greater resort to equity issues by large firms in developing countries, compared to those of advanced countries.

It is not the purpose of this study to explain this phenomenon, as this has been done elsewhere,[4] but rather to ask what lessons those who wish to establish an Islamic stock market should learn from the above experience of stock market financing in advanced and developing countries.

It should be noted that in advanced as well as developing countries, the significance of public stock markets has declined while that of private equity has greatly increased. The question therefore is whether a strong Islamic stock market should attempt to create a thriving public market with perhaps a small role for private equity markets, or sequence development the other way around: develop SMEs first and then the stock market as an exit mechanism.

An important question raised by the above discussion is why more companies do not list on the equity markets What measures should a future Islamic equity market take to expand its role to meet the financing needs of households and corporations?

Several reasons have been put forward to explain this deficit of firms to list on the stock market: fiscal discrimination against equity in favor of debt; the greater burden and expenses of listing on the public stock market than before; and the poor performance of the public equity markets.

The Kay Review suggests a more fundamental and deeper reason lies in the nature of financial intermediation itself, since it regards equity markets as a means of financial intermediation between savers and corporations. The latter enables savers to achieve diversification and liquidity. A successful intermediary enables savers to derive the benefits of diversification and liquidity by minimizing the disadvantages of control loss and information loss as the firms become bigger. The Review suggests that information asymmetry and principal-agent conflicts become more serious as the modern corporate economy evolves. The relationship between the investors and the corporations in large, impersonal, public equity markets is more distant and much less close (due to regulatory and information provision restrictions) than that between the management of a private equity-supported firm and its investors. The more distant the human relationship, the easier the moral dimension gets lost.

The Kay Review sums up the evidence on the U.K. stock market in relation to savings, and outlines an approach to resolving difficulties in this area in the following terms:

> Equity markets today should primarily be seen as a means of getting money out of companies rather than a means of putting it in. This does not mean that equity markets are not relevant to investment in U.K. business. But the relevance is indirect. Equity markets are one of the means by which investors who support fledgling companies can hope to realize value. Equity markets provide a means of oversight of the principal mechanism of capital allocation, which takes place within companies. Promoting stewardship and good corporate governance is not an incidental function of equity markets. The effectiveness of modern equity markets depends almost entirely on their effectiveness in promoting these goals of stewardship and governance. (28, para. **2.32**, emphasis added)

There are other weaknesses of non-Islamic stock markets that deserve attention. Notably, these include the short-termism of the stock markets. It is important to note that short-termism takes many different forms. Apart from not being concerned with the long-term value of the company, it can translate into lack of investment in the company's infrastructure, and reduction in expenditure on research and development and overall, a diminution of its reputation. It can also take the form of making quick profits on the stock market rather than staying the course with long-term investment in particular companies. In view of its many manifestations, the phenomenon of short-termism is commented upon at more than one place in this study. In chapter 12 of the *General Theory*, Keynes (1936, 160) adopted a straightforward definition of short-termism in terms of share turnover and observed as follows: "The spectacle of modern investment markets has sometimes moved me towards the conclusion that to make the purchase of an investment permanent and indissoluble, like marriage, except by reason of death or other grave cause, might be a useful remedy for our contemporary evils. For this would force the investor to direct his mind to the long-term prospects and to those only." However, Keynes abandoned this idea because if individual purchases of investments were rendered illiquid, they might adversely affect the propensity to invest.

The Porter Committee regarded short-termism as a major fault of U.S. capital markets. It proposed a tax on those who dispose of their shares quickly. Under this scheme, if an investor held the shares in a corporation for five or more years, he or she would be subject to a much lower level of taxation. Porter and his colleagues thought that such a change in the taxation of stock market returns would, over time, change the culture and ethos of the market and shift it toward long-termism.

The Kay Review proposed a third, radically different approach to short-termism and stock market reform. The remedy in the Kay Review is original and a major contribution to the theory of finance. It suggests that the answer lies in having long-term relationships among all the players: asset managers, asset holders, and corporate directors. It attributes short-termism to the decline of trust and misalignment of incentives. The Review suggests that a culture based on principles of stewardship, founded on respect for those whose funds are invested, is required as a long-term remedy for the problems of the stock market.

This approach fits in well with the basic ethos and culture of Islamic stock markets. It is, therefore, likely to be easier to implement the vision of the Kay Review in Islamic stock markets than in existing non-Islamic markets. Most commentators feel that it will not be easy to change existing stock markets due to resistance from those who would stand to lose from any major reform.

Stock Markets and Economic Efficiency: Further Lessons for Islamic Stock Markets

The Islamic stock market has the great advantage of being late on the scene and can therefore achieve fast growth and structural development much more speedily than would otherwise be the case. Moreover, the history of stock markets in non-Islamic countries and their analyses provide rich and varied narratives about the progress of the stock market, as well as its difficulties in these countries. The Islamic stock market must examine these narratives closely and learn the lessons that they provide. With that in mind, we shall consider some controversial issues in non-Islamic stock market economics and examine their implications for Islamic markets. The two main issues we shall focus on are the efficiency of the stock market prices, and the takeover mechanism, together with means such as bankruptcy, and delisting from the stock market as the disciplinary devices to increase economic efficiency.

Stock Market and Efficiency of Share Prices

Opinions differ on how "efficient" stock market prices are in theory and in practice. The orthodox paradigm of share price determination postulates that share prices are efficient because they emanate from perfect markets involving large numbers of well-informed buyers and sellers in which no one buyer or seller can influence the price and where there is a homogeneous product: namely, corporate shares. There is an alternative paradigm, however, indicated by the passage from Keynes cited earlier, that characterizes stock markets essentially as gambling casinos dominated by speculators. Allen and Gale (2000); Shiller (2000); Shleifer (2000); Singh and others (2005); Baker and Wurgler (2007); and Hong and Stein (2007), among others, have formalized the various elements of this paradigm.[5] In brief, this literature suggests that in the face of a highly uncertain future, share prices are likely to be influenced by the so-called noise-traders, and by whims, fads, and contagion. For similar reasons of psychology, investors may attribute much greater weight to near-term price forecasts rather than historical long-term performance, thus suggesting another reason for short-termism. Nevertheless, many economists believe that overall the best theory of share price determination is the one suggested by Keynes' famous "beauty contest" analogy. This points toward strategies adopted by probably a large number of investors on the stock market.

> [To] change the metaphor slightly, professional investment may be likened to those newspaper competitions in which the competitors have to pick out the six prettiest faces from a hundred photographs, the prize being awarded to the competitor whose choice most nearly corresponds to the average preferences of the competitors as a whole; so that each competitor has to pick, not those faces which he himself finds prettiest, but those of which he thinks likeliest to catch the fancy of the other competitors, all of whom are looking at the problem from the same point of view. It is not just a case of choosing those which, to the best of one's judgment, are really the prettiest, nor even those which average opinion genuinely thinks the prettiest. We have reached the third degree where we devote our intelligences to anticipating what average opinion expects the average opinion to be. And there are some, I believe, who practice the fourth, fifth and higher degree. (Keynes 1936, 156)

However, until recently, the empirical literature on the determination of share prices has been dominated by the so-called efficient market hypothesis (EMH), which argues that real world share prices are efficient in the sense that they incorporate all available information (Fama 1970). In the 1980s, 1990s, and 2000s, the EMH suffered fundamental setbacks against the empirical reality of the 1987 U.S. stock market crash, the meltdown in the Asian stock markets in the 1990s, the bursting of the technology stocks bubble in 2000, and the demise of the housing and subprime mortgages' bubble in 2007–09. None of these events is compatible with the fundamental valuation efficiency of the stock market. Alan Greenspan (1998) has commented on the reasons for the 1987 stock market crash and Asian stock market meltdown: "At one point the economic system appears stable, the next it behaves as though a dam has reached a breaking point, and water (read 'confidence') evacuates the reservoir. The United States experienced such a sudden change with the decline in stock prices of more than 20 percent on October 19, 1987. There is no credible scenario that can readily explain so abrupt a change in the fundamentals of long-term valuations on that one day." Kindleberger ([1978], 1989) similarly documented about 30 cases of unwarranted euphoria and excessive pessimism on the stock markets since the South Sea bubble of 1720. He termed these episodes manias, panics, and crashes.

James Tobin (1984) made an analytically useful distinction between two kinds of efficiency of stock markets. The first is information arbitrage efficiency, which ensures that all information concerning a firm's shares immediately percolates to all stock market participants, ensuring that no participant can make a profit on such public information. The second is fundamental valuation efficiency, which ensures that share prices accurately reflect a firm's fundamentals: namely, its long-term expected profitability. The growing consensus view is that, in these terms, stock markets may at best be regarded as being efficient in the first sense but are far from being efficient in the economically more important second sense. Thus the EMH, as identified in information arbitrage efficiency, is compatible with share prices not reflecting fundamental values. A prominent supporter of the EMH, Fischer Black (1986), observed this in his presidential address to the American Finance Association, noting that the efficient market theory of the stock market "seems reasonable" if we adopt the right definition of "efficient." He defined "efficient" to mean that individual company stock prices are between half true value and twice true value almost all the time, and he defined "almost all" the time to mean at least 90 percent (see Shiller 2012). This illustrates, at a very conservative level, the difference between theory and empirical reality in relation to the orthodox hypothesis. A more detailed discussion, as well as other examples of share prices evidently departing from their fundamentals for prolonged periods, is provided in Singh and others (2005).

Apart from the day-to-day mispricing of share prices on the stock market—which is particularly likely to be severe in developing countries because their firms do not have a long track record—share prices in developing countries are more volatile than in advanced countries (see El-Erian and Kumar 1995; Singh 1997). The volatility of share prices, however, is a negative feature of stock markets for several reasons. First, it reduces the efficiency of the price signals in allocating investment resources. Second, it increases the riskiness of investments and may discourage risk-averse corporations from financing their growth via equity issues and indeed from seeking a stock market listing at all. Third, at the macroeconomic level, a highly volatile stock market may lead to financial fragility for the entire economy (Singh 1997).

Takeovers and Bankruptcy as Disciplinary Mechanisms

It is important in this context for Islamic scholars favoring the establishment of stock markets to also bear in mind that the stock market often "spontaneously" leads to the development of a market for corporate control. Such a market exists in countries like the United States and the United Kingdom, and plays an active role in these economies. In developing countries, this market exists so far only in a rudimentary form. This is because in most of these countries, stock markets are immature and lack sufficient separation of ownership from control. Nevertheless, developing country governments come under pressure from big players in the system to establish a free market for corporate control. Parenthetically, this market for corporate control is regarded by traditional economics as the evolutionary end point of stock market development.

Empirical evidence, however, is all to the contrary. Research shows that the takeover mechanism as it works in the real world is highly flawed. Selection in the market for corporate control takes place not on the basis of performance alone, but on the basis of size, as well. Thus, a large relatively unprofitable firm has a greater chance of survival than a small profitable firm. This has adverse consequences for economic efficiency (see Scherer 2006; Singh 2008; Tichy 2002). The market for corporate control, instead of being a vehicle for economic efficiency, exacerbates the shortcomings of the stock markets by encouraging speculative takeovers of whole companies rather than just buying and selling of a few shares of individual companies. Thus, in the non-Islamic world, in conventional economic terms, neither the pricing mechanism nor the takeover mechanism are helpful to economic efficiency and development.

The third issue is the effectiveness of the exit mechanism for failed companies, such as delisting from the stock market or bankruptcy. The important disciplinarian role of the exit mechanism is that failed institutions should exit and that there are consequences for failure. Many emerging market stock markets do not work well because of the lack of enforcement of rules or not allowing more delisting and bankruptcy of failed companies. Indeed, in a number of cases, governments have been known to intervene in stock markets to bail out companies in trouble. However, not all interventions to prevent the closure of large firms in developed or developing economies are necessarily wrong. The orthodox view is that such action only engenders more moral hazard problems, eroding the disciplinary role of financial markets. However, a full cost-benefit analysis of the proposed intervention is required, including not just the financial outcomes but also the relevant social costs and benefits, before it can be concluded that the cost of intervention is too high in terms of erosion of financial market discipline. It is also worth noting that one way in which takeovers may be helpful is the case of a declining company that may be acquired before it fails.

Stock Market Efficiency in Non-Islamic Markets: Further Lessons for Islamic Markets

The main lesson that the architects of Islamic stock markets should draw from the complex literature on share price determination and the takeover mechanism is that there are broadly two kinds of agents who participate in the stock market. One of these is interested in maximizing the long-term value of the company in which he or she is investing. The second is a trader who is interested only in the share prices and whether he or she can make an immediate profit on the basis of the analysis of these prices and their movements over time. The second category of investor is not at all interested in the long-term value. Such investors try to forecast the psychology of the market and ascertain how they can profit from it. The main implication for the Islamic stock market is that in a conventional market, both kinds of individuals or economic agents will be present. In order to achieve its long-term goals, the Islamic stock market must encourage the former and attempt to discourage the latter type of activity. Short-termism will run counter to Shari'ah laws, but it is difficult to provide proof of this behavior because no one will admit that they were playing the market rather than seeking long-term maximization of the value of the firm in which they had invested. As suggested by the Kay Review, the ideas of trust, stewardship, and straightforward honesty will need to be brought to bear on this fundamental issue.

To avoid the difficulties of immature markets—which are bound to arise in developing countries due to the operations of a market for corporate control—an alternative form of regulation is to be much more cautious in allowing the takeover market to emerge. Research shows that takeovers represent a very costly mechanism for changing firm management, especially when takeover bids are contested. Even when they are not contested, the transaction costs tend to be high (see Peacock and Bannock 1991). Takeovers and mergers also greatly increase the dangers of short-termism, and encourage speculation and financial engineering, rather than the pursuit of the classic capitalist goals of reducing costs and producing new products. Importantly, neither Germany nor Japan nor any of the successful East Asian newly industrialized countries had a market for corporate control during their development.

Research also shows that such a market is arbitrary and uncertain in its effects. There is no perfect solution to the need for change in management and ownership. Proponents of the Anglo-American system argue that the Darwinian process of creative destruction requires takeovers as a means of accelerating change. Opponents argue that such bidding wars are costly and the change has not necessarily benefited investors, due to the asset-stripping behavior that regulators cannot always prevent. Developing countries must find a cheaper way of changing firm management than the takeover mechanism that currently works in countries like the United States and the United Kingdom.

Issues of Globalization and of Long-Term Growth for Islamic Stock Markets

The discussion that follows briefly considers the growth question first, as it is in some ways easier to answer. This is what was referred to earlier as the natural progression theory, which asserts that as economies grow, so does the stock market, which is therefore an emblem of development. It will take us too far afield to discuss this theory in depth. However, even broad-brush evidence on this issue is telling. For example, it is useful to note that the economic miracles that occurred in the second half of the twentieth century can hardly be ascribed to the stock market and its development. Thus, in Europe, the Italian miracle (very fast growth), the German miracle, and the Austrian miracle, and in Asia, the justly famous miracles of the Republic of Korea or Taiwan, China, did not depend conspicuously on the equity or bond markets in these countries. Similarly, an examination of comparative growth rates over a long hundred-year time span indicates that bank-based countries (such as Germany and Japan) have as good, if not better, a long-term record than the United States and the United Kingdom. Pagano (1993) notes that the Italian stock market was bigger 100 years ago than it was in 1990. The Italian economy evidently grew during these 100 years without any expansion of its stock market. There are wide inter-country differences in the size of the stock market relative to GDP in various European countries. In the United Kingdom, the ratio of stock market value to GDP is five times larger than in Denmark, Finland, France, and Germany, and six times larger than in Italy and Norway. Pagano (1993) reports that in Italy, not only has the number of listed companies stagnated for nearly a century, but the total worth of companies trading has not kept pace with the economy as a whole. At the turn of the century (1906), total market capitalization of Italian firms was 26.3 percent, compared to 12.1 percent in 1991. Explaining inter-country differences in the incidence of stock market capitalization, the number of companies listed on the stock market, and related questions are subjects for research that cannot be pursued here because these lie outside the scope of the present study.

The discussion now turns to the impact of globalization on Islamic stock markets. Simply and starkly put, Islamic stock markets cannot operate independently from non-Islamic financial markets.

First, contagion will always occur, due to arbitrage activities between markets, even though such arbitrage may not be either legal or permissible under Shari'ah rules.

Second, the fact that current global markets are highly distorted in terms of interest rates, exchange rates, different tax rates, and policy regimes means that there will be impact on Islamic stock markets.

Third, the regulatory rules governing Islamic stock markets and non-Islamic stock markets will be different, primarily because Islamic finance has Shari'ah rules that govern the moral foundations of Islamic markets. In the final analysis, the Islamic stock market is only as strong as its technical and legal infrastructure; the quality of listed companies' financial intermediaries; and the way that Islamic regulators, courts, and interpretation of Shari'ah laws reinforce trust in the Islamic financial system and avoid the moral hazard and egregious behavior that currently mar and undermine non-Islamic markets.

Fourth, if non-Islamic financial markets suffer from short-termism and lack of trust, can Islamic markets protect themselves from "infection"?

The bottom line is that currently, non-Islamic stock markets suffer from the curse that modern finance appears to be serving itself rather than serving the real sector. Being built on moral foundations, Islamic stock markets must demonstrate that they serve the real sector more effectively, more equitably, and more sustainably.

How can we induce the financial system to serve the real sector? The answer is that if the financial system makes money, while the real sector is losing money, finance is not symbiotic or aligned with the real sector. Finance as a service industry can prosper only when its principal, the real sector, prospers. Therefore, the incentives that drive finance must be aligned with the real sector, not just in the short term, but in the long term as well. To do so, the marginal revenue from serving the real sector must be equal to the marginal cost of doing so. In other words, profits from toxic excessive leverage should be taxed or regulated—and if need be, incentives should be provided for lending to the real sector. The current global regulatory reforms do not address this basic distortion in incentives.

In that regard, we are convinced that conventional finance theory and its practice has forgotten its institutional history. Finance grew out of serving the real sector, with a foundation in moral ethics and trust, and acting as the credit disciplinarian and corporate governance steward for borrowers and listed companies. Indeed, in the first decade of the last century, legal trusts were ubiquitous on the stock market and the dealings on the market were expected to be trustworthy, not just in a legal sense, but in terms of normal usage of the word "trust." To cite a small but pertinent example, at the beginning of the twentieth century in England, there were 19 provincial stock exchanges in cities like Birmingham and Manchester. Economic historians note that they performed very useful functions, including raising substantial amounts of equity capital for local firms, and worked on the basis of trust rather than formal legal rules. However, none of these provincial exchanges function today. Economies of scale enjoyed by the London stock market have overwhelmed all the small stock exchanges.[6] Indeed, with the arrival of modern finance theory and derivative financing, the game has become global, impersonal, and a celebration of private greed at public expense. When financial markets become impersonal and too large and too complex to manage, they can lose their moral bearings. Personal accountability becomes lost in impersonal "public responsibility." Everybody's money is nobody's money, so liberal monetary creation for all loses all sense of responsibility. It is as if inflation is good for all. It may be good for those with huge debt overhang, but the poor and those with holdings of paper assets will suffer.

This analogy of provincial stock exchanges with the Islamic stock market will be valid only if the latter remains small and relatively local. It does underscore the point that the role of financial intermediaries in safeguarding the moral bearings of Islamic finance is critical. They must start small in helping the SMEs to raise funds for trade, investments, and risk taking. This calls for a very different approach from the "mega-markets" of centralizing liquidity through sheer scale. The Islamic stock market will also have to discourage any strategic pricing that is not concerned with enhancing the long-term value of corporations; be on guard against the threat of contagion; and try to avoid any negative feedback loops that may arise from the interaction between the stock market and the foreign exchange market in a crisis situation.

Conclusion

Currently, there is widespread dissatisfaction with the stock markets in advanced countries, including the United States and the United Kingdom, where such markets have been historically important. The U.K. Equity Market (Kay) Review is most illuminating. It recommends a root and branch change in the conduct of the stock markets. It calls for long-term relationships among all participants in the equity chain: relationships that are based on respect and trust and involve notions of stewardship and mutual respect. The report also suggests that the whole ethos of the stock market should change to permit the exercise of appropriate values of trust, stewardship, and honesty.

In essence, since stock markets are systems, the long-term viability and sustainability of systems depend on the tradeoff among three overlapping but often conflicting objectives: efficiency in resource allocation; stability and resilience to internal and external shocks; and fairness and equity, enabling all to access the market in a competitive manner. The fact that stock markets, like all systems, require oversight and regulation, particularly during crises, means that government intervention is inevitable. The current crisis has amply demonstrated that the EMH assumed that efficiency would take care of stability and social equity.

It is the central contention of this study that the proponents of Islamic stock markets will find it easier to implement Kay's reform program for the stock market than their U.K. counterparts. The strong ethical basis of the Islamic stock market gives it a decisive edge in meeting the requirements of the Kay Review. Indeed, it may come to pass that the tutor and the pupil reverse their roles. The U.K. stock market may well learn from the experience of the Islamic stock market, with its strong ethical underpinnings.

The advocates of Islamic stock markets in various country settings should regard the project of establishing such markets a long-term commitment that may take two to three decades to complete.[7] They should begin by concentrating on the financing needs of the excluded, particularly SMEs, and by implementing the spirit of the Kay Review, which is very much in accord with Islamic ethics. It may also be useful to start the actual establishment of Islamic stock markets in a small number of Muslim countries on a national basis in the first instance.

However, as people come to know one another and as the knowledge base and experience expand, the national stock markets may integrate into regional or international Islamic stock markets. Developing markets is a process of learning and adapting.

The second major lesson is that advocates of Islamic stock markets should not permit a market for corporate control to arise either "spontaneously" or by design. This is because, as discussed, such a market leads to short-termism, speculation, rapid turnover of shares, and strategic pricing—all of which go against the grain of an Islamic stock market.

This raises an important question: If takeovers are not to be used to discipline errant or poorly performing firms, how should these firms be controlled? The answer is simple but extremely important. All firms should in the first instance be subject to the discipline of competition in their primary product and service markets. The exit mechanism in terms of bankruptcy laws and the court mechanisms should have higher priority in the policy agenda, rather than takeover mechanisms.

Islamic stock markets will have to devote more attention to the stability and equitable aspects of market systems through their ethical and moral base. Since Islamic finance investors and market participants are relatively new and inexperienced, it will take time to nurture the development of Islamic stock markets to balance the three objectives of stability, robustness, and fairness in a transparent and sustainable manner.

To put all the above into practice will not be easy, but this is a worthy exercise and challenge for Islamic finance practitioners. It is also a historic opportunity to enter the global market at a time when there is widespread dissatisfaction with the conduct of stock markets and related financial institutions in advanced countries.

Notes

1. Pareto optimal refers to the state of the world in which, while no person's welfare decreases, everyone else's welfare remains the same or increases. Alternatively, no one can be made better off without making at least one individual worse off.
2. For a full discussion of the issues, see Sheng and Singh (2012).
3. There is no consensus on the date of the beginning of the crisis. Many economists, however, suggest that the crisis began with the demise of the Lehmann Brothers in 2008. This volume views 2007–09 as the crisis period. Other economists extend the crisis period to include 2011–12, as well.
4. For a fuller analysis of this issue, see Glen and Singh (2003, 2005); Singh (2003); and Gügler, Mueller, and Yurtoglu (2003).
5. See also students of behavioral finance, such as contributions by Barberis and Thaler (2003).
6. It is also interesting to note in this context that banks and financial institutions in Canada fared far better than their counterparts in other advanced economies during the recent financial crisis because they stayed closer to their roots, did not overextend themselves either across borders or in terms of leverage, and continued to be very

conservative and traditional in their values. The authors are grateful to the editors for this point.

7. While there is only one basic concept of an Islamic stock market—which emphasizes trust and stewardship and prohibits speculative activity—the specific stock exchange rules will not necessarily be the same for each country; hence the discussion of "Islamic stock markets."

References

Allen, Franklin, and Douglas Gale. 2000. "Financial Contagion." *Journal of Political Economy* 108 (1): 1–33.

Baker, Malcolm P., and Jeffrey A. Wurgler. 2007. "Investor Sentiment in the Stock Market." *Journal of Economic Perspectives* 21 (2): 129–52.

Barberis, Nicholas, and Richard Thaler. 2003. "A Survey of Behavioral Finance." In *Handbook of the Economics of Finance*, edited by George M. Constantinides, Rene M. Stulz, Milton Harris, 1053–128. 1st ed. Vol. 1. Amsterdam: Elsevier.

Black, Fischer. 1986. "Noise." *Journal of Finance* 41 (3): 529–43. Also "Presidential Address." American Finance Association.

Blanchard, Olivier, 2009. "The Crisis: Basic Mechanisms and Appropriate Policies." *CESifo Forum*, Ifo Institute for Economic Research at the University of Munich 10 (1): 3–14. http://www.cesifo-group.de/portal/pls/portal/docs/1/1200909.PDF.

El-Erian, Mohamed, and Manmohan Kumar. 1995. "Emerging Equity Markets in Middle Eastern Countries." In *Development of Financial Markets in the Arab Countries, Iran and Turkey*, edited by Economic Research Forum (ERF) for Arab Countries, Iran and Turkey, 129–75. Cairo: Economic Research Forum (ERF) for Arab Countries, Iran and Turkey.

Fama, Eugene F. 1970 "Efficient Capital Markets: A Review of Theory and Empirical Work." *Journal of Finance* 25 (2): 383–417.

Glen, Jack, and Ajit Singh. 2003. "Capital Structure, Rates of Return and Financing Corporate Growth: Comparing Developed and Emerging Markets, 1994–00." Working Paper 265, ESRC Centre for Business Research, University of Cambridge, U.K.

———. 2005. "Corporate Governance, Competition, and Finance: Re-thinking Lessons from the Asian Crisis." *Eastern Economic Journal* 31 (2): 219–43.

Greenspan, Alan. 1998. "Risk Management in the Global Financial System." Speech before the Annual Financial Markets Conference of the Federal Reserve Bank of Atlanta, Miami Beach, Florida. http://www.federalreserve.gov/boarddocs/speeches/1998/19980227.htm.

Gügler, Klaus, Dennis C. Mueller, and B. Burcin Yurtoglu. 2003. "The Impact of Corporate Governance on Investment Returns in Developed and Developing Countries." *Economic Journal* 113 (491): F511–39.

Hong, Harrison, and Jeremy C. Stein. 2007. "Disagreement and the Stock Market." *Journal of Economic Perspectives* 21 (2): 109–128.

Kay, John. 2012. "The Kay Review of UK Equity Markets and Long-Term Decision Making." http://www.bis.gov.uk/kayreview.

Keynes, John Maynard. 1936. *The General Theory of Employment Interest and Money*. New York: Harcourt, Brace and Company.

Kindleberger, Charles. (1978) 1989. *Manias, Panics, and Crashes: A History of Financial Crises*. Reprint, New York: Basic Books. Revised and enlarged, 1989.

Metwally, Mokhtar M. 1984. "The Role of the Stock Exchange in an Islamic Economy." *Journal for Research in Islamic Economics* 2 (1): 21–30.

Mirakhor, Abbas. 2011. "Keynote Address: Epistemological Foundation of Finance: Islamic and Conventional." Foundations of Islamic Finance Conference Series, Epistemological Foundation of Finance: Islamic and Conventional, March 8–10.

Myers, Stuart C., and Nicholas S. Majluf. 1984. "Corporate Financing and Investment Decisions When Firms Have Information That Investors Do Not Have." *Journal of Financial Economics* 13 (2): 187–221.

Pagano, Marco. 1993. "Financial Markets and Growth: An Overview." *European Economic Review* 37 (2–3): 613–22.

Pagano, Marco, Fabio Panetta, and Luigi Zingales. 1998. "Why Do Companies Go Public? An Empirical Analysis." *Journal of Finance* 53 (1): 27–64.

Peacock, Alan, and Graham Bannock. 1991. "Corporate Takeovers and the Public Interest." Aberdeen University Press.

Porter, Michael E. 1992. "Capital Disadvantage: America's Failing Capital Investment System." *Harvard Business Review*. http://hbr.org/1992/09/capital-disadvantage-americas-failing-capital-investment-system/ar/1.

Scherer, Frederic M. 2006. "A New Retrospective on Mergers." *Review of Industrial Organization* 28 (4): 327–41.

Sheng, Andrew, and Ajit Singh. 2012. "The Challenge of Islamic Finance." http://www.project-syndicate.org/commentary/the-challenge-of-islamic-finance.

Shiller, Robert J. 2000. *Irrational Exuberance*. Princeton, NJ: Princeton University Press.

———. 2012. *Finance and the Good Society*. Princeton, NJ: Princeton University Press.

Shleifer, Andrei. 2000. *Inefficient Markets: An Introduction to Behavioral Finance*. New York: Oxford University Press.

Singh, Ajit. 1993. *The Stock Market and Economic Development: Should Developing Countries Encourage Stock Markets?* UNCTAD Review 4. http://cedeplar.ufmg.br/economia/disciplinas/ecn933a/crocco/Criacao_expansao_mercado_capitais/SINGH~31.PDF.

———. 1995. "Corporate Financial Patterns in Industrializing Economies: A Comparative International Study." IFC Scientific Paper 2, International Finance Corporation, Washington, DC.

———. 1997. "Financial Liberalisation, the Stock Market and Economic Development." *Economic Journal* (May): 771–82.

———. 2003. "Competition, Corporate Governance and Selection in Emerging Markets." *Economic Journal* 113 (491): 443–64.

———. 2008. "Stock Markets in Low- and Middle-Income Countries" Working Paper 377, ESRC Centre for Business Research.

Singh, Ajit, and Tabatabai Hamid, eds. 1993. *Economic Crisis and Third World Agriculture*. Cambridge, U.K.: Cambridge University Press.

Singh, Ajith., Jack Glen, Ann Zammit, Rafael De Hoyos, Alaka Singh, and Bruce Weisse. 2005. "Shareholder Value Maximisation, Stock Market and New Technology: Should the U.S. Corporate Model Be the Universal Standard?" Asia-Europe Papers, Discussion

Paper 1, July 2005. Also published as CBR Working Paper 315. Subsequently published in *International Review of Applied Economics* 19 (4): 419–37.

Solow, Robert M. 2009. "How to Understand the Disaster." *New York Review of Books* 56 (8). http://www.nybooks.com/articles/archives/2009/may/14/how-to-understand-the-disaster.

Tichy, Gunther. 2002. "What Do We Know about the Success and Failure of Mergers?" *Journal of Industry, Competition and Trade* 1 (4).

Tobin, James. 1984. "A Mean-Variance Approach to Fundamental Valuations." Cowles Foundation Discussion Papers 711R, Cowles Foundation for Research in Economics, Yale University, New Haven, CT.

PART 3

Policy Formulation

CHAPTER 11

A Survey of the Economic Development of OIC Countries

Hossein Askari and Scheherazade Rehman

Introduction

There are a number of generally accepted determinants of economic development and growth, including inputs (such as capital, labor, technology, entrepreneurship, and management) and conditions and policies (such as developed financial markets, free labor and product markets, moderate tax rates, low public debt, and consistent macroeconomic policies). More recently, in a return to the earlier writings of Adam Smith, sound and efficient institutions have become touted as an essential pillar, if not the very foundation, of economic development and growth. From time to time, other factors, such as religion and the work ethic, come into focus because a person's everyday decisions are in part influenced by belief systems; and religion could play a significant role in both individual and collective decision-making.

Has Islam been supportive or detrimental to economic development and growth in Muslim countries? While it may be tempting to answer this question by simply assessing the performance of countries that are classified as Muslim, that would be a mistake. The impact of Islam on development and growth can be correctly determined if, and only if, countries are first classified by their adoption and adherence to Islamic teachings, as elaborated in the Qur'an and exemplified by the traditions of the Prophet Mohammad—and only then assessed for the contribution of all factors in the context of a complete (not partial) model, including religion, to their development and growth. In other words, we must first determine whether these countries have truly adopted and practiced Islamic economic teachings and could be correctly classified as Islamic (at least in their economic and financial practice). Or do they only profess Islam and are Islamic in name only? Even if they adhere to Islamic teachings in their policies, practice, and governance, we must still demonstrate that it is these teachings, and not other factors, that have shaped and determined their economic performance over time.

The authors are professors at the George Washington University.

This chapter briefly discusses important and widely accepted Islamic teachings on economics, finance, and development. It then examines the broad economic performance of OIC (Organization of Islamic Conference) countries[1] to see how they have adhered to, and fared in, the economic dimensions that are important in Islam—in other words, it assesses their "economic Islamicity." The chapter concludes with some thoughts as to the efficacy of Islamic teachings regarding economics, finance, and development.

Fundamental Islamic Economic Doctrines

Islam advocates an environment where behavior is molded to support the goals of an Islamic society: societal welfare and socioeconomic justice, in the pursuit of making humankind one and supporting the Unity of Allah's Creation. It is generally accepted that the central economic tenant of Islam is to develop a prosperous economic and egalitarian social structure in which all people (men and women) can maximize their intellectual capacity, preserve and promote their health, and actively contribute to the economic and social development of society. To this end, economic development and growth and economic and social justice are the foundational elements of an Islamic economic system, and Islam gives detailed economic guidelines for creating such a prosperous and just community.

At the outset, we must emphasize the fact that Islam is a rule-based religion. Rule-compliance promotes material growth through higher productivity. Rules, or good institutions, are crucial for economic growth: property rights protection, the enforcement of contracts, and good governance are emphasized in both the Qur'an and in the traditions of the Prophet. Good institutions with transparent rules and compliance afford confidence to all market participants. But the rules to promote and support development and growth go further, and include the rules of seeking knowledge, avoiding waste, doing no harm or injury, working hard, and refraining from fraud, cheating, or abusing property. The internalization of the rules of conduct governing market participation and rule-compliance assures that the market will be an efficient mechanism to create a balance within an economy. Rules regarding the fair treatment of others assure that those who participate in the act of production receive just payment for their effort. Thus, market-based distribution guided by the price mechanism would also be fair. Rules governing income redistribution assure that the rights of others in access to resources are preserved before income becomes disposable. All economic transactions are governed by rules requiring strict faithfulness to the terms and conditions of contracts and promises. Hence, the probability of asymmetric information and moral hazard is minimized. Rules governing consumption assure that there is no opulent or wasteful consumption. Rules governing the use of disposable income and wealth assure that wealth is not hoarded and is made available in the form of investment and expenditures in the Way of Allah. Prohibition of interest assures the direct participation of wealth-holders in projects and with managers, as the Qur'an advocates risk-sharing finance to bring mankind together and enhance trust in a Muslim society. Governance, rules, and their practice are important facets of the Islamic economic and financial system, with sound institutions at its foundation. The Prophet warned that failure by members of society to correct ineffective governance would lead to a totalitarian nightmare. The consequences of noncompliance are so severe that the Prophet warned that prayers of the noncompliant would not be answered.

Islam unites ethical principles with institutional measures (laws and rules) to create a framework for how an Islamic-inspired economy and society should function. Institutions proposed by Islam relating to governance, social solidarity, cooperation, and justice are designed to achieve economic development and growth. Broad measures to address perceived resource scarcity and achieve an equitable distribution of wealth and resource under the rubric of justice are three-fold. They include the fostering of ethical and moral values such as justice, equality, and honesty; economic tools and instruments and inheritance and property laws; and the development of the institutional capacity and political will to insure that these principles and norms are adequately upheld and followed. At the core of the Islamic model is justice, while the principles of equity, fiscal prudence, sanctity of personal income and property rights, and hard work branch out from this core.

While justice and equity are at the foundation of an Islamic society and economy, it is also widely recognized that free markets, however functioning under certain prescribed laws, should play a prominent role in the distribution of goods and services. The laws of Islam unambiguously call for transparent and free markets, commercial fairness, and ethical business as basic standards of economic activities.

According to Islamic teachings, all able humans are encouraged to compete in business, work hard for economic gain that should accrue to them, and own private property. It is widely recognized in Islam that the economic and psychological pressure of poverty may induce some individuals to seek unethical means of earning an income. Thus all members of an Islamic society must be given the same opportunities to advance: that is, a level playing field and the opportunity to work. For those for whom there is no work and for those who cannot work, society must afford the minimum required for a dignified life: shelter, food, health care, and education. Thus the principles of an Islamic economic system were designed with this in mind, ensuring the availability of education and equal opportunity for employment for all, poverty reduction and prevention, and continuous social and intellectual development for all individuals.[2] In the end, the existence of absolute and relative poverty, along with significant income inequality, is direct evidence of ethical shortcomings, rule violation, and governance failure, for which members of society are responsible, individually and collectively, no matter how strong their pretensions to Islamicity.

According to Islam, there is a strong precedence for high moral standards, ethics, values, and norms of behavior, governing many aspects of economic life. Moreover, it has been clearly acknowledged that corruption and corrupt practices are un-Islamic and are specifically condemned in Islam. For example, one of the Prophet's sayings illustrates the severity with which corruption is viewed: "Damned is the bribe-giver (or 'corrupter'), the bribe-taker (or 'corrupted') and he who goes between them." The Prophet, in accordance with prescribed rules, prohibited theft, bribery, interest on money, the usurpation and confiscation of the property rights of others by force, and other ethically and morally forbidden activities as sources of income and wealth. These proscribed activities create instantaneous property rights without commensurate exertion of labor in production and are socially unproductive and harmful. These rules clearly establish the priority of the interests of society over those of the individual, without adverse impact on private initiative in production, exchange, and consumption. It is these same rules that modern Western-trained economists claim to be the basis for national economic success.

The Prophet clarified rules of property rights over natural resources. To protect the interests of society and maintain social order and stability, the Prophet enunciated rules, based on those already prescribed by the Qur'an, to give priority to the rights of society over those of the individual. These include the rule of no harm or injury, and prohibition of the waste and destruction of resources and products, of extravagance and opulence in production and consumption, of individual behavior that could create instability in the system, and of illegal, immoral, and unethical sources of income and wealth. These rules, while general, relate to property rights because while these individual rights are recognized and protected, they are not allowed to harm the interests of society.

The first principle of property rights acknowledges the permanent, constant, and invariant ownership of all property by Allah. The second principle acknowledges, in consonance with the Qur'an, the transfer by Allah of the right of possession to all of mankind. The third principle acknowledges equal opportunity of access by all to the natural resources provided by the Creator, to be combined with their labor to produce goods and services. Ownership of natural resources (such as raw land, water, and mineral deposits) is considered to be a gift bestowed to humanity by God, and only God has absolute ownership (Cummings, Askari, and Mustafa 1980). The logic here is that since humans did not actually create any of the world's natural resources, they cannot exert unequivocal ownership over them. They may own anything they produce with their work or gain through legitimate investment and inheritance. To ensure property rights for all members of society, property rights over natural resources (such as mines and oil deposits) were placed in trust of either the state to be used for the benefit of all or in the hands of society at large as commons (for example, surface and underground water). In the case of exhaustible resources, such as oil and natural gas, ownership is clearly vested in the state to manage these in a way that affords equal benefits to every member of society, be they able to work or handicapped. Furthermore, this benefit must accrue equally to all future generations. The notion of equity and social justice is of paramount importance for countries with large oil and gas resources. Economists long ago addressed this issue. As Nobel laureate Robert Solow

(1974, 41) has noted: "The finite pool of resources (I have excluded full recycling) should be used up optimally according to the general rules that govern the optimal use of reproducible assets. In particular, earlier generations are entitled to draw down the pool (optimally, of course!) so long as they add (optimally, of course!) to the stock of reproducible capital."

Note that Solow concludes that exhaustible resources should be optimally drawn down and replaced by reproducible capital (for future output) optimally for future generations. What if governments cannot, or will not, optimally add to the stock of reproducible capital? The clear need is to find an alternative to Solow's prescribed optimal draw down and optimal addition to reproducible capital. A viable option is to take all oil revenues and create a fund to address issues of equity. This may be the only way in which the interests of future as well as current generations can be preserved. For instance, if governments were to use oil revenues to build roads and bridges, it is highly unlikely that future generations of citizens would receive the same benefit as current generations. Moreover, as the government spends current oil revenues, some citizens among the current generation would benefit more than others. For instance, those who own construction companies and build the roads and bridges would benefit more than the rest of society. The only way to preserve equity is to make the same (real purchasing power) direct cash transfers to all citizens, in this and future generations.

In Islam, a clear distinction is made between the right of *ownership* and the right of *possession*, particularly in the case of land. Any individual could combine labor, capital, and available land to produce a commodity over which the person would have full property rights, a critical element for national economic prosperity. The land would remain in the person's possession as long as the land was in production. However, if the land was not used for continuous production (for a designated period, such as three consecutive years), the person would lose the right of possession, and another person would have the right to take possession of the land, and, in combination with labor and capital, to put the land to productive use. It is worth emphasizing that the Prophet underlined the rule that such opportunities were available to all members of society regardless of their gender or beliefs. In making such opportunities available to all members of society, Islam implicitly admonishes corrupt practices and any form of discrimination. In cases of criminal violations requiring judicial action, members of each faith were to refer to the procedures specified by their own faith, according to the Constitution of Medina.

Islam considers hard work on the part of any individual and society to be one of the most critical drivers of economic development and social progress. Thus Islamic rules are designed to foster labor, production, and economic commerce, and emphasize the prohibition of corruption, routine beggary, and freeloading, and any vocations that may promote social instability or political, economic, or social oppression.

Importantly for governments, no political authority can violate these prescribed rules and retain legitimacy, and no community can claim that it has remained a believing community while being ruled over by an authority that is noncompliant with and in violation of the prescribed rules. In short, it is the noncompliance with and violation of the duty of commending rule-compliance and of forbidding noncompliance, that leads to the emergence of corrupt, unjust, dictatorial, and totalitarian authority. The Prophet warned that nonobservance of this duty by individuals and the community creates the conditions that will result in Allah empowering the worst among the humans to rule over the community, and if noncompliance by the community and its members continues in the face of injustice by the illegitimate authority (that has lost legitimacy), this becomes a rule violation. Good and just governance is an essential element of an Islamic economic and financial system, and it is the duty of all Muslims to work toward a society that is rule-compliant and has good governance.

In sum, a truly Islamic economic system is a market-based system, but with entrenched Islamic behavior and goals (objectives/rules/institutions) attributed to consumers, producers, and to government (authorities), and with institutions and scaffolding that very much resemble the modern view of economic development—a view that was espoused by Adam Smith in his two books (1759, 1776) more than two centuries ago. Based on the Islamic vision, we expect the Islamic solution (if faithfully implemented) to emphasize and stress a number of important principles in comparison to the conventional Western economic and financial market-based system: a greater degree of justice in all aspects of economic management; a higher moral standard, and greater honesty and trust, exhibited in the marketplace and in all economic transactions; poverty eradication; a more even distribution of wealth and income; no hoarding of wealth; less opulence in consumption; no exploitive speculation; risk sharing as opposed to debt contracts; better social infrastructure and provision of social services; better treatment of workers; higher education expenditures relative to gross domestic product (GDP); higher savings and investment rates; a higher degree of environmental preservation; and more vigilantly supervised markets. It would be expected that these differences would be reflected in higher quantitative and qualitative economic growth if these goals and rules were adopted. In other words, if a community or country adhered to the Islamic prescription, one would, a priori, expect a higher rate of growth, flowing from a higher investment rate, higher educational expenditures, higher social awareness, better functioning markets, a higher level of trust, sanctity of legitimate income and wealth, and institutions that have empirically been shown to be critical for growth.

Before assessing the adherence of Muslim countries to Islamic teachings as outlined above, we would like to emphasize that Adam Smith, in his *Theory of Moral Sentiments*, long ago noted the role of religion and the importance of rules and rule-compliance in the proper functioning of an economic system ([1759] 2002, 186–98):

> The regard to those general rules of conduct is what is properly called a sense of duty, a principle of the greatest consequence in human life, and the only principle by which the bulk of mankind are capable of directing their actions. ... Without this

sacred regard to general rules, there is no man whose conduct can be much depended upon. It is this that constitutes the most essential difference between a man of principle and honor and a worthless fellow. ... Upon the tolerable observance of these duties depends the very existence of human society, which would crumble into nothing if mankind were not generally impressed with a reverence for those important rules of conduct. This reverence is still further enhanced by an opinion which is first impressed by nature, and afterward confirmed by reasoning and philosophy, that those important rules of morality are the commands and *Laws* of the Deity, who will finally reward the obedient, and punish the transgressors of their duty. ... The happiness of mankind as well as of all other rational creatures seems to have been the original purpose intended by the Author of Nature when he brought them into existence. No other end seems worthy of that supreme wisdom and benignity which we necessarily ascribe to him. ... But, by acting according to the dictates of our moral faculties, we necessarily pursue the most effectual means for promoting the happiness of mankind, and may therefore be said, in some sense to co-operate with the Deity, and to advance, as far as is in our power, the plan of providence. By acting otherwise, on the contrary, we seem to obstruct, in some measure, the scheme, which the Author of Nature has established for the happiness and perfection of the world, and to declare ourselves, if I may say so, in some measure the enemies of God. Hence we are naturally encouraged to hope for his extraordinary favor and reward in the one case, and to dread his vengeance and punishment in the other. ... When the general rules which determine the merit and demerit of actions comes thus to be regarded as the *Laws* of an all-powerful being, who watches over our conduct, and who, in a life to come, will reward the observance and punish the breach of them—they necessarily acquire a new sacredness from this consideration. That our regard to the will of the Deity ought to be the supreme rule of our conduct can be doubted of by nobody who believes his existence. The very thought of disobedience appears to involve in it the most shocking impropriety.

This brief discussion about the fundaments of a market economy and Islam should confirm a number of points. There is nothing in Islam that discourages economic prosperity and growth. Islam embraces capitalism, but a type of capitalism that incorporates a strong dose of morality and justice. Capitalism ensconced in morality is what Adam Smith endorsed in his less-quoted book. To our mind, the absence of morality, fairness, and justice is the Achilles' heel of today's capitalism, as being played out in the global crisis that has enveloped the world since 2007.

While it is near impossible to *directly* measure and assess the adherence of OIC countries to all these Islamic teachings on economic and financial governance and management, we can get an indirect insight into some of these: the quality of institutions; the quality of governance; market freedom (for goods, labor, and financial markets); economic freedom; the extent of corruption; progress in poverty eradication; the overall income distribution; the prevalence of wealth hoarding; the quality and availability of education; employment opportunities; the equity of benefits derived from natural resource depletion; the independence, effectiveness, and fairness of the legal system; and level of private and public debt.

The next section assesses how well OIC countries have performed relative to other country groups in some of these areas by examining existing indexes. The message is clear: If OIC countries have truly adopted and followed the Islamic prescription, they should demonstrate superior performance along these dimensions that are central to an Islamic economic system.

The Performance of OIC Countries

The discussion that follows assesses the broad economic performance of members of the OIC relative to other regional and country groupings, and investigates whether OIC members have delivered broad-based and sustained development and growth. In addition to analyzing a thirty-year trend of the United Nations Human Development Index (HDI)[3] as a broad-based measure for overall longitudinal development and growth, the investigation focuses on specific areas of education, gender, health, income (wealth), inequality, poverty, and environment/sustainability—important elements stressed in an Islamic system.[4]

Overall trends in human development. Figure 11.1 shows a thirty-year trend of overall human development for the OIC countries in comparison to other regional and country groupings. We use the HDI, which is a composite of three indexes: the Education Index (EI); the Health (Life Expectancy) Index (LEI); and the Income (Wealth) Index (II).[5] It is clear that over a long period of time, the OIC countries have consistently underperformed in comparison to the world average in broad-based economic and social development. What stands out in the figure is that the OIC countries as a group have consistently underperformed other country groupings. However, a subset of the OIC, the six countries of the Gulf Cooperation Council (GCC)—Bahrain, Kuwait, Oman, Qatar, Saudi Arabia, and the United Arab Emirates—have performed above the world average (although still below the average for the highly industrialized Organisation for Economic Co-operation and Development [OECD] countries) over this same thirty-year period.[6]

Education. Figure 11.2 follows the thirty-year educational progress of the OIC countries as measured by the U.N. Education Index.[7] Education is generally accepted as a major input into economic growth and development, as well as a reflection of a nation's economic progress, development, and quality of life, and is a variable reflecting a country's status as a developed, emerging, or underdeveloped country. Moreover, education (including its attributes, such as knowledge) is the second most oft repeated word in the Qur'an and was also repeatedly stressed by the Prophet. Over the last 30 years, it would appear that OIC performance has been consistently well below the world average. It should again be noted that a subset—the GCC countries—has performed above the world average, but have still remained well below the OECD average.

Gender equality. The empowerment of women and gender equality are key to achieving a healthy and sustainable economic and social development They not only promote economic efficiency, but, as the World Bank notes, aid in enhancing

Figure 11.1 U.N. Human Development Index (HDI) Trends

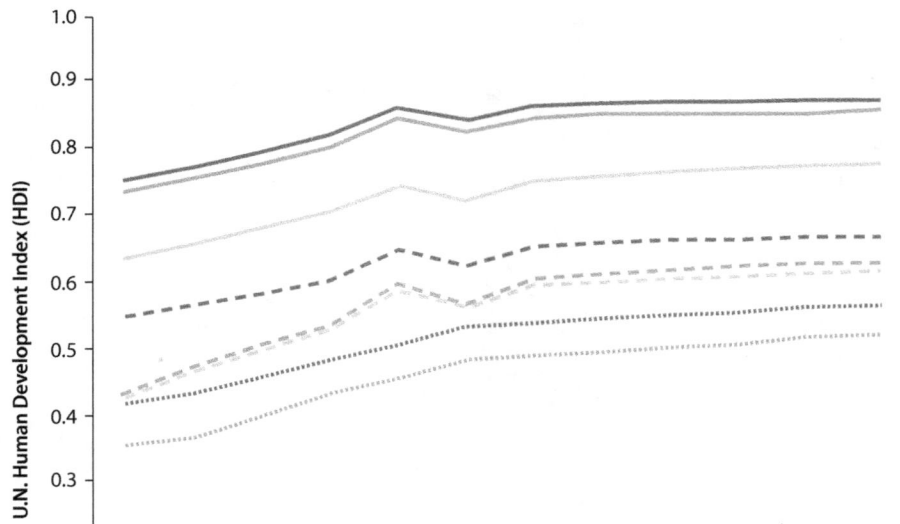

Source: http://hdr.undp.org/en/statistics/hdi/.
Note: The U.N. Human Development Index (HDI) measures development by combining the three dimensions of health, education, and living standards into a composite index, which is expressed as a number between 0 and 1. RB = regional briefing note; OECD = Organisation for Economic Co-operation and Development; OIC = Organization of Islamic Conference; GCC = Gulf Cooperation Council.

other types of development by "removing barriers that prevent women from having the same access as men to human resource endowments, rights, and economic opportunities. Giving women access to equal opportunities allows them to emerge as social and economic actors, influencing and shaping more inclusive policies. Improving women's status also leads to more investment in their children's education, health, and overall wellbeing."[8] Figure 11.3 measures gender equality by assessing how active women are in the labor force.[9] These results should be disaggregated by subregion. When it comes to women participating in the workforce and in the economy, the OIC countries have fared much better than the Arab region of the OIC—particularly the GCC countries. The gender performance of OIC countries, excluding the Arab countries, has been almost consistently above the world average and that of the OECD countries.

Figure 11.2 U.N. Education Index

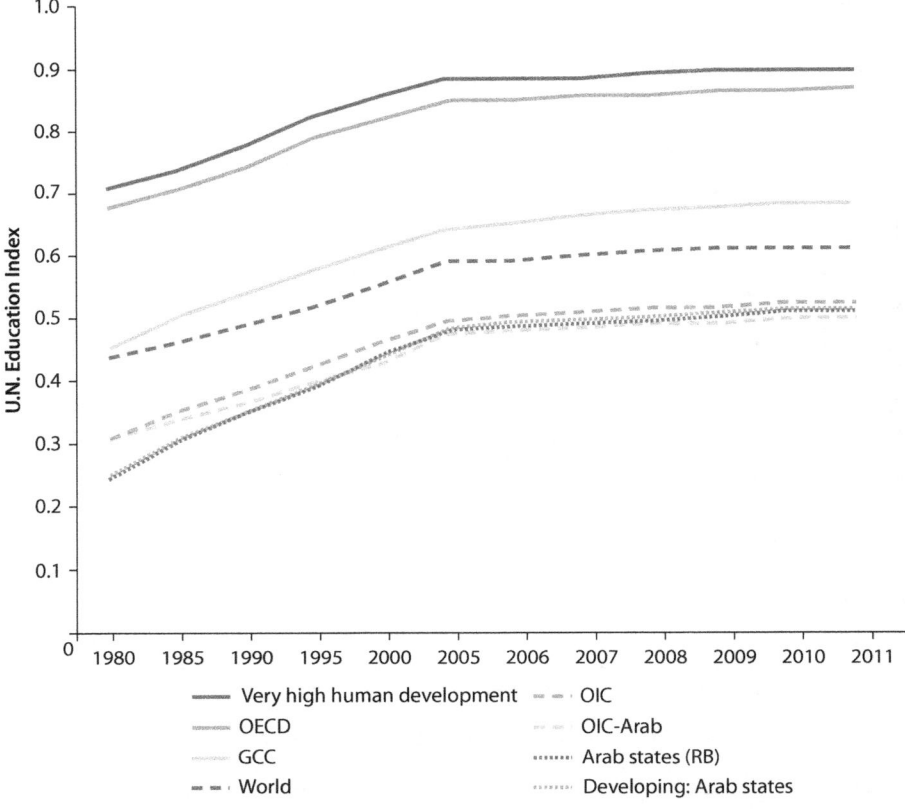

Source: http://hdr.undp.org/en/statistics/hdi/.
Note: The U.N. Human Education Index (EI) measures the adult literacy rate (with a two-thirds weight) and the combined primary, secondary, and tertiary gross enrollment ratio (with a one-third weight). The adult literacy rate gives an indication of the ability to read and write, while the tertiary gross enrollment ratio gives an indication of the level of education from nursery/kindergarten to post graduate education. The EI is expressed as a number between 0 and 1. RB = regional briefing note; OECD = Organisation for Economic Co-operation and Development; OIC = Organization of Islamic Conference; GCC = Gulf Cooperation Council.

While this is an impressive statistic, the performance of the Arab countries in fostering gender equality is equally disturbing: namely, lagging well behind the world average and all other regions.

Health and life expectancy. In order to address progress in addressing health issues over time, we use the U.N. Health Index,[10] which is measured as the life expectancy at birth. Figure 11.4 shows that human health conditions in the OIC countries are far below world standards. In this area, the Arab region (developing and developed) have consistently performed better than the non-Arab OIC countries.

Income and wealth distribution and poverty levels. To assess the income or wealth of a region or a country grouping, we use the Income (or Wealth) Index of the United Nations.[11] The Income Index measures the living standards of countries in

Figure 11.3 Gender Inequality

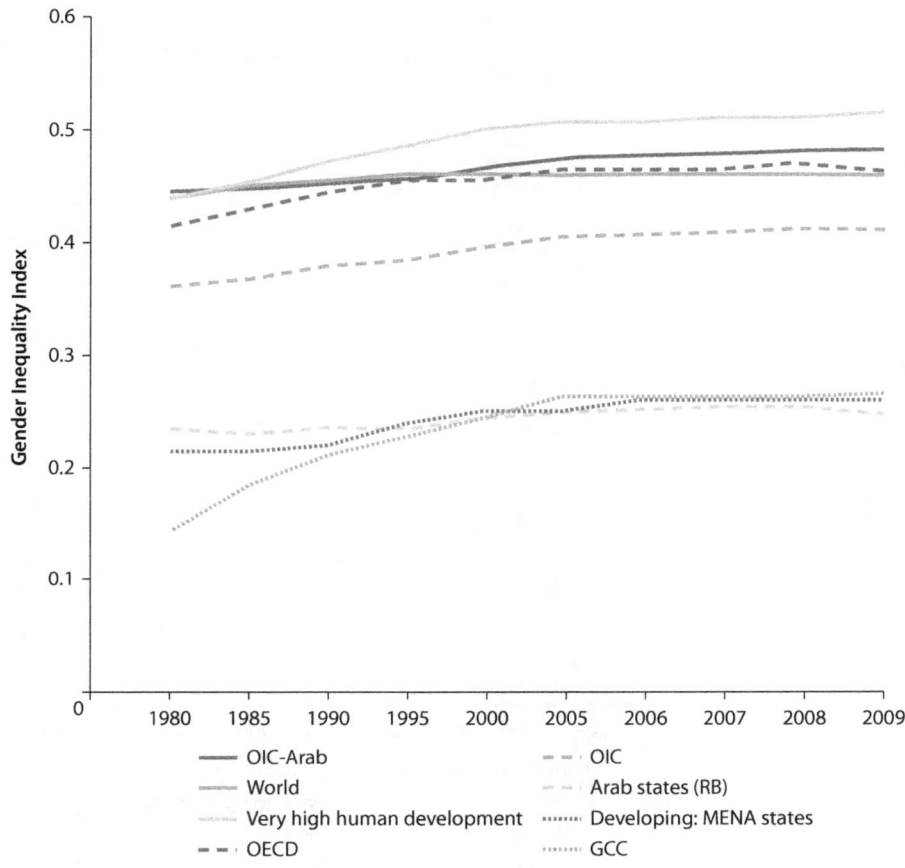

Source: http://data.worldbank.org/topic/gender.
Note: The data represent the average participation of females (ages 15+) in the total labor force. MENA = Middle East and North Africa; RB = regional briefing note; OECD = Organisation for Economic Co-operation and Development; OIC = Organization of Islamic Conference; GCC = Gulf Cooperation Council.

terms of GNI (gross national income) per capita in terms of purchasing power parity in U.S. dollars (PPP$). The results can be seen in figure 11.5. Overall OIC living standards are well below those of the developing Arab countries, as the per capita GNI of the GCC countries is on par with the highly developed countries of the world and the OECD.

To get a more comprehensive picture of the wealth of various regional and country groupings, we also examine income and wealth distribution. Again, as we have said many times before, economic and social justice is the heart of the Islamic system—equity and the eradication of poverty are absolutely central. Figure 11.6 presents the Gini coefficient of the regional and country groupings. The information concerning the Gini coefficient is mixed because of missing data, and as a result may be somewhat misleading. Although this should not negate the fact that income disparity in the OECD countries has risen and is

Figure 11.4 U.N. Health Index

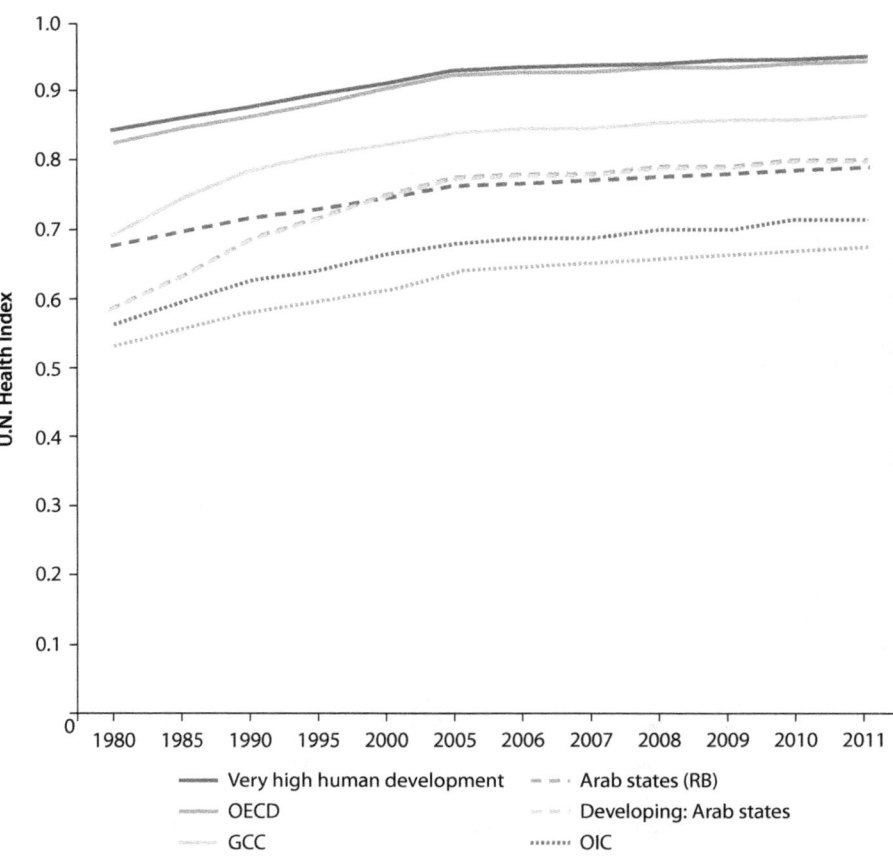

Source: http://hdrstats.undp.org/en/indicators/72206.html.
Note: The U.N. Health Index measures life expectancy at birth. The Health Index is expressed as a number between 0 and 1. RB = regional briefing note; OECD = Organisation for Economic Co-operation and Development; OIC = Organization of Islamic Conference; GCC = Gulf Cooperation Council.

now on par with the developing and emerging world, it should be underscored that income disparity in the OIC group, and in the Arab region, has remained constant over the last 30 years. To gain further insight into the overall income-wealth picture of various regional and country groupings, it may be helpful to look into prevailing poverty levels.[12] Figure 11.7 shows the poverty levels, as measured by the percentage of the population that lives on $1.25 (PPP) or less per day, in various regions and county groupings. By any measure, the OIC countries have not done well with respect to managing and lowering poverty levels over the last 30 years; poverty has not only been persistent but appears to have increased.

Environmental quality and sustainability. Turning to the environment/sustainability record of various regional and country groupings, data limitations

Figure 11.5 U.N. Income (Wealth) Index

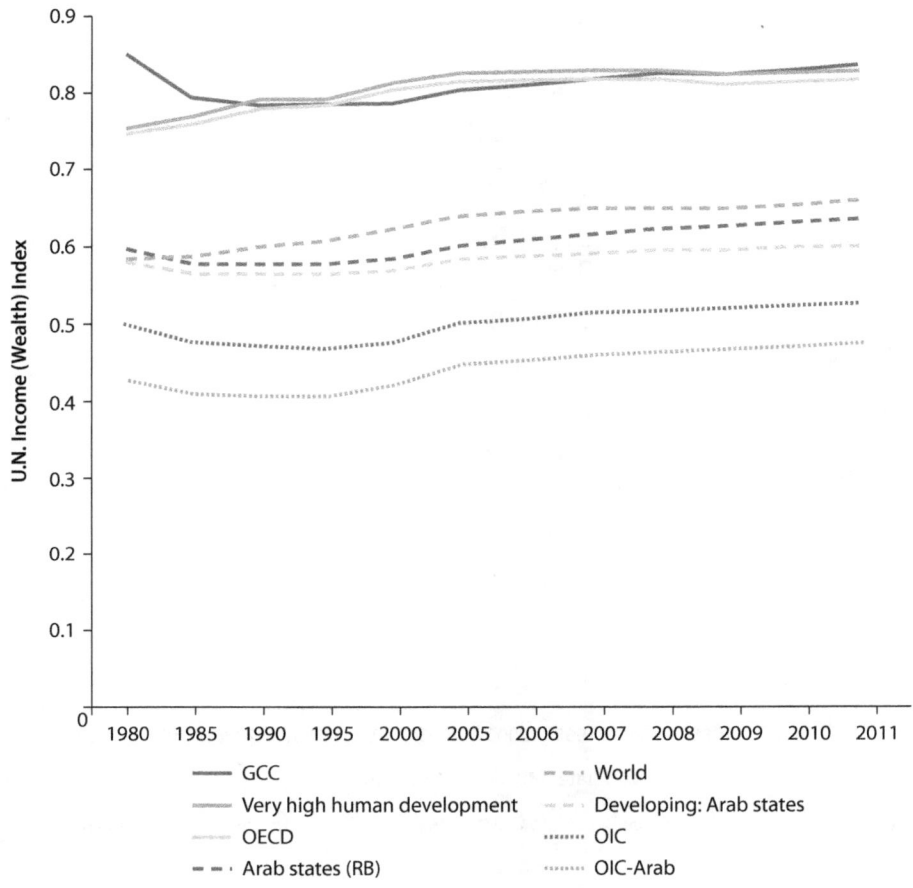

Source: http://hdrstats.undp.org/en/indicators/72206.html.
Note: The U.N. Income (Wealth) Index measures GNI per capita (PPP$). The Income Index is expressed as a value between 0 and 1. RB = regional briefing note; OECD = Organisation for Economic Co-operation and Development; OIC = Organization of Islamic Conference; GCC = Gulf Cooperation Council.

prevented us from conducting a longitudinal assessment. As a result, we can only examine the latest available data for the Environmental Performance Index (EPI) for 2010 (see figure 11.8). The "overall EPI rankings provide an indicative sense of which countries are doing best against the array of environmental pressures that every nation faces."[13] It represents both the environmental health and the ecosystem vitality of countries. The OIC countries clearly trail the world when it comes to environmental responsibilities.

A correlation of performance to Islamic fundamentals. While these indicators confirm the generally held belief that the economic performance of OIC countries has been below par for the last 30 years, there is no credible correlation to Islam or any other religion. While OIC countries profess Islam, they have not followed Islamic teachings as clearly indicated by these comparative results on economic

Figure 11.6 Gini Coefficient

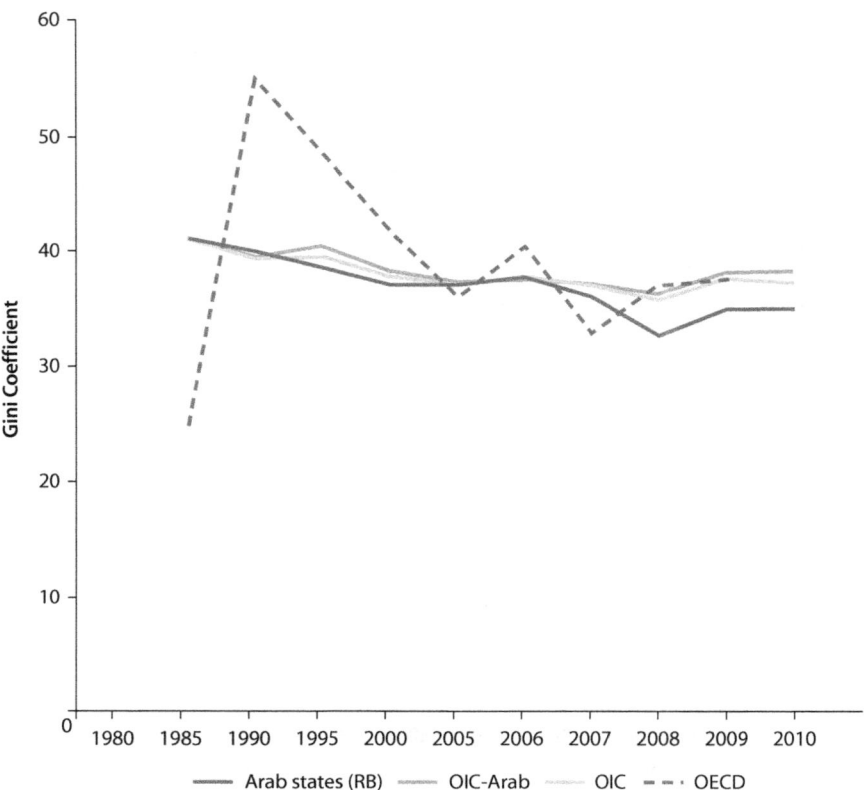

Source: Poverty and Inequality Database: Gini Index, World Development Indicators (WDI). http://povertydata.worldbank.org/poverty/home.
Note: The data represent the Gini coefficient. The following countries had no available data: Brunei Darussalem, Kuwait, Lebanon, Libya, Oman, Saudi Arabia, Somalia, the United Arab Emirates, and the West Bank and Gaza. Data for Iceland were also not available and thus not calculated with the OECD country grouping. Because data were missing for 1995 for the OECD countries, the data were derived by averaging the 1990 and 2000 data points. RB = regional briefing note; OECD = Organisation for Economic Co-operation and Development; OIC = Organization of Islamic Conference.

dimensions stressed in Islam—human development, excellence in education, health care provision, economic prosperity, poverty eradication, equality and justice, and environmental preservation for future generations. In contrast to this study—where we look at a few policies that countries professing Islam should adopt—in two earlier works (Rehman and Askari 2010a, 2010b), we made a first attempt to develop two very rough composite indexes (overall and economic Islamicity) covering adherence to overall and economic Islamic teachings. In other words, to what extent do countries that profess Islam follow its basic principles?

We have reproduced these results in tables 11.1–11.4. These are very preliminary results, but they do tend to indicate that the majority of Islamic countries have not adhered to Islamic principles, by and large. As indicated in tables 11.1

Figure 11.7 Poverty

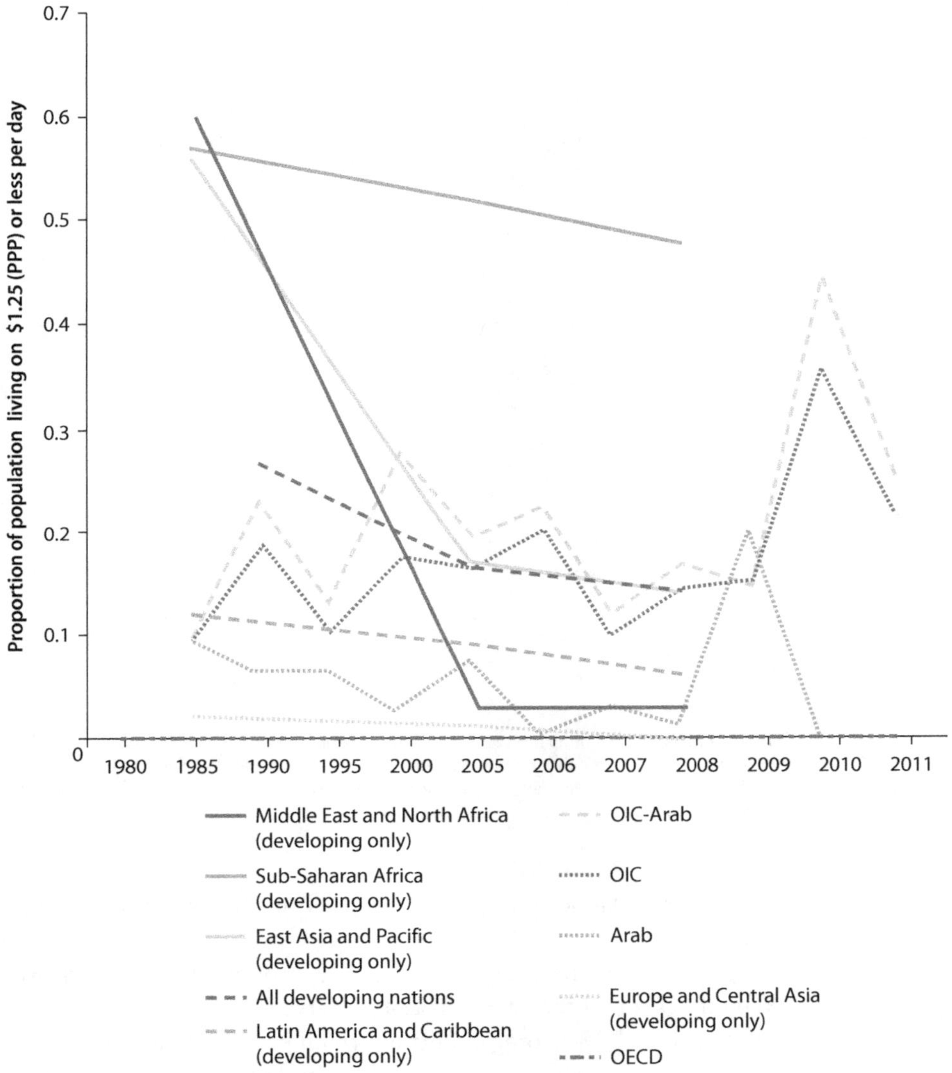

Sources: UNDP (http://hdr.undp.org) and World Bank (http://databank.worldbank.org/).
Note: The Poverty Headcount Ratio measures poverty at $1.25 a day (PPP) (as a percentage of the population). OECD = Organisation for Economic Co-operation and Development; OIC = Organization of Islamic Conference.

and 11.2, the average ranking of the 56 Islamic countries is 139, well below the average ranking of the 208 countries measured. If the Islamic countries (OIC) are compared with OECD countries, the disparities are even more pronounced. One could argue that a fairer comparison would be to the group of non-OECD or middle-income countries. However, even on this basis, the Islamic countries do not perform well as a group. When compared with the 178 non-OECD countries (average rank, 118), the 41 upper-middle-income countries (average rank, 85), and the 123 non-OECD, non-OIC countries (average rank, 108),

Figure 11.8 Environment Index, 2010

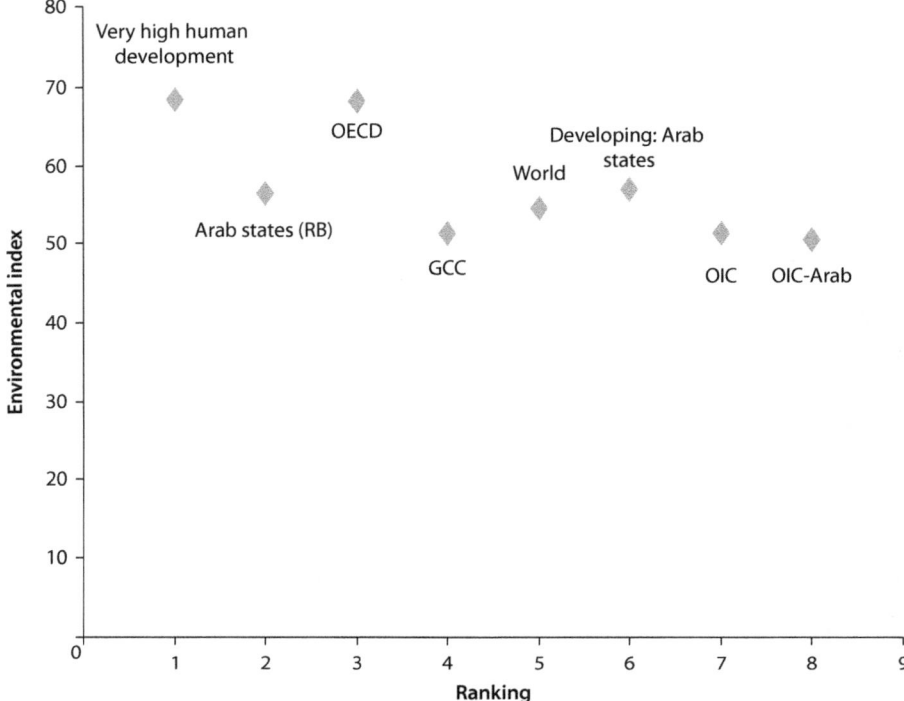

Source: http://www.carboun.com/wp-content/uploads/2010/04/EPI-2010-Full-report.pdf.
Note: The 2010 Environmental Performance Index measures the average of the Environmental Health and the Ecosystem Vitality Indexes of countries. RB = regional briefing note; OECD = Organisation for Economic Co-operation and Development; OIC = Organization of Islamic Conference; GCC = Gulf Cooperation Council.

the performance of the Islamic (OIC) countries performance is the worst, with an average rank of 139.

The degree of failure of the performance of OIC countries is most clearly demonstrated by the fact that the Islamic countries fared even worse on the ranking than the 55 lower-middle-income countries, which had an average ranking of 132. When we used a subset of the index, the Economic Islamicity Index (EI^2), the OIC countries performance was just as low. For example, the average EI^2 rank among the OECD countries is 24, while the average for the OIC is 133 (tables 11.3 and 11.4). Even when compared to non-OECD and middle-income countries, the Islamic countries do not perform well as a group. Of the 178 non-OECD countries (average rank, 118), the 41 upper-middle-income countries (average rank, 83), and the 123 non-OECD, non-OIC countries (average rank, 111), the performance of the Islamic (OIC) countries is the worst, with an average rank of 133.

By these measures, it could be argued that the non-Islamic countries, and especially those of the OECD, are adhering to a far greater extent to Islamic precepts than the self-described Islamic ones.

Table 11.1 Overall Islamicity Index Rank by Economy

Economies (208)	Overall Islamicity Index rank (OIC countries are highlighted)	Economies (208)	Overall Islamicity Index rank (OIC countries are highlighted)
New Zealand	1	St. Vincent and the Grenadines	44
Luxembourg	2	Namibia	45
Ireland	3	Greece	46
Iceland	4	Jamaica	47
Finland	5	Kuwait	48
Denmark	6	Uruguay	48
Canada	7	South Africa	50
United Kingdom	8	Botswana	51
Australia	9	St. Lucia	52
Netherlands	9	Ghana	53
Austria	11	Argentina	54
Norway	12	Brazil	55
Switzerland	13	Mexico	55
Belgium	14	Bulgaria	57
Sweden	15	El Salvador	58
Portugal	16	Philippines	59
Germany	17	Dominica	60
Bahamas, The	18	Israel	61
France	18	Monaco	62
Czech Republic	20	Lesotho	63
Estonia	21	Bahrain	64
Costa Rica	22	Brunei Darussalam	65
Spain	23	Romania	66
Barbados	24	United Arab Emirates	66
United States	25	Belize	68
Slovenia	26	Andorra	69
Hong Kong SAR, China	27	Cayman Islands	70
Latvia	28	Seychelles	71
Japan	29	Fiji	72
Malta	30	Uganda	73
Hungary	31	Tanzania	74
Slovak Republic	31	Antigua and Barbuda	75
Italy	33	Gabon	75
Chile	34	Jordan	77
Lithuania	35	Thailand	78
Cyprus	36	Grenada	79
Singapore	37	San Marino	79
Malaysia	38	China	81
Panama	39	Nicaragua	81
Trinidad and Tobago	40	Cape Verde	83
Poland	41	Macao SAR, China	83
Mauritius	42	Tunisia	83
Croatia	43		

table continues next page

Table 11.1 Overall Islamicity Index Rank by Economy *(continued)*

Economies (208)	Overall Islamicity Index rank (OIC countries are highlighted)	Economies (208)	Overall Islamicity Index rank (OIC countries are highlighted)
Colombia	86	Guatemala	127
Dominican Republic	87	Belarus	128
Peru	88	Malawi	129
India	89	Mali	130
Aruba	90	Saudi Arabia	131
Russian Federation	91	Burkina Faso	132
Honduras	92	Vanuatu	133
Greenland	93	Vietnam	134
Guyana	94	Rwanda	135
Netherlands Antilles	95	Paraguay	136
Mozambique	96	Kyrgyz Republic	137
Mongolia	97	Korea, Dem. People's Rep.	138
Macedonia, FYR	98	Virgin Islands (U.S.)	139
Oman	99	Indonesia	140
Suriname	100	Venezuela, RB	141
Bosnia and Herzegovina	101	Madagascar	142
Ukraine	102	Palau	143
Turkey	103	Kenya	144
Maldives	104	Guinea	145
Liechtenstein	105	Samoa	146
Korea, Rep.	106	Benin	147
Kazakhstan	107	Pakistan	147
Timor-Leste	107	Cuba	149
Senegal	109	New Caledonia	150
Albania	110	Nepal	151
Moldova	110	Bangladesh	152
Qatar	112	Egypt, Arab Rep.	153
Puerto Rico	113	Cambodia	154
Armenia	114	Tonga	155
Kiribati	115	Burundi	156
Sri Lanka	116	Swaziland	156
Georgia	117	Lebanon	158
St. Kitts and Nevis	117	Zimbabwe	159
Morocco	119	Algeria	160
Northern Mariana Islands	119	Micronesia, Fed. Sts.	161
Papua New Guinea	119	Cameroon	162
Zambia	119	Iran, Islamic Rep.	163
Bolivia	123	Myanmar	164
Gambia, The	124	Central African Republic	165
Azerbaijan	125	Bermuda	166
Ecuador	125	Bhutan	167
		Sierra Leone	168

table continues next page

Table 11.1 Overall Islamicity Index Rank by Economy (continued)

Economies (208)	Overall Islamicity Index rank (OIC countries are highlighted)	Economies (208)	Overall Islamicity Index rank (OIC countries are highlighted)
Afghanistan	169	Niger	189
Guam	170	Guinea-Bissau	190
Congo, Dem. Rep.	171	Solomon Islands	190
Togo	172	São Tomé and Príncipe	192
Turkmenistan	173	Djibouti	193
Nigeria	174	Liberia	194
Uzbekistan	174	Mauritania	195
Haiti	176	Libya	196
Tajikistan	176	Chad	197
American Samoa	178	Yemen, Rep.	198
Côte d'Ivoire	179	Angola	199
Ethiopia	180	Comoros	200
French Polynesia	181	Iraq	201
Congo, Rep.	182	Channel Islands	202
Equatorial Guinea	183	Sudan	202
Lao PDR	183	Eritrea	204
Serbia	185	Isle of Man	205
Syrian Arab Republic	186	Somalia	206
Marshall Islands	187	West Bank and Gaza	207
Faeroe Islands	188	Mayotte	208

Source: Authors' calculations.
Note: OIC members are shaded. 1 = Best; 208 = Worst performance in terms of Islamic precepts.

Concluding Remarks on Islam and Economic Performance and Prosperity

As we have emphasized a number of times, there is little evidence to attribute the sub-par economic performance of Muslim countries to Islamic teachings. Just because countries that profess Islam have had sub-par economic performance does not mean that Islamic teachings are the basis for their failure! To the contrary, as discussed, Islamic teachings are fully supportive of sustained growth and prosperity, and hold as central tenants efficient and sound institutions, free markets, market supervision, sound governance, equal opportunity, sanctity of honestly earned income and wealth, rule enforcement, transparency in all business dealings, the importance of education and good health, poverty eradication, financial stability (by embracing equity as opposed to debt financing), admonitions against corruption and hoarding, and so on.

In fact, we would argue that Islamic teachings on economic development and growth are similar to the foundational elements of capitalism, as espoused by Adam Smith, which are the evolving recommendations of modern economic development theories—but with a strong dose of justice.[14] OIC countries have

Table 11.2 Summary Results of the Islamicity Index (I^2) by Country Subgroup (the Lower the Ranking, the Better the Adherence to Islamic Precepts)

Subgroups (no. of countries)	EI^2	LGI^2	HPI^2	IRI^2	Overall I^2 rank
OECD[a] (30)	24	28	29	37	25
High-income[b] (60)	60	40	84	40	60
Upper-middle-income[c] (41)	83	84	88	87	85
All countries (208)	104	96	104	75	104
Non-OECD, non-OIC (123)	111	101	110	89	108
Persian Gulf (7)	94	104	138	109	112
Non-OECD (178)	118	112	116	99	118
Lower-middle-income[d] (55)	116	124	115	112	122
OIC[e] (56)	133	136	130	115	139
Low-income[f] (54)	170	154	126	107	153

Source: Authors elaborations, based on Rehman and Askari 2010a, 2010b.
Note: EI^2 = Economic Islamicity Index; LGI^2 = Legal and Governance Islamicity Index; HPI^2 = Human and Political Rights Islamicity Index; IRI^2 = International Relations Islamicity Index; I^2 = Islamicity Index = $EI^2 + LGI^2 + HPI^2 + IRI^2$.
a. The 30 OECD countries are Australia, Austria, Belgium, Canada, the Czech Republic, Denmark, Finland, France, Germany, Greece, Hungary, Iceland, Ireland, Italy, Japan, the Republic of Korea, Luxembourg, Mexico, the Netherlands, New Zealand, Norway, Poland, Portugal, the Slovak Republic, Spain, Sweden, Switzerland, Turkey, the United Kingdom, and the United States.
b. Economies are divided according to 2011 GNI per capita, calculated using the World Bank Atlas method. High-income countries are classified as having a GNI per capita of $12,476 or more.
c. Upper-middle-income countries are classified as having a GNI per capita of $4,036–12,475.
d. Lower-middle-income countries are classified as having a GNI per capita of $1,026–4,035.
e. Only 56 of the 57 OIC countries are included in this data set. Significant data on the West Bank and Gaza were not available and thus were not included.
f. Low-income countries are classified as having a GNI per capita of $1,025 or less as per the World Bank.

Table 11.3 Economic Islamicity Index (EI^2) Rankings by Economy[a]

Economies	EI^2 rank	Economies	EI^2 rank
Ireland	1	Iceland	20
Denmark	2	Japan	21
Luxembourg	3	Estonia	22
Sweden	4	Switzerland	23
United Kingdom	4	Lithuania	24
New Zealand	6	Czech Republic	25
Singapore	7	Germany	26
Finland	8	Israel	27
Norway	9	Spain	28
Belgium	10	Portugal	29
Austria	11	Slovenia	30
Hong Kong SAR, China	12	Korea, Rep.	31
Canada	13	Latvia	32
Australia	14	Malaysia	33
Netherlands	15	Italy	34
United States	15	Slovak Republic	35
France	17	Thailand	36
Cyprus	18	Costa Rica	37
Chile	19	Bahamas, The	38

table continues next page

Table 11.3 Economic Islamicity Index (EI²) Rankings by Economy[a] *(continued)*

Economies	EI² rank	Economies	EI² rank
Barbados	39	South Africa	84
Northern Mariana Islands	40	Ukraine	84
Hungary	41	Mongolia	86
Kuwait	42	Lebanon	87
Greece	43	Ghana	88
Malta	44	Puerto Rico	89
Russian Federation	45	Moldova	90
Cayman Islands	46	Saudi Arabia	91
Armenia	47	Turkmenistan	92
Poland	48	Jamaica	93
Mexico	49	Belarus	94
Croatia	50	Maldives	95
Seychelles	51	Kyrgyz Republic	96
Bosnia and Herzegovina	52	India	97
Panama	53	Bolivia	98
Kazakhstan	54	Uganda	99
Brunei Darussalam	55	Aruba	100
Colombia	56	Antigua and Barbuda	101
Monaco	57	Georgia	102
Bulgaria	58	St. Vincent and the Grenadines	103
Dominica	59	Indonesia	104
Mauritius	60	Albania	105
Bahrain	61	Korea, Dem. People's Rep.	106
China	62	Sri Lanka	107
Uruguay	63	Macedonia, FYR	108
Trinidad and Tobago	64	Guyana	109
United Arab Emirates	64	Vietnam	110
Botswana	66	Cambodia	111
Brazil	67	Qatar	111
Argentina	68	Cuba	113
Netherlands Antilles	69	Venezuela, RB	114
El Salvador	70	St. Kitts and Nevis	115
Turkey	71	Ecuador	116
Tunisia	72	Serbia	117
Namibia	73	Vanuatu	118
Jordan	74	Honduras	119
Romania	75	Morocco	120
New Caledonia	76	Fiji	121
San Marino	77	Madagascar	122
Peru	78	Nicaragua	123
St. Lucia	79	Faeroe Islands	124
Azerbaijan	80	Andorra	125
Philippines	81	Macao SAR, China	126
Oman	82	Guatemala	127
Kiribati	83	Dominican Republic	128

table continues next page

Table 11.3 Economic Islamicity Index (EI²) Rankings by Economy[a] *(continued)*

Economies	EI² rank	Economies	EI² rank
Egypt, Arab Rep.	128	Central African Republic	170
Grenada	130	Guinea	171
Algeria	131	Liechtenstein	172
Uzbekistan	132	Angola	173
Paraguay	133	Libya	174
Tonga	134	Lao PDR	175
Belize	135	Benin	176
Swaziland	136	Myanmar	177
Cape Verde	137	Burundi	178
Lesotho	138	Isle of Man	179
Iran, Islamic Rep.	139	Yemen, Rep.	180
Palau	140	Cameroon	181
Bangladesh	141	Mauritania	182
Mozambique	142	Zambia	183
Gabon	143	Papua New Guinea	184
Tanzania	144	Micronesia, Fed. Sts.	185
Pakistan	145	Zimbabwe	186
Ethiopia	146	Chad	187
Tajikistan	147	Niger	188
Iraq	148	West Bank and Gaza	189
Afghanistan	149	Sudan	190
Solomon Islands	150	Congo, Rep.	191
Gambia, The	151	Eritrea	191
Senegal	152	Marshall Islands	193
Virgin Islands (U.S.)	153	Haiti	194
Kenya	154	Togo	195
Djibouti	155	Liberia	196
Suriname	156	Comoros	197
Timor-Leste	157	Congo, Dem. Rep.	198
Nepal	158	Somalia	199
Bhutan	159	Sierra Leone	200
Nigeria	160	Côte d'Ivoire	201
Rwanda	160	Guinea-Bissau	202
Samoa	162	French Polynesia	203
Malawi	163	Guam	204
Mali	164	Bermuda	205
Channel Islands	165	Mayotte	206
Equatorial Guinea	166	American Samoa	207
Burkina Faso	167	Greenland	208
Syrian Arab Republic	168	*Average*	*104.46*
São Tomé and Príncipe	169		

Source: Authors' calculations.
Note: OIC members are shaded. EI² = Economic Islamicity Index; 1 = Best; 208 = Worst performance in terms of Islamic precepts.
a. Only 56 of the 57 OIC countries are included in this data set. Significant data on the West Bank and Gaza were not available and thus were not included.

Table 11.4 **Economic Islamicity (EI²) Index Ranking Averages of All Countries and Various Subgroups**

Subgroups (no. of countries)	Average EI² rank
OECD (30)	24.37
High-income (60)	60.27
Upper-middle-income (41)	83.10
Persian Gulf (7)	93.71
Non-OECD, non-OIC (123)	110.81
Lower-middle-income (55)	115.75
Non-OECD (178)	117.96
OIC (56)	132.82
Low-income (54)	160.48

Source: Authors' calculations.
Note: For definitions of county subgroups, see table 11.2. EI² = Economic Islamicity Index.

exhibited sub-par economic performance not because they have followed Islamic economic prescriptions and policies—good institutions, the rule of law, economic justice, and best practices—but precisely because they have not. It is worth repeating that Islamic teachings are similar to today's Western economic recommendations for sustained economic development and growth, with one difference. Islam inserts morality and justice into the core of societal development.

It would be incorrect to pick one or two elements from Islamic teachings and then go on to say that it is this or that reason why countries that profess Islam have fared badly. There are a host of reasons why countries do well or badly when it comes to economic development and growth, and good institutions are key. For instance, is it sensible to conclude that Islamic inheritance laws—affording each child an equal share of parental bequests, with male descendants receiving double that of females (as well as espousal rights to inheritance)—are the cause of sub-par performance because wealth becomes too dispersed? Is it not less dispersed in Islam than if parents were to give each child (male and female) an equal share, which most parents do in the West (or is there strong evidence that parents divide their bequests more unequally in the non-Muslim world)? Is not diversification, as with most things, better in reducing risk than a sole inheritor who could waste every cent of his or her inheritance? Or is there evidence that wealth disparity is the key to higher growth? Are not the inheritance laws of some countries, such as France (with the exception of the differential share of male and female children), similar to Islamic law (basically limiting inheritance to the spouse and children)? Similarly, is it reasonable to attribute sub-par performance to the Islamic prohibition against debt? Why not speculate that the frequency and length of Muslim prayers is the reason for sub-par economic growth in the OIC? We could go on and on. Again, there is no link between sub-par growth and Islam. Moreover, if any link was to be confirmed, it would have to be in the context of a complete model where all factors affecting development and growth are considered.

We attribute the sub-par performance of Muslim countries to their bad governance. These countries have been plagued by corrupt, unrepresentative, and oppressive governments, in many cases the relic of the colonial era. The rulers in a number of these countries continue to be supported by foreign powers and their influential elites, corporations, and individuals. Muslim rulers and their supporters (both domestic and foreign) have been motivated and driven by self-enrichment, with no incentive to develop and nourish effective institutions, which in turn would only undermine their own autocratic rule. Instead, military expenditures have ballooned to support their tight grip on power, exacerbating costly internal and regional conflicts and wars. The inflow of vast oil revenues in some countries has also been reflected in shortsighted policies, such as vast subsidies to buy domestic political support. This has led to failed governance and policies resulting in undemocratic societies caught in a vicious cycle of economic deprivation and injustice for the vast majority of the citizenry. These policies, practices, and fallouts, which are admonished by Islam, have been erroneously connected in some quarters to Islam. To our mind, the reason that OIC countries have exhibited sub-par economic performance is not that they have followed Islamic economic prescriptions and policies—good institutions, the rule of law, economic justice, and best practices—but precisely that they have not.

Notes

1. The OIC comprises 56 countries and the West Bank and Gaza: Afghanistan, Albania, Algeria, Azerbaijan, Bahrain, Bangladesh, Benin, Brunei Darussalam, Burkina Faso, Cameroon, Chad, the Comoros, Côte d'Ivoire, Djibouti, the Arab Republic of Egypt, Gabon, The Gambia, Guinea, Guinea-Bissau, Guyana, Indonesia, the Islamic Republic of Iran, Iraq, Jordan, Kazakhstan, Kuwait, the Kyrgyz Republic, Lebanon, Libya, Malaysia, Maldives, Mali, Mauritania, Morocco, Mozambique, Niger, Nigeria, Oman, Pakistan, Qatar, Saudi Arabia, Senegal, Sierra Leone, Somalia, Sudan, Suriname, the Syrian Arab Republic, Tajikistan, Togo, Tunisia, Turkey, Turkmenistan, Uganda, the United Arab Emirates, Uzbekistan, the West Bank and Gaza, and the Republic of Yemen. They have governments that have adopted Islam as the official state religion; or have Islam as their primary religion; or have a significant Muslim population; or have simply declared themselves an Islamic republic.

2. For further details, see Askari and Taghavi (2005).

3. The Human Development Index (HDI) measures development by combining the three dimensions of health, education, and living standards into a composite index. As such, it is a "single statistic which serves as a frame of reference for both social and economic development. The HDI sets a minimum and a maximum for each dimension, called goalposts, and then shows where each country stands in relation to these goalposts, expressed as a value between 0 and 1" (http://hdr.undp.org/en/statistics/hdi/).

4. All data for this study come from the United Nations data bank or the World Development Indicators (WDI). Because of the longitudinal nature of this study, the data for some countries in their regional and country grouping were sporadic or missing. This has been a significant limitation for the comparisons in this study.

A Survey of the Economic Development of OIC Countries   323

5. As explained on the HDR website, "The scores for [these] three HDI dimension indices are then aggregated into a composite index using geometric mean" (http://hdr.undp.org/en/statistics/hdi/).

6. The 34 member-countries of the Organisation for Economic Co-operation and Development (OECD) comprise the world's most highly industrialized economies.

7. The Education Index (EI) of the HDI is "measured by mean of years of schooling for adults aged 25 years and expected years of schooling for children of school entering age. Mean years of schooling is estimated based on educational attainment data from censuses and surveys available in the UNESCO Institute for Statistics database and Barro and Lee (2010) methodology. Expected years of schooling estimates are based on enrollment by age at all levels of education and population of official school age for each level of education. Expected years of schooling is capped at 18 years. The indicators are normalized using a minimum value of zero and maximum values are set to the actual observed maximum value of mean years of schooling from the countries in the time series, 1980–2010. Expected years of schooling is maximized by its cap at 18 years. The EI is the geometric mean of two indices" (http://hdr.undp.org/en/statistics/hdi/).

8. See http://data.worldbank.org/topic/gender.

9. The gender equality measures how active women are in the labor force by calculating the average of the labor force rate, female rate (percentage of female population ages 15+), and labor participation rate (percentage of total labor force).

10. The life expectancy at birth component of the HDI is calculated using a minimum value of 20 years and maximum value of 83.4 years. This is the observed maximum value of the indicators from the countries in the time series, 1980–2010. Thus, the longevity component for a country where life expectancy at birth is 55 years would be 0.552 (http://hdrstats.undp.org/en/indicators/72206.html).

11. "For the wealth component, the goalpost for minimum income is $100 (PPP) and the maximum is $107,721 (PPP), both estimated during the same period, 1980–2011. The decent standard of living component is measured by gross national income (GNI) per capita (PPP$) instead of GDP per capita (PPP$). The HDI uses the logarithm of income, to reflect the diminishing importance of income with increasing GNI" (http://hdr.undp.org/en/statistics/hdi/).

12. Poverty is measured by the poverty headcount ratio at $1.25 a day (PPP) (% of population). The following countries had no data available for any category in the Poverty Index: Brunei Darussalem, Kuwait, Lebanon, Libya, Oman, Saudi Arabia, Somalia, the United Arab Emirates, and the West Bank and Gaza. Data from OECD (http://hdr.undp.org) and WDI (http://databank.worldbank.org/).

13. The 2010 Environmental Performance Index was developed by the Yale Center of Environmental Law and Policy, Center for International Earth Science Information Network (CIESIN) in collaboration with the World Economic Forum and the Joint Research Center of the European Commission (http://www.carboun.com/wp-content/uploads/2010/04/EPI-2010-Full-report.pdf).

14. See Mirakhor and Askari (2010) and chapter 1 of this volume.

References

Askari, Hossein, and Roshanak Taghavi. 2005. "The Principal Foundations of an Islamic Economy." *Banca Nazionale Del Lavoro Quarterly Review* LVIII (235).

Barro, Robert J., and Jong-Wha Lee. 2010. "A New Data Set of Educational Attainment in the World, 1950–2010." NBER Working Paper No. 15902, April. National Bureau of Economic Research, Cambridge, MA.

Cummings, Thomas J., Hossein Askari, and Ahmad Mustafa. 1980. "Islam and Modern Economic Change." In *Islam and Development*, edited by John L. Esposito. New York: Syracuse University Press.

Mirakhor, Abbas, and Hossein Askari. 2010. *Islam and the Path to Human and Economic Development*. New York: Palgrave Macmillan.

Rehman, Scheherazade, and Hossein Askari. 2010a. "How Islamic Are Islamic Countries?" *Global Economy Journal* 10 (2).

———. 2010b. "An Economic Islamicity Index." *Global Economy Journal* 10 (3).

Smith, Adam. (1759) 2002. *The Theory of Moral Sentiments*. Reprint, edited by Knud Haakonssen. Cambridge, U.K.: Cambridge University Press. Citations refer to the 2002 Cambridge University Press edition.

———. (1776) 1977. *An Inquiry into the Nature and Causes of the Wealth of Nations*. Reprint, Chicago, IL: University Of Chicago Press. Citations refer to the 1977 University of Chicago Press edition.

Solow, Robert M. 1974. "Intergenerational Equity and Exhaustible Resources." *The Review of Economic Studies* 41: 29–45, Symposium on the Economics of Exhaustible Resources.

CHAPTER 12

Islam and Development: Policy Challenges

Azura Othman and Abbas Mirakhor

Introduction

The basic premise of economic development has been focused on achieving material growth. Traditionally, macroeconomic policies have been devised to achieve economic growth with price stability. More recently, however, the growth of an economy has been thought of in terms of improving the quality of life. There have been more calls for ethical production and consumption than ever before. Increasingly, contemporary discussions on economic development have placed more emphasis on human development as a prerequisite to attaining economic development.

Economists such as Mahbub ul Haq and Amartya Sen have changed the focus of thinking about development to expanding human capabilities and well-being. At the same time, many social and environmental problems have shifted the focus to human beings as the end of development rather than as means of achieving progress. The symbiotic relationship between humankind, the Creator, and the environment can no longer be ignored in achieving sustained and civilized development. Macroeconomic policies are taking cognizance of social and environmental elements as integral parts of the decision process (Mirakhor and Askari 2010).

The many discourses on the subject are not surprising considering the repercussions of the crises that have hit the world economy of late and the high incidence of world poverty—despite the rapid economic progress of past few decades. In the pursuit of economic growth, social aspects have often been compromised. In the wake of the recent financial crisis, for example, astronomical sums of public tax money have been poured into the affected economies to avert a complete breakdown. Whether or not bailouts are justified, the risk of reckless leveraging for high private profits was shifted ultimately to taxpayers,

---

Azura Othman is a PhD candidate at the International Centre for Education in Islamic Finance (INCEIF), Malaysia. Abbas Mirakhor is the First Holder of the INCEIF Chair in Islamic Finance.

as they have had to bear the costs. In the process, economic justice has suffered.

A policy design that favors a rich minority over an increasingly impoverished majority is not a credible economic policy for social equality. If the social aspects of economic growth are a matter of central concern, then the adequacy and appropriateness of the policies currently being implemented to regulate the economy need to be reviewed. The weaknesses in the current system can be pinned down to policies and practices that encourage excessive creation of debt and pay little attention to the social and ethical aspects of market practices. The existence of "rentiers" (rent seekers), which thrive on such policies and extract excessive private profits at the expense of the public, further widens the divergence between the financial and real sector of the economy. Therefore, policy tools that provide an incentive structure for closing the gap between the financial and real sector of the economy and at the same time enhance social solidarity through the mutual sharing of risks and returns are needed to achieve economic justice.

One of the main challenges to "reforming" the current policy structure is steering out of the "path-dependency" created by the elements of interest ingrained in the financial system in the economy.[1] This chapter highlights a new path. It presents an approach to monetary and fiscal policy that addresses the current weakness and argues that the potential benefits of implementing it outweigh the perceived costs of reform.

This new approach builds on the foundational principles of Islamic economy, which places its greatest emphasis on the development of an individual's active moral consciousness in all social interactions. Spiritual achievements are not separable from legitimate economic pursuits. Every person is accountable for all of her/his actions in this world. Therefore, rule-compliance is a prerequisite to achieving social order on earth. Social order is achieved when there is social and economic justice within the society. One of the bases of economic justice is equality in opportunity of access to and distribution of resources. Distributive justice is achieved through instruments of redemption of the rights of the less able. The approach and policy tools advocated in this chapter build on this foundation.

The Islamic Economy and the Role of the State

In all economic systems, the state plays a role in the economy. Only the extent of the state's involvement differs, depending on the common values and belief system shared by the individuals that make up the particular society. The role of the state in an Islamic economy is to ensure that everyone has equal access to resources and means of livelihood, the markets are supervised so that justice is attained and transfers takes place from the more able to the less able—and that distributive justice is ensured for the next generation (Al-Hasani and Mirakhor 2003). As is mentioned in a number of essays in this book, Islam is a rule-based system. In such a system, the state regulates, supervises, and provides an incentive structure for rule-compliance, all within the framework prescribed by the Qur'an and *Sunnah*.

Islam uses the market as a mechanism to solve part of the coordination problem within the economy. The state enters the market as the supervisor/regulator of economic activity. It is the combination of state supervision/regulation and free enterprise that will be used to maximize social welfare. The state must actively complement market forces to ensure that individual initiative does not degenerate into a private greed for gains, especially when the gains are nonproductive. The capstone rule in Islam is urging compliance with the rules and discouraging rule violation. Compliance with this rule is required of all members of society.

The role of the government is only that of a trustee to society, and it is to act according to the rules prescribed in the Qur'an and *Sunnah*. Therefore, the foundation for legitimacy of the government is rule-compliance. In Islam, legitimacy of a government is initiated through a contract of *mubaya'ah*—a contract of exchange between the government (the ruler) and the people. The government makes a commitment to strict adherence to rules prescribed by the Qur'an in exchange for the loyalty of the people, so long as that government remains rule-compliant. Repeatedly, both the Qur'an and the Beloved Messenger emphasize that members of the society must remain vigilant in exercising their duty of "urging rule compliance and discouraging rule violation" (*al 'amr i bi al Ma'ruf wa anNahi 'anil Munkar*) with respect to one another and with respect to the government. In former times, the act of *mubaya'ah* was performed directly between those who were to rule and the people, or it was done by their representatives, where distance prohibited direct contact between rulers and the people. It is presumed that this function is performed by election in contemporary times. If so, then it is the responsibility of the people in society to participate fully in the election of the government. Hence, the duty of electing and voting out a government is given to society, where every individual has equal political rights and the responsibility of participation.

The role of the government is broadly divided into two functions: a policy function that ensures that private interest does not diverge too far from public interest; and a function to design and implement an incentive structure to encourage rule-compliance, coordination, and cooperation. The presence of market failures can impair economic relations and transactions. In such a situation, government intervention is justified to protect the public interest. The state, through the government, is empowered to use all available means permitted by law to achieve the objectives and duties prescribed for the society, including synchronization of individual and public interests. An important function of government is to reduce uncertainty for members of society to allow them to overcome the obstacles in decision making caused by lack of information. The rules prescribed specify what kind of conduct is most appropriate in achieving just results when individuals face alternative choices. The degree of effectiveness of rule enforcement is determined by the degree to which the members of the society internalize the objective of social justice.

Policy Tools in Macroeconomic Management

Policies are decisions of the government to undertake certain actions directed toward achieving certain objectives. At a macro level, policies have been traditionally designed to achieve the objective of the economic system consistent with the world view of the society. In most cases, the achievement of growth and development in the economy is seen as the primary objective of macroeconomic policies.

In an idealized model, macroeconomic policies create inducements that elicit desired responses from sectors of the economy reflecting the desired level of income, prices, and employment. Two main policy tools are utilized to achieve this. Monetary policy uses the instrument of the interest rate to increase or reduce the level of supply of money, and thus spending and production in the economy. Fiscal policy uses the power of the government to tax and spend as a means of influencing aggregate demand and the level of economic activity. Whenever there is a shock to the economy, these tools are used, independently or in combination, to stabilize the economy. An important consequence of the global financial crisis has been the increasing challenge in managing the macro-economy and sustaining economic growth. In this context, uncertainty has been growing about the adequacy of current policy regimes, whose central anchor is the interest–based debt system.

The Interest-Based Financial System

At the core of a conventional economic system is the interest-based financial system. Banks are the main institution that operates the financial system. The traditional function of a bank is to accept deposits from the surplus sector of the economy and channel them to the deficit sector in the form of lending. This financial intermediation has an important function in the economy in that it facilitates the circulation of surplus wealth for productive use within the economy. Over time, the fractional reserve banking system emerged, which allows lending activities to be a multiple of the deposits held by the banks.

An intrinsic feature of the interest-based system is that the risks of a debt transaction are transferred from the lender to the borrower. The rate of return to the lender is guaranteed, regardless of the outcome of the business undertaking of the borrower. The property right to the money lent remains with the borrower, as the lender must return the principal together with the interest.

The interest-based financial system creates a phenomenon known as "financialization" that results in a divergence between the real sector and the financial sector of the economy. The current fractional banking system allows multiple amounts of money to be created out of a given amount of deposits received, enhancing the process of creating debt. The development of complex financial derivatives has resulted in credit expansion outpacing the growth of the real sector of the economy. As layer upon layer of securitization decouples the connection between the financial and real sectors, an inverted credit pyramid is created to the extent that the liabilities of the economy becomes a large multiple of real assets needed to validate them (Mirakhor 2011). Additionally, such a system is characterized by mismatched maturity and values of asset and liability structure of balance sheets of banks. These institutions borrow short and lend long. When subjected to asset price shocks, the liability side of the balance sheet is very slow to adjust, while the asset side adjusts rapidly. Both mismatches create a potential for instability that can spread rapidly through contagion. The result can be an increase in the frequency, contagion, and severity of financial and economic crises (Askari and others 2012).

Monetary Policy and the Transmission Mechanism

Monetary policy is a process undertaken by the monetary authority in controlling the money supply and cost of money in achieving the stability of the economy. It relies on the relationship between the rate of interest and the supply of money to influence economic growth, inflation, exchange rates, and unemployment. The central bank is normally the institution that manages the economy's money supply, currency and interest rates. It has control over the country's monetary base and regulates the financial system through the operation of monetary policy. The operation of monetary policy is conducted through open market operations, buying and selling financial instruments, and setting the reserve requirement and the discount rate. Central banks serve the function of being the lender of last resort to the banking sector.

In undertaking an expansionary monetary policy, the central bank will seek to expand the monetary base—consisting of money in circulation, as well as the banking sector reserve with the central bank—by injecting liquidity in the economy. This can be done by reducing the reserve requirements of the banking sector or through open market operations: either through large purchases of financial instruments such as government bonds, or direct lending to the banking system with low discount rates, thereby increasing the amount of cash in the system. This mechanism works through the banking sector as the transmission agent for the expansionary monetary policy. A reduction in the discount rate or reserve requirement signals a "green light" for the banking sector to expand balance sheets and increase lending, which in turn aims at increased spending by consumers. An illustration of this transmission mechanism is presented in figure 12.1.

Monetary policy must meet certain challenges: notably, dealing with the flexibility of the financial system to react, and ensuring the timing and credibility of announcements. The latter depends on the success of the previously implemented monetary policies, as reputation is an important element in the implementation of a successful monetary policy. The success of this policy also depends on the effectiveness of the transmission mechanism and the independence of the central bank from the rest of government. The objectives of the government as policy makers and the private banking sector may not converge. When the banking sector does not transmit the increased liquidity to the rest of the private sector and consumers, but instead uses the liquidity to expand its own bottom line, then the transmission mechanism has failed. Within the context of a

Figure 12.1 A Transmission Mechanism in a Conventional Economy

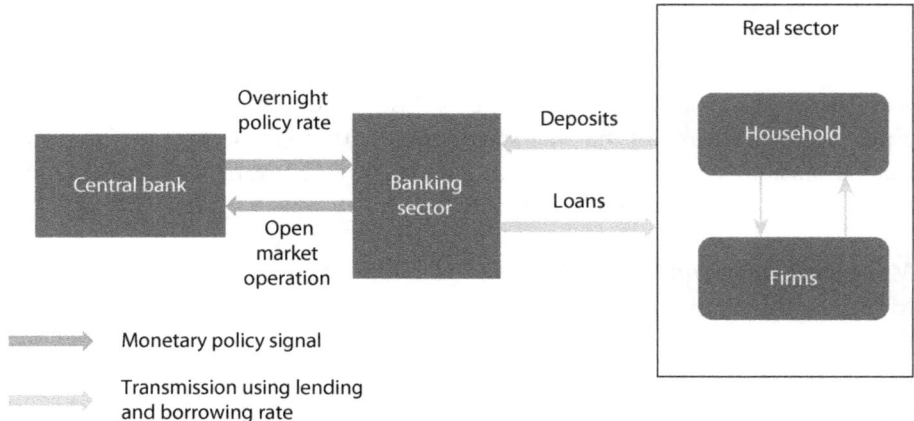

fractional reserve banking system, the role of the central bank in the course of implementing its monetary policy makes the current conventional financial system unstable and vulnerable to financial turmoil through the expansion of credit out of "thin air." Interest rates set by the central bank create a wedge between the money interest rate and the natural rate of interest.[2] It allows money capital to multiply independently of real or physical output. Creation of credits not backed by real economy diverts real savings from productive activities to nonproductive activities that in turn weaken the process of real wealth expansion.

Fiscal Policy

Fiscal policy is the use of the government's power to tax and spend to influence economic activities. In most situations, when government spending has increased and revenues have not increased commensurately, governments have financed the resulting shortfalls (budget deficits) by increasing borrowing, raising taxes, or both. In theory, a stimulus to spur economic activity during slow-downs is supposed to be financed by subsequent growth. More often than not, the current and prospective rates of growth of the economy are lower than the interest rate on the growing debt. Growth may not be large or fast enough to validate debt levels that may exceed 100 percent of gross domestic product (GDP), as is the case today in many advanced countries. The solution of austerity, higher taxes, and lower spending suggested by the dominant policy regime, requires a strong political consensus. Increased borrowing by issuing bonds or long-term government borrowing also does not appear to be a desirable solution, as it increases vulnerability to shocks, creates a burden on future taxpayers, and has adverse distributional implications.

The current public sector borrowing policy in a conventional economy that is based on interest is putting countries in a highly leveraged position. As borrowing increases, the country runs the risk of producing income only to service the interest on debt. The problem of debt repayment must be passed on to the public, as tax revenue must increase in order to pay for the debt. As borrowing continues to fund increasing government spending, the problem will be passed on to future generations of taxpayers. When government borrowings are funded externally, the problem is exacerbated by the outflow of resources on debt servicing that will add pressure to the balance of payments. So far the solution to the problem has come in the form of providing more loans to help countries out of their debt problem. A question that arises is whether solving a debt crisis with more debt is the right solution to the problem.

The Prohibition of Interest and the Promotion of Risk Sharing

Islam ordains fair and equitable dealings among humans. Accordingly, Islam specifically provides a clear prohibition against interest (or *riba*) in a number of verses in the Qur'an.[3] No rule violation is ever scorned more than engaging in interest rate–based transactions (*riba*).[4]

Islam considers an interest rate–based contract unfair and inequitable because it shifts the risks of financial transactions to the borrower. The loan transaction itself violates the basic principle of protecting property rights, as the right of ownership of the money lent is not fully transferred. The lender retains property rights to the principal, in addition to collateral, but has claims on the property of the borrower in the form of the principal plus interest.

Instead of interest-based transactions, Islam ordains equitable exchange, thus encouraging sharing both the risk and the rewards (or losses) of transactions. Equity finance is an example of financing that is not based on interest rates. The return to the equity asset is not known at the time of investing; it depends on the performance of the underlying real sector project. Thus the risk (and any future rewards or losses) of the asset are shared by the investor and entrepreneurs.

The Concept of Risk Sharing

The concept of risk sharing is central to the tenants of fair and equitable finance. Risk and uncertainty are ever-present facts of life. In contemporary societies, people face two types of risk: systematic risk and idiosyncratic risk (Mirakhor 2011). The first type of risk relates to risks that are widely shared (such as war, natural disasters, contagious diseases, famines, and in the economic sphere, macroeconomic fluctuations). Such risk cannot be diversified. However, in the economic sphere, such risks can be mitigated through sound macroeconomic policies that strengthen economic fundamentals, effective international policy coordination, and steps to make the financial system more stable. Idiosyncratic risk relates to risks that are specific to individuals (such as risk of sickness and accidents). Such risks are diversifiable and hence insurable.

The presence of risk makes life uncertain, and lack of certainty can lead to paralysis in decision making. Uncertainties of life can be mitigated by complying with the rules of behavior as provided in the Qur'an. These rules promote risk sharing. Sharing of risk intensifies human interaction and increases solidarity among members of the society.

In the economic sphere, the rule prescribing exchange allows the risk of transactions to be shared. Idiosyncratic risks such as variability of income and consumption can be mitigated through risk-sharing arrangements that allow consumption smoothing. The rich in the society are mandated to share the risk of life with the poor. When the rich shirk on their duty to share by refusing to redeem the rights of the poor in the wealth they possess, poverty increases in the society.

Public policy plays a crucial role in creating an effective incentive structure to promote risk sharing and strengthen an institutional framework that assists in reducing individual risks. Clear and secure property rights, contract enforcement, and trust among people and between people and the government can reduce risk and uncertainty, strengthen social solidarity, and bring private and public interests into closer harmony. Islamic finance instruments of risk sharing can help cushion the impact of economic shocks and suffering of individuals by dispersing their effects among a large number of people.

In a society, risk can be shared among its members and/or between its members and the state. An example of a risk-sharing instrument that has been popular with governments is the public-private partnership. This is a cooperative venture between the government and the private sector in which risks and returns are shared through a long-term contract.

The same concept can be replicated between the government and the public. For example, public policy can be devised to mobilize savings of poor households (for example, in the form of *Takaful*, or financial cooperatives) and reduce vulnerability to income shocks (see chapters 7 and 8).

Contemporary governments have become ultimate risk managers of their societies. Precepts of Islamic finance and development add the dimension to this role to promote social justice and equality. As the agent (*wakil*) of their people, governments can take steps to involve the citizens in sharing the risks and rewards of financing government activities more directly and on a much wider scale that has been the practice.

Policy Instruments in an Islamic Economy

The foundational principles of Islamic finance are that all transactions must be based on contracts of exchange and that interest-rate-based contracts are prohibited. The role of the government and hence the policies adopted include promotion of risk sharing, while simultaneously increasing the effectiveness of monetary policy and creating greater fiscal space and a stable macroeconomic environment (Askari and others 2010, 2012; Debrun and Kapoor 2010; Duval, Elmeskov, and Vogel 2006).

A distinctive feature of the Islamic financial system is that monetary policy influences portfolio adjustments of the private sector directly through the expansion and/or contraction of the money supply through the capital market investment, rather than through the money market through the lending process, as in the conventional economy. As a result, expansion in money supply has a much greater chance of being accompanied by increase in real production. This feature makes the Islamic financial system relatively more stable (Siddiqi 2001). Concerns have been raised, however, regarding the ability of governments to deal with severe fiscal constraints where borrowing is not permitted. Therefore, alternative policy instruments that move away from interest-based borrowing to those based on risk sharing must be considered. The result of these reforms would lead to a change in the design and implementation of fiscal and monetary policies. The objective of these reforms would be the stability and growth of the real economy, without losing sight of the goal of achieving justice and equity among members of the society.

Monetary Policy in an Islamic Economy

The challenge for monetary policy in an Islamic framework is to design instruments that satisfy the requirements of an effective monetary policy while meeting the rule of exchange-based transactions without resorting to the interest rate mechanism. The solution to the problem is to devise financial instruments that rely on the risk-sharing features of equity finance. Where monetary policy in a conventional economy uses interest rates to regulate the money supply, in an Islamic economy money supply is altered through asset mark activities. As discussed, the incentive structure intended by monetary authorities to induce portfolio adjustment may be distorted if signals are not transmitted to the private sector by the banking sector. For example, the excess in reserves arising from a lowering of the reserve requirements may be used by the banking sector to buy government bonds instead of lending to the private sector to increase consumption and investment. As a result, the effect of the monetary policy may not be fully achieved. The use of the interest rate as a tool for monetary policy creates incentives for financial decoupling.

Risk-sharing instruments can avoid this problem. Such instruments, issued by the government to finance its operations and used by the monetary authority to affect portfolio adjustment by the private sector, can achieve the objectives of monetary policy while promoting greater resilience of the economy to shocks.

Equity Participation Shares

The first-best instrument of risk sharing is the stock market. With an active stock market, individuals can buffer idiosyncratic liquidity shocks by selling equity shares in the stock market. When risk is spread among a large number of participants through an efficient stock market, closer coordination between the financial and real sector is promoted. Moreover, the benefits of economic growth and financial system stability are better shared. Risk sharing through equity finance will ensure that Islamic finance is anchored to the real sector at all times.

Using the same concept, the liquidity in the economy through the monetary policy mechanism can be controlled through the issuance of financial instruments, such as equity participation shares, which provide participation in financing of government expenditure, such as in development projects. The papers must have low enough denominations and be traded in secondary markets so that ordinary citizens—not just institutional investors—can have access to them. In an exercise to contract the money supply, these papers would be issued directly to the market to mop up excess liquidity in the market. The effect would be immediate and leakages arising from intermediation would be reduced. Conversely, if the goal is to increase money supply, the monetary authority would buy these papers from the private sector.

The rate of return on these papers would be referenced to the rate of return to the real sector of the economy. The rate could be benchmarked against the average rate of return of the stock market, which is generally higher than the interest rate in the economy; hence this presents investors with a better return on their idle income. For example, the current interest rate of government securities in Malaysia is approximately 3 percent, while the rate of return on bank deposits is 2 percent. If the rate of return on the equity participation shares could be set to reflect the equity premium in the stock market, it could potentially earn 5–7 percent. An alternative could be that the rate of return to these papers could be benchmarked on the return to the real sector of the economy.[5] Either way would represent a better investment alternative for investors. In countries such as Malaysia where private savings are high, resources that are currently earning 2 percent return could be mobilized to productive use in the economy for a higher rate of return. The effect of this policy measure would be not only to achieve the same monetary policy impact as in the conventional economy, but also to serve as a measure of improving income distribution of the society by providing better access to all members of the society to the benefits from the growth of the economy. It would also serve as a consumption-smoothing instrument (to mitigate idiosyncratic risk) for small investors.

The papers must be allowed to be openly traded in the secondary market so that the holders could redeem or liquidate them by selling them at the prevailing market price. This means the institutional investor such as banks would have to pay the market price in order to have access to this instrument for the purposes of managing their asset portfolios. In this way, the economic opportunity would be equally available to all and would not only concentrate among the more financially able. At the same time, the opportunity (risk-reward profile) in economic activity would be available according to the level of financial capability of each investor. Such monetary policy instruments would also enhance governance, as the government would be more accountable to the general public with regard to their investments in the risk-sharing instruments.

Fiscal Policy in an Islamic Economy

Rules governing an Islamic economy can address the persistent budget deficit and rising level of government debt. The high level of debt constrains government's ability to take on additional risk in its balance sheet. Apart from the threat of a credit rating downgrade, persistent fiscal deficits also impair the ability of the policymakers to respond effectively to future shocks. Additionally, increasing the debt burden could have adverse distributional impacts for the current and future generations. This is due to the fact that the middle- and lower-income classes carry the burden of the taxes that are needed to service government debt held by either higher-income groups or foreign investors. The design of policy instruments for fiscal policy in an Islamic economy should reflect concerns such as distributive justice.

Relatively stable fiscal revenue is essential for macroeconomics management and in turn for sustained growth (Askari, Iqbal, and Mirakhor 2009). A fiscal deficit is a common phenomenon in many nations, including the developed industrialized countries. This suggests that the policy prescriptions that had been put in place were not sufficient to create a sustainable fiscal position. This may have been due to either multiple structural weaknesses in the current tax system or to a breakdown in fundamentals. In either case, a new policy configuration that would lead to a more sustainable and growth-supportive fiscal position would be in order.

An alternative approach to the current policy dilemma would propose a two-pronged solution: reform of the tax system, and a radical change in the way governments finance their spending. The tax system needs to be simplified to induce voluntary declaration from taxpayers, and widened to include a tax on wealth. At the same time, financing of economic activities should move away from the current interest-based system to one based on risk sharing through utilization of funds available to the public at large. Therefore, it is imperative that the policies to increase revenue are put in place in tandem with a policy to mobilize debt-free public sector financing.

Taxation

The focus of taxation is on increasing government revenue. *Zakat* in Islam and taxation in conventional terms have similarities in terms of ensuring that resources of a country are fairly enjoyed by all members of the society. *Zakat* is imposed on Muslims from their surpluses to redeem the rights of others in the society who are less able. The difference between *zakat* and taxation is that distribution of *zakat* is prescribed to only eight categories of people,[6] whereas taxes are collected to support government spending for the provision of public goods and development. *Zakat* is also compulsory according to Divine Law, while taxation is a policy imposed by the government. According to Muslim scholars, the state is authorized to collect additional amounts in taxes if *zakat* is not sufficient to meet the needs of those requiring assistance and to produce public goods.

While there are many reasons for tax avoidance in many countries and in different systems of governments, including complex governance issues (some of which are discussed in chapters 1, 3, 5, and 11 in this volume) in general, a good tax policy is one that balances simplicity, efficiency, fairness, and revenue sufficiency. The tax structure needs to be reformed in such a way that the people will be willing to pay taxes without much enforcement, as they believe a fair amount of their income will be given away. The tax structure should also be easy to administer and capable of generating the revenue required. A complex system of taxation poses a challenge for taxpayers to comprehend and comply with. At the same time, a complex tax system provides incentive for shrewd taxpayers to identify loopholes to reduce payment of taxes or avoid taxes altogether.

Simplifying the tax system will also reduce costs both to the government, of auditing taxpayers and enforcing compliance, and to the taxpayer, of engaging tax consultants and tax lawyers to defend contentious tax positions. With a simple tax system, investors can have certainty about the tax costs of doing business. A simple tax system based on the ability to pay is also capable of bringing more taxpayers into the tax net. This could reduce the perception of injustice attached to a tax system that captures only a small segment of the society in the tax net. A simple tax system can be designed around a flat tax, reflecting the structure of *zakat* and other charges prescribed in the Qur'an.

Flat Tax. A flat tax system is simple, as there is only one tax rate applicable to all. A simple tax system would naturally lead to efficient tax collection. Implementing a flat tax system would increase compliance by taxpayers and thereby increase tax revenue. A flat tax system, because it is a fairer tax system than a progressive tax system,[7] could lead to less tax evasion. To address the issue of the tax burden of the low-income earners who currently may be paying a low tax rate, a minimum exemption level of income could be determined, before taxes would be payable. As mentioned in chapters 1, 5, and 11 in this volume, Islam places a great deal of emphasis on human dignity. Therefore, the amount determined for the minimum bracket is one that could enable a person to live in the society with dignity. This usually translates into sufficient income to guarantee "basic needs." This minimum level is called the "Nisab limit."

Two of the well-known proponents of the flat tax system, Robert Hall and Alvin Rabushka (1995), have developed a flat tax system that taxes income and eliminates double taxation by excluding tax on investment. It is advocated as a simple tax system that would generate greater tax compliance, as tax filing would become a less painful process. It would reduce tax evasion while raising high levels of revenue for the government.

This is not a new tax system. A flat tax has been adopted in a number of economies, including several eastern European nations, Mongolia, and Hong Kong SAR, China, and has come to be featured prominently in policy debates in Western Europe, the United States, and Australia.

Wealth Tax. As a matter of equity, it is argued that taxes should be levied according to the ability to pay. The current focus on taxing income may impose undue burdens on income earners who need the income for their day-to-day living. Income alone may not be a sufficient measure of well-being or taxable capacity. The possession of wealth adds to the capacity to pay tax, over and above the income yielded by that wealth.

Taxing wealth means making those who are more financially able contribute more in tax. Wealth represents accumulated assets owned, and not just income earned. Therefore, in the interests of equity, it is justifiable to tax wealth in addition to income. Moreover, as wealth generally represents a much larger tax base than income, the rate of taxation can be kept low but still raise substantial tax revenue. In addition, advocates of a wealth tax argue that such a tax may encourage the better-off to transfer their assets from less productive uses to more productive ones, and from idleness to income-producing ventures.

The wealthiest segment of the population, which holds assets in the form of properties and stocks, will probably be paying a relatively low tax as a proportion of their wealth compared to those whose wealth consists mainly of their monthly salary. Collecting tax revenue from the segment of the population with the most wealth could promote equality, as the wealth that is currently concentrated in the hands of a few would become revenue for the government to be used for social development.

Under an Islamic economic system, a flat tax system consisting of an income tax component and a wealth tax component has the potential to be ideal. It reflects the rate structure of *Khums* (literally, a "one-fifth" charge levied on war booty during the earliest period in Islamic history)[8] and *zakat* prescribed by the Qur'an and the *Sunnah*. The optimum flat tax rate may differ from country to country, depending on the unique economic situation. As a general guideline, it is proposed here that the tax structure be composed of a 20 percent income tax and a 2.5 percent wealth tax.

The flat tax system of 20 percent on income may represent a reduction in the marginal tax rate from the tax rate prevailing in most countries. The reduction in marginal tax rate would incentivize people and firms to work and increase production. The reduction in tax rates also represents an increase in disposable income to individuals that would lead to increased consumption in the economy. With a simple tax system in force, tax administration would be much easier, and government resources could be released to attend to other matters more important and productive to the economy.

Public Sector Financing

When revenue is not sufficient to cover a budget deficit, the government must borrow. Due to the prohibition of interest, in an Islamic economy the policy instrument for public sector borrowing policy should be based on risk sharing. The benefits of risk sharing are manifold, as discussed. Instead of borrowing, the government could issue equity participation shares to finance development projects. This would mobilize higher private sector savings in many countries to support productive public sector investment projects. By issuing risk-sharing instruments to fund development expenditures, the burden of debt could be reduced. At the same time, the household sector would be able to enjoy a higher rate of return on its savings because the rate of return on the papers would be driven by the return to the real sector.

The equity participation shares would have a rate of return that would be tied to the growth of the national income or to the real rate of return in the real sector of the economy. The issues should be in small enough denominations and traded

Figure 12.2 A Transmission Mechanism in an Islamic Economy

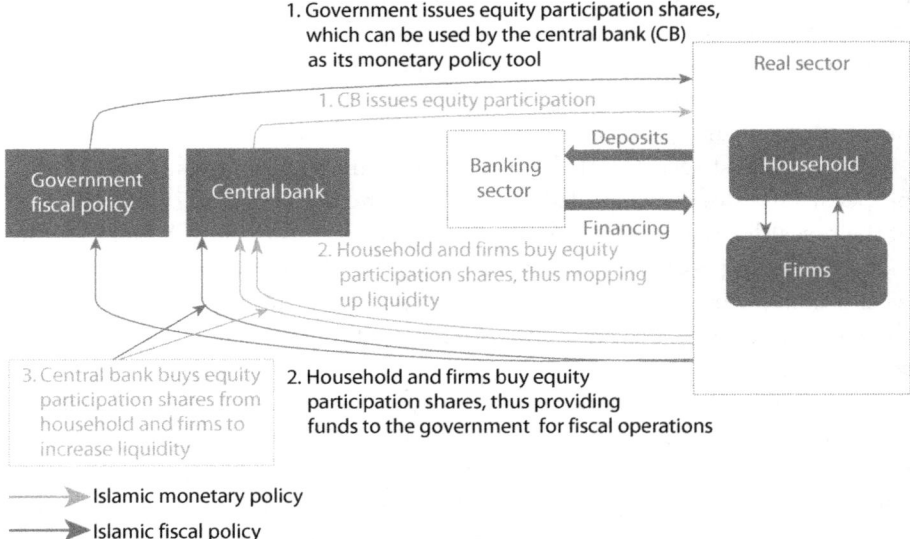

on the secondary market so they would be more accessible and affordable to the general public. This would unlock the revenue potential hidden in idle resources. At the same time, it would provide investment opportunities at a higher rate of return for the public than that currently earned in saving deposits. By tapping these resources, the government would not only avail itself of a source of funding for its expenditures, but also provide a more equitable opportunity for the public to have access to the wealth of the nation. The economic pie could now be shared among a larger segment of the economy, and not only by the more financially able few. This distributional implication of this policy instrument would further strengthen social solidarity.

The cost to the government of raising financing through equity participation shares would not be much higher than the current rate of interest paid on debt instruments, but it would provide a better impetus to the growth of the economy by mobilizing funds otherwise sitting in deposits. At the same time, these papers could also serve as an ideal instrument for monetary policy measures. To expand the money supply, the papers could be bought from the open market, thereby increasing the amount of money in circulation to increase consumption. An illustration of the mechanism of the Islamic monetary and fiscal policy instruments is provided in figure 12.2.

Challenges in Policy Implementation

Even though an Islamic economic system could yield many benefits, there is a lack of real life examples and precedence that can demonstrate the benefits. The litmus test for an Islamic system is how well it reduces poverty. Existence of wide-spread poverty is prima facie evidence of an absence of compliance with rules governing Islamic behavior and a strong signal of shirking of the duty of sharing ordained by Islam. A number of Muslim countries are listed among the poorest in the world as shown in *The World Factbook 2009* by the U.S. Central Intelligence Agency. Afghanistan and Niger are the two Muslim countries among the world's top ten poorest countries in 2011 (IMF 2012). On the other hand, the richest country in the world on a per capita basis is Qatar, according to the IMF 2012 database. Other Muslim countries in the top 15 are Brunei Darussalam, Kuwait, and the United Arab Emirates. While income inequality is low in most non-Muslim countries, including various European nations, Australia, and Canada, income inequality in Muslim countries leaves much to be desired (U.S. CIA 2009). This situation is not reflective of the distributive justice that should be present in an Islamic economy. Instead, it is the Scandinavian countries, with the lowest Gini coefficient, that have the top positions in terms of the best quality of life index compiled by the Organisation for Economic Co-operation and Development (OECD) (see chapter 11).

The Move toward Social and Economic Justice in Islamic Countries

Of late, Islamic countries in the Middle East have been in the spotlight for political unrest. The Arab Republic of Egypt, Libya, the Syrian Arab Republic, Bahrain, and the Republic of Yemen are among the countries that have been or are still undergoing turmoil at the time of writing. Tunisia, Egypt, and Libya have seen a change in government and political leaders. Unrest has been triggered by dissatisfaction with the injustice perpetrated by the people in power. What has happened is an example of collapse of trust, breach of contract, and transgressions of property rights.

As discussed, the people elect governments through the transaction of exchange of commitments to rule-compliance: that is, *mubaya'ah*. The main point to note is that Islam has laid down rules for humans. Rule-compliance is expected of all humans to ensure harmony, social solidarity, and justice. When contracts are not fulfilled and trust collapses, coordination and cooperation become difficult, and can lead to a breakdown in communal harmony. Lack of full transparency in dealings will promote the people in power and the people who have responsibilities toward others to shirk their responsibilities.

As mentioned, an imbalanced distribution of income leads to the concentration of wealth among the rich, while the poor fall deeper into poverty. The case of extreme poverty in many societies is a case of failure of rule-compliance by those in authority, as well as the members of the society at large. The latter fail to internalize the rules and act accordingly. The former fail to uphold the rules such as property rights, faithfulness to the terms and conditions of contracts, transparency, good governance, primacy of human dignity, and risk sharing. The unrest underway in various Islamic countries is a move toward greater social and economic justice. It is hoped that as the search for political legitimacy and a fair and just system of government evolves in these countries, greater attention will be focused on finding contemporary ways and means of compliance with rules prescribed in the Qur'an that ensure social solidarity and justice.

Building Blocks for an Islamic Economy

The biggest challenge in any shift in paradigm is path-dependency. In the case of the move away from conventional finance to a model adopting more aspects of Islamic finance or a hybrid of the two, the paradigm to be shifted is an economy gripped by interest rate–based debt financing. To steer away from path-dependency, there must be a change in mindsets (or world views, as discussed in the overview to this volume). There must be a firm commitment to rule-compliance as the way of life. The focus will then change from a self-interested agenda to an other-regarding program, with social solidarity, unity, justice, and equity at the center of the public's attention. This requires giving full recognition to dignity as the most important gift of Allah (swt) to humans that must be protected. Recognition of human dignity requires cognizance that poverty erodes dignity. Human dignity cannot be protected in the face of poverty. Recognition of the importance of dignity must confer basic rights to humans that must be formalized as constitutional rights. At minimum, these should include the right to a reasonable quality of living and the rights to education, security, and health.

Framing the Benefits

Contemporary societies are pluralistic, if not in terms of race, language, or ethnicity, then in terms of world views, and understanding of values and norms. The benefits accrued to a rule-compliant society must be carefully framed and explained in order to elicit the widest possible social legitimacy for economic policy measures that promote risk sharing.

In the face of risk, people respond to two mechanisms (Mirakhor 2011). Their response to a risky situation depends on how they form their perception of a given situation and how the events are framed. The same situation framed differently will give rise to different responses. People will also base their responses on their perception of the prospect of gains or losses attached to the decisions. In order to move forward, Islamic finance must be framed in terms of the benefits and prospects of gain, rather than loss that it brings to the society. The prospects of gains, such as efficient capital mobilization, risk allocation, contracting, transparency, and governance, should be highlighted.

Islamic finance is not as much about advancing a system of thought as it is offering a financing mode that places human relations, irrespective of religious affiliation, as the foundation of development. Framing is crucially important because to achieve the objective of social and distributive justice in the pursuit of economic growth requires solid commitment from various stakeholders—including financial institutions, central banks, regulators, the government, the legal system, and the public at large, which ultimately must legitimize all those institutions—to a path that leads to its achievement. The interests of different stakeholders must be realigned toward the same objective of growth with stability and justice.

The way forward does not necessarily entail drastic change, but a multistage implementation path of cumulative changes needed to achieve an objective. An example of a master plan is the Malaysian Financial Sector Master Plan (FSMP) and Financial Sector Blueprint (FSB), each of which is a 10-year road map toward achieving a more vibrant financial services sector, including an Islamic financial sector (see box 12.1).

Box 12.1 The Malaysian Financial Services Master Plan (2001–10) and the Malaysian Financial Sector Blueprint (2011–20)

The Financial Sector Master Plan (FSMP) is a 10-year plan outlining the strategic focus, common goals, and sequence of measures to develop a more resilient, competitive, and dynamic financial system with best practices that support and contribute positively to the growth of the Malaysian economy. It is focused on creating forward-looking and robust domestic financial institutions that are more technologically driven and ready to face the challenges of liberalization and globalization. The implementation was done in three phases. Phase one aimed to enhance domestic capacity and develop strategic and nascent sectors. Phase two aimed to diversify the financial sector through intensifying competitive pressure and gradual liberalization of the market. Phase three aimed to liberalize domestic competition through introduction of new foreign competition and enhance international positioning in areas of competitive advantage. One of the sectors focused upon is the Islamic finance industry. Its promising growth over the last 30 years has placed Malaysia as one of the role models in many aspects of Islamic finance. This growth is spearheaded further by the Malaysia International Islamic Financial Centre (MIFC) initiative, which has introduced a spate of enabling legislation and incentives to take the industry to the next level of its development. The gradual and sequenced approach of FSMP enabled the introduction of the liberalization package in 2009 that aimed at strengthening Malaysia's linkages with international economies.

With the establishment of a more mature financial sector as a result of FSMP, the subsequent 10-year plan, the Financial Sector Blueprint (FSB), was introduced to further facilitate Malaysia's economic transformation toward becoming a high value-added and high-income economy by 2020. The FSB is an integrated approach focused on greater participation of the Malaysian financial sector in facilitating regional financial flows, especially in supporting regional trade, investment, and financial integration, as well as the internationalization of Islamic finance. The formulation of FSB draws important lessons from the recent global financial crisis, which highlighted that financial stability is an important prerequisite in ensuring the orderly and sustainable development of the financial sector and the economy as a whole. The FSB signals new trends and expectations. In particular, there is a growing demand for socially responsible investments and ethical financial products and services that hinges on fairness, transparency, and risk sharing. This will undoubtedly drive the financial sector to relook and rethink its product and business strategies to adapt to the new competitive landscape.

The central bank's master plan and blueprints have been instrumental in communicating its regulatory stance and driving the financial services industry forward. This is an example of a viable multistage development plan that can be implemented in achieving a macroeconomic objective.

Meeting the Challenge of Global Integration

Better interaction between and among countries to achieve the social justice is needed to reduce global poverty. Countries can attempt to mitigate the risk of exposure to shocks by developing strong equity markets open to foreign investors, limiting external borrowing to that denominated in domestic currency, accumulating foreign reserves, and developing ways to invest in foreign asset markets to allow a diversification of income. The equity participation shares as discussed can be issued to external investors, thereby promoting collaboration among countries in their economies. Imagine the benefits that would accrue to the international solidarity, stability, and growth if the debts of countries such as Greece were financed through equity participation instruments sold on the international markets, backed by the credibility of international financial institutions like the International Monetary Fund (IMF), the European Central Bank, and the members of G-20, with a rate of return based on the rate of growth of the GDP of the country.

Summary

The focus of this chapter has been the theory and implementation of macroeconomic policies in the context of Islamic teachings. Monetary and fiscal policies in the conventional and Islamic contexts were defined and explained, to highlight the differences between the two approaches. It was argued that interest rate–based debt finance forms the foundation of financial transactions in conventional finance. This system, perpetuated by fractional reserve banking, government deposit insurance, and the potential for high leverage, is prone to instability. It was explained that the organizing principles of Islamic economic and financial systems are exchange and avoidance of interest rate–based debt financing. As has been well known since the time of classical economics, exchange promotes specialization, division of labor, and gains from the act of exchange. In the process, the two sides of the exchange share the risk of specialization.

It was further explained that monetary and fiscal policies must rely on risk-sharing instruments to implement policies aimed at growth with stability and justice. In an Islamic approach, the government relies on equity-sharing instruments to finance any revenue shortfalls, rather than resorting to borrowing. These instruments, in turn, become mechanisms of monetary policy transmission. In the conventional system, signals emitted by monetary authority to induce private sector portfolio adjustment must be transmitted by the money market, where financial institutions are the main players. The monetary authority and the private sector financial institutions have different objective functions, however. Private sector financial institutions may have incentives not to pass through the central bank's signals to the private sector, leading to the impairment of monetary policy. By contrast, in an Islamic approach, when monetary authorities use risk-sharing instruments that have small denominations and are traded in the secondary market, the transmission mechanism becomes the asset or capital market, where the authorities have the opportunity to influence private sector portfolio adjustments directly. This invests monetary policy with greater potency than in the conventional system.

In an Islamic approach, fiscal policy will rely on tax structure that resembles those prescribed in the Qur'an and *Sunnah*. The appropriate tax structure advocated here is a flat tax system, with an income tax component and a wealth tax component. The mix advocated here calls for a 2.5 percent wealth tax and a 20 percent income tax.

If there is need to finance budget shortfalls, the government could raise funds by issuing shares representing an equity position in a portfolio of public sector projects. In turn, these instruments would be at the disposal of the monetary authority to use to send signals to the private sector when and if needed. These instruments have a number of benefits. In particular, they create flows that are not based on debt and that allow broad-based participation of the public in the activities of government. They also have positive distributional implications for the current and future generations. The current generation, through the ownership of these instruments, will have an opportunity to pass on wealth rather than debt to future generations.

It is necessary to frame Islamic-based policies correctly and seek public participation that is as wide as possible. Islamic finance must be understood as a mode of financing that promotes human dignity, social solidarity, close correspondence between the real and financial sectors, and potent fiscal and monetary policies. This framing is necessary in order to achieve a strong social consensus and commitment to rule-compliance from a broad spectrum of stakeholders in the society.

Notes

1. Path-dependency is the continued use of a product or practice based on historical preference or use. This persistent pattern holds true even if newer, more efficient products or practices are available because of the previous commitment made. Path-dependency occurs because it is often easier or more cost-effective to simply continue along an established and known path than to create an entirely new one (see Investopedia, http://www.investopedia.com).
2. Thornton [1802] (1939) distinguished between a market (loan) rate of interest and the interest rate (the marginal rate of profit, or the natural rate of interest), which equilibrates savings and investment. According to Thornton's theory of two interest rates, inflation results from a divergence between the two rates.
3. Al Qur'an Al Baqarah, verses 275–279; Al Imran, verse 3:130; An Nisa, verse 4:161; Ar Rum, verse 30:39.
4. Al Qur'an Al Baqarah, verse 2:278–279.
5. This is an approximate rate of return based on the average rate of return of 11 percent after taking into account cost of issuance and the risk premium.
6. The eight categories are: the poor; the needy; collectors and administrators of the *zakat*; those whose hearts lean toward the love for Allah; for freeing humans from worldly bondage; those who are overburdened with debts (for example, those who

have gone bankrupt); expenditure for removing obstacles in the path of humans toward their Creator; and for the wayfarer (see the Qur'an, chapter 9, verse 60).

7. A progressive tax system is a tax system where the tax rate increases as the taxable base amount increases.

8. See the Qur'an, chapter 8, verse 41.

References

Al-Hasani, Baqir, and Abbas Mirakhor. 2003. *Iqtisad–The Islamic Approach to Economic Problems*. New York: Global Scholarly Publications.

Askari, Hossein, Zamir Iqbal, and Abbas Mirakhor. 2009. *New Issues in Islamic Finance and Economics: Progress and Challenges*. Singapore: John Wiley & Sons.

Askari, Hossein, Zamir Iqbal, Noureddine Krichene, and Abbas Mirakhor. 2010. *The Stability of Islamic Finance: Creating a Resilient Financial Environment for a Secure Future*. Singapore: John Wiley & Sons.

———. 2012. *Risk Sharing in Finance: The Islamic Finance Alternative*. Singapore: John Wiley & Sons.

Debrun, Xavier, and Radhicka Kapoor. 2010. "Fiscal Policy and Macroeconomic Stability: New Evidence and Policy Implications." *Nordic Economic Review* 37: 1457–82.

Duval, Romain, Jörgen Elmeskov, and Lukas Vogel. 2006. "Structural Policies and Resilience to Shocks." Working Paper 567, Economics Department, Organisation for Economic Co-operation and Development (OECD), Paris.

Hall, Robert E., and Alvin Rabushka. 1995. *The Flat Tax*. Stanford, CA: Hoover Institution Press, Stanford University.

IMF (International Monetary Fund). 2012. "World Economic Outlook Database (October)." International Monetary Fund, Washington, DC.

Mirakhor, Abbas. 2011. "Risk Sharing and Public Policy." 5th International Islamic Capital Market Forum, Securities Commission of Malaysia, November 10.

Mirakhor, Abbas, and Hossein Askari. 2010. *Islam and the Path to Human Economic Development*. Palgrave Macmillan.

Siddiqi, Muhammad Nejatullah. 2001. *Economics: An Islamic Approach*. U.K.: Institute of Policy Studies and Islamic Foundation.

Thornton, Henry. (1802) 1939. *An Inquiry into the Nature and Effects of the Paper Credit of Great Britain*. Edited by F. R. von Hayek. Reprint, New York: Rinehart.

U.S. CIA (United States Central Intelligence Agency). 2009. *The World Factbook 2009*. Directorate of Intelligence.

Glossary of Arabic Terms

Ádl Justice.

Akhlaq Personal, moral, and behavioral disposition of a person.

Amana Trust. Placing something valuable in trust with someone for custody or safekeeping.

Aqidah Faith and beliefs of a Muslim

Ariya Lending for gratuitous use. Lending of an asset takes place between a lender and the borrower with the agreement that the former will not charge anything for the use of the thing he lent out.

Barakah Blessings and returns for performing virtuous acts.

Bay' Sale of a property or commodity for a price.

Bay' al-Istisna Sale in order to manufacture or construct.

Bay-mua'jjal Sale contract where the price of the product or underlying asset is agreed but the payment in lumpsum or installments is deferred to a specified future date.

Bay' al-Salam Sale by immediate payment against future delivery. Similar to conventional forward contract but requires full payment at the time of contract.

Bay' al-'Arabun Payment of a portion of full sale price paid in good faith as earnest money.

Bay' al-Dayn Sale of debt or liability.

Bay' Bithamin Ajil (BBA) Sale contract where payment is made in installments after delivery of goods. Sale could be for long-term and there is no obligation to disclose profit margins.

Gharar Any uncertainty or ambiguity created by the lack of information or control in a contract.

Hadith Report of statement or actions of Prophet Muhammad (pbuh).

Howala Transfer of a debt or an obligation from one debtor to another.

Ibadat The *Shari'ah* rules guiding the practicalities of ways to perform rites and rituals.

Iijarah wa 'iqtina'   A hire-purchase contract which is similar to conventional lease-purchase agreements. In addition to a regular contract of *Ijarah*, another contract is added which includes a promise by the lessor/owner to sell the leased asset to the lessee at the end of the original lease agreement.

Ijarah   A sale contract that is not the sale of a tangible asset but rather a sale of the *usufruct* (the right to use the object) for a specified period of time.

Ijma'   Consensus on legal opinion.

Ijtihad   The efforts expanded by jurists to extract solutions to problems based on the principles of primary and secondary sources where rules of behavior are not explicitly addressed by the primary sources, that is, the *Qur'an* and *Sunnah*.

Istihsan   Juristic preference of one alternative to another.

Jo'ala   Agreement with an expert in a given field to undertake a task for a predetermined fee or commission (as in a consultancy agreement or contract).

Khilafah   Stewardship.

khiyanah   Betrayal of trust. Faithlessness.

Kifala   Suretyship. Assuming someone's liability in case the principal fails to meet their obligation.

Ma'ad   Believing in returning to Allah (swt) for final, definite, and complete account of one's actions.

Madhahib   Different schools of thought in understanding, interpreting, and formulating the precepts of *Shari'ah*.

Maslaha   Public welfare.

Maysir   Impermissibile games of chance.

Mu'amelat   Rules of behavior governing practicalities of day-to-day life in social, political, and economic activities.

Mudarabah   An economic agent with capital *(rabbul-mal)* can develop a partnership with another agent (*mudarib*) with skills to form a partnership with the agreement to share the profits. Although losses are borne by the capital owner only, the *mudarib* may however be liable for a loss in case of misconduct or negligence on his part.

Mudarib   Economic agent with entrepreneural and managements skills who partners with *rabbul-mal* (owner of capital) in a *Mudarabah* contract.

Murabahah   A cost-plus-sale contract where a financier purchases a product, that is, a commodity, raw material or supplied, for an entrepreneur who does not have its own capital to do so. The financier and the entrepreneur agree on a profit margin, often referred to as a mark-up which is added to the cost of the product. The payment is delayed for a specified period of time.

Musharaka Aqed   Granting the partner ownership rights to value of assets without any specific linkage to any real asset.

Musharaka Mulk   Ownership rights given to a partner to a specific real asset.

Musharaka Mutanaqisah   Contract of diminishing partnership. Usually, one partner buys out share of others over time.

Musharakah   Equity partnership. It is a hybrid of *Shiraka* (partnership) and *Mudarabah* combining the act of investment and management.

Nafs   Soul, psyche.

niyya   Intention.

Nubuwwa   Believing that Mohammed (pbuh) is the last and the final Messenger of *Allah* (swt) bringing to mankind the most perfect set of rules of conduct required for the perfect life in this world.

pbuh   An English abbreviation often appended when writing the name of Prophet Muhammad. It stands for "Peace Be upon Him."

Qard-al-hassan   Charitable loans with no interest and low expectations of return of principal.

Qimar   Gambling.

Qiyas   Analogical reasoning.

Qur'an   The Divine book revealed to Prophet Mohammed (pbuh).

Rabbul-mal   Provider of funds/capital in Mudarabah contract.

Rahn   The contract of *rahn* or pledge is to make a property a security provided by the borrower against a loan so that in case of the borrower's inability to make the payment, liability may be recovered from the value of the pledged property.

Riba   The premium (interest) that must be paid by the borrower to the lender along with the principal amount as a condition for the loan or for an extension.

Riba al-Fadl   *Riba in* hand-to-hand or barter exchange.

Riba al-Nasi'ah   *Riba* in money-to-money exchange provided exchange is delayed or deferred and additional charge is associated with such deferment.

Sadaqah   Voluntary charity.

Sarf   Sale by exchange of money for money at spot.

Shari'ah   Islamic Law.

Suftaja   Bills of exchange or letters of credit.

Sukuk   Plural of the Arabic word *Sakk* meaning certificate, reflects participation rights in the underlying assets.

Sunnah   The practice of Prophet Mohammed (pbuh).

swt   An Arabic abbreviation often appended when writing the name of *Allah* (God). It stands for "Subhanahu Wa Ta'ala" ("May He Be Glorified and Exalted").

Takaful   Insurance contract through mutual or joint guarantee.

Taqwa   Ever-present consciousness of the presence of Allah (swt)

Tawhid   The Unity and Oneness of the Creator—Allah (swt)

Wadi'ah   Deposit of one's property with another person for safekeeping with permission to use it without the intention of receiving any return from it.

Wikala   Representation. Entrusting a person or legal entity (*Wakil*) to act on one's behalf or as one's representative.

Environmental Benefits Statement

The World Bank is committed to reducing its environmental footprint. In support of this commitment, the Office of the Publisher leverages electronic publishing options and print-on-demand technology, which is located in regional hubs worldwide. Together, these initiatives enable print runs to be lowered and shipping distances decreased, resulting in reduced paper consumption, chemical use, greenhouse gas emissions, and waste.

The Office of the Publisher follows the recommended standards for paper use set by the Green Press Initiative. Whenever possible, books are printed on 50% to 100% postconsumer recycled paper, and at least 50% of the fiber in our book paper is either unbleached or bleached using Totally Chlorine Free (TCF), Processed Chlorine Free (PCF), or Enhanced Elemental Chlorine Free (EECF) processes.

More information about the Bank's environmental philosophy can be found at http://crinfo.worldbank.org/crinfo/environmental_responsibility/index.html.

Economic Development and Islamic Finance • http://dx.doi.org/10.1596/978-0-8213-9953-8

www.ingramcontent.com/pod-product-compliance
Lightning Source LLC
Chambersburg PA
CBHW081757300426
44116CB00014B/2148